SOCIETY WITHIN THE BRAIN

Society within the Brain presents scientific research linking social connection with brain and cognitive aging through state-of-the-art research. This involves comprehensive social network analysis, social neuroscience, neuropsychology, psychoneuroimmunology, and sociogenomics. This book provides a scientific discourse on how a society, community, or friends and family interact with individuals' cognitive aging. Issues concerning social isolation, as well as controversy around the origins of individual differences in social brain and behavior, are discussed. An integrative framework is introduced to explicate how social networks alleviate the effects of aging in brain health and reduce dementia risks. This book is of interest and useful to a wide readership: from gerontologists, psychologists, clinical neuroscientists, and sociologists; to those involved in developing community-based interventions or public health policy for brain health; to people interested in how social life influences brain aging or in the prevention of dementia.

JEANYUNG CHEY is the current president of the Korean Psychological Association and the director of the Clinical Neuroscience Lab at Seoul National University, where she has led numerous projects on cognitive aging and protective and risk factors for dementia, such as education, social connection, and stress, using a multidisciplinary approach and longitudinal data. A founding leader of the Korean Society for Neuropsychological Research, she opened South Korea's first hospital clinical neuropsychology lab and has developed many neuropsychological tools, including the first dementia test in the country. She was awarded the South Korean government's National Prize for Contribution in Overcoming Dementia in 2022.

SOCIETY WITHIN THE BRAIN

How Social Networks Interact with Our Brain, Behavior, and Health as We Age

EDITED BY

JEANYUNG CHEY
Seoul National University

Shaftesbury Road, Cambridge CB2 8EA, United Kingdom

One Liberty Plaza, 20th Floor, New York, NY 10006, USA

477 Williamstown Road, Port Melbourne, VIC 3207, Australia

314–321, 3rd Floor, Plot 3, Splendor Forum, Jasola District Centre, New Delhi – 110025, India

103 Penang Road, #05–06/07, Visioncrest Commercial, Singapore 238467

Cambridge University Press is part of Cambridge University Press & Assessment, a department of the University of Cambridge.

We share the University's mission to contribute to society through the pursuit of education, learning and research at the highest international levels of excellence.

www.cambridge.org
Information on this title: www.cambridge.org/9781009663977

DOI: 10.1017/9781108974325

© Cambridge University Press & Assessment 2023

This publication is in copyright. Subject to statutory exception and to the provisions of relevant collective licensing agreements, no reproduction of any part may take place without the written permission of Cambridge University Press & Assessment.

First published 2023
First paperback edition 2025

A catalogue record for this publication is available from the British Library

Library of Congress Cataloging-in-Publication data
NAMES: Chey, Jeanyung, editor.
TITLE: Society within the brain : how social networks interact with our brain, behavior and health as we age / edited by Jeanyung Chey.
DESCRIPTION: Cambridge ; New York : Cambridge University Press, 2023. | Includes bibliographical references and index.
IDENTIFIERS: LCCN 2022056932 | ISBN 9781108838290 (hardback) | ISBN 9781108974325 (epub)
SUBJECTS: LCSH: Cognition in old age. | Older people–Social networks. | Brain–Aging. | Social perception in old age. | Social interaction. | Geriatric psychiatry.
CLASSIFICATION: LCC BF724.85.C64 S63 2023 | DDC 155.67–dc23/eng/20230217
LC record available at https://lccn.loc.gov/2022056932

ISBN 978-1-108-83829-0 Hardback
ISBN 978-1-009-66397-7 Paperback

Cambridge University Press & Assessment has no responsibility for the persistence or accuracy of URLs for external or third-party internet websites referred to in this publication and does not guarantee that any content on such websites is, or will remain, accurate or appropriate.

To my mother and aunts.
And to all the aurushin *who have participated in our studies since 1996*
J. C.

Contents

List of Figures	*page* ix
List of Tables	xi
List of Contributors	xii
Preface	xiii
Introduction *Jeanyung Chey*	1

PART I APPROACHES TO SOCIETY WITHIN THE BRAIN

1. A Case of a Rapidly Aging Society and Its Dementia Population — 11
   Jeanyung Chey

2. Social Network Positions and Health Status in Older Adults — 50
   Yoosik Youm and Junsol Kim

3. The Social Brain and How It Links Social Intelligence and Well-Being — 69
   Sunhae Sul and Isu Cho

4. The Genomics of Cognitive Aging in Social Isolation — 105
   Sung-Ha Lee and Seyul Kwak

PART II SOCIETY INTERACTING WITH BRAIN, COGNITION, AND HEALTH IN LATE LIFE

5. The Life Course Approach to Cognitive Aging and Dementia — 119
   Jeanyung Chey and Seyul Kwak

6. Enriched Social Connectedness and Brain Function — 141
   Seyul Kwak, Jeanyung Chey, and Yoosik Youm

7 Psychoneuroimmunology Linking Social Isolation with
   Cognitive Aging   162
   Sung-Ha Lee

8 Loneliness and Psychological Health in Late Life   175
   Hairin Kim and Jeanyung Chey

PART III AN INDIVIDUAL'S COGNITIVE AGING WITH
OTHERS: KEY FINDINGS, ISSUES, AND IMPLICATIONS

9 Social Relationships and Cognitive Function in Older Adults   195
   Hoyoung Kim

10 Social Network and the Brain   217
   Yoosik Youm and Junsol Kim

11 Origins of Individual Differences in Social Behavior and the
   Social Brain   231
   Isu Cho and Sunhae Sul

12 Preventing Dementia with Social Connection   269
   *Jeanyung Chey, Isu Cho, Hairin Kim, Hoyoung Kim, Seyul Kwak,
   Sunhae Sul, Sung-Ha Lee, and Yoosik Youm*

Index   297

Figures

1.1a A family picture taken in Iksan, a small town in Jeollabuk Province, by photographer Joo Myung Duck (1971) *page* 13
1.1b A young family walking country lane in Gapyeong, a rural region in Gyeonggi Province, photographed by Joo Myung Duck (1972) 14
1.1c A coal-briquette deliverer in Seoul, 1973 15
1.2a Years of education of Koreans in age brackets 20
1.2b Years of education for Korean women and men over 65 years old 21
1.3 Conceptual errors on the Clock Drawing Test 30
2.1 Ego-centric social networks and complete social networks 51
2.2 Closure position (*k*-core score): A hypothetical network graph of ten people 53
2.3 Example of a brokerage position 55
2.4 Village-level complete social networks from the KSHAP 62
3.1 Brain regions involved in social behavior 81
5.1 Representation of the cognitive reserve hypothesis 125
5.2 Comparison of the brain metabolism and network characteristics of the low and high education groups of women, utilizing graph theoretical analysis 128
5.3 A schematic model of how social connection interacts with neural resource undergoing aging to modulate the manifestation of clinical dementia 132
6.1 Brain regional correlates of social connectedness and their corresponding social brain system 145
6.2 Possible pathways of how social connectedness and brain characteristics influence one another 153

8.1	Path model of the proximal and distal characteristics of the social network	180
10.1	Regions of interest in the amygdala network	219
10.2	Regions of interest in the mentalizing network	221
11.1	The influence of genetic and environmental factors on human social behavior and the social brain	232

Tables

1.1	Dementia prevalence in developed and developing countries	page 23
1.2	Prevalence of dementia in Korean men and women	26
2.1	Ego-centric network measures by selected variables in the KSHAP and the NSHAP	57
2.2	The hazard ratios of loneliness, social disengagement, and group-level segregation from Cox proportional hazard regression models and Cox MSMs (n = 679)	63
3.1	Hypotheses explaining the evolution of the human social brain	75
11.1	Neurotransmitters, related function, social behavior, genes, and brain regions	233

Contributors

ISU CHO, PH.D. isucho@brandeis.edu Post-Doctoral Associate, Department of Psychology, Brandeis University

HAIRIN KIM, PH.D. hairin.kim@gmail.com Research Fellow, Emocog Corporation

HOYOUNG KIM, PH.D. hykimpsy@jbnu.ac.kr Associate Professor, Department of Psychology, Jeonbuk National University

JUNSOL KIM junsolkim@gmail.com Ph.D. candidate, Department of Sociology, University of Chicago

SEYUL KWAK, PH.D. seyul88@gmail.com Assistant Professor, Department of Psychology, Pusan National University

SUNG-HA LEE, PH.D. sunghalee@gmail.com Senior researcher, Center for Happiness Studies, Seoul National University

SUNHAE SUL, PH.D. ssul@pusan.ac.kr Associate Professor, Department of Psychology, Pusan National University

YOOSIK YOUM, PH.D. yoosik@yonsei.ac.kr Underwood Distinguished Professor, Full Professor of Sociology Department, Yonsei University

Preface

This book came to be from a series of collaborations with my graduate students and colleagues conducted over the past twenty-eight years. I am especially grateful to have worked with Dr. Yoosik Youm and his lab for the past decade on the Korean Social Life, Health and Aging Project (KSHAP) as well as all the colleagues of the KSHAP team, particularly Drs. Hyeon Chang Kim, Yeong-Ran Park, and Eun Lee, with whom I had the pleasure of collaborating and discussing our studies. Many chapters were contributed by previous students from the Clinical Neuroscience Lab at Seoul National University (CNS@SNU) and the Social Network Lab at Yonsei University, who have conducted studies in rural villages, metropolitan areas, and at CNS and the MRI center at SNU for many years. Unique contributions were made by social neuroscientists and psychologists Drs. Sunhae Sul and Isu Cho, and psychoneuroimmunologist Sung-Ha Lee, which allowed more elaborate discussions with regard to social impact pathways on cognition and brain aging. I am very grateful to all the authors for accepting the invitation to write the chapters and for contributing significant time and effort to finish the book together. It should be mentioned, however, that many more past and current students have contributed indirectly in valuable ways, including conducting and writing up our studies for publication and also assisting me in the editorial process. I owe Jihyeon Jo and Hankyung Lee much gratitude for their dedication for the latter.

I was very fortunate to have met Steve Acerra from Cambridge University Press at the 2019 Annual International Neuropsychological Society Meeting in New York. He kindly suggested that I write a book on my research on the cognitive and brain aging of older Koreans, which might shed light on the recent sharp increase in the global incidence of dementia, especially in developing countries. He has supported me throughout the whole process, from deliberation on the book's theme to the conceptual design of its cover. I am very grateful to Steve, and also to

Rowan Groat, Anne Rufina Raymond, Robert Holden, and Mark Fox, who have been very helpful in improving the manuscript and making progress toward publication.

I thank my daughters Solho and Jinho and my husband Jae-Wook Yoon for their patience and support so that I could concentrate on writing and editing a book removed from a busy household for a good period of time. I am also grateful to my sister Kae-Ryung Chey and my dear friend Janet Levoff for their emotional support in embarking on a new adventure of organizing and writing a book with my colleagues. I confess that without any one of the supports and contributions I have received during this process, this book would not have been possible.

Lastly, this book owes incalculable debt to colleagues, scientists, and scholars in the field. I hope our contribution will be helpful and meaningful for the scientific and professional communities interested in cognitive and/or brain aging and dementia, especially during this era of increased loneliness and social isolation.

Introduction

Jeanyung Chey

The global population is growing older, and aging and its associated health conditions are challenging individuals, families, and societies. Social isolation has been recognized as a health risk, especially for older adults. More recently, its adverse effects on cognitive and brain health have been reported. On the other hand, various social activities and social networks have been found to have beneficial effects on behavioral as well as brain functions in older adults. It has been difficult, however, to comprehend the full extent and impact of such activities and networks on health, partly due to the complexity of social interactions and human relationships as well as the multilayered aging processes.

Society Within the Brain has been written to introduce the burgeoning interdisciplinary field that has investigated the relationship between social connection and cognitive or brain health in older adults, which could contribute in reducing the risk of dementia in late life. The interdisciplinary nature of the findings and multiple levels of data in this field make it challenging to integrate and understand those findings. Moreover, the brain structures and functions associated with social behaviors have been identified only recently. Before we review and discuss research that examines how social interaction and relationships influence the brain functions and how social brain structures mediate our interactions with other people in the context of aging and dementia, we first introduce the major approaches and their key findings that have contributed to the discussions in this field. In order to lay a foundation for explicating the findings from this multilevel analysis, Part I, titled Approaches to Society within the Brain, will introduce the main approaches (e.g., sociology, psychology, epidemiology, neuroimaging, neuroimmunology, and genomics) that engage at different levels on a spectrum of data or observations, which will serve as the background to the research introduced in the book.

Challenges of Brain Aging in Modern Societies

People are living much longer in modern societies with advanced medical care and better supply of food and resources. In general, longer life expectancy has been a blessing for many people and societies, but it also comes with challenges that individuals, families, and societies have to overcome or deal with. The risk of dementia is one of the most significant concerns reported by aging individuals, and the recent increase in the prevalence of dementia has been recognized as such a major public health challenge as to be called a dementia pandemic. In modern societies with weaker family and community support, loneliness or social isolation is another concern of old age as people tend to retire and experience loss of friendship or family members.

In Chapter 1, Jeanyung Chey begins Part I with the case of South Korea, the most rapidly aging country in the world. According to a study utilizing statistical modeling to project life expectancy from World Health Organization data, South Korean girls born in 2030 will be the first group of people in world history to live to an average age of ninety years (Kontis et al., 2017). The chapter's brief history of the country, which experienced dynamic changes in its social structure and fabric in the last half of the twentieth century through political upheaval and economic reforms, some of which many developing countries share in common, could provide a benchmark model or a cautionary case to learn from. As it transformed from a mostly agricultural society to a major industrial player in the global economy in less than half a century, South Korea experienced exponential growth in economic indices and well-being indicators, such as the average number of years in education and the life expectancy of the younger generations. One of the unexpected side effects of the rapid transformation, however, was becoming the fastest aging population in world history. One of the major challenges the country has been tackling since the mid-1990s is the swiftly increasing prevalence of dementia. The history of compulsory education in South Korea and its neighboring countries are compared in the discussion of the role of formal education in the development of dementia. The effects of a lack of formal education on cognitive and brain development in older Koreans are discussed, as well as the need to develop valid dementia tools for older adults with minimal education.

The Korean Social Life, Health, and Aging Project (KSHAP), a longitudinal study involving sociological, psychological, and biological approaches, was begun in 2011 to examine the complex paths and processes involved in aging and health, which have become important agendas in the rapidly aging country. Many studies introduced in this volume focus on the psychological and brain science data regarding the social networks of older adults from the KSHAP, and in Chapter 2, Yoosik Youm (the project's principal investigator) and his colleague Junsol Kim review the project to provide readers with a bird's eye view of the multidisciplinary project that has developed over a decade. With an annual survey and comprehensive social network analysis of the villagers who were aged over sixty at the baseline, the KSHAP provides both objective and subjective measures of social connections between villagers, which helps making interpretation of their effects on health and aging less ambiguous. Developed several years prior to KSHAP, the National Social Life, Health, and Aging Project examined the ego-centric social networks and health of older adults in the U.S.. Despite differences in the methods and scope of the data, one of the more consistent findings from these projects was that a larger social network was associated with better self-rated physical and psychological health and well-being in late life. The mechanisms and pathways of the protective effects, however, have been less clear and elusive at times.

One hypothesis raised was the social brain hypothesis, which argues that human intelligence has evolved to solve social problems to increase survival and reproduction rates, and it predicts that people with better social brain capacity would have larger social networks and better position in the hierarchical structure of social relationships. In Chapter 3, social neuroscientists Sunhae Sul and Isu Cho review the psychological and evolutionary perspectives of human sociality, focusing on belongingness and the social intelligence hypothesis. The social brain, the neural basis of the latter hypothesis, is further examined to illustrate how people perceive and process the social world and adjust their behavior, which is followed by an introduction to the psychological aspects of the social network, socio-cognitive functions, and the socio-emotional selectivity in late life and their neural correlates. The chapter concludes with a discussion on the scientific studies linking the social brain and well-being in late life.

An implicit assumption of the social brain hypothesis is the genetic contribution of the social brain capacity, which is expressed differently in individuals. In Chapter 4, psychoneuroimmunologist Sung-Ha Lee and neuropsychologist Seyul Kwak take a more direct approach to the question of to what extent genes and environment contribute to a person's social relationship and cognition by introducing the genomic biomarkers of social isolation and cognitive aging. The chapter reviews the genomics of social relationship and cognitive aging separately from the genome-wide association studies (GWAS) of the respective fields. Sociogenomics, recently pioneered by Steven Cole and others, is introduced, demonstrating alterations in the expression of genes regulating inflammation and immune responses in people exposed to chronic adverse environments, captured in the term Conserved Transcriptional Response to Adversity (CTRA). Similarly, altered gene expression patterns associated with the development of the prefrontal cortex have been found. These findings from the relatively new field of genomics confront common misconceptions regarding biological factors, especially those that are regulated by genes, that they are innate and determined at birth or conception and, therefore, unchangeable. The chapter concludes with discussions on the protective factors against adverse gene expression patterns, such as prosocial behavior or having meaning in life, and the future directions of this new field.

How Does Society Interact with Our Brain as We Age?

In recent years, it has become clear that various life experiences and the state of one's physical health could either protect us from or increase the risk of dementia (Livingston et al., 2017). For instance, formal education in earlier years, including literacy, has been found to protect the effects of neurodegeneration in late life, while not receiving adequate education accounted for 8% of the risk of developing dementia. In midlife, major stress or adversity has been found to be a significant risk factor, while enriched social life in late life is being recognized as a protective factor. In Chapter 5, the first chapter of Part II Society Interacting with Brain, Cognition, and Health in Late Life, the life course approach to cognitive aging and dementia is introduced by Chey and Kwak, who briefly review the modifiable risk factors of dementia that have been recognized and focuses on two major neural resources (i.e., cognitive reserve and brain maintenance) that have demonstrated resilience and resistance to aging and its associated neurodegeneration. Reserve, or cognitive reserve, is the moderating concept that explains the discrepancy between the amount of brain degeneration and the clinical manifestation observed in dementia. Although it cannot be directly measured, numerous studies have confirmed its moderating effects using proxies, such as education, premorbid intelligence, and occupation. Maintaining the integrity of brain structures and functions throughout aging is another important neural resource to be recognized in terms of preventing dementia. A schematic model is introduced of how these neural resources interact with social connection to yield the cognitive status of older adults, which in some cases results in dementia. The following Chapters 6, 7, and 8 discuss the components and pathways in detail. In Chapter 6 by Kwak, Chey, and Youm, major features of the social network that were found to promote or pose risk for brain health in late life are discussed, along with the neural mechanisms involved in this interaction. Cognitive stimulation and the mitigation of inflammatory responses provided by social connectedness, as well as the neural resource–constrained social connectedness (i.e., the capacity of the social brain), are discussed with supporting evidence.

Lee, in Chapter 7, introduces findings from a relatively new field of psychoneuroimmunology that has identified chronic systemic inflammation from stress and adversity as well as aging, which can partly explain the link between social isolation and cognitive aging. Proinflammatory markers, such as interleukin (IL) 1B and 6, C-reactive protein (CRP), and tumor necrosis factor (TNF-α) have been mostly used to measure the level of inflammation in the reviewed studies. Gut microbiome, however, has been reviewed as an alternative marker for inflammation in recent investigations. Moreover, protective factors that have been found to reduce inflammation, such as social integration or a sense of purpose in life, are reviewed.

Loneliness, being a significant risk factor for ill health in late life, is examined in terms of psychological well-being by Hairin Kim and Chey in Chapter 8, which starts with a conceptual clarification and examines the unique significance of loneliness in late life. Social disconnection contributes to loneliness as a state, whereas dispositional conditions and genetics have been associated with "trait loneliness." Various risk factors for loneliness, such as loss of significant relationships and low socioeconomic status, are reviewed, as well as the characteristics of social networks that have been found to be significant predictors for loneliness. Further, loneliness postulated as a psychological experience of threat to one's existence is investigated with a review of findings that demonstrate association between stress response, including the hypothalamus-pituitary axis, and loneliness throughout a lifetime and extended to a chronic state appears to result in depression or other psychiatric illnesses.

Do Others Matter in Cognitive Aging of Individuals?

The last part of the book, Part III An Individual's Cognitive Aging with Others, makes efforts to answer how much social relationships contribute to an individual's cognitive aging process, first by reviewing the major findings of cognitive aging and its influence from social relationships. This is followed by a discussion on the social brain hypothesis that would argue for the crucial constraint that the social brain has on the social networks of an individual, which has been controversial not only for its grave implications but also for the reductionist view that could overlook important contributions, such as socioeconomic and psychosocial factors. Genetic and environmental factors influencing major social behavior and their interactions are discussed in Chapter 11, and concludes with evidences for late-life modulation of early development of social behavior. The part and volume conclude with the last chapter, which summarizes psychosocial interventions effective for facilitating social connectedness as well as strategies and policies that were translated from evidence that found the moderating and preventive effects of social life on cognitive aging or dementia.

In Chapter 9, Hoyoung Kim, a clinical neuropsychologist, addresses the importance of cognitive health for quality of life and functional independence in older adults with a review of the age-associated changes in cognitive function and social relationships in late life and the interrelationship between the two factors. As social relationships have emerged as a protective factor against neurocognitive disorders and cognitive decline in old age, a more accurate description of the interrelationship is necessary for preventive interventions to be effective. Structural and functional aspects of social relationships on dementia risk and cognitive function in older adults are discussed as they tap into different features of social relationships, utilizing quantitative and qualitative approaches, respectively. The chapter also reviews studies that found modulating effects on the interrelationship between cognition and social life owing to individuals' demographic characteristics and the types of activities and relationships the older adults engage in, which would have significant implications for the effectiveness of interventions.

What Contributes to Social Network Position and Size?

Questions or issues were raised from the findings regarding the connection between social networks and cognitive aging or brain health; most importantly, what is the origin of individual differences in social network positions and size? Youm and J. Kim, in Chapter 10, introduce the social brain hypothesis, originally proposed by evolutionary psychologists, which was adopted to account for the beneficial effect of richer and bigger social networks with greater social brain capacity. Although association between the social brain and social network has been consistently reported, the directionality of the cause and effect is not clear, especially in humans. In order to provide a broader perspective on this issue, Cho and Sul in Chapter 11 review a host of contributing factors that have been found to influence individuals' social behavior and social brain, roughly categorized into genetics, environment, and their interaction.

Staying Connected and Healthy as We Age

In the last chapter, Chey and colleagues make efforts to integrate the implications of the research covered in the book and discuss the possible psychosocial interventions, strategies and policies that could promote healthier aging by maintaining or developing supportive social connections in communities and societies.

While this book is by no means a comprehensive review of all the research that has been done to date in the field, it introduces in some detail studies from the KSHAP, the first interdisciplinary aging study to collect the complete social network of villages. Therefore, the project allowed the studies to capture ecologically relevant social characteristics that are difficult to capture with self-reported surveys. It further made it possible to integrate different levels of data in the studies, such as socio-economic information, psychological functioning, and cognitive and brain measures. It is hoped that the book will offer an integrated yet unique perspective in examining the relationship between social life and cognitive aging or brain health in older adults around the world.

REFERENCES

Kontis, V., Bennett, J. E., Mathers, C. D., Li, G., Foreman, K., & Ezzati, M. (2017). Future life expectancy in 35 industrialised countries: Projections with a Bayesian model ensemble. *The Lancet, 389*(10076), 1323–1335.

Livingston, G., Sommerlad, A., Orgeta, V., Costafreda, S. G., Huntley, J., Ames, D., Ballard, C., Banerjee, S., Burns, A., Cohen-Mansfield, J., Cooper, C., Fox, N., Gitlin, L. N., Howard R., Kales, H. C., Larson, E. B., Ritchie, K., Rockwood, K., Sampson, E. L., ... & Mukadam, N. (2017). Dementia prevention, intervention, and care. *The Lancet, 390*(10113), 2673–2734.

PART I

Approaches to Society within the Brain

CHAPTER 1

A Case of a Rapidly Aging Society and Its Dementia Population

Jeanyung Chey

1.1 Introduction

Global aging is one the most significant challenges we are facing today, although aging trajectories differ from country to country (United Nations [UN], 2017, 2019a). In general, population aging takes a socioeconomic toll on a society, and the subsequent rise in the prevalence of dementia is a serious health burden and difficult social issue most aging countries are now confronted with (Patterson, 2018). Dementia is an emotionally difficult illness not only for the patient but also for family members and caregivers. As the patients lose memory, visuospatial abilities, and other cognitive functions, care often becomes a daunting task. It has been estimated that the worldwide cost of dementia was one trillion U.S. dollars in 2016, and this will likely double in 2030 (Patterson, 2018). Fifty million people, approximately the population of South Korea or Spain, live with dementia around the world, and the number has been projected to triple by 2050.

Since age is the most significant risk factor for dementia, with prevalence significantly increasing after 65 years old (Cummings & Benson, 1992), countries with faster population-aging trajectories are likely to experience greater challenges in tackling issues concerning dementia. A country is classified as an "aging society" when 7% of its population are over 65 and as an "aged society" when 14% are, and the rate of its population aging is often gauged by the time it took to become an aged society from an aging society. For instance, France took 115 years, the U.S. 69, Spain 45, and Japan 25 to become an aged society from an aging one (Higo & Khan, 2015), but it took only 18 years for South Korea to transform from an aging to an aged society, making it the fastest-aging country in the world (Korean Statistical Information Service [KOSIS], 2021a; Ogawa & Matsukura, 2007; UN, 2019b). Another measure of population aging, the percentage increase of its population 65 years old and older during a period of time, also illustrates that South Korea would experience a 23% increase from 2019 to

2050, the greatest increase in the world (UN, 2017, 2019b). According to the UN, however, many low- to middle-income countries (i.e., LMICs in Asia and Latin America) are on a similar track, as it has been projected that population aging is growing at a faster pace in these countries than the aged countries in Europe and North America.

In this chapter, the significance of South Korea as a case of interest for understanding global and regional population aging and the associated increasing dementia population is introduced and discussed. A brief history of South Korea, transforming from an agricultural society to a major industrialized nation in less than half a century is introduced, along with major societal changes that would have a major impact on the cognitive aging of older Koreans and their risk for dementia. Earlier studies of cognitive aging of elderly Koreans are introduced, which have demonstrated strong effects of education or literacy on cognitive tests evaluating dementia. Further, the chapter discusses the role of formal education in cognitive development and its moderating effects on neurodegeneration, which would have significant consequences on the prevalence of dementia in older Koreans, especially women. This has important implications on global aging and dementia epidemiology, as well as other health risks associated with rapid modernization, as the current increase in global dementia population is most concentrated in the LMIC countries in Latin America and Asia (Livingston et al., 2020; Patterson et al., 2018).

1.2 From an Agricultural Society to an Industrialized Modern Nation

Today, it is difficult for the younger generation to imagine a post-war Korea with mass poverty, but older Koreans have vivid memories of growing up in small villages scarred by wars and foreign occupation (see Figures 1.1a, 1.1b, 1.1c). The Republic of Korea, better known as South Korea, was established in 1948 amid political turmoil involving foreign interference and clashes of political ideology, resulting in the division of the Korean peninsula into North and South that precipitated the Korean War of 1950–1953. A decade after the war, South Korea initiated the transformation of an age-old agricultural economy heavily reliant on rice farming to a highly industrialized global economy in less than half a century. Sociologist Kyung-Sup Chang characterized the transformation as the "compressed modernization" process of South Korea, and analyzed the sociopolitical, economic, and cultural risks embedded in this rapid transformation (Chang, 1999, 2010).

A Rapidly Aging Society and Its Dementia Population

(a)

Figure 1.1a A family picture taken in Iksan, a small town in Jeollabuk Province, by photographer Joo Myung Duck (1971). It was very common for Korean families to live in a household with three generations, especially in rural villages during the early phase of Korean Economic Development Plan (1962–1996). Copyright provided by Datz Museum of Art.

Historically, Koreans had been mainly rice farmers since the fifth century BC, living in small villages in the Korean peninsula and ruled by monarchs from a number of dynasties until the last one, Chosun, which ended with the Japanese occupation of the peninsula in 1910. Despite the introduction of sporadic industrialization in the early twentieth century by foreign countries and the establishment of a modern republic in 1948, until the early 1960s South Korea remained mostly an agricultural country with a patriarchal infrastructure heavily steeped in Confucianist tradition. After a successful military coup led by Park Jung-Hee in 1961 that overturned the young democracy, the subsequent authoritarian government led by Park and his successors embarked on a very bold economic development plan from 1962 to 1996: the Korean Economic Development Plan (KEDP) (Ko, 2007; Park, 2009). Many agree that the economic overhaul was very effective and efficient in transforming an inert economy into a vibrant one, making Korea an important player in the global market (Park, 2009; Vogel, 1991). Three decades of planned economic development, however, was something similar

(b)

Figure 1.1b A young family walking country lane in Gapyeong, a rural region in Gyeonggi Province, photographed by Joo Myung Duck (1972). Mother is carrying a baby on her back and a basket on her head, following her husband in Gapyeong, a northern rural region.
Copyright provided by Datz Museum of Art.

to a grand-scale social experiment that resulted in a society with a significant number of tensions and asymmetries in its social fabric (Chang, 1999).

1.2.1   Korean Economic Development: Planned and Unintended Outcomes

As the KEDP was implemented to ensure expeditious growth in the economy, Korean society was under perpetual reconstruction. Moreover,

(c)

Figure 1.1c A coal-briquette deliverer in Seoul, 1973. In Kang Woon-gu (2008). Chance or Destiny. Paju, Gyeongido: Yeolhwadang.
Copyright provided by the photographer.

because it was planned and assessed by the authoritarian government with very little oversight, the plan was executed in a regimented military style with minimal consideration for civil rights or the psychological well-being of its citizens (Han & Sharp, 1997). Efficiency was perhaps the most important guiding principle to ramp up the economy in a short period of time, practically a generation, partly due to the fact that the authoritarian dictatorship had to earn its legitimacy through economic growth (Jeon, 2019; Kim, 1997; Ko, 2007). The plan and its execution were very successful in enlarging the Gross National Income (formerly Gross National Product or GNP), jumping from 2.9 billion dollars in 1962 to 608 billion in 1996, a 210-fold increase (World Bank, 2021a), while the Gross Domestic Product per capita increased from $90 in 1962 to $13,398 in 1996 (KOSIS, 2021b). As capital resources to build the economy were extremely scant initially, the industrial infrastructure was built in selected regions and concentrated in selected industries. Businesses, factories, and transportation were built in and around the biggest city and capital, Seoul, with the first highway built to connect Seoul with the biggest port city,

Busan. During the KEDP phase, these urban areas enjoyed huge population growth as the major workforce from farming communities flowed from rural areas into industrial cities (Park, 2009). Further concentration of financial and economic resources was given to a number of big companies or conglomerates that could follow and cooperate with the government's economic plan focused on an export-driven economy (Kim, 1997). Even educational resources were concentrated in the elite or higher education institutions, such as national science and engineering institutes and universities funded by the government and the conglomerates, which were established to educate the future techno-elites who would lead the technology-driven Korean economic development (Jeon, 2019). In comparison, public education at the community level was delegated to private sectors, except the compulsory elementary education that had been established in 1949 (Yang et al., 2010). The implementation of the economic development plan that concentrated on selected fields and sectors of society for three decades would have a lasting imprint on the social fabric and structure of South Korea, which would create unintended outcomes alongside the successful achievement of economic goals.

Interestingly, birth control policy was an important component of the planned economic development, which, although unintended, would have a significant consequence on the population aging of South Korea due to its aggressive and prolonged implementation. Initially, it was established to curb the post-war baby boom that peaked at six births per woman in 1960 and exacerbated the poverty of post-war Korea. With the success of the population control policy, the birth rate decreased significantly every decade, reaching the replacement rate of two in 1984. Unfortunately, the policy continued until 1996 and a reverse policy encouraging people to have children was introduced only in 2006, although a strong downward trend in the birth rate was already becoming established in Korea and its neighboring region (Chang et al., 2010). South Korea's birth rate dropped below one in 2018, and it is currently the lowest in the world at 0.8 (KOSIS, 2021d; UN, 2019b) and expediting population aging as life expectancy increased at the same time.

With the growing economy, the life expectancy of South Koreans increased as public hygiene improved and health-care systems were built. More specifically, average Koreans lived to just fifty-five years old in 1960; however, in 1969 they lived to over sixty, in 1988 to seventy, and to over eighty years old since 2010 (World Bank, 2021b). It has been reported that reductions in infant mortality, diseases related to infection, and cardiovascular disease were the three major factors that contributed to improving the life expectancy of South Koreans (Yang et al., 2010), which was partly possible due to the rapid expansion of the health-care system. Since the first introduction of health insurance for workers in large-scale companies with 500 or more employees in 1977, it was expanded to cover all citizens in just twelve years (Lee, 2003). The national health insurance system, introduced in 1989, no doubt has improved the overall health and quality of life of Koreans significantly. With the dropping birth rate and increasing life expectancy, however, the South Korean population has been growing older speedily. Considering that the percentage of the population aged sixty-five or older was only 2.9% in 1960, the rapid climb to 7% in 2000, officially becoming an aging country, was a major change in the country's social demographics in just forty years since the KEDP took off (Kim, Won, et al., 2003; National Archives of Korea, 2021). Today, one of the most important population policy agendas of the South Korean government is to address and solve the problem of the so-called "demographic cliff" by moving the birth rate upward in order to slow down population aging (Ministry of Health & Welfare, Republic of Korea, 2021), a policy that has not been successful so far.

Rural areas have been hit the hardest in terms of population loss and aging. As business and industrial hubs were being developed, young workers found service and factory jobs in urban areas. Moreover, young students and sometimes their families moved to cities for secondary and higher education, resulting in a significant migration of the younger population to urban areas. Hence, the population aged rapidly and eventually decreased in small agricultural and fishing villages. Just thirty years after the government-led economic development plan had been implemented, prevalence and clinical studies in South Korea started to find an alarming rate of dementia in the growing older population, especially in the rural areas (Park et al., 1994; Woo et al., 1998).

1.2.2 *Education during the Modernization Period*

The Republic of Korea started off with an ambitious plan to introduce compulsory primary education in 1948, and this was implemented right before the war in early 1950. The national elementary school system recovered relatively quickly after the war, but it took many years, in fact half a century, to expand compulsory education to secondary level. Considering that modernized industrialization would require an educated workforce, it is somewhat puzzling that a government initiating an ambitious economic development plan did not expand the compulsory education established in 1950 to middle school and beyond as they embarked on the plan. Unfortunately, it remained solely at primary level until 2002, when middle school was included (Yang et al., 2010). This was partly due to the whole-hearted support of Korean families to educate their children in formal institutions from elementary school to college. For example, the enrollment in primary schools tripled, secondary school enrollment increased more than eight-fold, and higher education by ten times from 1945 to 1960 (Seth, 2017), a trend that continued during the latter part of the twentieth century. According to sociologist Kyungsup Chang (2010), the *social investment family* in Korea, compared to the *social investment state* in the advanced modern countries in Europe and North America, fertilized the social basis for sustained economic development in Korea. Confucian tradition, manifested as "industrial neo-Confucianism," has been proposed as the root of the high motivation of Korean families in educating their children, which contributed to the steep increase in the average number of years of education for younger generations. The entrance exam for higher education and elite institutions was characterized as a common cultural tradition in Eastern countries such as South Korea (Vogel, 1991).

Chang (2010), on the other hand, took note of the significant role education had on the new social ordering in post-war Korean society, in which traditional social order based on land ownership had all but vanished (Kim, 2016). In the new social order, families strived to educate their children so that they would achieve higher social status, mounting to the famous "education fervor" in modern Korea (Seth, 2002). Thanks to the strong motivation and efforts of Korean families to educate the younger generation, the government and businesses were able to get a workforce with higher education without significant investment. Further, the economic development plan from the 1960s relied on low wages to gain competitiveness in exporting goods that required labor-intensive systems, such as in the textile industries (Seth, 2017). Therefore, it is hard to deny that the early exponential growth in the Korean economy benefited from the low labor costs of young workers with little formal education and mostly from the rural areas, who would endure harsh working conditions (Chang, 1995).

Despite its effectiveness in increasing the average years of education (see Figure 1.2a), formal education supported by the *social investment family* had serious side effects. Perhaps the most important was that it failed to provide social mobility for socioeconomically disadvantaged citizens, since it depended on fierce competition between individuals and families and was at odds with the fair provision of educational opportunities (Chang, 2010). It was especially disadvantageous for girls from rural or poor families wanting to receive secondary level education or beyond, as not only did traditional Confucian social order propel more boys to further their education in cities, but also the girls who remained in small rural villages did not have access to public education beyond elementary school. Many girls left their home villages to work in the cities as teenagers in the early stages of the KEDP, which maintained the significant disparity between the education received by women and men before the twenty-first century (Chang, 1995; Sung, 2003). As illustrated in Figure 1.2b, the vast majority of women over sixty-five received only primary education or less in 2005, which contrasts with more than half of men who received secondary education or more. The level of secondary and higher education in older women has risen significantly in the past decade, yet more than half of them did not receive secondary education (KOSIS, 2021c). Surprisingly, young women have entered college more frequently than men in the past eight years, as socioeconomics and culture related to family have changed drastically during the compressed modernization period. Still, the fact that a significant gender disparity in formal education has remained among older Koreans has had somber implications for the dementia risk in women.

1.3 Population Aging, Dementia, and Education

Average South Korean women born in 2030 are projected to live into their nineties for the first time in world history (Kontis et al., 2017). Considering that longevity is one of the most sought-after human desires, especially for Koreans, who have suffered war and life-threatening hardship in their modern history, this news merited great celebration in Korea, yet it was met with ambivalence. The increasing socioeconomic burden and health issues associated with population aging caused more apprehension than jubilation. A recent survey by the National Health Insurance found that dementia is the fourth most important health concern among Koreans (Health Insurance Review & Assessment Service, 2016).

Dementia has been generally defined as an acquired syndrome of intellectual impairment produced by brain dysfunction (Cummings & Benson, 1992), and it is caused by various diseases of the brain. Although memory impairment has been most frequently associated with dementia, the cognitive and behavioral symptoms of dementia vary depending on the brain regions affected by the disease. Most

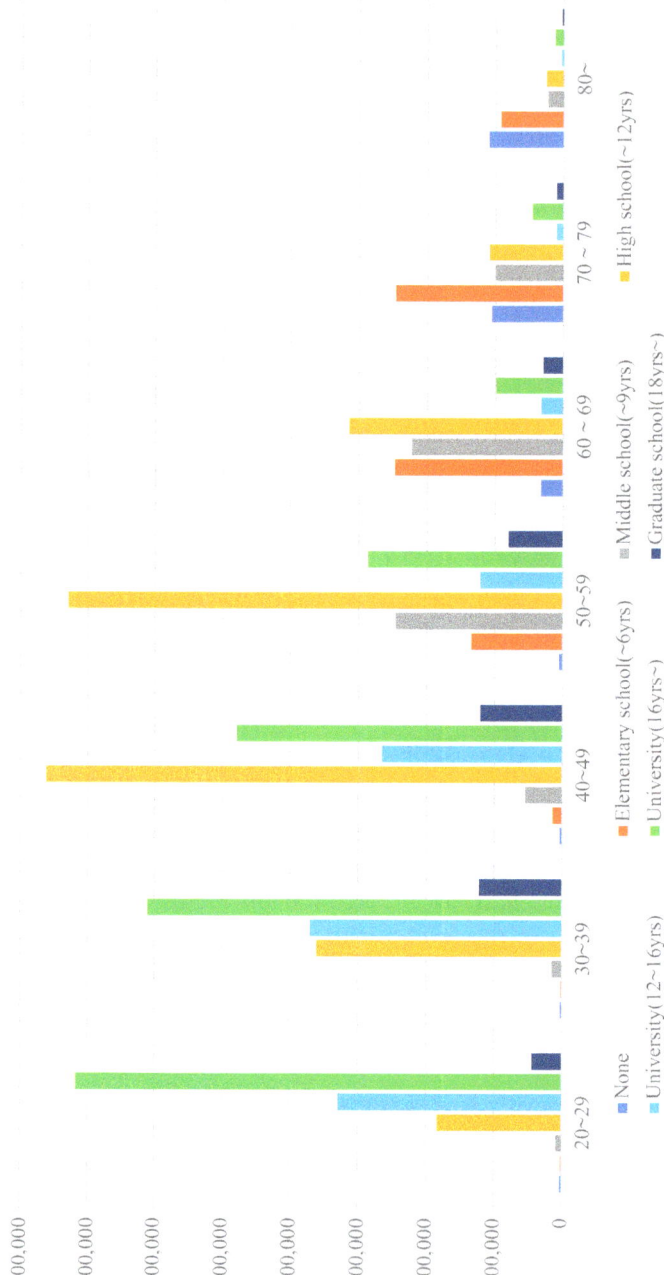

Figure 1.2a Years of Education of Koreans in age brackets – the number of Koreans who received secondary education or higher has increased dramatically over each decade.

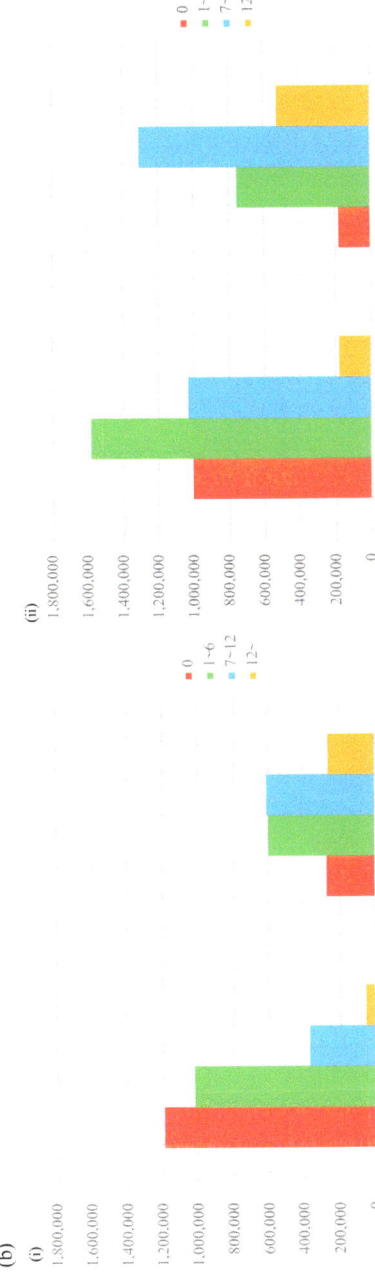

Figure 1.2b Years of education for Korean women and men over 65 years old in 2005 (i) and 2015 (ii), illustrates significant increase in secondary education in older Koreans over a decade.

epidemiological studies have shown Alzheimer's disease to be the most common cause of dementia, followed by vascular diseases or other brain conditions, such as alcoholism-related brain damage, depending on the age, gender, geographical location, and education of the elderly population (Cao et al., 2020; Rizzi et al., 2014).

Concern over increasing dementia prevalence in South Korea became apparent from the 1990s, when studies began reporting levels higher than the world average of 5% in older Koreans (Ferri et al., 2005; Kim et al., 2003; Youn et al., 2005), and 10.8% in a rural area in Gyeongbuk province (Park et al., 1994). Moreover, the numbers were significantly higher than other Asian countries and similar to the more advanced aged countries in Europe and North America. It was particularly noteworthy that dementia prevalence in Taiwan was reported to be 1.7-4.3% (Fuh & Wang, 2008) from 1980 to 2007. Considering that Taiwan has been comparable to South Korea in terms of its economic development and its history of Japanese occupation in the early twentieth century (Vogel, 1991; World Bank, 2021a), the marked disparity in dementia prevalence between the two countries observed in the early 1990s was puzzling (see Table 1.1 for details). Moreover, until recently, Japan, whose population aging was more advanced, reported lower prevalence than Korea, around 6-7% (Ohara et al., 2017). At first glance, it was not clear why the prevalence of dementia in Korea had risen at an alarming rate since population aging started in the 1990s. On closer inspection, however, the prevalence statistics of older Koreans was striking in that women were two to five times more at risk of developing dementia than men (Kim et al., 1999; Lee et al., 2002; Park et al., 1994; Shin et al., 2002; Suh et al., 2003; Woo et al., 1998. See Table 1.2 for details). Although women had been reported to be at increased risk for dementia, especially the Alzheimer's type, a prevalence of this magnitude had not been reported in countries more advanced in aging, such as the U.S., Japan, and France.

The socioeconomic status of an individual, especially their years of formal education, has been found to have a major impact on their risk of dementia (Chapko et al., 2018; Meng & D'Arcy, 2012; Valenzuela & Sachdev, 2006). Formal education has been found to be protective against dementia consistently in numerous studies and has been recognized as one of the proxies of cognitive reserve that can moderate the effects of brain damage or degeneration on cognitive functioning (Varangis & Stern, 2020). As demonstrated in Figure 1.2b, many elderly Koreans, especially women, had low education and some were illiterate. Although many of the uneducated women learned to read and write at home or through the adult

Table 1.1 Dementia prevalence in developed and developing countries

country		references	year	age	area/sample	sample size	prevalence (adjusted/standardized/estimated prevalence) (%)		
							overall	men	women
U.S. and Canada	U.S.	Folstein et al., 1991	1981	65+	Eastern Baltimore	923	(4.5)	(5.2)	(4.0)
		Koller & Bynum, 2015	2008	65+	Medicare Fee-for-Service beneficiaries	4,800,000	8.5 (8.2)	6.4	9.9
		Langa et al., 2017	2012	65+	HRS* cohort	10,511	8.8 (8.6)	–	–
		Matthews et al., 2019	2014	65+	Medicare Fee-for-Service beneficiaries	28,027,071	11.5 (10.9)	9.2 (8.6)	13.3 (12.2)
	Canada	Canadian Study of Health and Aging Working Group, 1994	1991–1992	65+	Medicare lists in nine provinces or Enumeration Composite Record in Ontario and Institutions	10,263	(8.0)	(6.9)	(8.6)
		Public Health Agency of Canada, 2017	2013–2014	65+	Canada excluding Saskatchewan	–	7.1	5.6	8.3
Europe	U.K.	Matthews et al., 2013	1989–1994 2008–2011	65+ 65+	Cambridgeshire, Newcastle, Nottingham	7,635 7,796	(8.3) (6.5)	(7.4) (4.9)	(9.4) (7.7)
	Portugal	Nunes et al., 2010	2003–2004	55–79	Sao João da Madeira, Arouca	1,146	2.7	3.2	2.3
		Gonçalves-Pereira et al., 2017	2012–2013	65+	Fernão Ferro, Mora/Cabeção	1,397	3.7	–	–
		Ruano et al., 2019	2013–2015	55+	Porto	730	1.0 (1.3)	0.4	1.3

Table 1.1 (cont.)

country	references	year	age	area/sample	sample size	prevalence (adjusted/standardized/estimated prevalence) (%)		
						overall	men	women
Spain	Pi et al., 1996	1990	65+	Catalunya (La Selva del Camp)	516	14.9	–	–
	Lobo et al., 2007	1994–1996	65+	Zaragoza	3,715	5.9 (3.9)	3.8 (2.3)	7.4 (5.0)
	Virués-Ortega et al., 2011	1990–2003	75+	Composite population study (Arosa, Bidasoa, Cantalejo, Gerona, Leganes, NEDICES, PRATICON, Santiago, Toledo, Zaragoza)	546	9.0 (7.5)	6.8	10.3
	Tola-Arribas et al., 2013	2009	65–104	Valladolid	2,170	8.5 (5.5)	4.9	11.2
Italy	Ferini-Strambi et al., 1997	1991	60+	Vescovato	673	9.1 (9.8)	–	–
	Prencipe et al., 1996	1992	65+	Poggio Picenze, Scoppito, Tornimparte	968	8.0	7.9	8.2
	Spada et al., 2009	2005–2006	60–85	Sicily (San Teodoro)	280	7.1	–	–
Greece	Tsolaki et al., 1999	1993	70+	Pylea	380	9.6	6.3	12.1
	Kosmidis et al., 2018	–	65+	Larissa, Maroussi, and nearby towns	1,792	5.0	5.6	4.6

Region	Country	Reference	Year	Age	Location	N			
Asia	Japan	Shibayama et al., 1986	1982	65+	Aichi Prefecture	3,106	5.8	—	—
		Okamura et al., 2013	1980–2008 (review)	60+	—	—	2.9–12.5	—	—
		Ninomiya et al., 2020	2016–2018	65+	Research institutions (Tokyo, Fukuoka, Shimane, Ishikawa, Aomori, Iwate, Kumamoto, Ehime)	11,410	8.5	6.6	9.8
	China	Zhang et al., 1990	1987	65+	Shanghai	3,888	(4.6)	(2.0)	(6.6)
		Chiu et al., 1998	1995	65+	Hong Kong	1,034	(4.0)	—	—
		Wu et al., 2018	1989–2016 (review)	65+	Hong Kong	—	7.2	—	—
				60+	—	—	5.3	—	—
		Wang et al., 2019	1985–2018 (review)	60+	—	—	4.9	3.8	5.6
	Taiwan	Fuh & Wang, 2008	1987–1993 (review)	65+	—	—	1.7–4.3	—	—
		Wu et al., 2018	1989–2016 (review)	65+	—	—	6.0	—	—

HRS: Health and Retirement Study

Table 1.2 Prevalence of dementia in Korean men and women

references	year	area	age	sample size	overall	men	women
						prevalence (adjusted/standardized/estimated prevalence) (%)	
Suh et al., 2021	2017	Nationwide	65+	2,972	(8.5)	(5.3)	(10.6)
Jang et al., 2021	2015	Nationwide	60+	352,869	6.7 (5.3)	4.5	8.0
Kim et al., 2014	1990–2013 (review)	–	65+	–	9.2	6.8	10.7
Kim et al., 2011	2008	Nationwide	65+	6,141	9.2 (8.1)	8.0	9.9
Kim et al., 2003	2001	Busan	65+	1,101	7.4 (8.0)	2.4 (2.7)	10.5 (10.0)
Lee et al., 2002	1999–2000	Seoul	65+	643	(8.1)	–	–
Park et al., 1994	1990	Yungil-Gun, Kyungbook	65+	692	10.8	7.2	14.5

literacy program, such as Hangul School, later in life, the cognitive development of these older adults cannot be the same as those who were educated during childhood, which would have made a significant difference in the socioeconomic status and cognitive reserve of these women throughout their adult life. Therefore, it could be hypothesized that the high prevalence of dementia in elderly Korean women is largely due to their higher risk of dementia from insufficient formal education. This hypothesis is somewhat consistent with the observed prevalence of dementia and compulsory education history in South Korea and its regional neighbors with similar economic development during the twentieth century. For instance, Taiwan introduced compulsory education, including elementary and middle school education, in 1968 (Ministry of Education, Republic of China, 2021), while Japan added three years of middle school in 1947 to their compulsory primary education, which was established in the early twentieth century. Hence, most older adults who enjoyed longer life expectancy in these two countries during and after industrialization would have had at least nine years of formal education. In comparison, middle school became compulsory in Korea much later, in 2002 (Yang et al., 2010), and many older Koreans who had been disadvantaged in youth were not able to receive secondary education, most of these being women.

Most of the illiterate and minimally educated Korean women grew up in rural communities steeped in strong patriarchal traditions where women's education was discouraged, or they may have grown up in families that could not afford education for all their children (Park, 1993). Therefore, the preventive effect of compulsory secondary education would have been greater in older adults who grew up in small rural villages where the schools were all but absent, compared to those in cities where public middle schools were more accessible. Albeit in hindsight, the number of older Koreans with dementia would have been much lower, especially in women, if compulsory secondary education had been introduced one generation earlier. It should be mentioned, however, that more recent prevalence studies in both Taiwan and Japan found increased prevalence as the life expectancy has continually increased in both countries (Liu et al., 2019; Ninomiya et al., 2020; Sun et al., 2014).

On the other hand, dementia prevalence has been observed to be relatively high and increasing quickly in the low- and middle-income countries (LMICs), primarily situated in Latin America and South East Asia, which are mostly in the early stage of population aging (Prince et al., 2004, 2013). In fact, about two thirds of people with dementia live in

LMICs, while most new incidences (71%) are expected to occur in these countries (Prina et al., 2019; World Health Organization, 2017). Global investigations on the risk factors of dementia including the LMICs, where secondary education is mostly not compulsory, found that less education is a risk factor for dementia (Livingston et al., 2020), which is consistent with findings in South Korea.

1.3.1 Education, Cognitive Development, and Dementia Diagnosis

One of the first studies to reveal the cognitive functioning of older Koreans was the first project to establish norms for a dementia screening test in Korea. The Korean version of the Dementia Rating Scale (Chey, 1998; Mattis, 1988), a popular test to assess the general cognitive functioning of older adults in North America, was developed and standardized for older Koreans over 55 years old (Chey et al., 1999). It was a small-scale study with 148 community-residing older adults in the Seoul-Gyeonggi region, recruited carefully from diverse districts so that their education and income were representative of the entire area. The normative study demonstrated that on average older Koreans (mean = 125.1, standard deviation [SD] = 9.5) performed significantly lower than their North American counterparts (mean = 137.3, SD = 6.9) and also revealed a greater range of performance. A strong education effect was also found in the Korean sample, in addition to the usual age effect found in the North American elderly population (Chey et al., 1999). These results were consistent with other studies with a wider range of education than the U.S. sample (Schmidt et al., 1994), and were later replicated with a larger Korean sample (Suk et al., 2010). In the first study, older Koreans who received higher education performed on par with their North American counterparts (men and women equally), but those who did not finish elementary education performed poorly on the tests. Moreover, men performed significantly better than women on average, but this disparity disappeared when the education effect was removed. Another interesting finding was the wider range of cognitive performance observed in older adults with low education, especially those with no education, with scores ranging from 68 to 140, a range that narrowed as the years of education increased (primary education 98-144; secondary education 110-144; higher education 120-144; Chey et al., 1998), which could reflect the "scaffolding effect" of early education on people's cognitive and brain development (Vygotsky, 1978), particularly for children living in environments not conducive to learning and cognitive development. Extremely low scores on cognitive tests were frequently observed in individuals with little formal education, who were often illiterate. Upon interviewing the participant and her family members, however, no significant cognitive or functional decline would be reported among illiterate women. Many of these older adults living in rural areas didn't know or didn't care about their addresses, frequently asked in mental state tests, but they were efficient in working at the farm or taking care of the household.

An urgent issue was raised, therefore, concerning the validity of dementia tools or neuropsychological tests developed in North America and Europe when assessing older Koreans with few years of education (Chey et al., 1998, 1999, 2002; Cho et al., 2002). Since the items in dementia tests were matched to cognitive functioning for normal North American adults who had typically finished secondary education, limited performance due to lack of education or illiteracy had not been considered as a possibility when the tests were originally developed. It was a challenge to discriminate between mild dementia from a low cognitive performance due to lack of education (Chey et al., 2006).

Hence, in-depth investigation of the relationship between mind and brain was necessary not only at an individual but also at the population level. Findings from the Clock Drawing Test (CDT) performance of older adults with little education was a good example of how cautious an evaluator should be when testing older adults with little formal education, and this is especially true for those who are illiterate (Kim & Chey, 2010). Despite involving multiple cognitive functions, the simplicity of CDT earned its popularity as a dementia screening tool in North America. A number of Korean clinicians, therefore, had expected the test to be a short but effective test for dementia screening in older Koreans. Compared to the automatic process of clock reading, it has been found that drawing a clock upon a verbal command with hands consistent with a specific time requires a complex array of neuropsychological functions, such as language comprehension, visuospatial abilities, executive functions, and the representation of a clock and its retrieval (Freedman et al., 1994). Therefore, the rationale of the test was that performance or errors on the CDT would be informative of the older testee's overall cognitive functioning. Findings from dementia and other neurological patients in North America and Europe supported this assumption (Shulman, 2000).

A study investigating the CDT performance of normal elderly Koreans, however, found significant effects of education in this apparently simple test, most dramatically demonstrated in the illiterate older adults. More specifically, illiterate individuals not only scored very low on the CDT, but also

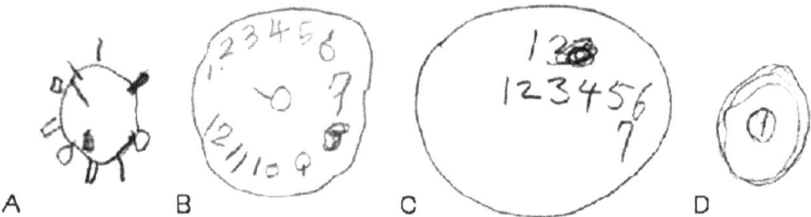

Figure 1.3 Conceptual errors on the Clock Drawing Test of uneducated older adults without dementia (A & B) and patients with dementia of the Alzheimer's type (C & D). (Adapted from Kim & Chey, 2010).

made "conceptual errors," which is characterized by the absence of the representation of a clock, namely, the conceptualization error (Kim & Chey, 2010), which had been formally regarded as a hallmark of dementia of the Alzheimer's type (see Figure 1.3). An illiterate elderly individual, however, would commit the error not because she had lost the representation of a clock but because she had never acquired it in her life (see Figure 1.3).

Concept formation and other higher cognitive functions depend on the integrity of the prefrontal cortex and its connecting brain regions as well as on lengthy formal education (Chey & Park, 2011). In the study, a number of older women who grew up in rural villages did not know how to tell the time from a clock at home nor read destinations on a bus or street signs throughout their lives (Kim & Chey, 2010). Despite a significant limitation of mental faculty in modernized Korea, illiteracy had been very common in Korea and throughout the world until the nineteenth century. For instance, only 12% of the global population could read and write in 1820 (Roser & Ortiz-Ospina, 2016).

Most importantly, the clinical validity of the CDT was investigated in the study by comparing the test performance of mild Alzheimer's dementia patients with those of normal controls. The comparison illustrated that the test performance did not adequately discriminate between the two groups in older adults with less than six years of education (Kim & Chey, 2010). Further, the results showed that nonverbal tests could be as challenging for older adults with low education as the verbal tests. This was consistent with other observations of tests of visuospatial functioning, which were thought to be independent of culture and education. For example, copying and recalling nonverbal material, such as the Rey Complex Figure, proved to be too complicated and difficult for most older Koreans with less than high school education, and the figure stimuli needed to be simplified to be suitable for the population (Kim, 2001; Park et al., 2011).

Despite the numerous challenges involved in developing dementia assessment tools that would be valid and reliable for an elderly population with a wide spectrum of education, a number of screening tools as well as more refined neuropsychological tests were developed in Korea during a short period of time (see for reviews; Chey & Park, 2011; Kim & Chey, 2016). Most recently, the Korean version of the Harmonized Cognitive Assessment Protocol (K-HCAP; Chey et al., 2022; Lee et al., 2020) has been developed, which can be utilized in international comparison between the Health and Retirement Study and its sister projects around the world (Langa et al., 2020; Lee et al., 2019).

1.3.2 Cognitive Aging and Dementia in Older Adults with Low Education

As standardized cognitive tests with age and education norms became available in Korea from the late 1990s, clinicians faced a difficult dilemma of whether to diagnose minimally educated individuals with low cognitive performance (LCP) as cases of mild cognitive impairment (MCI), a possible preclinical stage of dementia that was proposed as a clinical entity that could be prime for treatment (Petersen et al., 1999). More specifically, questions were raised whether the community-residing elderly individuals demonstrating a below-normal range of cognitive performance but not meeting dementia diagnosis criteria (Winblad et al., 2004) should be classified as MCI, which progresses to dementia in approximately 40% of cases (Mitchell & Shiri-Feshki, 2009), two to seven times higher than those with normal cognition (Boyle et al., 2006). As neuroimaging technologies advanced to measure neuropathologies in vivo (Mintun et al., 2006), studies found that the neuropathology of Alzheimer's disease, the main disease to cause dementia, developed much earlier than its clinical symptoms, sometimes more than a decade before (Convit et al., 1997; Fox et al., 1996; Jack et al., 2010; Kaye et al., 1997; Vemuri et al., 2009; Wolf et al., 2004). Therefore, understanding the nature of the LCP observed in older Koreans with no or minimal formal education became imperative and urgent to improve the diagnostic accuracy in a country where over 70% of adults over sixty-five years old received six or fewer years of formal education (KOSIS, 2006). Utilizing magnetic resonance imaging (MRI)-based volumetry, Chey et al. (2006) examined the medial temporal lobe, which typically shows the first signs of atrophy in Alzheimer's disease in community-residing older adults who have received no more than six years of education. Based on the fact that individuals with MCI show smaller medial temporal structures, such as the entorhinal cortex and the hippocampus (Convit et al., 1997; Wolf et al., 2004), it was reasoned that if the minimally educated older adults with LCP showed smaller volumes in the entorhinal cortex or hippocampus than those with normal cognitive performance, they are likely to be similar to the MCI cases observed in North America and should be classified as having MCI. Critical for storing information experienced by the individual (i.e., episodic memory), the volumes of these structures were compared in the two groups of older adults with minimal education but who did not show functional decline in everyday life. The study found no significant difference in the two medial temporal lobe structures when corrected with the size of the cranium, which suggested that the memory structures of the LCP did not show more atrophy in the brain regions vulnerable to Alzheimer's disease, as found in the MCI cases. Moreover, upon one- and three-year follow-up evaluations, the LCP elderly individuals generally improved on the cognitive scores as they familiarized themselves with the paper-and-pencil tests, while the older adults with normal cognitive performance did not show such gains. These findings suggested that the LCP elderly individuals were unlikely to be MCI cases, who should have shown cognitive decline in the following assessment and converted to dementia at the rate of 5–10% annually (Mitchell & Shiri-Feshki, 2009).

Whole brain volumes of the LCP older adults measured with the intracranial cavity volume, however, were significantly smaller than those with normal cognitive performance. Though unexpected, the finding was consistent with studies that reported significant correlation between whole brain size and education (Mortimer et al., 2003) and also intelligence (Pietschnig et al., 2015; Willerman et al., 1991; Witelson et al., 2006). A later study, utilizing automatic regional volumetry of the whole brain, found that the older adults with LCP had significantly smaller volumes in the bilateral precuneus and prefrontal cortices, both of which are cortical hubs with rich structural connections to associative cortices and regions closely associated with intelligence, self-awareness, and higher cognitive functions (Chey et al., 2016).

These findings significantly helped to reduce the ambiguity of interpreting the LCP of community-residing older adults who received little formal education. More specifically, the LCP older adults were not preclinical dementia patients but those who had low overall cognitive capacity throughout their lifetime, mostly due to lack of formal education. Since the two cognitive performance groups were matched in years of education and all participants had received no more than six years of education, it is likely that even informal education had not been available to the LCP individuals. This is consistent with the fact that more than half of them were illiterate, while none of the normal cognitive performance group were.

Although LCP in community-residing older adults with low education does not indicate incipient dementia, smaller whole brain and certain regional volumes could pose a risk for earlier manifestation of dementia in these individuals once neurodegeneration starts in the brain (Mori et al., 1997; Wolf et al., 2004). Indeed, after six years of follow-up, older adults with LCP demonstrated more frequent cognitive decline and dementia, despite the fact that their cognitive performance improved in the first three years (Shin, 2017; Shin, Chey, & Lee, 'Is low cognitive performance a risk for dementia in elderly people who lack formal education?' Unpublished manuscript). As LCP was only observed in older adults with few years of education and often illiterate, these results were consistent with studies that found greater risk of dementia in people with less education and illiteracy (Ashby-Mitchell et al., 2017; Norton et al., 2014; Rentería et al., 2019; Spada et al., 2009). Formal education, a proxy of the cognitive reserve, moderates the clinical manifestation of dementia, delaying it by increasing the reserve capacity of the brain (Stern, 2012). Similarly, low cognitive functioning or lower intelligence can also pose a risk for dementia (Russ, 2018). Therefore, the risk of dementia for older Koreans would be high as a population, as a significant number of older women received no or minimal education and many had low cognitive functioning throughout their lifetime. More detailed discussions regarding the moderating effects of cognitive reserve, whose proxies include years of education and intelligence, will be discussed in Chapter 5.

1.3.3 Other Modifiable Risks Associated with Compressed Modernization

Rapid societal change can accompany psychological and physical challenges and adversities for its constituents that can be harmful to their brain health. Instability in social positions, unsafe working and living environments that could result in brain injuries and exposure to neurotoxins, and air pollution are modifiable social factors that increase the risk of dementia.

Financial Insecurity and Social Isolation in Late Life
Many older Koreans face economic hardship after retirement, as the introduction of the pension system has been slow and spotty with slim

support that is frequently insufficient to support late life. Weak social investment by the state and heavy reliance on families for the care and support of the older generation, amid financial crisis and the emergence of new social paradigms characterized by nuclear families and dense urbanization, have left Koreans very vulnerable in late life (Chang, 2018). Traditionally, the eldest son and his family lived with his parents and supported and took care of his parents in late life (*mosigi*), as he inherited the land or means of living. A family system based on Confucian agricultural society had to go through major change under the compressed modernization process. The migration of children to cities and the rising urban real-estate prices made cohabitating with adult children for support and care very difficult if not impossible for many parents. Moreover, the first financial crisis in the late 1990s, which required IMF intervention, devastated the South Korean economy and drove many companies and families into bankruptcy. Many disadvantaged adult children could not support nor take care of their aging parents as the economy became unfavorable, and the aging parents at the turn of the century found themselves with insecure support or care from their adult children for the first time in Korean history. A majority of aging Koreans were shattered in that they were not prepared financially, socially, or emotionally to be independent in late life. It was possible that they may have invested too heavily in their children's education, and many were left with little or no financial reserve to support themselves in late life. In fact, the poverty rate of elderly Koreans is around 43.4%, the highest among the Organisation for Economic Co-operation and Development (OECD) member countries and about three times the average of 14.8% (OECD, 2021). But most importantly, this seismic shift in the familial system was accompanied by frequent conflicts and estrangement between family members, accelerating the disintegration of the traditional social fabric of the country.

Today, 35% of older South Koreans report that they have no one to discuss matters with during difficult times, the highest among OECD member countries, whose average is 11.5% (OECD, 2021). Undoubtedly, social isolation among older Koreans stems from disconnection from family members, including their adult children. Being estranged from one's children has been found to be a particularly significant stressor among older Koreans in studies investigating the role of stress in cognitive decline in community-residing older adults (Lee, 2005). Considering the traditional parental expectation towards adult children, this was frequently accompanied by significant grief, depression, and disappointment, which contributed to cognitive decline in many older Koreans (Kwak, 2006; Lee, 2005; Park et al., 2014). Especially vulnerable were older adults who moved to the city in their late life for health and financial reasons or those with low education who had weaker social support from neighbors and relatives, whom they could rely on when family members were unavailable.

Although social isolation and loneliness have been a significant social problem in high-income countries, such as Japan, Denmark, and the U.K., it has been recognized as a serious issue in South Korea only recently. Increasingly, social isolation among older citizens is being recognized as a major social issue, as a significant number of older adults have been found dead alone by strangers, referred to as *godoksa*, meaning solitary death. Various risk factors, such as economic hardship, chronic illness, alcoholism, social isolation, unemployment, estranged family relations, single-person households, and living in an urban area (Kim & Park, 2017), have been associated with *godoksa* or suicide among older Koreans. It is undeniable that these tragedies stem from a rapid disintegration of the family-based social support system that would have provided care and support for older citizens in previous generations. The ironic "individualization of the older adults without the individualism" proposed by Chang (2018, p. 108) aptly characterizes the socially disconnected and lonely plight many older Koreans are confronted with today, especially those with lower socioeconomic standing. The following chapters, especially Chapter 7, review and discuss dementia and other health risks posed by loneliness and social disconnection in late life, while Chapter 12 reviews social programs and policies that are geared to reduce social isolation and its ill-health effects, especially dementia.

High-Risk Environment for Brain Injury and Damage
Considering that traumatic brain injury is a major risk for dementia (Plassman et al., 2000; Shively et al., 2012), older Koreans who have experienced a moderate to severe head injury (e.g., in factories, on construction sites, or in vehicular accidents) would be two to four times higher at risk for dementia. Moreover, the risk of dementia increases exponentially with repeated injuries, as the risk increases twofold with a single injury but fourfold for the second injury (Li et al., 2017; Schneider et al., 2021). Although studies reporting detailed and accurate statistics were not available for traumatic brain injury, the fact that South Korea has maintained high rates of death due to both traffic and industrial accidents until very recently suggests that a history of brain injury would be quite prevalent among older Koreans. It is unfortunate that necessary

precautions to prevent major injuries or exposure to toxic chemicals have not been seriously enforced in Korea, partly due to ignorance, but also for the sake of efficiency or productivity. Frequent traffic accidents have endangered the brain health of pedestrians due to automobile-centered traffic regulations in the past. Moreover, construction sites with scant safety precautions have been major sites for falls and injuries, which if not fatal would have resulted in head injuries. Safety regulations have changed in recent years, but the history of brain injuries among older adults remains, and it is likely to have significantly increased the risk of dementia for elderly Koreans.

Korean farmers were not safe from the hazards of industrialization, since they were exposed to pesticides that were introduced extensively from the 1960s when the "new village movement" (*saemael undong*) began. The pesticides that were imported and distributed widely since the time of the KEDP purported to increase the productivity of the crops significantly, but without adequate precautions concerning the toxicity of the chemicals. Organophosphate pesticide (OPP), one of the most common pesticides around the world, has been found to contain neurotoxins and was banned for residential use in the U.S.A. in 2001. Considering that rice, the major crop in Korea, requires labor-intensive farming, it is likely that rice farmers had been exposed to the chemicals quite heavily in the past when the health risks of the pesticides were unknown to the public. Prolonged exposure to OPP has been found to increase the risk for dementia (Killin et al., 2016), in addition to the increased risks for cardiovascular and respiratory diseases (Hung et al., 2015; Peiris-John et al., 2005) and cancer (Alavanja et al., 2004; Lerro et al., 2015). Since the detrimental effects of the pesticides on dementia risks tend to be stronger in less educated people (McDowell et al., 1994), the increased risk for dementia posed by the OPP should be examined more seriously in rural Korea.

Recently, air pollution and particulate pollutants have been found to be detrimental to brain health and to accelerate neurodegeneration, which appears to increase the risk of dementia (Livingston et al., 2020). In a systematic review of studies from many countries, exposure to fine ambient particulate matter (PM2.5), nitrogen dioxide (NO2), and carbon monoxide, very common air pollutants from traffic exhaust fumes and thermal power generation in South Korea (Wolf et al., 2022), have been found to be consistently associated with dementia risks (Peters et al., 2019). In recent years, air pollution has become a major health hazard and stressor for South Koreans, as the nation's air quality ranks 119 among 180 countries and is likely to be a significant risk for dementia in the future.

1.4 Conclusions

Recently, the World Health Organization (2017) announced the "Global action plan on the public health response to dementia 2017–2025." As global population aging is advancing quickly, the number of people with dementia is increasing rapidly. It is projected to be 75 million in 2030 and 132 million by 2050, compared to 47 million in 2015. Further, about 60% of people with dementia live in LMICs, and most new incidences (71%) are expected to occur in these countries. Rapid aging following compressed modernization and industrialization in South Korea appears to make it the foremost case of the global trend of speedy population aging in LMICs. Although South Korea has been recently categorized as an advanced economy and a high-income country (World Bank, 2021a), its case bears similarity with the more recently aging countries.

South Korea is one of the fastest-aging countries in world history, and its dementia population is growing swiftly. The events were in large part inadvertent results of the expeditious economic development plan and compressed modernization carried out in the latter part of the twentieth century. The government-driven economic development plan that spanned a generation from 1962 to 1996 was extremely successful economically but would have significant side effects, such as rapid population aging and high dementia prevalence. Moreover, the Korean government's heavy reliance on the family and private sectors for important social investment, such as education and care, inadvertently resulted in disintegration of social support from family that would contribute to the increasing public health problems.

The unintended outcomes of expeditious industrialization have been discussed in terms of population aging. The role of education in cognitive test performance and in preventing dementia during cognitive aging has been illustrated with cognitive and brain aging studies on older Koreans with a wide range of education levels. Further, other modifiable risks of dementia associated with compressed modernization, such as financial insecurity and social isolation in late life, which have not been addressed sufficiently in South Korea, needed mentioning.

The case of South Korea has implications for LMICs, which are now experiencing rapid aging and alarming incidence of dementia. There is an argument for pacing industrialization to ensure social infrastructures do not disintegrate without the introduction of alternative systems so that older adults can be adequately supported in their late life. Further, having policies to establish compulsory secondary education accessible to both girls and boys as well as to protect adults' brain health from environmental and industrial hazards appear to be important measures to reduce the incidence of dementia in the future.

REFERENCES

Alavanja, M. C., Hoppin, J. A., & Kamel, F. (2004). Health effects of chronic pesticide exposure: Cancer and neurotoxicity. *Annu. Rev. Public Health*, *25*, 155–197.

Ashby-Mitchell, K., Burns, R., Shaw, J., & Anstey, K. J. (2017). Proportion of dementia in Australia explained by common modifiable risk factors. *Alzheimer's Research & Therapy*, *9*(1), 1–8.

Boyle, P. A., Wilson, R. S., Aggarwal, N. T., Tang, Y., & Bennett, D. A. (2006). Mild cognitive impairment: Risk of Alzheimer disease and rate of cognitive decline. *Neurology*, *67*(3), 441–445.

Canadian Study of Health and Aging Working Group. (1994). Canadian Study of Health and Aging: Study methods and prevalence of dementia. *Can. Med. Assoc. J.*, *150*(6), 899–913.

Cao, Q., Tan, C. C., Xu, W., Hu, H., Cao, X. P., Dong, Q., Tan, L., & Yu, J. T. (2020). The prevalence of dementia: A systematic review and meta-analysis. *Journal of Alzheimer's Disease*, *73*(3), 1157–1166.

Chang, K. S. (1995). Gender and abortive capitalist social transformation: Semi-proletarianization of South Korean women. *International Journal of Comparative Sociology*, *36*(1), 61.

(1999). Compressed modernity and its discontents: South Korean society in transition, *Economy and Society*, *28*(1), 30–55.

(2010). *South Korea under Compressed Modernity: Familial Political Economy in Transition*. Routledge.

(2018). *The End of Tomorrow: Familial Liberalism and the Crisis of Reproduction*. Jipmudang.

Chang, Y. S., Kim, N. Y., Lee, S. Y., & Chin, D. R. (2010). *Trends and Projections on Korean Population*. Korea Institute for Health and Social Affairs (KIHASA).

Chapko, D., McCormack, R., Black, C., Staff, R., & Murray, A. (2018). Life-course determinants of cognitive reserve (CR) in cognitive aging and dementia – a systematic literature review. *Aging & Mental Health*, *22*(8), 921–932.

Chey, J. (1998). *Korean-Dementia Rating Scale*. Hakjisa.

Chey, J., Kim, M. J., Stern, Y., Shin, M., Byun, H., & Habeck, C. (2016). Neural substrates of reserve observed in a non-demented aging population. *Journal of Alzheimer's Disease & Parkinsonism*, *6*(7), 294.

Chey, J., Kim, S. Y., Cho, B., & Park, M. (2002). Normative study of the Computerized Dementia Screening Test (CDST). *Korean Journal of Clinical Psychology 21*(2), 445–460.

Chey, J., Lee, D., Kwak, S., & Lee, J. (2022). Validation study of the Korean version of Harmonized Cognitive Assessment Protocol (K-HCAP). Paper presented at the INS 2022 Meeting in Barcelona Spain.

Chey, J. Lee, S., Park, S., & Park, E. (1998, February). Development of the Norms for the Korean-Dementia Rating Scale [presentation]. International Neuropsychological Society (INS) Meeting, Honolulu, Hawaii

Chey, J., Na, D. G., Tae, W. S., Ryoo, J. W., & Hong, S. B. (2006). Medial temporal lobe volume of nondemented elderly individuals with poor cognitive functions. *Neurobiology of Aging, 27*(9), 1269–1279.

Chey, J., Na, D. R., Park, S., Park, E., & Lee, S. (1999). Effects of education in dementia assessment: Evidence from standardizing the Korean-Dementia Rating Scale. *The Clinical Neuropsychologist, 13*(3), 293–302.

Chey, J., & Park, H. (2011). Neuropsychology in Korea. In D. Fuji (ed.), *The Neuropsychology of Asian Americans*, pp. 247–267. Psychology Press.

Chey, J. Y., & Lee, S. A. (1997). Development of the norms for the Korean-Dementia Rating Scale. *Korean Journal of Clinical Psychology, 16*, 423–433.

Chiu, H. F. K., Lam, L. C. W., Chi, I., Leung, T., Li, S. W., Law, W. T., Chung, D. W., Fung, H. H., Kan, P. S., Lum, C. M., Ng, J., & Lau, J. (1998). Prevalence of dementia in Chinese elderly in Hong Kong. *Neurology, 50*(4), 1002–1009.

Cho, B., Yang, J., Kim, S., Yang, D. W., Park, M., & Chey, J. (2002). The validity and reliability of a Computerized Dementia Screening Test developed in Korea. *Journal of the Neurological Sciences, 203*, 109–114.

Convit, A., De Leon, M. J., Tarshish, C., De Santi, S., Tsui, W., Rusinek, H., & George, A. (1997). Specific hippocampal volume reductions in individuals at risk for Alzheimer's disease. *Neurobiology of Aging, 18*(2), 131–138.

Cummings, J. L., & Benson, D. F. (1992). *Dementia: A Clinical Approach.* Butterworth-Heinemann Medical.

Ferini-Strambi, L., Marcone, A., Garancini, P., Danelon, F., Zamboni, M., Massussi, P., Tedesi, B., & Smirne, S. (1997). Dementing disorders in north Italy: Prevalence study in Vescovato, Cremona Province. *European Journal of Epidemiology, 13*(2), 201–204.

Ferri, C. P., Prince, M., Brayne, C., Brodaty, H., Fratiglioni, L., Ganguli, M., Hall, K., Hasegawa, K., Hendrie, H., Huang, Y., Jorm, A., Mathers, C., Menezes, P. R., Rimmer, E., & Scazufca, M. (2005). Alzheimer's Disease International. Global prevalence of dementia: A Delphi consensus study. *Lancet, 366*(9503), 2112–2117. https://doi.org/10.1016/s0140-6736(05)67889-0

Folstein, M. F., Bassett, S. S., Anthony, J. C., Romanoski, A. J., & Nestadt, G. R. (1991). Dementia: Case ascertainment in a community survey. *Journal of Gerontology, 46*(4), M132–M138.

Fox, N. C., Warrington, E. K., Freeborough, P. A., Hartikainen, P., Kennedy, A. M., Stevens, J. M., & Rossor, M. N. (1996). Presymptomatic hippocampal atrophy in Alzheimer's disease: A longitudinal MRI study. *Brain, 119*(6), 2001–2007.

Freedman, M., Leach, L., Kaplan, E., Winocur, G., Shulman, K., & Delis, D. C. (1994). *Clock Drawing: A Neuropsychological Analysis*. Oxford University Press.

Fuh, J. L., & Wang, S. J. (2008). Dementia in Taiwan: Past, present, and future. *Acta Neurol Taiwan*, *17*(3), 153–161.

Gonçalves-Pereira, M., Cardoso, A., Verdelho, A., da Silva, J. A., De Almeida, M. C., Fernandes, A., Raminhos, C., Ferri, C. P., Prina, A. M., Prince, M., & Xavier, M. (2017). The prevalence of dementia in a Portuguese community sample: A 10/66 Dementia Research Group study. *BMC geriatrics*, *17*(1), 1–11.

Han, G. S., & Sharp, R. (1997). Economic development in South Korea: By-product of military regimes. *Policy, Organisation and Society*, *14*(1), 23–39.

Health Insurance Review & Assessment Service. (2016). Korea's diseases of most concern http://www.hira.or.kr/bbsDummy.do?brdBltNo=9243&brdScnBltNo=4&pgmid=HIRAA020041000100#none

Higo, M., & Khan, H. T. (2015). Global population aging: Unequal distribution of risks in later life between developed and developing countries. *Global Social Policy*, *15*(2), 146–166.

Hung, D. Z., Yang, H. J., Li, Y. F., Lin, C. L., Chang, S. Y., Sung, F. C., & Tai, S. C. (2015). The long-term effects of organophosphates poisoning as a risk factor of CVDs: A nationwide population-based cohort study. *PLoS ONE*, *10*(9), e0137632.

Jack, C. R., Knopman, D. S., Jagust, W. J., Shaw, L. M., Aisen, P. S., Weiner, M. W., Petersen, R. C., & Trojanowski J. Q. (2010). Hypothetical model of dynamic biomarkers of the Alzheimer's pathological cascade. *The Lancet Neurology*, *9*(1), 119–128.

Jang, J. W., Park, J. H., Kim, S., Lee, S. H., Lee, S. H., & Kim, Y. J. (2021). Prevalence and incidence of dementia in South Korea: A nationwide analysis of the National Health Insurance Service senior cohort. *Journal of Clinical Neurology*, *17*(2), 249.

Jeon, J. (2019). Economic efficiency debate on state interventionism: How could Korea in Park Chung Hee regime achieve economic growth despite corruption? *Humanities Social Science Research*, *20*(3), 1–31.

Kaye, J. A., Swihart, T., Howieson, D., Dame, A., Moore, M. M., Karnos, T., Camicioli, R., Ball, M., Oken, B., & Sexton, G. (1997). Volume loss of the hippocampus and temporal lobe in healthy elderly persons destined to develop dementia. *Neurology*, *48*(5), 1297–1304.

Killin, L. O., Starr, J. M., Shiue, I. J., & Russ, T. C. (2016). Environmental risk factors for dementia: A systematic review. *BMC Geriatrics*, *16*(1), 1–28.

Kim, D. H., Na, D. L., Yeon, B. G., Kang, Y., Min, K. B., Lee, S. H., Lee, S. S., Lee, M. R., Pyo, O. J., Park, C. B., Kim, S., & Bae, S. S. (1999). Prevalence of dementia in the elderly of an urban community in Korea. *Korean Journal of Preventive Medicine*, *32*(3), 306–316.

Kim, E. (2001). *A Normative Study of the Simple Rey Figure Test*. Master's Thesis, Sungshin Women's University.

Kim, E. M. (1997). *Big Business, Strong State: Collusion and Conflict in South Korean Development, 1960–1990.* Suny Press.

Kim, H., & Chey, J. (2010). Effects of education, literacy, and dementia on the Clock Drawing Test performance. *Journal of the International Neuropsychological Society, 16*(6), 1138–1146.

Kim, I. (2016). Land reform in South Korea under the US military occupation, 1945–1948. *Journal of Cold War Studies, 18*(2), 97–129.

Kim, J., Jeong, I., Chun, J. H., & Lee, S. (2003). The prevalence of dementia in a metropolitan city of South Korea. *International Journal of Geriatric Psychiatry, 18*(7), 617–622.

Kim, K. W., Park, J. H., Kim, M. H., Kim, M. D., Kim, B. J., Kim, S. K., Kim, J. L., Moon, S.W., Bae, J. N., Woo, J. I., Ryu, S. H., Yoon, J. C., Lee, N. J., Lee, D. Y., Lee, S. B., Lee, J. J., Lee, J. Y., Lee, C. U., Chang, S. M., ... & Cho, M. J. (2011). A nationwide survey on the prevalence of dementia and mild cognitive impairment in South Korea. *Journal of Alzheimer's Disease, 23* (2), 281–291.

Kim, M., & Park, J. M. (2017). Factors affecting cognitive function according to gender in community-dwelling elderly individuals. *Epidemiology and Health, 39*.

Kim, M. S., & Chey, J. (2016). Clinical neuropsychology in South Korea. *The Clinical Neuropsychologist, 30*(8), 1325–1334.

Kim, M. S., Won, J. W., Suh, M. H., Kang, B. G., & Lim, Y. K. (2003). *Socioeconomic Problems of an Aging Society and Policy Responses: Experience of OECD Member Countries.* KIHASA.

Kim, Y. J., Han, J. W., So, Y. S., Seo, J. Y., Kim, K. Y., & Kim, K. W. (2014). Prevalence and trends of dementia in Korea: A systematic review and meta-analysis. *Journal of Korean Medical Science, 29*(7), 903–912.

Ko, J. Y. (2007). The South Korean experience in economic development. *Making world development work: Scientific alternatives to neoclassical economic theory, 127–141.*

Koller, D., & Bynum, J. P. (2015). Dementia in the USA: State variation in prevalence. *Journal of Public Health, 37*(4), 597–604.

Kontis, V., Bennett, J. E., Mathers, C. D., Li, G., Foreman, K., & Ezzati, M. (2017). Future life expectancy in 35 industrialised countries: Projections with a Bayesian model ensemble. *The Lancet, 389*(10076), 1323–1335.

Korean Statistical Information Service (KOSIS). (2006). *Statistics of Education.* [Data set]. https://kosis.kr/statHtml/statHtml.do?orgId=101&tblId=DT_1IN0504&conn_path=I3

(2021a). *Statistics Korea, Population Projections for Korea.* [Data set]. https://kosis.kr/statHtml/statHtml.do?orgId=101&tblId=DT_1BPA002&conn_path=I2

(2021b). *Gross Domestic Product.* [Data set]. https://kosis.kr/statHtml/statHtml.do?orgId=101&tblId=DT_2KAA904_OECD&conn_path=I2

(2021c). *Statistics of Education.* [Data set]. https://kosis.kr/statHtml/statHtml.do?orgId=101&tblId=DT_1PM1501&conn_path=I3

(2021d). *Statistics of Birth Rate.* https://kosis.kr/statHtml/statHtml.do?orgId=101&tblId=DT_1B81A21&checkFlag=N

Kosmidis, M. H., Vlachos, G. S., Anastasiou, C. A., Yannakoulia, M., Dardiotis, E., Hadjigeorgiou, G., Sakka, P., Ntanasi, E., & Scarmeas, N. (2018). Dementia prevalence in Greece. *Alzheimer Disease & Associated Disorders*, *32*(3), 232–239.

Kwak, Y. (2006). *Perceived Stress is Associated with Decreased Posterior Cingulate Metabolism and Poor Episodic Memory.* Master's thesis, Seoul National University.

Langa, K. M., Larson, E. B., Crimmins, E. M., Faul, J. D., Levine, D. A., Kabeto, M. U., & Weir, D. R. (2017). A comparison of the prevalence of dementia in the United States in 2000 and 2012. *JAMA Internal Medicine*, *177*(1), 51–58.

Langa, K. M., Ryan, L. H., McCammon, R. J., Jones, R. N., Manly, J. J., Levine, D. A., Sonnega, A., Farron, M., & Weir, D. R. (2020). The health and retirement study harmonized cognitive assessment protocol project: Study design and methods. *Neuroepidemiology*, *54*(1), 64–74.

Lee, D., Kwak, S., Lee, J., & Chey, J. (2020). Validation of Korean-Harmonized Cognitive Assessment Protocol (K-HCAP): A Pilot Study. Poster presentation, 2020 Annual Conference of the Korean Psychological Association (KPA), Korea.

Lee, D. Y., Lee, J. H., Ju, Y. S., Kang Uk Lee, M. D., Kim, K. W., Jhoo, J. H., Yoon, J. C., Ha, J., & Woo, J. I. (2002). The prevalence of dementia in older people in an urban population of Korea: The Seoul study. *Journal of the American Geriatrics Society*, *50*(7), 1233–1239.

Lee, J., Banerjee, J., Khobragade, P. Y., Angrisani, M., & Dey, A. B. (2019). LASI-DAD study: A protocol for a prospective cohort study of late-life cognition and dementia in India. *BMJ Open*, *9*(7), e030300.

Lee, J. C. (2003). Health care reform in South Korea: Success or failure? *American Journal of Public Health*, *93*(1), 48–51.

Lee, S. (2005). *Stress and Cognitive Aging.* Master's thesis, Seoul National University.

Lerro, C. C., Koutros, S., Andreotti, G., Friesen, M. C., Alavanja, M. C., Blair, A., Hoppin, J. A., Sandler, D. P., Lubin, J. H., Ma, X., Zhang, Y., & Freeman, L. E. B. (2015). Organophosphate insecticide use and cancer incidence among spouses of pesticide applicators in the Agricultural Health Study. *Occupational and Environmental Medicine*, *72*(10), 736–744.

Li, Y., Li, Y., Li, X., Zhang, S., Zhao, J., Zhu, X., & Tian, G. (2017). Head injury as a risk factor for dementia and Alzheimer's disease: A systematic review and meta-analysis of 32 observational studies. *PLoS ONE*, *12*(1), e0169650.

Liu, C. C., Li, C. Y., Sun, Y., & Hu, S. C. (2019). Gender and age differences and the trend in the incidence and prevalence of dementia and Alzheimer's disease in Taiwan: A 7-year national population-based study. *Biomed Research International*, 2019.

Livingston, G., Huntley, J., Sommerlad, A., Ames, D., Ballard, C., Banerjee, S., Brayne, C., Burns, A., Cohen-Mansfield, J., Cooper, C., Costafreda, S. G., Dias, A., Fox, N., Gitlin, L. N., Howard, R., Kales, H. C., Kivimäki, M., Larson, E. B., Ogunniyi, A., ... & Mukadam, N. (2020). Dementia prevention, intervention, and care: 2020 report of the Lancet Commission. *The Lancet, 396*(10248), 413–446.

Lobo, A., Saz, P., Marcos, G., Dia, J. L., De-la-Camara, C., Ventura, T., Montañes, J. A., Lobo-Escolar, A., Aznar, S., & ZARADEMP Workgroup. (2007). Prevalence of dementia in a southern European population in two different time periods: The ZARADEMP Project. *Acta Psychiatrica Scandinavica, 116*(4), 299–307.

Matthews, F. E., Arthur, A., Barnes, L. E., Bond, J., Jagger, C., Robinson, L., Brayne, C., & Medical Research Council Cognitive Function and Ageing Collaboration. (2013). A two-decade comparison of prevalence of dementia in individuals aged 65 years and older from three geographical areas of England: Results of the Cognitive Function and Ageing Study I and II. *The Lancet, 382*(9902), 1405–1412.

Matthews, K. A., Xu, W., Gaglioti, A. H., Holt, J. B., Croft, J. B., Mack, D., & McGuire, L. C. (2019). Racial and ethnic estimates of Alzheimer's disease and related dementias in the United States (2015–2060) in adults aged≥ 65 years. *Alzheimer's & Dementia, 15*(1), 17–24.

Mattis, S. (1988). *Dementia Rating Scale: Professional Manual*. Psychological Assessment Resources.

McDowell, I., Hill, G., & Lindsay, J (1994) The Canadian study of health and aging: Risk factors for Alzheimer's disease in Canada. *Neurology, 44*(11), 2073–2080.

Meng, X., & D'Arcy, C. (2012). Education and dementia in the context of the cognitive reserve hypothesis: A systematic review with meta-analyses and qualitative analyses. *PLoS ONE, 7*(6), e38268.

Ministry of Education, Republic of China. (2021). *Educational System*. https://english.moe.gov.tw/cp-126-17722-3fb83-1.html

Ministry of Health & Welfare, Republic of Korea (2021). Policies: Challenges & Tasks Ahead. http://www.mohw.go.kr/eng/pl/plo103.jsp?PAR_MENU_ID=1003&MENU_ID=100326

Mintun, M. A., Larossa, G. N., Sheline, Y. I., Dence, C. S., Lee, S. Y., Mach, R. H., Klunk, W. E., Mathis, C. A., DeKosky, S. T., & Morris, J. C. (2006). [11C]PIB in a nondemented population: Potential antecedent marker of Alzheimer disease. *Neurology, 67*(3), 446–452.

Mitchell, A. J., & Shiri-Feshki, M. (2009). Rate of progression of mild cognitive impairment to dementia–meta-analysis of 41 robust inception cohort studies. *Acta Psychiatrica Scandinavica, 119*(4), 252–265.

Mori, E., Hirono, N., Yamashita, H., Imamura, T., Ikejiri, Y., Ikeda, M., Kitagaki, H., Shimomura, T., & Yoneda, Y. (1997). Premorbid brain size as a determinant of reserve capacity against intellectual decline in Alzheimer's disease. *American Journal of Psychiatry, 154*(1), 18–24.

Mortimer, J. A., Snowdon, D. A., & Markesbery, W. R. (2003). Head circumference, education and risk of dementia: Findings from the Nun Study. *Journal of Clinical and Experimental Neuropsychology*, 25(5), 671–679.
National Archives of Korea. (2021). *Population Policies: Yesterday and Today*. https://theme.archives.go.kr/next/populationPolicy/policy1980.do
Ninomiya, T., Nakaji, S., Maeda, T., Yamada, M., Mimura, M., Nakashima, K., Mori, T., Takebayashi, M., Ohara, T., Hata, J., Kokubo, Y., Uchida, K., Taki, Y., Kumagai, S., Yonemoto, K., Yoshida, H., Muto, K., Momozawa, Y., Akiyama, M., & Kiyohara, Y. (2020). Study design and baseline characteristics of a population-based prospective cohort study of dementia in Japan: The Japan Prospective Studies Collaboration for Aging and Dementia (JPSC-AD). *Environmental Health and Preventive Medicine*, 25(1), 1–12.
Norton, S., Matthews, F. E., Barnes, D. E., Yaffe, K., & Brayne, C. (2014). Potential for primary prevention of Alzheimer's disease: An analysis of population-based data. *The Lancet Neurology*, 13(8), 788–794.
Nunes, B., Silva, R. D., Cruz, V. T., Roriz, J. M., Pais, J., & Silva, M. C. (2010). Prevalence and pattern of cognitive impairment in rural and urban populations from Northern Portugal. *BMC Neurology*, 10(1), 1–12.
Ogawa, N., & Matsukura, R. (2007). Ageing in Japan: The health and wealth of older persons. *United Nations Expert Group Meeting on Social and Economic Implications of Changing Population Age Structure*, 31, 199–220.
Ohara, T., Hata, J., Yoshida, D., Mukai, N., Nagata, M., Iwaki, T., Kitazono, T., Kanba, S., Kiyohara, Y., & Ninomiya, T. (2017). Trends in dementia prevalence, incidence, and survival rate in a Japanese community. *Neurology*, 88(20), 1925–1932.
Okamura, H., Ishii, S., Ishii, T., & Eboshida, A. (2013). Prevalence of dementia in Japan: A systematic review. *Dementia and Geriatric Cognitive Disorders*, 36(1–2), 111–118.
Organisation for Economic Co-operation and Development. (2021), Lack of social support (indicator). https://doi.org/10.1787/1c4df204-en
Park, H., Chey, J., & Kim, S.E. (2014). Basal cortisol level and functional level and asymmetry of the hippocampus. *Journal of Psychology: General*, 33(4), 815–834.
Park, J., Ko, H. J., Park, Y. N., & Chul-Ho, J. (1994). Dementia among the elderly in a rural Korean community. *The British Journal of Psychiatry*, 164(6), 796–801.
Park, J. G. (2009). *Primary Economic Policy of Administrations in South Korea*. Korea Economic Research Institute (KERI).
Park, K. A. (1993). Women and development: The case of South Korea. *Comparative Politics*, 25(2), 127–145.
Park, S., Kim, E., Kim, H., & Chey, J. (2011). Effects of age and education on the Simple Rey Figure Test in elderly Koreans. *Korean J. Psychol. Gen*, 30, 99–115.

Patterson, C. (2018). *The State of the Art of Dementia Research: New Frontiers. World Alzheimer Report 2018.* Alzheimer's Disease International.

Peiris-John, R. J., Ruberu, D. K., Wickremasinghe, A. R., & van-der-Hoek, W. (2005). Low-level exposure to organophosphate pesticides leads to restrictive lung dysfunction. *Respiratory Medicine, 99*(10), 1319–1324.

Peters, R., Ee, N., Peters, J., Booth, A., Mudway, I., & Anstey, K. J. (2019). Air pollution and dementia: A systematic review. *Journal of Alzheimer's Disease, 70*(s1), S145–S163.

Petersen, R. C., Smith, G. E., Waring, S. C., Ivnik, R. J., Tangalos, E. G., & Kokmen, E. (1999). Mild cognitive impairment: Clinical characterization and outcome. *Archives of Neurology, 56*(3), 303–308.

Pi, J., Olivé, J. M., Roca, J., & Masana, L. (1996). Prevalence of dementia in a semi-rural population of Catalunya, Spain. *Neuroepidemiology, 15*(1), 33–41.

Pietschnig, J., Penke, L., Wicherts, J. M., Zeiler, M., & Voracek, M. (2015). Meta-analysis of associations between human brain volume and intelligence differences: How strong are they and what do they mean? *Neuroscience & Biobehavioral Reviews, 57*, 411–432.

Plassman, B. L., Havlik, R. J., Steffens, D. C., Helms, M. J., Newman, T. N., Drosdick, D., Phillips, C., Gau, B. A., Welsh-Bohmer, K. A., Burke, J. R., Guralnik, J. M., & Breitner, J. C. S. (2000). Documented head injury in early adulthood and risk of Alzheimer's disease and other dementias. *Neurology, 55*(8), 1158–1166.

Prencipe, M., Casini, A. R., Ferretti, C., Lattanzio, M. T., Fiorelli, M., & Culasso, F. (1996). Prevalence of dementia in an elderly rural population: Effects of age, sex, and education. *Journal of Neurology, Neurosurgery & Psychiatry, 60*(6), 628–633.

Prina, A. M., Mayston, R., Wu, Y. T., & Prince, M. (2019). A review of the 10/66 dementia research group. *Soc. Psychiatry Psychiatr. Epidemiol., 54*, 1–10. https://doi.org/10.1007/s00127-018-1626-7

Prince, M., Graham, N., Brodaty, H., Rimmer, E., Varghese, M., Chiu, H., Acosta, D., & Scazufca, M. (2004). Alzheimer Disease International's 10/66 Dementia Research Group – One model for action research in developing countries. *International Journal of Geriatric Psychiatry, 19*(2), 178–181.

Prince, M., Bryce, R., Albanese, E., Wimo, A., Ribeiro, W., & Ferri, C. P. (2013). The global prevalence of dementia: A systematic review and metaanalysis. *Alzheimer's & Dementia, 9*(1), 63–75.

Public Health Agency of Canada. (2017). *Dementia in Canada, including Alzheimer's disease: Highlights from the Canadian chronic disease surveillance system* [Fact sheet]. https://www.canada.ca/content/dam/phac-aspc/documents/services/publications/diseases-conditions/dementia-highlights-canadian-chronic-disease-surveillance/dementia highlights-canadian-chronic-disease-surveillance.pdf

Rentería, M. A., Vonk, J. M., Felix, G., Avila, J. F., Zahodne, L. B., Dalchand, E., Frazer, K. M., Martinez, M. N., Shouel, H. L., & Manly, J. J. (2019).

Illiteracy, dementia risk, and cognitive trajectories among older adults with low education. *Neurology, 93*(24), e2247–e2256.

Rizzi, L., Rosset, I., & Roriz-Cruz, M. (2014). Global epidemiology of dementia: Alzheimer's and vascular types. *BioMed Research International, 2014*.

Roser, M., & Ortiz-Ospina, E. (2016). Literacy. *Our World in Data*. https://ourworldindata.org/

Ruano, L., Araújo, N., Branco, M., Barreto, R., Moreira, S., Pais, R., Cruz, V. T., Lunet, N., & Barros, H. (2019). Prevalence and causes of cognitive impairment and dementia in a population-based cohort from northern Portugal. *American Journal of Alzheimer's Disease & Other Dementias®, 34*(1), 49–56.

Russ, T. C. (2018). Intelligence, cognitive reserve, and dementia: Time for intervention? *JAMA Network Open, 1*(5), e181724–e181724.

Schmidt, R., Freidl, W., Fazekas, F., Reinhart, B., Grieshofer, P., Koch, M., Eber, B., Schumacher, M., Polmin, K., & Lechner, H. (1994). The Mattis Dementia Rating Scale: Normative data from 1,001 healthy volunteers. *Neurology, 44*(5), 964–964.

Schneider, A. L., Selvin, E., Latour, L., Turtzo, L. C., Coresh, J., Mosley, T., Ling, G., & Gottesman, R. F. (2021). Head injury and 25-year risk of dementia. *Alzheimer's & Dementia, 17*(9), 1432–1441.

Seth, M. J. (2002). *Education Fever*. University of Hawaii Press.

(2017). South Korea's economic development, 1948–1996. *Oxford Research Encyclopedia of Asian History*.

Shibayama, H., Kasahara, Y., & Kobayashi, H. (1986). Prevalence of dementia in a Japanese elderly population. *Acta Psychiatrica Scandinavica, 74*(2), 144–151.

Shin, I. S., Kim, J. M., Yoon, J. S., Kim, S. J., Yang, S. J., Kim, W. J., Lee, S. H., Kwak, J. Y., & Lee, H. Y. (2002). Prevalence rate and risk factors of dementia compared between urban and rural communities of the metropolitan Kwangju area. *Journal of Korean Neuropsychiatric Association, 41*(6), 1165–1173.

Shin, M. (2017). *Risk for Cognitive Aging and Dementia in the Elderly Korean Population with Baseline Low Cognitive Performance*. Doctoral dissertation, Seoul National University.

Shively, S., Scher, A. I., Perl, D. P., & Diaz-Arrastia, R. (2012). Dementia resulting from traumatic brain injury: What is the pathology? *Archives of Neurology, 69*(10), 1245–1251.

Shulman, K. I. (2000). Clock-drawing: Is it the ideal cognitive screening test? *International Journal of Geriatric Psychiatry, 15*(6), 548–561.

Spada, R. S., Stella, G., Calabrese, S., Bosco, P., Anello, G., Guéant-Rodriguez, R. M., Romano, A., Benamghar, L., & Guéant, J. L. (2009). Prevalence of dementia in mountainous village of Sicily. *Journal of the Neurological Sciences, 283*(1–2), 62–65.

Stern, Y. (2012). Cognitive reserve in ageing and Alzheimer's disease. *The Lancet Neurology, 11*(11), 1006–1012.

Suh, G. H., Kim, J. K., & Cho, M. J. (2003). Community study of dementia in the older Korean rural population. *Australian and New Zealand Journal of Psychiatry, 37*(5), 606–612.

Suh, S. W., Kim, Y. J., Kwak, K. P., Kim, K., Kim, M. D., Kim, B. S., Kim, B. J., Kim, S. G., Kim, J. L., Kim, T. H., Moon, S. W., Park, K. W., Park, J. I., Park, J. H., Bae, J. N., Seo, J., Seong, S. J., Son, S. J., Shin, I. S., . . . & Kim, K. W. (2021). A 9-Year Comparison of Dementia Prevalence in Korea: Results of NaSDEK 2008 and 2017. *Journal of Alzheimer's Disease, 81*(2), 821–831.

Suk, J. S., Chey, J. Y., & Kim, H. Y. (2010). An additional normative study of the Korean-dementia rating scale. *Korean J Clin Psychol, 29*(2), 559–572.

Sun, Y., Lee, H. J., Yang, S. C., Chen, T. F., Lin, K. N., Lin, C. C., Wang, P. N., Tang, L. Y., & Chiu, M. J. (2014). A nationwide survey of mild cognitive impairment and dementia, including very mild dementia, in Taiwan. *PLoS ONE, 9*(6), e100303.

Sung, S. (2003). Women reconciling paid and unpaid work in a Confucian welfare state: The case of South Korea. *Social Policy & Administration, 37* (4), 342–360.

Tola-Arribas, M. A., Yugueros, M. I., Garea, M. J., Ortega-Valín, F., Cerón-Fernández, A., Fernández-Malvido, B., San José-Gallegos, A., González-Touya, M., Botrán-Velicia, A., Iglesias-Rodríguez, V., & Díaz-Gómez, B. (2013). Prevalence of dementia and subtypes in Valladolid, northwestern Spain: The DEMINVALL study. *PLoS ONE, 8*(10), e77688.

Tsolaki, M., Fountoulakis, C., Pavlopoulos, I., Chatzi, E., & Kazis, A. (1999). Prevalence and incidence of Alzheimers disease and other dementing disorders in Pylea, Greece. *American Journal of Alzheimer's Disease, 14*(3), 138–148.

United Nations, Department of Economic and Social Affairs, Population Division (2017). *World Population Aging 2017.*

(2019a). *World Population Ageing 2019: Highlights* (ST/ESA/SER.A/430).

(2019b). *World Population Prospects 2019, Volume I: Comprehensive Tables* (ST/ESA/SER.A/426).

Valenzuela, M. J., & Sachdev, P. (2006). Brain reserve and dementia: A systematic review. *Psychological Medicine, 36*(4), 441–454.

Varangis, E. & Stern, Y. (2020). Cognitive Reserve. In A. K. Thomas & A. Gutchess, (eds.), *The Cambridge Handbook of Cognitive Aging: A Life Course Perspective (Cambridge Handbooks in Psychology)*, pp.32–46. Cambridge University Press. https://doi.org/10.1017/9781108552684

Vemuri, P., Wiste, H. J., Weigand, S. D., Shaw, L. M., Trojanowski, J. Q., Weiner, M. W., Knopman, D. S., Petersen, R. C., & Jack, C. R.; Alzheimer's Disease Neuroimaging Initiative (2009). MRI and CSF biomarkers in normal, MCI, and AD subjects: Diagnostic discrimination and cognitive correlations. *Neurology, 73*(4), 287–293.

Virués-Ortega, J., de Pedro-Cuesta, J., Vega, S., Seijo-Martínez, M., Saz, P., Rodríguez, F., Rodríguez-Laso, A., Reñé, R., de las Heras, S. P., Mateos, R., Martínez-Martín, P., Mahillo-Fernandéz, M., López-Pousa, S., Lobo, A., Reglà, J. L., Gascón, J., García, F. J., Fernandéz-Martínez, M., Boix, R.,... & del Barrio, J. L.; Spanish Epidemiological Studies on Ageing Group. (2011). Prevalence and European comparison of dementia in a ≥75-year-old composite population in Spain. *Acta Neurologica Scandinavica*, *123*(5), 316–324.

Vogel, E. F. (1991). *The Four Little Dragons: The Spread of Industrialization in East Asia*, vol. 3. Harvard University Press.

Vygotsky, L. S. (1978). *Mind in Society: The Development of Higher Psychological Processes*. Harvard University Press.

Wang, Y. Q., Jia, R. X., Liang, J. H., Li, J., Qian, S., Li, J. Y., & Xu, Y. (2019). Dementia in China (2015–2050) estimated using the 1% population sampling survey in 2015. *Geriatrics & Gerontology International*, *19*(11), 1096–1100.

Willerman, L., Schultz, R., Rutledge, J. N., & Bigler, E. D. (1991). In vivo brain size and intelligence. *Intelligence*, *15*(2), 223–228.

Winblad, B., Palmer, K., Kivipelto, M., Jelic, V., Fratiglioni, L., Wahlund, L. O., Nordberg, A., Bäckman, L., Albert, M., Almkvist, O., Arai, H., Basun, H., Blennow, K., de Leon, M., DeCarli, C., Erkinjuntti, J., Giacobini, E., Graff, C., Hardy, J., ... & Petersen, R. C. (2004). Mild cognitive impairment–beyond controversies, towards a consensus: Report of the International Working Group on Mild Cognitive Impairment. *Journal of Internal Medicine*, *256*(3), 240–246.

Witelson, S. F., Beresh, H., & Kigar, D. L. (2006). Intelligence and brain size in 100 postmortem brains: Sex, lateralization and age factors. *Brain*, *129*(2), 386–398.

Wolf, H., Hensel, A., Kruggel, F., Riedel-Heller, S. G., Arendt, T., Wahlund, L. O., & Gertz, H. J. (2004). Structural correlates of mild cognitive impairment. *Neurobiology of aging*, *25*(7), 913–924.

Wolf, M. J, Emerson, J. W., Esty, D. C., de Sherbinin, A., Wendling, Z. A., et al. (2022). 2022 Environmental Performance Index. New Haven, CT: Yale Center for Environmental Law & Policy. epi.yale.edu

Woo, J. I., Lee, J. H., Yoo, K. Y., Kim, C. Y., Kim, Y. I., & Shin, Y. S. (1998). Prevalence estimation of dementia in a rural area of Korea. *Journal of the American Geriatrics Society*, *46*(8), 983–987.

World Bank (2021a). Gross National Income, Republic of Korea. https://data.worldbank.org/indicator/NY.GNP.MKTP.CD?locations=KR

(2021b). Life expectancy, Republic of Korea. https://data.worldbank.org/indicator/SP.DYN.LE00.IN?locations=KR

World Health Organization. (2017). Global action plan on the public health response to dementia 2017–2025.

Wu, Y. T., Ali, G. C., Guerchet, M., Prina, A. M., Chan, K. Y., Prince, M., & Brayne, C. (2018). Prevalence of dementia in mainland China, Hong Kong and Taiwan: An updated systematic review and meta-analysis. *International Journal of Epidemiology, 47*(3), 709–719.

Yang, S. S., Gong, B. H., & Kim, H. J. (2010). *A Research on the World Trend in Compulsory Education and its Development Strategies.* Korean Educational Development Institute (KEDI).

Youn, J. C., Lee, D. Y., Kim, K. W., & Woo, J. I. (2005). Epidemiology of dementia. *Psychiatr. Invest., 2*(1), 28–39.

Zhang, M. Y., Katzman, R., Salmon, D., Jin, H., Cai, G. J., Wang, Z. Y., Qu, G. Y., Grant, I., Yu, E., Levy, P., Klauber, M. R., & Liu, W. T. (1990). The prevalence of dementia and Alzheimer's disease in Shanghai, China: Impact of age, gender, and education. *Annals of Neurology, 27*(4), 428–437.

CHAPTER 2

Social Network Positions and Health Status in Older Adults

Yoosik Youm and Junsol Kim

2.1 Introduction

Since the 1970s, a large body of studies has investigated how social relationships are associated with physical health, mental health, cognitive health, and even mortality (Berkman & Syme, 1979; Blazer, 1982; Cassel, 1976; Cobb, 1976; Haber et al., 2007; House et al., 1982, 1988). However, due to the limitations in data and methodology, earlier studies focused on how one's perception of social support (e.g., emotional, instrumental, and financial support) is related to health (Berkman & Glass, 2000; Smith & Christakis, 2008).

It is only recently that researchers have conducted "social network analysis," which enables them to measure social relationships quantitatively and estimate their effects systematically on older adults' health status. Social network analysis allows us to investigate a variety of patterns in social relationships, such as social network positions (e.g., closure and brokerage positions) and resources that flow through social networks (e.g., social supports, information, contagion of behaviors), and their roles in older adults' health status (Berkman et al., 2000, Smith & Christakis, 2008).

In this chapter, we are going to explore various types of social network positions and their associations with health status in older adults. Specifically, we focus on the Korean Social Life, Health, and Aging Project (KSHAP) and the National Social Life, Health, and Aging Project (NSHAP) studies. The KSHAP and NSHAP have collected longitudinal datasets of older adults' social networks and health status in South Korea and the United States, respectively. Based on the KSHAP and NSHAP studies, we are going to describe, compare, and discuss social networks and health among older adults in South Korea and the United

This work was supported by the Ministry of Education of the Republic of Korea, the National Research Foundation of Korea (NRF-2022S1A3A2A02089737), and the Yonsei University Research Grant of 2022.

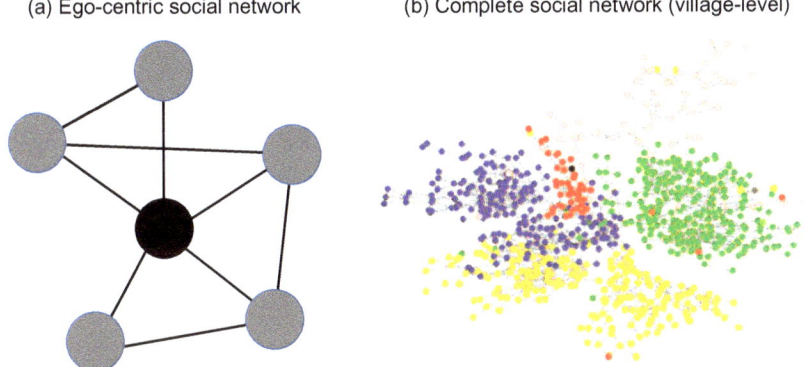

Figure 2.1   Ego-centric social networks and complete social networks.
Note: In Panel B, colors of nodes indicate one's affiliation in a sub-village (Ri).

States. After that, we will expand on the relationships between village-level complete social networks, a range of biomarkers, and psychological and brain measures based on multidisciplinary KSHAP studies. By doing so, we discover how social networks shape common as well as unique pathways in aging in both countries.

2.2   Three Types of Social Network Positions: Size, Closure, and Brokerage

A social network is the web of social relationships among individuals (Berkman & Glass, 2000; Wasserman & Faust, 1994). Social network analyses include both ego-centric social networks at the individual level and complete social networks at the level of communities. Figure 2.1(a) is an example of an ego-centric social network, which consists of an individual at the center and his/her friends. Each node (circle) indicates each individual, and each edge (tie) between nodes indicates a relationship between individuals.

By collecting ego-centric social networks from every individual in a community, one can construct complete social networks at the level of communities, as shown in Figure 2.1(b). The figure depicts complete social networks between older adults residing in a South Korean rural village, as collected in the KSHAP (Youm et al., 2014). Using these social network data, we can examine a variety of social network positions that older adults occupy, any valuable information emerging from these social network positions, and their impacts on older adults' health status.

Traditionally, the *size* (also known as degree) of the social network has been considered as an important health determinant. The size of the social network is measured by the number of interpersonal contacts or amount of social interaction, which also reflects the amount of social support one can receive (Blazer, 1982; Seeman et al., 1993; Welin et al., 1985). A larger social network size is known to buffer stress, preserve one's psychological well-being, and protect one's health (Cobb 1976; Seeman et al., 1993). On the other hand, social isolation (i.e., structural isolation due to small social network size) has been found to be a critical risk factor in older adults' health (Cacioppo & Hawkley, 2003; House, 2001; Waite & Cornwell, 2009). Studies show that older adults expand their social network by beginning novel social relationships to recover from their loss of social ties due to bereavement (Van Tilburg, 1998; Youm et al., 2014). Such a recovery of social network size is associated with an increase in self-rated health and a decrease in depressive symptoms (Cornwell & Laumann, 2015).

Another important social network characteristic is the *closure* position, also known as embeddedness (Burt, 2001; Coleman, 1988; Joo, Kwak, et al., 2017). Older adults' closure positions can be beneficial for their health for three reasons. First, people in closure positions belong to a very cohesive core group where the members share similar values, attitudes, and behaviors (Festinger et al., 1950). In turn, they receive various types of social support in a more consistent and coordinated way (Festinger et al., 1950, Joo, Kwak, et al., 2017). Second, people in closure positions are friends with each other. Therefore, regardless of a couple of members who are sick or become hostile in a closure position, the whole friendship circle can be maintained to exchange valuable support (Coleman, 1988). Third, since people in closure positions are strongly connected to each other and are more likely to act together as a group, they are likely to maintain their cognitive health and deal with the challenge of planning and coordinating collective actions of diverse members (Joo, Kwak, et al., 2017).

To measure closure position, *density* is often used, which is the number of social connections that exist among social network members, or friends, divided by the maximum possible number of connections (Wasserman & Faust, 1994).

$$A's\ density = \frac{actual\ connections\ among\ A's\ social\ network\ members}{maximum\ possible\ connections\ among\ A's\ social\ network\ members}$$

In Figure 2.2, A has three social network members, and there exist three connections among the three members. The number of maximum possible connections between the three members is three. Thus, A's density is

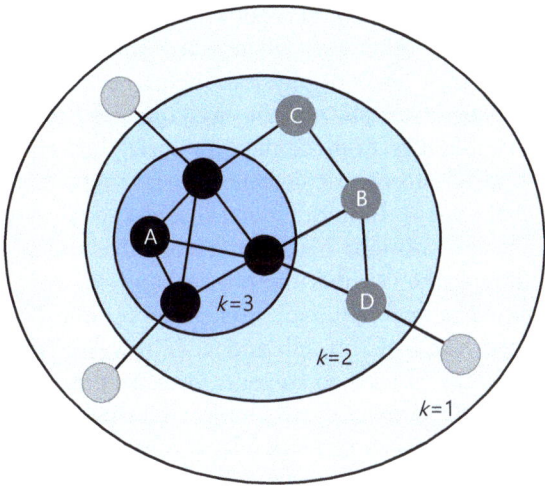

Figure 2.2 Closure position (k-core score): A hypothetical network graph of ten people. Closure position was measured by k-core score, the highest value of k among k-core groups to which people belonged. A k-core group consists of people who have at least k social connections with group members. Even though A's and B's social network sizes are the same (3), only A can be a member of the 3-core group and has a higher k-core score than B (3 vs. 2).

$3 \div 3 = 1$. A higher density indicates that an individual is more likely to be in the closure position.

The k-core score is another popular measure of closure position (Wasserman & Faust, 1994). A k-core group refers to a group of people who have at least k social connections with other group members. Given that one person can be affiliated in several nested k-core groups, one's k-core group is usually defined as the k-core group in which the value of k is the highest. For example, in Figure 2.2, A is simultaneously affiliated in a 1-core group composed of all ten people in the graph, a 2-core group of seven people, and a 3-core group of four people. Therefore, A's k-core score is three, which is the maximum possible value of k. On the other hand, B's k-core score is two given that B is not affiliated in the 3-core group. More specifically, even though A's and B's social network sizes are identical, B does not hold three social connections with 3-core group members. In this case, A is more likely to be in the closure position than B.

Last, another important type of social network position is *brokerage* (Burt, 2000, 2002; Cornwell, 2009a; Kim et al., 2019). This captures a very different, almost opposite, characteristic of social networks compared to closure positions (Burt et al., 2009). Brokerage positions refer to positions that connect otherwise unconnected others. Being in brokerage positions requires high levels of physical, mental, and cognitive capacities because two groups of people who are not connected to each other have different and sometimes even conflicting social backgrounds, such as contradictory social norms or beliefs (Burt, 2000, 2002; Cornwell, 2009a; Kim et al., 2019). Indeed, Cornwell et al. (2009) suggest that older adults in brokerage positions have better cognitive and physical health. This may be due to the fact that the physical and cognitive activities and capacities required to maintain one's brokerage position allow older adults to maintain good health (Cornwell, 2009a; Cornwell, 2009b).

Bridging potential is used to measure brokerage position. It is often measured as a binary variable of whether there existed any social network member in the respondent's network who was not connected to any other network members (Cornwell, 2009a; Cornwell, 2009b). Network constraint is also used to measure the extent of brokerage (Burt, 2009; Kim et al., 2019). Network constraint is an inverse measure of brokerage because the network constraint reduces one's brokerage potential (Burt, 2009; Kim et al., 2019). It is measured as follows: the network constraint exercised by person j on person i consists of two distinct parts. First, person i is constrained by person j as much as person i invests resources and energies into a relationship with person j. The value p_{ij} is the ratio of the social tie between i and j to the total ties of i, and it is assumed that p_{ij} indicates the amount of resource that i invested in a relationship with j. For instance, if i has two friends j and k, p_{ij} is assumed to be 1/2. Second, person i is constrained by a relationship with person k who has a connection with person j. Thus, p_{ik} (the resources that i invested in a relationship with k) and p_{jk} (the resources that j invested into a relationship with k) are calculated for every k, and the formula to obtain an individual i's network constraint is calculated as follows: $c_i = \sum_{j, j \neq i} \left(p_{ij} + \sum_{k, k \neq i, k \neq j} p_{ik} p_{kj} \right)^2$.

In a more constrained network such as A in Figure 2.3, an individual is constrained by the strong demands from surrounding people because they are in closure positions. In closure positions, people are connected to each other, share similar norms and attitudes, and exert social influences of assimilation on other people. On the other hand, in a less constrained network such as B, an individual occupies a brokerage position where he/she enjoys fewer constraints. However, he/she needs to interact with other people from diverse social backgrounds who have diverse and even incompatible norms and demands. These require physical, mental, and cognitive

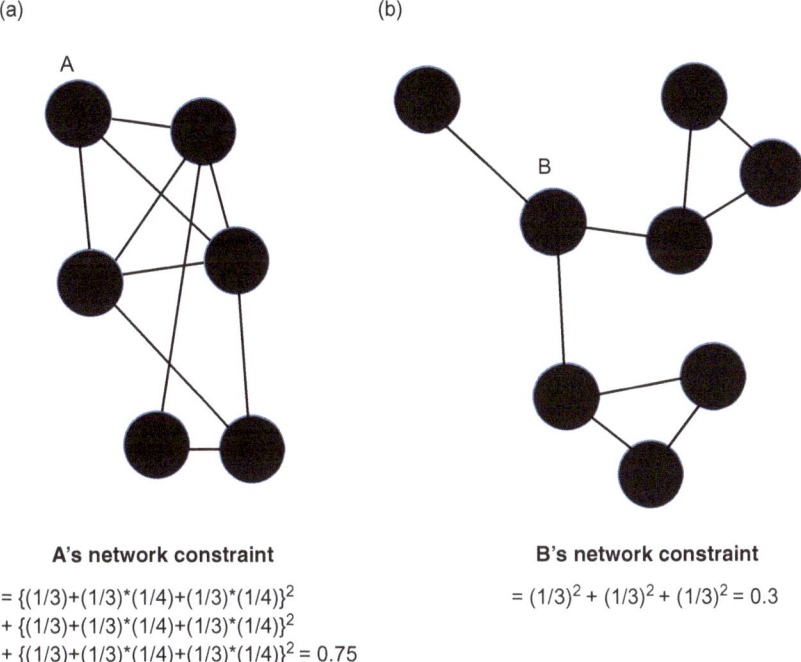

Figure 2.3 Example of a brokerage position. B has a better opportunity for the brokerage role than A. A larger circle size represents more opportunity for brokerage. Brokerage opportunity refers to the smaller network constraint on an individual. The bottom panel shows the equation for each individual's social network constraint.

capacities and can lead to several health benefits (Cornwell, 2009a, Cornwell, 2009b).

As discussed in this section, social network positions enable researchers to investigate a variety of dimensions in social networks that cannot be captured by traditional self-rated perceived social support measures. While social network positions focus on quantifying the structure of social networks, perceived social support measures quantify how one perceives his/her quality of social relationships.

2.3 Comparisons of Social Network Positions and Self-Rated Health between South Korea and the United States

In this section, we are going to review how the various social network positions described in the previous section are related to older adults' health status in South Korea and the United States. We specifically focus on recent studies from the KSHAP and NSHAP.

The NSHAP collected information about ego-centric social networks and health among older adults. Specifically, the NSHAP collected a national representative sample of older adults in the United States (Lichtenberg, 2014). The NSHAP collected longitudinal ego-centric social network data and included a module that enabled respondents to provide information about their social network members (people who discuss important matters) and the relationships among them (Cornwell et al., 2009). The module measured social networks by asking this question:

> From time to time, most people discuss things that are important to them with others. For example, these may include good or bad things that happen to you, problems you are having, or important concerns you may have. Looking back over the last 12 months, who are the people with whom you most often discussed things that were important to you?

The participants listed the names of at most five people and described the type of relationship with each social network member (e.g., spouse, child, neighbor). Based on these social network data, a large body of studies found that social network characteristics were associated with physical and psychological health, such as subjective well-being, depressive symptoms, hypertension, erectile dysfunction, health behaviors, and health-care utilization (Cornwell & Laumann, 2011; Cornwell et al., 2009; Cornwell & Waite, 2012; Litwin, 2011).

The KSHAP collected data on ego-centric social networks among older South Korean adults using the same module (Youm et al., 2014). The difference between the NSHAP and the KSHAP is that the KSHAP mandatorily includes an older adult's spouse as a member of his/her social networks given that older adults have spouses. This was because spouses play a particularly important role in South Korean older adults' health (Youm et al., 2014). However, while the NSHAP collected a national representative sample of American older adults, the KSHAP collected a community sample that selected the entire population of older adults in Township K, a South Korean rural community.

Table 2.1 compares the participants' characteristics in the NSHAP and the KSHAP, allowing us to examine the differences in ego-centric social networks and health between American and South Korean older adults. The table shows several noteworthy discrepancies. First, KSHAP respondents maintained smaller (3.07 vs. 3.65) yet denser (0.98 vs. 0.85) social networks compared to NSHAP respondents. This is surprising given that

Table 2.1 *Ego-centric network measures by selected variables in the KSHAP and the NSHAP*

		KSHAP (N, proportion)	NSHAP (N, proportion)	Network size (spouse + alters [a])		Overall volume of contact (per year)		Network density		Bridging potential	
				KSHAP	NSHAP	KSHAP	NSHAP	KSHAP	NSHAP	KSHAP	NSHAP
Age	≤64	(151, 0.19)	(1020, 0.34)	3.25	3.71	717.28	780.34	0.99	0.86	0.00	0.06
	65–74	(367, 0.45)	(1092, 0.36)	3.17	3.65	717.26	720.25	0.98	0.84	0.01	0.08
	≥75	(296, 0.36)	(893, 0.30)	2.85	3.57	668.97	690.48	0.98	0.84	0.02	0.09
	p-value			<0.01	0.27	0.23	<0.01	0.59	0.07	0.35	0.23
Gender	Male	(342, 0.42)	(1455, 0.48)	3.28	3.41	734.53	675	0.99	0.87	0.00	0.06
	Female	(472, 0.58)	(1550, 0.52)	2.92	3.88	674.47	797.33	0.97	0.84	0.02	0.09
	p-value			<0.01	<0.01	0.03	<0.01	0.02	<0.01	0.01	0.01
Marital status	Living with spouse	(612, 0.76)	(1801, 0.60)	3.33	3.75	760.91	780.08	0.98	0.88	0.01	0.03
	Separated/divorced/widowed	(196, 0.24)	(1204, 0.40)	2.31	3.46	523.38	653.91	0.96	0.79	0.03	0.16
	p-value			<0.01	<0.01	<0.01	<0.01	0.08	<0.01	<0.01	<0.01
Education	<High school	(242, 0.30)	(699, 0.23)	2.77	3.19	647.06	722.69	0.99	0.88	0.01	0.07
	Elementary school/*Seodang*[b]	(334, 0.41)	(793, 0.26)	3.11	3.55	746.87	750.14	0.98	0.88	0.01	0.07
	≥Middle school	(230, 0.29)		3.33		689.66		0.97		0.01	
	Some college		(856, 0.28)		3.79		756.31		0.84		0.08
	≥Bachelor's		(657, 0.22)		3.96		713.92		0.81		0.08
	p-value			<0.01	0	0.01	0.18	0.23	0	1	0.97

Table 2.1 (cont.)

			Network size (spouse + alters)[a]		Overall volume of contact (per year)		Network density		Bridging potential	
	KSHAP (N, proportion)	NSHAP (N, proportion)	KSHAP	NSHAP	KSHAP	NSHAP	KSHAP	NSHAP	KSHAP	NSHAP
Self-rated health	Poor/somewhat poor (353, 0.43)	(856, 0.27)	2.85	3.48	646.11	736.8	0.98	0.85	0.01	0.08
	Good (399, 0.49)	(956, 0.30)	3.21	3.54	739.63	732.18	0.97	0.86	0.01	0.08
	Very good/excellent (62, 0.08)	(1281, 0.43)	3.42	3.83	747.89	742.33	0.99	0.85	0	0.07
	p-value		<0.01	<0.01	<0.01	0.81	0.65	0.76	0.7	0.49
Overall weighted mean			3.07	3.65	699.7	738.04	0.98	0.85	0.01	0.08
Standard deviation			1.23	1.47	386.43	354.39	0.12	0.23	0.1	0.26
Skewness			0.43	−0.42	1.04	0.57	−6.81	−1.60	9.54	3.22

Note: In the KSHAP, some college and bachelor's degrees were not differentiated in the survey. a. "Alter" indicates people connected to the self (i.e., ego) in ego-centric social networks. b. Seodang is a traditional village-based elementary school in South Korea.

the KSHAP mandated the inclusion of a spouse in one's social network, which could lead to higher social network sizes. The KSHAP respondents had a lower volume of contact with their social network members (699.70 vs. 738.04) while showing a smaller bridging potential (0.01 vs. 0.08). In addition, older men in the NSHAP showed smaller networks (3.41 vs. 3.88) and lower volumes of contact (675.00 vs. 797.33) compared to older women in the NSHAP. In contrast, older men in the KSHAP showed larger networks (3.28 vs. 2.92) and more frequent contact with network members (734.53 vs. 674.47) compared to the older women in the KSHAP. Note that the average brokerage potential was close to zero among older men in the KSHAP, which indicates that South Korean rural men tend to be in closure positions rather than brokerage positions.

In both countries, older adults with a high social network size showed better self-rated health. This shows that stronger, more intimate, and more communicative social relationships can produce valuable social support, which will be beneficial for one's health and gives some protection from diseases.

These analyses lead to several notable insights. First, larger social networks resulted in better self-rated health in both the NSHAP and the KSHAP, consistent with previous studies conducted in the United States (Cornwell et al., 2009; Schafer, 2011). Second, while age difference in terms of social network size was not significant among American older adults, age difference in social network size was significant among South Korean older adults. Specifically, American older adults maintained their social network size regardless of their age, but South Korean older adults showed a decrease in their network size as they grew older.

Third, American older women reported larger social network size compared to American older men. In contrast, South Korean older women reported smaller social network size compared to South Korean older men. This may reflect the strong patriarchal norms still present in rural South Korea. It seems that South Korean people are confined to their socially constructed roles of men as the leader or representative of the household who should communicate with nonfamily neighbors and visitors (*ga-jang* in Korean) and women as family care providers and household managers (Jeon et al., 2007; Wei-Ming, 1996). More specifically, compared to the United States, where older women are more prone to sustain a larger social network, the social networks of South Korean rural older women seem to be constrained by household chores and farming. These differences suggest that aging processes are not universal across different countries and cultures. The aging pathway should be understood in the context of gender roles and other societal milieux of older adults.

Last, South Korean older adults maintained smaller yet denser networks compared to American older adults. Social network members were strongly limited to family and relatives among South Korean older adults. American older adults, however, sustained more relationships with people who were not their relatives. Given that the KSHAP collected the sample from remote rural villages in South Korea, we cannot generalize these results to the entire South Korean elderly population. The examination of social network characteristics among South Korean older adults in urban areas will be required in future studies.

2.4 Village-Level Complete Social Networks and Mortality

The previous section showed how ego-centric networks were related to self-rated health and discussed the similarities and differences between South Korean and American older adults' social networks and health. In this section, we are going to examine how we can expand on the role of social relationships in health, using village-level complete social network data.

When KSHAP researchers collected social network data, they asked respondents to provide the actual names of their social network members (Lee et al., 2014; Youm et al., 2014). By doing so, they were able to construct a complete map of the social network of all older adults residing in Township K. This allowed them to examine not only the ego-centric social network of each respondent but also the complete network of an entire village in South Korea as shown in Figure 2.1(b).

Most recently, Youm et al. (2021) examined how three distinctive characteristics of social relationships, namely, loneliness, social disengagement, and group-level segregations, are related to all-cause mortality (Youm et al., 2021). First, loneliness refers to one's "perception" of social isolation. More specifically, loneliness aims to measure the difference between one's desired and actual social connectedness (Cacioppo et al., 2006; Youm et al., 2021). On the other hand, social disengagement is defined as an objective condition in which an individual is disconnected from social relationships, social life, and social activities (Sabin, 1993).

The third aspect of social relationships, which is particularly interesting, is group-level segregation. Youm et al. (2021) defined group-level segregation as affiliation in a social group that is disconnected from the larger social community. The diameter of a social group is the length of the largest geodesic path within the social group. For example, if a social group's diameter is one, every group member should be each other's friends. If a group's diameter is two, every group member should be each other's friends or friend's friends. While the aforementioned two measures, loneliness and social disengagement, quantify whether an individual is segregated from other individuals, this measure focuses on whether *a social group in which an individual is affiliated* is segregated from other groups. If an individual is segregated at group level, one may have many friends, but the total number of people one can reach via his/her social ties is relatively limited. Also, people may classify group-level segregated individuals as lonely and socially disengaged individuals based on the characteristics of their social groups, regardless of the actual number of social connections they occupy. We can measure group-level segregation only when community-level complete social network data are collected, as in the KSHAP (see Figure 2.4).

Racial segregation in the United States can be an example of group-level segregation. It is well known that people in some racial/ethnic groups in the United States do not have social ties with people outside their racial/ethnic group (Youm et al., 2021). As such, complete social networks data allow us to better understand the mechanisms of how macro-level phenomena, such as racial segregation and the disintegration of rural communities from larger urban communities discussed in Chapter 1, shape our health.

While loneliness, social disengagement, and group-level segregations are expected to affect mortality, it is difficult to estimate the causal effects of these three measures on mortality. First, it is possible that bad health conditions that cause mortality affect social relationships (i.e., reverse causality). Second, time-invariant and time-variant covariates, such as education, gender, and income, may affect both social relationships and mortality, driving the spurious relationships between the two (i.e., the omitted variable bias).

To deal with these two issues, based on five models, Table 2.2 illustrates the effects of each of the three social relationship measures on all-cause mortality among older adults throughout the eight-year period. Model 1 presents the results from a Cox proportional hazard model that controls for none of the covariates. Model 2 presents the results from a Cox proportional hazard model that controls for time-invariant covariates, which are education, gender, and various measures at the baseline, such as loneliness, social disengagement, segregation, living with spouse, yearly income, smoking, drinking, depression, physical health, cognitive health, and comorbidity. Model 3 presents a Cox proportional hazard model that additionally controls for the time-variant covariates of loneliness, social

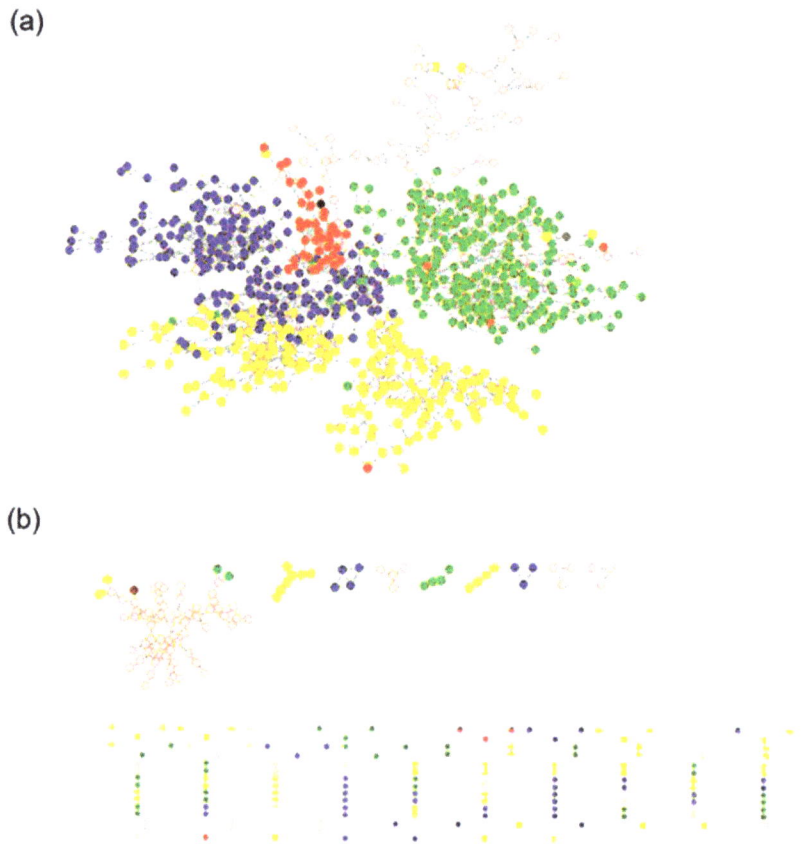

Figure 2.4 Village-level complete social networks from the KSHAP. Panel A indicates the largest group in the village; Panel B indicates individuals segregated from the largest group in the village (group-level segregation). Colors of nodes indicate one's affiliation in a sub-village (Ri).

disengagement, segregation, living with spouse, yearly income, smoking, drinking, depression, physical health, cognitive health, and comorbidity.

To control for circular relationships in which bad health affects social relationships and social relationships reversely affect health and even death, Model 4 presents a Cox marginal structural model (MSM) that estimates the average treatment effects (ATE) while controlling both time-variant and time-invariant covariates. Model 5 presents a Cox MSM that estimates average treatment effects among treated (ATT) while controlling both time-variant and time-invariant covariates.

Table 2.2 *The hazard ratios of loneliness, social disengagement, and group-level segregation from Cox proportional hazard regression models and Cox MSMs (n = 679)*

Model	Variable	Hazard ratio (95% confidence interval)	p-value
1. Cox proportional hazard model (unadjusted)	Loneliness	1.92 (1.18-3.12)	0.008
	Social disengagement	2.06 (1.26-3.36)	0.004
	Group-level segregation	1.94 (1.13-3.33)	0.016
2. Cox proportional hazard model without time-varying covariates	Loneliness	1.88 (1.11-3.17)	0.019
	Social disengagement	2.09 (1.21-3.62)	0.008
	Group-level segregation	2.21 (1.27-3.85)	0.005
3. Cox proportional hazard model with time-varying covariates	Loneliness	1.31 (0.68-2.52)	0.411
	Social disengagement	1.80 (1.00-3.24)	0.049
	Group-level segregation	1.76 (1.00-3.11)	0.051
4. Cox MSM (ATE)	Loneliness	1.50 (0.73-3.09)	0.274
	Social disengagement	1.75 (0.97-3.15)	0.062
	Group-level segregation	2.01 (1.13-3.56)	0.018
5. Cox MSM (ATT)	Loneliness	1.01 (0.43-2.36)	0.980
	Social disengagement	1.53 (0.82-2.84)	0.182
	Group-level segregation	2.38 (1.16-4.86)	0.017

The results suggest that loneliness and social disengagement are correlated with mortality, but they do not cause mortality when controlling for time-variant confounders (see Table 2.2 for details). As shown in Model 1, if we did not control for any covariates, lonely people were almost twice as likely to die (95% CI: HR 1.18-3.12). Socially disengaged older adults were two times more likely to die as well (95% CI: HR 1.26-3.36). As presented in Model 2, when controlled for time-constant covariates, lonely people were still 1.88 times more likely to pass away (95% CI: HR 1.11-3.17), and socially disengaged people were twice as likely to die (95% CI: HR 1.21-3.62). However, Model 3 showed that the effect of loneliness (p = 0.411) was not statistically significant, and the effect of social disengagement was only marginally significant (p = 0.049) when controlled for time-varying covariates. Consistent with the results of Model 3 results, the two Cox MSM Models 4 and 5 also showed that the effects of loneliness and social disengagement are not statistically significant.

Group-level segregation, however, showed robust effects on mortality. As shown in Model 3, group-level segregated individuals were 80% (95%

CI: HR 1.00-3.11) more likely to die even when we controlled for time-varying covariates. Similarly, the two Cox MSM Models 4 and 5 showed that the effect of group-level segregation was statistically significant. In Model 4, group-level segregated individuals were twice as likely to die (95% CI: 1.13-3.56). In Model 5, group-level segregated individuals were also 2.38 times more likely to die (95% CI: 1.16-4.86).

This study is an effective example of how complete social networks further our understanding about the links between social relationships and health. As shown in the study, complete social networks allow us to measure important patterns in social relationships that are not available in perceived social supports or ego-centric social network measures. Also, the longitudinal study design, combined with counterfactual causal inference methods like Cox MSMs, enabled us to show robust influence of social networks on health after controlling for reverse causality and omitted variable bias.

2.5 Social Networks, Biomarkers, and the Mind

In this section, we demonstrate how studies can benefit from integrating social network approaches into a multidisciplinary study design in aging studies. The KSHAP study conducted multidisciplinary data collections, including social network data, survey interviews, physical examinations, functional assessment, biomarkers, and even brain imaging data to comprehensively investigate a variety of social, psychological, and physical characteristics among older South Korean adults. Moreover, by employing a variety of biomarkers, the KSHAP studies were able to elucidate detailed biological mechanisms of how the two are interrelated.

Joo, Lee, et al. (2017) showed how individuals' brokerage potential in their social networks were related to coronary artery calcium (CAC) scores, a reliable cardiovascular risk marker (Joo, Lee, et al., 2017). This finding was carried out utilizing the Cardiovascular and Metabolic Disease Etiology Research Center – High Risk Cohort (CMERC-HI) data, which collected high-risk patients' social networks using the social network module used in the KSHAP. They found that higher brokerage potential was associated with lower CAC scores, and this association was stronger among older and female participants (Joo, Lee, et al., 2017). This study showed that the use of biomarkers may allow us to further explore the biological mechanisms that link social networks and health.

Also, the combination of social network data and neuroimaging data can open up exciting discussions about the biological mechanisms that link social networks to cognitive health. Using village-level complete social network data from the KSHAP, Joo, Kwak, et al. (2017) found that individuals' closure positions, or embeddedness, in their social networks lead to long-distance functional connectivity in their brain networks. It is possible that closure positions may provide positive cognitive stimulation that is protective for cognitive health (Joo, Kwak, et al., 2017).

Furthermore, we can examine how physical, cognitive, and social health are intermingled by combining physical and cognitive health data, neuroimaging data, and social network data. Bang et al. (2019) found the evidence that systemic inflammation negatively constrains social behaviors and relationships among older adults by altering the brain functional state (Bang et al., 2019). Specifically, using village-level complete social network data from the KSHAP, they found the relationships between systemic inflammation, measured by high-sensitivity C-reactive protein (hsCRP); frontotemporal brain functional connectivity; and social network size. They found that hsCRP levels were associated with a decrease in frontotemporal brain functional connectivity, which, in turn, was significantly associated with smaller network size. By showing that bad health measured by inflammation leads to changes in the functional state of our brain, which eventually leads to small social network size, the research suggests that our mind may be an important mediator that links our health and our social relationships.

As such, our social network is linked to our health, and possibly linked by our states of mind and brain. Therefore, to comprehensively understand the aging process, it is necessary to understand the complex interactions between physical, psychological, and social health via a combination of social network approaches and multidisciplinary approaches.

REFERENCES

Bang, M., Kim, J., An, S. K., Youm, Y., Chey, J., Kim, H.C., Park, K., Namkoong, K., & Lee, E. (2019). Associations of systemic inflammation with frontotemporal functional network connectivity and out-degree social-network size in community-dwelling older adults. *Brain, Behavior, and Immunity*, 79, 309–313.

Berkman, L. F., & Glass, T. (2000). Social integration, social networks, social support, and health. *Social Epidemiology*, 1, 137–173.

Berkman, L. F., Glass, T., Brissette, I., & Seeman, T. E. (2000). From social integration to health: Durkheim in the new millennium. *Social Science & Medicine*, 51, 843–857.

Berkman, L. F., & Syme, S. L. (1979). Social networks, host resistance, and mortality: A nine-year follow-up study of Alameda County residents. *American Journal of Epidemiology*, 109, 186–204.

Blazer, D. G. (1982). Social support and mortality in an elderly community population. *American Journal of Epidemiology*, 115, 684–694.

Burt, R. S. (2000). The network structure of social capital. *Research in Organizational Behavior*, 22, 345–423.

 (2001). Structural holes versus network closure as social capital. In N. Lin, K. Cook, & R. S. Burt (eds.), *Social Capital: Theory and Research*, pp. 31–56. Routledge.

 (2002). Bridge decay. *Social Networks*, 24, 333–363.

 (2009). *Structural Holes: The Social Structure of Competition*. Harvard University Press.

Burt, R. S., Bartkus, V. O., & Davis, J. H. (2009). Network duality of social capital. In V. O. Bartkus & J. H. Davis (eds.), *Social Capital. Reaching Out, Reaching* pp. 39–65. Edward Elgar.

Cacioppo, J. T., & Hawkley, L. C. (2003). Social isolation and health, with an emphasis on underlying mechanisms. *Perspectives in Biology and Medicine*, 46, S39–S52.

Cacioppo, J. T., Hawkley, L. C., Ernst, J. M., Burleson, M., Berntson, G.G., Nouriani, B., & Spiegel, D. (2006). Loneliness within a nomological net: An evolutionary perspective. *Journal of Research in Personality*, 40, 1054–1085.

Cassel, J. (1976). The contribution of the social environment to host resistance: The Fourth Wade Hampton Frost Lecture. *American Journal of Epidemiology*, 104, 107–123.

Cobb, S. (1976). Social support as a moderator of life stress. *Psychosomatic Medicine*, 38(5), 300–314.

Coleman, J. S. (1988). Social capital in the creation of human capital. *American Journal of Sociology*, 94, S95–S120.

Cornwell, B. (2009a). Good health and the bridging of structural holes. *Social Networks*, 31, 92–103.

 (2009b). Network bridging potential in later life: Life-course experiences and social network position. *Journal of Aging and Health*, 21, 129–154.

Cornwell, B., & Laumann, E. O. (2011). Network position and sexual dysfunction: Implications of partner betweenness for men. *American Journal of Sociology*, 117, 172–208.

 (2015). The health benefits of network growth: New evidence from a national survey of older adults. *Social Science & Medicine*, 125, 94–106.

Cornwell, B., Schumm, L. P., Laumann, E. O., & Graber, J. (2009). Social networks in the NSHAP study: Rationale, measurement, and preliminary findings. *Journals of Gerontology Series B: Psychological Sciences and Social Sciences*, 64, i47–i55.

Cornwell, E. Y., & Waite, L. J. (2012). Social network resources and management of hypertension. *Journal of Health and Social Behavior*, 53, 215–231.

Festinger, L., Schachter, S., & Back, K. (1950). *Social Pressures in Informal Groups: A Study of Human Factors in Housing*. Harper.

Haber, M. G., Cohen, J. L., Lucas, T., & Baltes, B. B. (2007). The relationship between self-reported received and perceived social support: A meta-analytic review. *American Journal of Community Psychology*, 39, 133–144.

House, J. S. (2001). Social isolation kills, but how and why? *Psychosomatic Medicine*, 63, 273–274.

House, J. S., Landis, K. R., & Umberson, D. (1988). Social relationships and health. *Science*, 241, 540–545.

House, J. S., Robbins, C., & Metzner, H. L. (1982). The association of social relationships and activities with mortality: Prospective evidence from the Tecumseh Community Health Study. *American Journal of Epidemiology*, 116, 123–140.

Jeon, G.-S., Jang, S.-N., Rhee, S.-J., Kawachi, I., & Cho, S.-I. (2007). Gender differences in correlates of mental health among elderly Koreans. *The Journals of Gerontology Series B: Psychological Sciences and Social Sciences*, 62, S323–S329.

Joo, W.-t., Kwak, S., Youm, Y., & Chey, J. (2017). Brain functional connectivity difference in the complete network of an entire village: The role of social network size and embeddedness. *Scientific Reports*, 7, 1–12.

Joo, W.-t., Lee, C. J., Oh, J., Kim, I.-C., Lee, S.-H., Kang, S.-M., Kim, H. C., Park, S., & Youm, Y. (2017). The association between social network betweenness and coronary calcium: A baseline study of patients with a high risk of cardiovascular disease. *Journal of Atherosclerosis and Thrombosis, 40469*.

Kim, H., Kwak, S., Kim, J., Youm, Y., & Chey, J. (2019). Social network position moderates the relationship between late-life depressive symptoms and memory differently in men and women. *Scientific Reports*, 9, 1–10.

Lee, J.-M., Lee, W. J., Kim, H. C., Choi, W., Lee, J., Sung, K., Chu, S. H., Park, Y.-R., & Youm, Y. (2014). The Korean Social Life, Health, and Aging Project: Health examination cohort. *Epidemiology and Health*, 36, e2014003.

Lichtenberg, P. A. (2014). Sexuality and physical intimacy in long-term care. *Occupational Therapy in Health Care*, 28, 42–50.

Litwin, H. (2011). The association between social network relationships and depressive symptoms among older Americans: What matters most? *International Psychogeriatrics*, 23, 930.

Sabin, E. P. (1993). Social relationships and mortality among the elderly. *Journal of Applied Gerontology*, 12, 44–60.

Schafer, M. H. (2011). Health and network centrality in a continuing care retirement community. *Journals of Gerontology Series B: Psychological Sciences and Social Sciences*, 66, 795–803.

Seeman, T. E., Berkman, L. F., Kohout, F., Lacroix, A., Glynn, R., & Blazer, D. (1993). Intercommunity variations in the association between social ties and mortality in the elderly: A comparative analysis of three communities. *Annals of Epidemiology*, 3, 325–335.

Smith, K. P., & Christakis, N. A. (2008). Social networks and health. *Annual Review of Sociology*, 34, 405–429.

Van Tilburg, T. (1998). Losing and gaining in old age: Changes in personal network size and social support in a four-year longitudinal study. *The Journals of Gerontology Series B: Psychological Sciences and Social Sciences*, 53, S313–S323.

Waite, L., & Cornwell, E. (2009). Social disconnectedness, perceived isolation, and health among older adults. *Journal of Health and Social Behavior*, 50, 31–48.

Wasserman, S., & Faust, K. (1994). *Social Network Analysis: Methods and Applications*. Cambridge University Press.

Wei-Ming, T. (1996). Confucian traditions in East Asian modernity. *Bulletin of the American Academy of Arts and Sciences*, 12–39.

Welin, L., Svärdsudd, K., Ander-Peciva, S., Tibblin, G., Tibblin, B., Larsson, B., & Wilhelmsen, L. (1985). Prospective study of social influences on mortality: The study of men born in 1913 and 1923. *The Lancet*, 325, 915–918.

Youm, Y., Baldina, E., & Baek, J. (2021). All-cause mortality and three aspects of social relationships: An eight-year follow-up of older adults from one entire Korean village. *Scientific Reports*, 11, 1–11.

Youm, Y., Laumann, E. O., Ferraro, K. F., Waite, L. J., Kim, H. C., Park, Y.-R., Chu, S. H., Joo, W.-t., & Lee, J. A. (2014). Social network properties and self-rated health in later life: Comparisons from the Korean Social Life, Health, and Aging Project and the National Social Life, Health, and Aging Project. *BMC Geriatrics*, 14, 1–15.

CHAPTER 3

The Social Brain and How It Links Social Intelligence and Well-Being

Sunhae Sul and Isu Cho

3.1 Introduction

What we ... consider most valuable in the human character is essentially nothing more than the fulfilment of the conditions that arise from the social needs of mankind.

Alfred Adler (1928/2014)

Human beings are among the most sophisticated social animals. Cooperation with conspecifics is essential for our survival and reproduction. We are dependent on each other in acquiring resources, securing safety, and raising offspring. From birth to death, we put considerable time and effort in forming and maintaining social bonds with close others and social groups, namely, a social network. The importance of social resources shapes strong motivation for social affiliation and cognitive capacity for sophisticated social computation. Decades of psychological and neuroscientific studies provide evidence supporting basic motivation for social affiliation and high social intelligence in humans. In this chapter, we first summarize psychological perspectives on human sociality, centering around the belongingness hypothesis – that is, human minds have evolved to have a universal tendency to form and maintain lasting, positive, and significant social bonds (Baumeister & Leary, 1995) – and the social intelligence hypothesis – that is, human intelligence is evolved to solve complex social problems uniquely relevant to humans (Dunbar, 1998; Humphrey, 1976; Johnson-Ulrich, 2017). In the following sections, we examine the social brain in order to explore how our brain processes information about our social world and how we adjust our behavior to the perceived social world. After a brief review on aging in the social brain, we will discuss behavioral and neuroscientific studies linking the social brain and well-being.

This work was supported by the National Research Foundation of Korea (NRF 2018R1C1B6007059 granted to Sunhae Sul).

3.2 The Need to Belong: A Fundamental Human Motivation

Human motivation for social affiliation has been extensively studied throughout the history of psychology. Early on, Adler (1928/2020) insightfully pointed out that humans are indisputably social beings and their intellect is attuned to communal living. Many influential psychologists, including Maslow (1968) and Bowlby (1969), made similar suggestions that the need to belong should be considered as a fundamental human motivation. Conceptualizing the belongingness hypothesis, Baumeister and Leary (1995) defined the need to belong as "a need to form and maintain at least a minimum quantity of interpersonal relationships" (p. 499). They suggested that it is a basic human motivation for the following reasons: the need to belong is universal and innate; is not derivative of other motives; has affective, cognitive, and behavioral consequences; elicits goal-oriented behavior to satisfy it; decreases when satiated and should be substituted when deprived; and is critically linked to one's health, adjustment, and well-being.

According to the belongingness hypothesis, natural selection preferred the need to belong and the relevant psychological mechanisms because forming social bonds and long-lasting relationships has high survival and reproductive benefits. As a result, human minds have evolved to have a universal tendency to form and maintain social bonds to satiety, specialized cognitive systems to process information about close relationships and group memberships, and affective systems to reinforce social relatedness and to inhibit social deprivation. Although the process of evolution is difficult to be empirically tested, indirect evidence supports the idea that social relatedness is essential for adaptation and well-being. For example, social relatedness has a salutary effect on stress coping (Cohen & Wills, 1985) and facilitates positive affect (Bachorowski & Owren, 2001). Individuals with greater social resources tend to overcome everyday stress more easily, to be healthier, to have better quality of life (Cohen, 2004), and to live longer (Carter, 1998; House et al., 1988). Consistently, sociability or extraversion (Lucas & Diener, 2001), utilization of social resources (Sul et al., 2013, 2016), and quality of social life (Diener & Seligman, 2002) are correlated with subjective well-being. The need to belong has also been linked to self-esteem, a subjective evaluation of oneself, which is highly correlated with subjective well-being and mental health. Leary (2003) viewed self-esteem as a "sociometer" that gauges the degree to which one's need to belong is satisfied. This sociometer theory suggests that the balance between positive and negative inputs about social acceptance or belongingness determines the subjective feeling of self-worth. Higher self-esteem indicates greater subjective feelings of being accepted by others, while being ignored or rejected lowers one's self-esteem (Leary, 2003).

Studies on the size and structure of social groups imply the point of satiation for the need to belong. The optimal group size can be determined by the balance between the benefits and the costs – cognitive demand – of being affiliated in the group (Hill & Dunbar, 2003; Sutcliffe et al., 2012). Statistics from different studies point to 150 as the "optimal" group size. An average size of various human social groups from hunter-gatherer communities to modern military companies tend to converge around 150. Data from ego-centric social networks point to the same number; individuals on average have an active network of 150 people who they know as persons, reciprocate each other, and maintain personalized lasting relationships. The social network with approximately 150 people consists of three to four layers divided by the relationship closeness and social functions: the innermost circle of four or five best friends and a group of twelve to fifteen close friends, followed by casual friends and acquaintances (Hill & Dunbar, 2003; Roberts et al., 2009). In terms of the need to belong, the most influential relationship is the innermost network. The closer the relationship is, the greater impact it has on one's health and well-being. The innermost relationships, or social bonds, provide mutual emotional and instrumental support that reduces stress and promotes subjective well-being, whereas the outermost weak links have their utility in resource control (e.g., information exchange, resource buffering, group defense, etc.; Sutcliffe et al., 2012). Therefore, having a support clique of four or five friends extending to a sympathy group of twelve to fifteen friends could satisfy one's need to belong. Yet, maintaining a larger active network is necessary for successful social adaptation as well.

The theories on the fundamental human motivation for belongingness provide a common prediction that there should be neural mechanisms that measure the balance between social acceptance and rejection (Bartolo, 2019; Baumeister & Leary, 1995; Eisenberger et al., 2011). These mechanisms are associated with social sensitivity, which makes people respond to social feedback such as rejection and acceptance (e.g., DeWall et al., 2010; Eisenberger et al., 2011; Fareri & Delgado, 2014; Kross et al., 2007), and social functions that lead to positive social relationship, such as empathy and prosociality (e.g., Engen & Singer, 2013; Hein et al., 2010), which in turn may lead to the development of socially appropriate behavior and better social life. We will review some of recent findings on the neural mechanisms later in this chapter.

3.3 The Evolution of the Human Social Brain

The exceptionally large brain size of primates, especially humans, is puzzling because developing a large brain and high intelligence requires tremendous evolutionary cost in terms of energy metabolism, the risk of childbirth, and prolonged period of parenting. Scientists proposed different hypotheses explaining why primates, especially humans, evolved to have larger brains than other species. Here, we review some of these hypotheses that focus on human sociality: the social intelligence hypothesis, the ecological intelligence hypothesis, and the cultural intelligence hypothesis.

The social intelligence hypothesis, or social brain hypothesis, posits that human intelligence is evolved to solve complex social problems uniquely relevant to humans (Dunbar, 1998; Humphrey, 1976; Johnson-Ulrich, 2017). Because successful cooperation with other conspecifics is essential for survival and reproduction, primates need to establish long-term trustworthy partnerships and to engage in Machiavellian politics (Whiten & Byrne, 1988). Distinctive characteristics of human social networks – large size and complexity – introduce challenging problems such as detecting deception, finding trustworthy partners (Fiddick et al., 2000; Seyfarth & Cheney, 2015), recognizing others' mental states (Call & Tomasello, 2011), tracing and predicting long-term interactions (de Waal & Tyack, 2009), and making optimal strategic decisions. For humans with exceptionally complex social structures, cognitive challenges from the social world are often much greater than those from the physical world. Even the challenges from the physical world can be overcome by cultural transmission of knowledge and skills through social learning. The high computational demands of the complex social systems worked as selection pressure that favored a larger brain and higher intelligence.

Empirical evidence supporting the social intelligence hypothesis can be primarily found in primate research. For example, Dunbar and his colleagues (Barton & Dunbar, 1997; Dunbar & Shultz, 2007; Gowlett et al., 2012; Kudo et al., 1999; Sawaguchi & Kudo, 1990) found that the relative size of the neocortex is positively correlated with the social group size in primates, including humans. The ratio of the neocortex to the rest of the brain was consistently found to be positively correlated with different indices of social complexity, such as grooming clique size (Kudo & Dunbar, 2001), tactical deception (Byrne & Corp, 2004), social play (Lewis, 2000), long-term stable bonds (Dunbar, 1998; Dunbar & Shultz, 2007), and social learning (Reader & Laland, 2002). In an attempt to find direct relationships between the brain size and social and nonsocial intelligence, Reader and Laland (2002) analyzed the ratio of brain regions associated with the executive function (i.e., the relative size of neocortex and striatum to brain stem) and found that the larger ratio was associated with greater frequency of social learning, innovation, and tool use. The researchers also reported that social learning was positively correlated with innovation and tool use, implying that social intelligence covaries with nonsocial intelligence. Intraspecies analysis also supports the link between social complexity and intelligence. Research on the relationship between sociality and the evolutionary benefit of both birds (Ashton et al., 2018) and primates (Kamil, 2004) suggests that individuals with larger social groups and higher sociality tend to have better cognitive performance and greater reproductive success.

The social intelligence hypothesis is often contrasted with the ecological intelligence hypothesis, which emphasizes foraging cognition for acquiring food resources, such as spatial memory, value-based decision-making, and executive control (Ashton et al., 2018; Holekamp, 2007; Rosati, 2017). The ecological hypothesis assumes that the nonsocial environment, such as dietary ecology, can also operate as selective pressure for greater brain size and higher intelligence. This hypothesis suggests that human intelligence may have been evolved to solve ecological problems unique to our ancestors in the hunter-gatherer society. The human dietary ecology can be uniquely characterized by extractive, central-place, and high-risk foraging of spatially and temporally dispersed resources, which requires high nonsocial cognitive capacity, including spatial memory, self-control, and executive function (Rosati, 2017). Human sociality intertwines with the ecology at this point. Rosati (2017) suggested that both sociality and ecology contribute to the evolution of the human social brain because human ecology requires cooperation for buffering risk (e.g., high frequency of food sharing) and social learning of sophisticated foraging skills and knowledge, which in turn requires individuals to belong to a large social group. The social complexity of the large group could be another selection pressure, as the social intelligence hypothesis suggests. Similarly, Atzil et al. (2018) proposed that the human brain is evolved to regulate allostasis (ongoing physiology) and that the "social brain" emerged because social affiliation is essential for successfully maintaining physiological resources given the characteristics of human dietary ecology.

It is worth noting that whether there is domain-specific intelligence for social cognition is still under debate. Also, whether social complexity is the major selection pressure for human intelligence remains controversial. Conservative forms of the social intelligence hypothesis argue that complex social groups favor intelligence specialized for social cognition. However, recent integrative perspectives propose that domain-specificity is not necessarily a prerequisite for the social intelligence hypothesis because ecological problems that humans face can often be solved socially (Atzil et al., 2018; Rosati, 2017).

The cultural intelligence hypothesis suggests that cultural learning is a key to solving complex ecological problems, including social interactions. It focuses on the human uniqueness in cultural transmission processes rather than social interactions in general (Herrmann et al., 2007, 2010; Tomasello & Moll, 2013). Unlike the social intelligence hypothesis that places humans on a par with other primates and pays relatively more attention to strategic social interactions (e.g., Machiavellian intelligence; Byrne & Whiten, 1988), the cultural intelligence hypothesis centers around cognitive abilities that are unique to humans: humans have brains about three times larger than the great apes (Harvey et al., 1987) and have much more sophisticated cognitive skills (including language, symbolic mental operation, and scientific thinking and reasoning) than other primates (Herrmann et al., 2007). It argues that humans are the only species that must participate and exchange knowledge in cultural groups to develop far more complex cognitive skills. Herrmann et al. (2007) points out that social learning of humans is distinctive in terms of the way they learn from social interactions and established cultural practices. According to this argument, individuals deprived of these cultural interactions would not be able to develop distinctively human cognitive skills. In other words, humans are born with "species-specific" social cognitive skills that lead them to participate in cultural learning. This, in turn, triggers a cascade of developmental processes to acquire highly sophisticated cognitive abilities. Empirical evidence supporting this idea mostly comes from human developmental studies. For example, Herrmann et al. (2007) found that 2.5-year-old children had more sophisticated social cognitive skills than chimpanzees and orangutans, whereas their general cognitive skills for the physical world did not differ from their primate relatives. Moll (2018) further verified the idea by showing that children learned problem-solving significantly better when an adult model delivered cues in a pedagogical manner than incidentally.

Taken together, despite nontrivial differences in the assumptions and predictions of the different hypotheses (see Table 3.1), a common conclusion is that the human brain is attuned to the social environment and that

Table 3.1 *Hypotheses explaining the evolution of the human social brain*

Hypothesis	Evolutionary pressure	Relevant social behavior	Empirical evidence
Social intelligence hypothesis	Strategic social interactions	Machiavellian politics	Correlation between social complexity and intelligence (often measured by neocortex size)
Ecological intelligence hypothesis	Dietary ecology	Social cooperation for risk management and foraging high-value foods Social learning of skills and knowledge for acquiring high-value foods	Correlation between foraging characteristics and cognitive abilities (e.g., spatial memory, value-based decision-making, delayed gratification, self-control, etc.)
Cultural intelligence hypothesis	Social learning	Cultural learning	Unique learning processes of human infants and children

we are experts in solving social problems. In the following section, we will explore how our brains interact with the social world.

3.4 Social Brain Networks

Our understanding of the neural mechanisms of social behavior has improved dramatically with recent advances in noninvasive neuroimaging techniques, especially functional magnetic resonance imaging (fMRI). Now scientists can simultaneously obtain behavioral data and neural data by applying sophisticatedly designed experimental paradigms involving fMRI that indirectly measures blood oxygen level with the spatial resolution of approximately 1–3 mm and the temporal resolution of approximately 1–3 seconds. Because invasive neuroscientific methods such as single-unit recording, optical imaging, or lesion studies are not eligible for most healthy human participants and human social behavior is far more sophisticated than that of animals, the development of noninvasive neuroimaging technique has benefited research on human socio-cognitive processes the most.

A vast amount of evidence accumulated over the last two decades has revealed how our brain processes information about the social world and how we adjust our behavior to the perceived social world (Adolphs, 2009; Atzil et al., 2018; Insel & Fernald, 2004; Kingsbury & Hong, 2020; Molapour et al., 2021; Thornton et al., 2019). A set of brain regions involved in this process is called the "social brain" (Adolphs, 2009; Blakemore, 2008; Dunbar & Shultz, 2007; Frith, 2007). The social brain consists of the systems shared by social and nonsocial information processing, for example, the valuation system and the systems specialized for socio-cognitive processing, such as social perception and mentalizing networks (Amodio & Frith, 2006; Behrens et al., 2008; Carter & Huettel, 2013; Parkinson & Wheatley, 2015; Sul et al., 2015). Human social behavior is a result of coordinated functioning of these neural systems. Domain-specificity of the social brain network is controversial, as already mentioned, but we will not discuss it further in this chapter. The following sections focus on the neural systems supporting the social bonding to satisfy the need to belong and the socio-cognitive functions to understand and interact with the social world.

3.4.1 *Neural Mechanisms Supporting Social Bonding, Empathy, and Prosocial Behaviors*

Assumptions regarding the fundamental human motivation for belongingness predict that our brain should be designed to reinforce behaviors that facilitate *social bonding* with positive/appetitive reactions to social acceptance and negative/aversive reactions to social rejections (Baumeister & Leary, 1995). Indeed, the human brain seems to process social rejection as pain and social acceptance as reward. Brain regions involved in pain processing, such as dorsal anterior cingulate cortex (dACC) and anterior insula (Cacioppo et al., 2013; Kross et al., 2011; Woo et al., 2014), are associated with the experience of social rejection, whereas the experience of social acceptance activates the frontostriatal reward processing circuit, including the ventromedial prefrontal cortex (VMPFC), subgenual ACC (sgACC), and ventral striatum (e.g., Izuma et al., 2008; Morelli et al., 2015; see Figure 3.1).

In a typical fMRI study, participants perform an experimental task designed to examine a psychological process of interest in an MRI scanner and the blood oxygen level dependent (BOLD) signals from the MRI data are analyzed to identify neural correlates of the targeted psychological processes, such as the need to belong. For example, in the seminal study by Eisenberger et al. (2003), participants in the scanner played a virtual ball-tossing game (e.g., CyberBall) that was designed to elicit a social exclusion experience. The fMRI data showed that dACC and anterior insula, the brain regions known to be associated with subjective feelings of pain, were more active during the social exclusion condition (when other players tossed the ball only between the two of them) than the social inclusion condition (when other players tossed the ball to the participants). The self-reported distress for social exclusion was positively correlated with the dACC activation. Studies using different paradigms to examine neural responses to social rejection have consistently revealed that the regions involved in emotional distress and pain are also associated with the experience of negative social feedback or social exclusion (DeWall et al., 2010; Eisenberger et al., 2011; Kross et al., 2007). However, these findings do not necessarily mean that our brain processes social pain and physical pain in the same way. There is evidence that the overlapping anatomical regions carry different information for physical pain and social pain. For example, an fMRI study using multivariate pattern analysis showed that the activation patterns of dACC and anterior insula distinguish social rejection from physical pain (Woo et al., 2014). In addition, some researchers suggested that dACC and anterior insula may not be specific to social rejection or pain. Somerville et al. (2006) suggested that neural activation of dACC reflects expectation violation when processing social feedback. More recently, Perini et al. (2018) suggested a possibility that dACC and anterior insula are involved in processing the salience of self being judged by others rather than in processing social pain.

Contrary to social rejection, social acceptance and approval elicit reward-related responses in the brain (Fareri & Delgado, 2014). For instance, Izuma et al. (2008) conducted an fMRI study to compare the neural correlates of monetary reward and social reward. Participants performed a gambling task in which they could earn monetary reward and a social feedback task in which they were presented impression evaluations for themselves and others in the scanner. The researchers found that both monetary reward and social reward (i.e., positive reputation) activated the same reward-related regions, namely the striatum. Similarly, being liked by others (Davey et al., 2010; Somerville et al., 2006) increases BOLD activation in the ventral ACC, including sgACC, another brain region known to be associated with reward value. Other socially desirable outcomes, such as possessing a high position in a social hierarchy (Zink et al., 2008), achieving social conformity (Klucharev et al., 2009; Wu et al., 2016), or engaging in prosocial behavior that is potentially expected to increase one's reputation (Harbaugh et al., 2007; Izuma et al., 2010; Sul et al., 2015), elicit increased BOLD activation in the frontostriatal reward circuit, consisting of the ventral striatum, ventral ACC, and VMPFC. These findings suggest that our brain is designed to motivate us to form social bonds and to satisfy the basic need for belongingness.

In addition to the neural systems supporting appetitive and aversive responses to social acceptance and rejection, respectively, the neural systems supporting empathy are as important in terms of forming and maintaining social bonds. Empathy is the sharing of others' experiences, especially sharing of feelings. It should be noted that empathy is not restricted to affective components (see Baron-Cohen & Wheelwright, 2004; Lamm et al., 2019). Empathy often refers to cognitive inference of others' mental states as well (e.g., Davis, 1980), but in this chapter, we use empathy to specifically indicate shared experience of others' feelings in order to distinguish socio-affective processes from socio-cognitive processes (see Section 3.4.2 on mentalizing for conceptualization; Luyten et al., 2020).

Early fMRI studies of empathy were rooted in the research on the mirror neuron system. Mirror neurons were originally found in a monkey study, in which researchers found a set of neurons in the premotor cortex firing both at the movement of the monkey's own hand and at the observation of another monkey's hand movement (Ferrari et al., 2003; Rizzolatti et al., 1996). Subsequent fMRI studies with human participants revealed a similar mirror neuron system, a set of brain regions that are activated both by the participants' own experience and by vicarious experience through observation of others (Iacoboni & Dapretto, 2006). Although it is still debated whether the mirror neuron system forms a basis of simulation and understanding of others' mind beyond the mere representation of others' actions (Heyes & Catmur, 2021), it is worth noting that the idea of the mirror neuron system contributed to the neuroimaging research on empathy that emphasizes shared neural representation of self and other.

The neural basis of empathy has mostly been studied in the context of vicarious pain. Researchers obtained fMRI images while showing participants other persons' body parts receiving pain, painful facial expressions, or symbolic displays indicating others experiencing painful stimuli (Hein et al., 2010; Jackson et al., 2005; Lamm et al., 2007; Singer et al., 2004, 2006). They found that the brain regions involved in the firsthand experience of pain, such as dACC extending to the anterior middle cingulate cortex (aMCC), anterior insula, and somatosensory cortex, were associated with the vicarious experience of pain. In other words, people empathize with others in pain by recruiting a shared neural representation for firsthand and vicarious pain (Lamm et al., 2007; Singer et al., 2006). The same was true for social pain. In a recent study (Novembre et al., 2015), participants observed others undergoing social exclusion or experienced themselves being socially excluded. The results showed that the firsthand and vicarious experiences of social pain recruited the same brain regions, including the pain network. Meta-analysis research suggests that dACC, aMCC, supplementary motor area (SMA), and bilateral anterior insula consist of a core network for empathy (Engen & Singer, 2013; Fan et al., 2011). More recently, another meta-analysis study showed that bilateral anterior insula, aMCC, somatosensory, and inferior frontal regions are the overlapping brain regions recruited by both empathy and nociception (Fallon et al., 2020). In other words, the human brain seems to support empathy via shared experience of pain (both social and physical) between self and other.

Prosocial behaviors are as essential as empathy for social boding because they help establish, consolidate, and maintain social relationships. As empathy is an important predictor of prosocial behaviors by eliciting other-regarding motivation (Batson, 2011), researchers have investigated the association between empathy-related brain activity and prosocial behaviors. In an fMRI study, Masten et al. (2011) had participants watch another person experiencing social exclusion and measured the neural activity associated with the vicarious social pain. The results showed that participants with higher self-reported trait empathy showed greater brain activity in the pain network (i.e., anterior insula and dACC) and in the mentalizing network (i.e., medial prefrontal cortex and precuneus) while observing social pain, and the empathy-related neural responses predicted subsequent prosocial behavior toward the victim. In another interesting study conducted by Hein et al. (2010), soccer fans observed a fan of their favorite team (ingroup) or a rival team (outgroup) experiencing pain and were given an opportunity to help the others by reducing their pain at the cost of enduring pain themselves. The fMRI data revealed that participants who showed greater empathy-related activation in anterior insula for ingroup members in pain than outgroup members in pain were more likely to help ingroup members than outgroup members. In a recent intervention study (Kim et al., 2021), participants in a compassion promotion condition, compared to those in a control condition, showed reduced empathic distress and increased activity in VMPFC. The decreased empathic distress among participants in the compassion promotion condition was also associated with increased functional connectivity between the VMPFC and inferior parietal lobule, which was predictive of greater prosociality (i.e., greater intention of helping others).

In addition to the pain-related empathy, recent studies with a computational approach have shown that shared and distinct neural coding for self-regarding and other-regarding information during reward-based learning is also linked to empathy and prosocial behavior. Sul et al. (2015) used a prosocial learning task in which participants could earn points for self or other by choosing one of two options that had different reward probabilities. They found that participants with prosocial propensity performed better than participants with proself propensity when they learned for another person. Moreover, the prosocial participants showed overlapping neural representations of chosen value for self and other within the VMPFC and sgACC, while clear self–other distinction was observed among proself participants. In another fMRI study using a similar prosocial learning task, participants with higher self-reported trait empathy showed greater prediction error signals in the ventral striatum when they learned for another person than for themselves (Lockwood et al., 2016). These findings suggest that shared neural representations for self and other form the basis of empathy and prosocial behavior.

3.4.2 Neural Mechanisms Supporting Social Cognition, from Perception to Mentalizing

To maintain successful social relationships and adapt to the social world, we need to make predictions about others' actions based on our knowledge and inference about their mental states. Such cognitive processes to acquire knowledge and make predictions about social situations are called social cognition. Neuroimaging studies have revealed a set of brain regions involved in social cognition including social perception (e.g., fusiform gyrus [FFG], superior temporal sulcus [STS], temporal pole [TP]), mentalizing (e.g., temporoparietal junction [TPJ], medial prefrontal cortex [MPFC]), social learning (e.g., ventral striatum, MPFC), and social evaluation and socio-emotional regulation (e.g., amygdala, ventral striatum including nucleus accumbens [NAC], VMPFC, and lateral prefrontal cortex) (Figure 3.1).

Social cognition comprises multilayered processes from low-level perception to higher-level inference. The first step is *perceiving and evaluating others*. Neuroimaging studies have revealed the brain regions engaged in the perception of facial identity, facial expression, body movements, eye gaze, and voice (Kanwisher & Yovel, 2006; Pitcher & Ungerleider, 2021). Haxby and Gobbini (2011) suggested an integrative model for facial perception in which extrastriate visual regions interact with nonvisual systems involved in person knowledge, motor simulation, and emotion processing. The core visual system for facial perception includes the

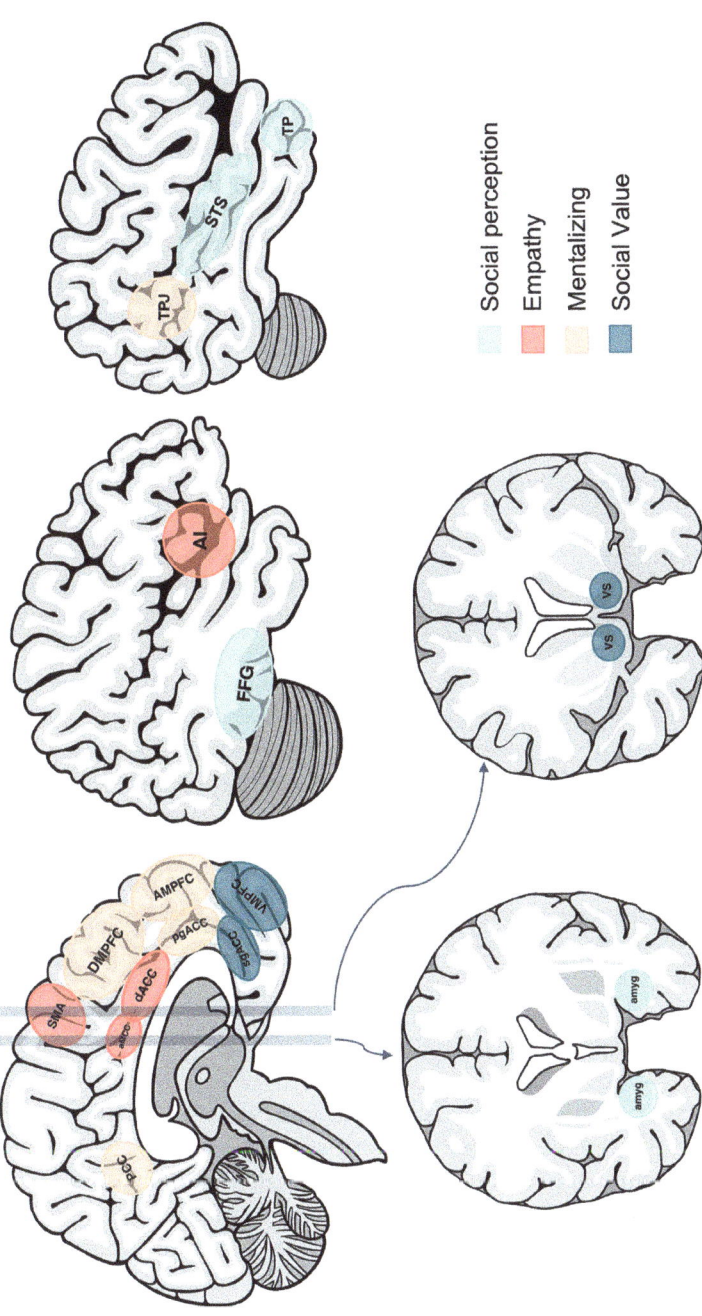

Figure 3.1 Brain regions involved in social behavior.

FFG: fusiform gyrus; STS: superior temporal sulcus; TP: temporal pole; amyg: amygdala; AI: anterior insula; SMA: supplementary motor area; dACC: dorsal anterior cingulate cortex; aMCC: anterior middle cingulate cortex; DMPFC: dorsomedial prefrontal cortex; AMPFC: anterior medial prefrontal cortex; pgACC: pregenual anterior cingulate cortex; PCC: posterior cingulate cortex; VMPFC: ventromedial prefrontal cortex; sgACC: subgenual anterior cingulate cortex; VS: ventral striatum. Different colors indicate different functions, which are categorized into four groups for simplicity. However, note that these categories are not exclusive to each other; one region can be involved in different social functions, and vice versa. Figure courtesy of Gaeun Yang.

inferior occipital gyrus and fusiform gyrus (i.e., fusiform face area), which process invariant facial features for identification, and the posterior STS, which processes dynamic features of facial gestures. More recently, Pitcher and Ungerleider (2021) took it a step further and suggested a "third visual pathway," distinguished from the canonical ventral and dorsal visual pathways. The researchers argued that there is an anatomically and functionally segregated third pathway, which projects from the early visual cortex to the STS, that is specialized for social perception and higher-level socio-cognitive functions processing dynamic social cues, such as moving faces and bodies, and eye gaze; integrating audiovisual information of speech; and interpreting others' behavior.

While the visual regions and the STS process perceptual features of social stimuli, the amygdala, NAC, and VMPFC are responsible for evaluating the value of social stimuli (Adolphs, 2009; Mende-Siedlecki et al., 2013). The amygdala has been known to respond to emotional facial expressions and show greater activation to negative than positive expressions or undesirable than desirable traits that are inferred from the face (Mende-Siedlecki et al., 2013; Morris et al., 1996; Todorov & Engell, 2008). However, some researchers have pointed out that the amygdala responds not only to emotional or social stimuli but also to uncertainty or reward, suggesting its role in vigilance for meaningful stimuli in the social world. By contrast, the NAC and VMPFC have been related to positive evaluation of social stimuli (Mende-Siedlecki et al., 2013). The activation of the NAC and VMPFC is known to be positively correlated with the perceived trustworthiness or attractiveness of another person. Yet, similar to the amygdala, the NAC has also been suggested to encode saliency rather than positive valence (Schmidt et al., 2019). In addition, recent findings suggest that our brain encodes information about others' position in a social network (see Chapter 10 for details).

Another important part of social cognition is mentalizing, the cognitive processes of inferring of others' mental states and deriving abstract knowledge about social situations. Mentalizing, theory of mind (ToM), perspective-taking, and empathy are often used interchangeably in the literature. Clear distinctions may not be possible because we need to integrate perceptual, affective, and cognitive information about self and others in order to understand and make predictions about the social world. Some researchers use empathy to refer to both sharing of affective experiences (affective empathy) and cognitive inference of mental states (cognitive empathy) (e.g., Davis, 1980), while others use mentalizing to indicate representing both affective and cognitive components of others' mental states (e.g., Luyten et al., 2020). Here, we use mentalizing to refer to cognitive processing of others' mental states and empathy to indicate shared experiences of others' feelings. ToM is an internal model or propositional knowledge about others' minds, and perspective-taking is a process of putting oneself in other's shoes, both of which are the cognitive processes relevant to mentalizing (Hein & Singer, 2008).

Although there are different perspectives on conceptualizing and defining these terms, researchers seem to agree on distinguishing the affective and cognitive components of understanding others' mental states (Baron-Cohen & Wheelwright, 2004; Corradi-Dell'Acqua et al., 2020; Davis, 1980; Healey & Grossman, 2018; Hein & Singer, 2008; Luyten et al., 2020; Perry & Shamony-Tsoory, 2013; see Section 3.4.1. for the neural correlates of affective empathy). Indeed, research on clinical populations with social deficits suggests that either empathy or mentalizing can be selectively impaired. For example, patients with Williams syndrome show deficits in social interactions despite their high sociability and empathy for others due to the impaired ability to infer others' beliefs and intentions (Meyer-Lindenberg et al., 2006). On the other hand, psychopaths show an absence of empathy while their mentalizing ability for manipulating others remains intact (Blair, 2005). Similarly, lesion studies suggest dissociable neural substrates for affective and cognitive components of sharing and understanding others' mental states (Corradi-Dell'Acqua et al., 2020; Healey & Grossman, 2018; Perry & Shamony-Tsoory, 2013), such that lesions in the prefrontal cortex and insula result in selective deficits in mentalizing (cognitive) and empathy (affective) respectively (Corradi-Dell'Acqua et al., 2020). From a motivational perspective, empathy has often been related to prosocial behavior and altruism (Batson, 2011), whereas mentalizing has been associated with cognitive understanding of the social world and, sometimes, with strategic interactions (Coricelli & Nagel, 2009; Kliemann & Adolphs, 2018; Saxe & Kanwisher, 2003).

The core network for mentalizing includes bilateral TPJ, along with the MPFC and the adjacent paracingulate cortex. A series of meta-analysis studies have shown that these regions are commonly recruited when people think about others' mental states almost across different experimental paradigms (Amodio & Frith, 2006; Denny et al., 2012; Schurz et al., 2014; Van Overwalle, 2011).

The TPJ has been suggested as a core region of the mentalizing network. As its name indicates, the TPJ is located at the intersection between the temporal and parietal lobes of the cortex and comprises parts of the angular gyrus and supramarginal gyrus, in which biological motion, gaze, and facial expressions are processed (Pitcher & Ungerleider, 2021) and neural activity related to attention-reorienting (Corbetta & Shulman, 2002) is found. Accumulating evidence suggests that the TPJ, especially the inferior and posterior regions in the angular gyrus, has a unique function in processing higher-level socio-cognitive information for mentalizing, in addition to lower-level social perceptual processing and domain-general attentional processing (Carter & Huettel, 2013). The unique function of the TPJ in mentalizing has been suggested by numerous studies. In an early fMRI study (Saxe & Kanwisher, 2003), participants read different stories in a scanner. Some of the stories described a character's false beliefs or intentions, which requires the ToM, while others were non-ToM stories. The researchers found that the bilateral TPJ showed greater BOLD response when the participants read the stories involving ToM than when they read non-ToM stories. They proposed that the TPJ might be uniquely involved in the processing of others' beliefs, which requires perspective-taking.

The role of the TPJ has also been studied in the context of strategic decisions. Using a computational modeling approach, Carter et al. (2012) invited participants to play a poker game with human or computer opponents in a scanner. The researchers used the multivariate patterns of the fMRI data from different brain regions measured at the time of deliberation to predict participants' decisions. They found that the TPJ provided information about the upcoming decisions when the decisions were made against human opponents who were relevant for future behavior. This result suggests the unique contribution of the TPJ to the integration of social information for strategic decisions. Similarly, Park et al. (2019) found that the right TPJ tracked one's belief about the probability of others' decisions during public-good games in which the outcome of one's decision depended on other group members' decisions. The TPJ is not only engaged in "cold" strategic inferences but also associated with perspective-taking for prosocial decisions, such as charitable giving. Another fMRI study showed that the BOLD activity patterns in the TPJ predicted the degree of cognitive perspective-taking that individuals endorsed during charitable giving decisions, while the anterior insula encoded affective empathy for beneficiaries (Tusche et al., 2016). In addition, a recent study using a three-person hyperscanning (i.e., measuring BOLD activities of brain from three participants at the same time) showed that the intersubject synchronization of the neural activity in the right TPJ was associated with collaborative interactions and team performance (Xie et al., 2020).

Another core region of the mentalizing network is the MPFC (Brodmann areas 9, 10, and 11), a large region of the prefrontal cortex located along the midline extending from the outermost neocortex to the adjacent paracingulate area. The MPFC has been consistently known to be activated when people think about their own mental state or others' mental states, regardless of the contents – whether thinking about personal dispositions, emotional states, desire and intention, or beliefs and thoughts (Frith & Frith, 2006). In-depth investigation over the last decade into the specific roles of the MPFC in mentalizing and recent meta-analyses consistently indicate topographically different functions along the ventral to dorsal axis. In brief, it has been suggested that the ventral part of the MPFC (VMPFC or BA11 and AMPFC or BA10) is relatively more involved in self-relevant, value-related, or affective processing, whereas the dorsal part of the MPFC (DMPFC or BA9) is more likely to be associated with other-relevant or cognitive processing (Denny et al., 2012; Frith & Frith, 2006; Lieberman et al., 2019; Sul et al., 2015).

Earlier fMRI studies using a self-referential paradigm, in which participants made judgments about personality traits or mental states of self and others, found that thinking about self and others commonly recruited a large area in the MPFC (e.g., Ochsner et al., 2004). Later research further revealed the functional distinction between the ventral and dorsal part of the MPFC. Mitchell et al. (2006) asked participants to predict the feelings and attitudes of two target individuals who were introduced as having opposite political attitudes. After scanning, participants' own political attitudes were measured to determine similar and dissimilar targets. The results showed that the ventral part of MPFC (AMPFC in Figure 3.1) was associated with thinking about the similar other, while the dorsal part of MPFC (DMPFC in Figure 3.1) was involved in thinking about the dissimilar other who had a different political attitude from the participant. The relationship between the DMPFC and mentalizing of unfamiliar others was found in another fMRI study conducted by Kang et al. (2013). In this study, participants made guesses about the preferences of unfamiliar target individuals in a scanner. The researchers found that participants with greater activity in the DMPFC during the judgment about others' preferences showed higher accuracy. In addition, a recent study using multivariate analysis reported that representational similarity between self and other in the AMPFC during a self- and other-reflection task (a variant of the self-referential paradigm in which participants considered the personality traits of self, close others, acquaintances, and celebrities) reflected subjective closeness between the participant and the target person (Courtney & Meyer, 2020). In addition to comparing self-reflective and other-reflective processes, some researchers tried to map the contents of mentalizing in the MPFC. Hynes et al. (2006) asked participants to make inferences about the thoughts and feelings of other people in an fMRI scanner and found that mentalizing about others' feelings activated the VMPFC, whereas mentalizing about others' thoughts was associated with the DMPFC.

Other social brain regions, such as the posterior STS, TP, and precuneus extending to the posterior cingulate cortex (PCC), are also known to be engaged in mentalizing processes. However, the most consistently and commonly observed regions regardless of the types of experimental tasks are the MPFC and TPJ. Functionally and structurally connected within the mentalizing network (Wang et al., 2021), these two regions seem to support our socio-cognitive functions in concord with each other (Baumgartner et al., 2015; Kang et al., 2013). Yet, there is ongoing debate about which of the two regions is the core structure of the mentalizing network and what distinctive roles the MPFC and TPJ play in mentalizing. Heretofore, both regions seem to play pivotal roles in mentalizing. Although it needs to be further determined, the evidence thus far suggests that the TPJ is more associated with cognitive perspective-taking and shifting mode of processing during social interactions (Carter & Huettel, 2013) while the MPFC is engaged in more general processing of socially relevant information and social value (Behrens et al., 2008; Saxe & Powell, 2006; Schurz et al., 2014; Sul et al., 2015).

3.5 The Social Brain and Aging

Before we move on to the association between the social brain and well-being, we will briefly review how the social brain changes with age from early to late adulthood. People undergo substantial changes in their social life in the course of life. For example, a meta-analytic research (Wrzus et al., 2013) reviewed 277 studies with more than 170,000 participants from adolescence and late adulthood to examine how the size and composition of social networks differ with age. It revealed that the size of social networks increased from adolescence to young adulthood and steadily decreased from then on. Specifically, while the size of the family network was stable irrespective of age, the size of personal and friendship networks was negatively associated with age.

There are two opposing perspectives on the changes in social relationships and social behavior during late adulthood: age-related decline in socio-cognitive abilities and age-related increase in prosociality and socio-emotional selectivity. Some researchers suggest that the decrease in the size of social networks and limited social interactions in older age are related to decreased socio-cognitive abilities, which may be accompanied by overall decline of cognitive functions (Lecce et al., 2017). In different studies using ToM tasks, older adults showed impaired ToM. For example, older adults, compared to young adults, showed worse performance when they were asked to give reasons for a character's behavior in the stories that involved the ToM (Charlton et al., 2009; Sullivan & Ruffman, 2004), or to infer another person's beliefs, which could be different from their own or reality (German & Hehman, 2006; Phillips et al., 2011). Recent findings, however, propose another possibility: that the age-related difference in the ToM task may reflect the task difficulty rather than the decline of socio-cognitive functions. Indeed, older adults showed intact ToM when the task that does not make high cognitive demands (i.e., an eye-tracking task) was used (Cho & Cohen, 2019). Consistent with the behavioral data, neuroimaging studies comparing young and older adults' social brain report inconsistent findings. In fMRI studies using different ToM tasks, older adults showed lower performance and decreased activations in the DMPFC (Moran et al., 2012). Similarly, in another study using an empathy-inducing task, older adults showed reduced activation in the anterior insula and anterior mid-cingulate cortex in response to others' physical pain (Chen et al., 2014). However, there is also evidence that does not support age-related changes in neural responses in the mentalizing network (Castelli et al., 2010).

In contrast, there is evidence that some of the socio-cognitive functions remain intact or even increase in late adulthood. For example, Cho et al. (2020) used a social decision-making paradigm and computational models to compare young and older adults' other-regarding preferences. They found that although older adults considered others' intentions less than did young adults when making a fairness-related decision, they showed a greater preference for other-regarding outcomes than young adults. In other words, older adults showed a greater tendency to take others' benefit into consideration during social decision-making compared to young adults. This result is consistent with recent findings on the age-related increase in prosociality and ego-transcending tendencies (Bailey et al., 2020; Beadle et al., 2015; Freund & Blanchard-Fields, 2014; Sparrow et al., 2021), all of which play pivotal roles in building social resources.

Moreover, older adults show a positivity effect, a tendency to focus on positive socio-emotional experiences and show greater selectivity toward positive emotional stimuli including positive intimate relationships (Mather & Carstensen, 2005), which can improve their well-being and the quality of social life. For example, older adults are less likely to process and remember emotionally negative stimuli than positive ones (Mather & Carstensen, 2005). The socio-emotional selectivity theory (SST; Carstensen, 1992) proposes that individuals with limited time perspectives are more likely to pursue emotionally meaningful goals and resources than individuals with abundant time perspectives. Older adults, who presumably have limited time perspectives compared to young adults, have such motivation, possibly leading to their tendency to narrow their social networks and dedicate resources primarily to emotionally meaningful relationships (i.e., close others). For instance, the age-related reduction in social network size is mainly due to the change in peripheral relationships, while close relationships are relatively intact (English & Carstensen, 2014; Fung et al., 2001). Older adults reported greater satisfaction about their network sizes compared to young adults (Lansford et al., 1998). On reviewing neuroimaging studies on these age-related changes in the socio-emotional experience, Nashiro et al. (2012) contrasted the aging brain model and the cognitive control model (i.e., SST). The aging brain model proposes that a reduced emotional reactivity to negative experiences among older adults (i.e., the positivity effect) comes from reduced sensitivity of the amygdala compared to young adults. On the other hand, the cognitive control model suggests that older adults are better at regulating negative emotion than young adults. According to Nashiro et al. (2012), neuroimaging data supports the latter. That is, the amygdala of older adults is structurally not different from that of young adults, and the reduced amygdala responses to negative stimuli among older adults seems to be the result of more effective emotion regulation via increased prefrontal activity.

3.6 Individual Differences in the Social Brain and Well-Being

As the brain regions involved in socio-cognitive processes were discovered, researchers began to turn their attention to the relationships between individual differences in the social brain, quality of social life, and well-being. First of all, it is well-known that quality of social life is tightly associated with well-being. Positive social relationships bring about frequent experiences of positive feelings, provide social support under stressful situations, and help replenish psychological resources for resilience. Numerous studies have consistently shown the importance of social relationships in one's physical and psychological well-being (Carter, 1998; Cohen, 2004; Cohen & Wills, 1985; Diener & Seligman, 2002; House et al., 1988; Sul et al., 2013, 2016). Behavioral evidence shows that individuals with better social relationships are healthier and happier (Campbell-Sills & Barlow, 2007; Mennin et al., 2007).

Second, the social abilities that we have reviewed so far in this chapter, including empathy, mentalizing, and prosociality, enable us to generate adaptive responses in different social situations and to build and utilize social resources, and they ultimately influence one's well-being. For instance, empathy helps people feel greater connectedness and experience positive emotions (Wei et al., 2011). The link between individual differences in empathy and subjective well-being has been reported in diverse samples across internal medicine residents (Shanafelt et al., 2005), college students (Choi et al., 2016), and adolescents (Vinayak & Judge, 2018). Similarly, mentalizing ability is beneficial for positive social relationships by facilitating better understanding of social contexts and reducing the possibility of miscommunication. Children who perform better in ToM tasks were more likely to have peer popularity (Slaughter et al., 2015) and showed higher peer acceptance and lower peer rejection later in life (Caputi et al., 2012; Fink et al., 2015). Such a relationship is also found in the elderly. Older adults with higher scores on ToM tasks had better social relationships with friends (Lecce et al., 2017). Both empathy and mentalizing contribute to adaptive social behavior that establishes and maintains positive social relationships, which eventually provide social resources and increase well-being. Prosociality is also tightly associated with well-being. Individuals who prioritize prosocial value over self-centered value report greater happiness (Dambrun & Ricard, 2011; Moynihan et al., 2015). Altruistic individuals are known to be happier, healthier, and live longer than selfish individuals (Post, 2005). Helping others increases life satisfaction and positive emotions. Individuals who volunteered to help others more often reported higher quality of life (Wheeler et al., 1998) and higher subjective well-being (Weinstein & Ryan, 2010). Dunn and colleagues conducted a series of carefully designed experiments to show that prosocial spending made people happier. Specifically, participants who were asked to spend money for others experienced a greater increase in subjective well-being than those who were asked to spend money for themselves (Dunn et al., 2008, 2014). Even two-year-old children expressed greater positive emotions when they shared cookies with a stuffed animal friend than when they kept them all to themselves (Aknin et al., 2012).

Thus far, we have seen behavioral evidence linking social abilities, social relationships, and well-being. In Section 3.4, we also reviewed the social brain networks supporting our ability to establish and maintain social relationships. It would be natural, then, to ask whether and how individual differences in the social brain are associated with social life and well-being. For example, Park et al. (2017) examined the neural mechanisms that link generosity and happiness. Participants were asked to spend money for others (prosocial spending group) or themselves (control group) for four weeks and then invited to the lab again to perform a decision-making task where they made decisions about sharing money with others in an MRI scanner. The prosocial spending group became happier and more generous than the control group. This change coincided with greater TPJ activity and TPJ-ventral striatum connectivity during the decision-making task among the prosocial spending group than in the control group.

Although direct links between individual differences in the social brain and behavioral outcomes in daily life need to be studied further in much broader domains, the emerging evidence supports at least some of the links in this association. One line of research is on connecting the social brain and social resources, namely social network properties. For instance, the volume of the MPFC, orbitofrontal cortex (OFC), PCC, and ACC, which are often implicated in mentalizing, has been reported to predict the ability to understand others and social network size (Kwak et al., 2018; Lewis et al., 2011; Noonan et al., 2018; Powell et al., 2012). Social network size is also known to be associated with the structural and functional differences in the emotion-related brain regions, such as the amygdala and paralimbic regions (Von Der Heide et al., 2014), and the amygdala-cortical functional connectivity (Bickart et al., 2012). In addition, structural and functional coupling of different social brain regions, such as fronto-temporal structural connectivity and functional connectivity between the default mode network, ACC, and dorsolateral prefrontal cortex, has been linked to social network size (Noonan et al., 2018).

Another line of research investigates the neural correlates of happiness and the overlap between the happiness-related brain regions and the social brain. Berridge and Kringelbach (2011) integrated neuroscientific research on reward and pleasure with the positive psychology framework, which proposes two components of well-being: hedonia (positive affect or pleasure) and eudaimonia (meaningfulness or engagement in life). In this review, hedonia was found to be associated with a pleasure circuit including the nucleus accumbens in the ventral striatum and the OFC/VMPFC. The source of pleasure could be not only appetitive sensory stimuli but also socially rewarding stimuli, such as pictures of a loved one (Bartels & Zeki, 2000). Thinking of loved ones could mitigate subjective experience of pain intensity by activating the NAC (Younger et al., 2010). On the other hand, eudaimonic well-being was linked to the default mode network comprising mentalizing regions. These findings suggest an overlap between the social brain and the neural correlates of well-being.

Functional and structural variability in these brain regions seems to be associated with individual differences in well-being. Experiments using fMRI found that individuals with higher subjective well-being showed increased activity in the brain regions involved in positive emotion and reward, such as the sgACC, when processing negative information (van Reekum et al., 2007) and in the striatum in response to positive stimuli (Heller et al., 2013). Individuals with lower self-esteem, which is highly correlated with lower subjective happiness, were more responsive to social exclusion and displayed greater activations within the dACC and stronger functional connectivity between dACC and the MPFC (Onoda et al., 2010). A structural MRI study reported that individuals with higher quality of life had smaller gray matter volumes in the dACC and left rostrolateral prefrontal cortex, the regions associated with processing negative emotions (Takeuchi et al., 2014). Regarding the hedonic vs. eudaimonic distinction, Luo et al. (2017) measured the relative dominance of eudaimonic over hedonic well-being within an individual and examined how this individual tendency is reflected in the brain. They found that individuals with greater eudaimonic than hedonic tendency showed stronger functional connectivity between the VMPFC and precuneus and had greater precuneus gray matter volume.

Although MRI research on individual differences might seem to be in line with the findings from task-based fMRI studies we reviewed above, caution is needed, especially when we interpret the results of structural MRI and resting-state fMRI studies. We cannot tell which of the different socio-cognitive processes associated with the abovementioned brain regions contributes to one's social relationships or well-being. Many links in the association between social brain and individual differences are yet to be discovered. For example, we cannot know whether individuals who have a larger MPFC have larger social networks because they are more empathic, because they mentalize better, or even because they are more sensitive to social reward. There is no one-to-one match between a certain brain region and a specific function. We do not have strong evidence linking the size of a brain structure and its associated functions. Further, neurodevelopment of a person is influenced by one's social relationships and experiences during childhood and adolescence, as we will see in Chapter 11. Therefore, interpreting causality between the social brain, social life, and well-being warrants caution.

3.7 Conclusion

In this chapter, we explored the psychological, evolutionary, and neuroscientific perspectives on human sociality. We have learned that basic motivation for social affiliation and high social intelligence have evolved owing to the uniqueness of human ecology, which requires complex social interactions. The belongingness hypothesis states that humans are born with innate motivation for forming and maintaining social bonds and networks. This idea is supported by the evidence that neural circuits for appetitive (reward) and aversive (pain) responses are tightly associated with the experience of social acceptance and rejection, respectively. The social intelligence hypothesis, ecological intelligence hypothesis, and cultural intelligence hypothesis commonly point to the necessity of high social intelligence, which might have evolved to solve complex social problems. The social brain, a network of brain regions involved in socio-cognitive functions, seems to support understanding and predicting the highly sophisticated social world. The empathy-related regions overlap with the pain pathway, and the mentalizing network involves the TPJ and MPFC. The social network, socio-cognitive function, and social brain change with age. Last, we reviewed the studies suggesting the link between the social brain and the neural correlates of happiness. Although it provides rich insights into human sociality, it should be noted that neuroimaging studies are mostly correlational and, thus, any causal inference should be made with caution, especially when associating neural data to the individual differences in social network properties, socio-cognitive functions, social life, and well-being.

REFERENCES

Adler, A. (1928/2014). *Understanding Human Nature: The Psychology of Personality*. Oneworld Publications.

Adolphs, R. (2009). The social brain: Neural basis of social knowledge. *Annual Review of Psychology*, 60, 693–716.

Aknin, L. B., Hamlin, J. K., & Dunn, E. W. (2012). Giving leads to happiness in young children. *PLoS ONE*, 7(6), e39211.

Amodio, D. M., & Frith, C. D. (2006). Meeting of minds: The medial frontal cortex and social cognition. *Nature Reviews Neuroscience*, 7(4), 268–277.

Ashton, B. J., Thornton, A., & Ridley, A. R. (2018). An intraspecific appraisal of the social intelligence hypothesis. *Philosophical Transactions of the Royal Society B: Biological Sciences*, 373(1756), 20170288.

Atzil, S., Gao, W., Fradkin, I., & Barrett, L. F. (2018). Growing a social brain. *Nature Human Behaviour*, 2(9), 624–636.

Bachorowski, J. A., & Owren, M. J. (2001). Not all laughs are alike: Voiced but not unvoiced laughter readily elicits positive affect. *Psychological Science, 12* (3), 252–257.
Bailey, P. E., Brady, B., Ebner, N. C., & Ruffman, T. (2020). Effects of age on emotion regulation, emotional empathy, and prosocial behavior. *The Journals of Gerontology: Series B, 75*(4), 802–810.
Barton, R. A., & Dunbar, R. I. M. (1997). Evolution of the social brain. In A. Whiten & R. W. Byrne (eds.), *Machiavellian Intelligence II*, pp. 240–263. Cambridge University Press.
Batson, C. D. (2011) *Altruism In Humans*. Oxford University Press.
Baumeister, R. F., & Leary, M. R. (1995). The need to belong: Desire for interpersonal attachments as a fundamental human motivation. *Psychological Bulletin, 117*(3), 497–529.
Baumgartner, T., Nash, K., Hill, C., & Knoch, D. (2015). Neuroanatomy of intergroup bias: A white matter microstructure study of individual differences. *NeuroImage, 122*, 345–354.
Baron-Cohen, S., & Wheelwright, S. (2004). The empathy quotient: An investigation of adults with Asperger syndrome or high functioning autism, and normal sex differences. *Journal of Autism and Developmental Disorders, 34*(2), 163–175.
Bartels, A., & Zeki, S. (2000). The neural basis of romantic love. *Neuroreport, 11* (17), 3829–3834.
Bartolo, P. (2019). Belong and Flourish – Drop Out and Perish, in S. Vella, R. Falzon, & A. Azzopardi (eds.), *Perspectives on Wellbeing*. Brill.
Beadle, J. N., Sheehan, A. H., Dahlben, B., & Gutchess, A. H. (2015). Aging, empathy, and prosociality. *Journals of Gerontology Series B: Psychological Sciences and Social Sciences, 70*(2), 213–222.
Behrens, T. E., Hunt, L. T., Woolrich, M. W., & Rushworth, M. F. (2008). Associative learning of social value. *Nature, 456*(7219), 245–249.
Berridge, K. C., & Kringelbach, M. L. (2011). Building a neuroscience of pleasure and well-being. *Psychology of Well-Being: Theory, Research and Practice, 1*(1), 1–26.
Bickart, K. C., Hollenbeck, M. C., Barrett, L. F., & Dickerson, B. C. (2012). Intrinsic amygdala–cortical functional connectivity predicts social network size in humans. *Journal of Neuroscience, 32*(42), 14729–14741.
Blair, R. J. R. (2005). Responding to the emotions of others: Dissociating forms of empathy through the study of typical and psychiatric populations. *Consciousness and Cognition, 14*(4), 698–718.
Blakemore, S. J. (2008). The social brain in adolescence. *Nature Reviews Neuroscience, 9*(4), 267–277.
Bowlby J. (1969). *Attachment and Loss*, vol. I: Loss. Basic Books.
Byrne. R., & Whiten, A. (eds.) (1988). *Machiavellian Intelligence*. Oxford University Press.
Byrne, R. W., & Corp, N. (2004). Neocortex size predicts deception rate in primates. *Proceedings of the Royal Society of London. Series B: Biological Sciences, 271*(1549), 1693–1699.

Cacioppo, S., Frum, C., Asp, E., Weiss, R. M., Lewis, J. W., & Cacioppo, J. T. (2013). A quantitative meta-analysis of functional imaging studies of social rejection. *Scientific Reports*, *3*(1), 1–3.

Call, J., & Tomasello, M. (2011). Does the chimpanzee have a theory of mind? 30 years later. *Human Nature and Self Design*, 83–96.

Campbell-Sills, L., & Barlow, D. H. (2007). Incorporating emotion regulation into conceptualizations and treatments of anxiety and mood disorders. *Handbook of Emotion Regulation*, *2*, 542–559.

Caputi, M., Lecce, S., Pagnin, A., & Banerjee, R. (2012). Longitudinal effects of theory of mind on later peer relations: The role of prosocial behavior. *Developmental Psychology*, *48*(1), 257–270.

Carstensen, L. L. (1992). Social and emotional patterns in adulthood: Support for socioemotional selectivity theory. *Psychology and Aging*, *7*(3), 331–338.

Carter, C. S. (1998). Neuroendocrine perspectives on social attachment and love. *Psychoneuroendocrinology*, *23*(8), 779–818.

Carter, R. M., Bowling, D. L., Reeck, C., & Huettel, S. A. (2012). A distinct role of the temporal-parietal junction in predicting socially guided decisions. *Science*, *337*(6090), 109–111.

Carter, R. M., & Huettel, S. A. (2013). A nexus model of the temporal–parietal junction. *Trends in Cognitive Sciences*, *17*(7), 328–336.

Castelli, I., Baglio, F., Blasi, V., Alberoni, M., Falini, A., Liverta-Sempio, O., Nemni, R., & Marchetti, A. (2010). Effects of aging on mindreading ability through the eyes: An fMRI study. *Neuropsychologia*, *48*(9), 2586–2594.

Charlton, R. A., Barrick, T. R., Markus, H. S., & Morris, R. G. (2009). Theory of mind associations with other cognitive functions and brain imaging in normal aging. *Psychology and Aging*, *24*(2), 338–348.

Chen, Y. C., Chen, C. C., Decety, J., & Cheng, Y. (2014). Aging is associated with changes in the neural circuits underlying empathy. *Neurobiology of Aging*, *35*(4), 827–836.

Cho, I., & Cohen, A. S. (2019). Explaining age-related decline in theory of mind: Evidence for intact competence but compromised executive function. *PLoS ONE*, *14*(9), e0222890.

Cho, I., Song, H. J., Kim, H., & Sul, S. (2020). Older adults consider others' intentions less but allocentric outcomes more than young adults during an ultimatum game. *Psychology and Aging*, *35*(7), 974–980.

Choi, D., Minote, N., Sekiya, T., & Watanuki, S. (2016). Relationships between trait empathy and psychological well-being in Japanese university students. *Psychology*, *7*(09), 1240–1247.

Cohen, S. (2004). Social relationships and health. *American Psychologist*, *59*(8), 676–684.

Cohen, S., & Wills, T. A. (1985). Stress, social support, and the buffering hypothesis. *Psychological Bulletin*, *98*(2), 310–357.

Corradi-Dell'Acqua, C., Ronchi, R., Thomasson, M., Bernati, T., Saj, A., & Vuilleumier, P. (2020). Deficits in cognitive and affective theory of mind relate to dissociated lesion patterns in prefrontal and insular cortex. *Cortex*, *128*, 218–233.

Corbetta, M., & Shulman, G. L. (2002). Control of goal-directed and stimulus-driven attention in the brain. *Nature Reviews Neuroscience, 3*(3), 201–215.
Coricelli, G., & Nagel, R. (2009). Neural correlates of depth of strategic reasoning in medial prefrontal cortex. *Proceedings of the National Academy of Sciences, 106*(23), 9163–9168.
Courtney, A. L., & Meyer, M. L. (2020). Self-other representation in the social brain reflects social connection. *Journal of Neuroscience, 40*(29), 5616–5627.
Dambrun, M., & Ricard, M. (2011). Self-centeredness and selflessness: A theory of self-based psychological functioning and its consequences for happiness. *Review of General Psychology, 15*(2), 138–157.
Davey, C. G., Allen, N. B., Harrison, B. J., Dwyer, D. B., & Yücel, M. (2010). Being liked activates primary reward and midline self-related brain regions. *Human Brain Mapping, 31*(4), 660–668.
Davis, M. (1980). A multidimensional approach to individual differences in empathy. *Catalog of Selected Documents in Psychology, 10*, 1–17.
De Waal, F. B., & Tyack, P. L. (eds.) (2009). *Animal Social Complexity: Intelligence, Culture, and Individualized Societies*. Harvard University Press.
DeWall, C. N., MacDonald, G., Webster, G. D., Masten, C. L., Baumeister, R. F., Powell, C., Combs, D., Schurtz, D. R., Stillman, T. F., Tice, D. M., & Eisenberger, N. I. (2010). Acetaminophen reduces social pain: Behavioral and neural evidence. *Psychological Science, 21*(7), 931–937.
Denny, B. T., Kober, H., Wager, T. D., & Ochsner, K. N. (2012). A meta-analysis of functional neuroimaging studies of self-and other judgments reveals a spatial gradient for mentalizing in medial prefrontal cortex. *Journal of Cognitive Neuroscience, 24*(8), 1742–1752.
Diener, E., & Seligman, M. E. (2002). Very happy people. *Psychological Science, 13*(1), 81–84.
Dunbar, R. I. (1998). The social brain hypothesis. *Evolutionary Anthropology: Issues, News, and Reviews, 6*(5), 178–190.
Dunbar, R. I., & Shultz, S. (2007). Evolution in the social brain. *Science, 317*(5843), 1344–1347.
Dunn, E. W., Aknin, L. B., & Norton, M. I. (2008). Spending money on others promotes happiness. *Science, 319*(5870), 1687–1688.
(2014). Prosocial spending and happiness: Using money to benefit others pays off. *Current Directions in Psychological Science, 23*(1), 41–47.
Eisenberger, N. I., Inagaki, T. K., Muscatell, K. A., Byrne Haltom, K. E., & Leary, M. R. (2011). The neural sociometer: Brain mechanisms underlying state self-esteem. *Journal of Cognitive Neuroscience, 23*(11), 3448–3455.
Eisenberger, N. I., Lieberman, M. D., & Williams, K. D. (2003). Does rejection hurt? An fMRI study of social exclusion. *Science, 302*(5643), 290–292.
Engen, H. G., & Singer, T. (2013). Empathy circuits. *Current Opinion in Neurobiology, 23*(2), 275–282.
English, T., & Carstensen, L. L. (2014). Selective narrowing of social networks across adulthood is associated with improved emotional experience in daily life. *International Journal of Behavioral Development, 38*(2), 195–202.

Fallon, N., Roberts, C., & Stancak, A. (2020). Shared and distinct functional networks for empathy and pain processing: A systematic review and meta-analysis of fMRI studies. *Social Cognitive and Affective Neuroscience, 15*(7), 709–723.

Fan, Y., Duncan, N. W., de Greck, M., & Northoff, G. (2011). Is there a core neural network in empathy? An fMRI based quantitative meta-analysis. *Neuroscience & Biobehavioral Reviews, 35*(3), 903–911.

Fareri, D. S., & Delgado, M. R. (2014). Social rewards and social networks in the human brain. *The Neuroscientist, 20*(4), 387–402.

Ferrari, P. F., Gallese, V., Rizzolatti, G., & Fogassi, L. (2003). Mirror neurons responding to the observation of ingestive and communicative mouth actions in the monkey ventral premotor cortex. *European Journal of Neuroscience, 17*(8), 1703–1714.

Fiddick, L., Cosmides, L., & Tooby, J. (2000). No interpretation without representation: The role of domain-specific representations and inferences in the Wason selection task. *Cognition, 77*(1), 1–79.

Fink, E., Begeer, S., Peterson, C. C., Slaughter, V., & de Rosnay, M. (2015). Friendlessness and theory of mind: A prospective longitudinal study. *British Journal of Developmental Psychology, 33*(1), 1–17.

Freund, A. M., & Blanchard-Fields, F. (2014). Age-related differences in altruism across adulthood: Making personal financial gain versus contributing to the public good. *Developmental Psychology, 50*(4), 1125–1136.

Frith, C. D. (2007). The social brain? *Philosophical Transactions of the Royal Society B: Biological Sciences, 362*(1480), 671–678.

Frith, C. D., & Frith, U. (2006). The neural basis of mentalizing. *Neuron, 50*(4), 531–534.

Fung, H. H., Carstensen, L. L., & Lang, F. R. (2001). Age-related patterns in social networks among European Americans and African Americans: Implications for socioemotional selectivity across the life span. *The International Journal of Aging and Human Development, 52*(3), 185–206.

German, T. P., & Hehman, J. A. (2006). Representational and executive selection resources in "theory of mind": Evidence from compromised belief-desire reasoning in old age. *Cognition, 101*(1), 129–152.

Gowlett, J., Gamble, C., & Dunbar, R. (2012). Human evolution and the archaeology of the social brain. *Current Anthropology, 53*(6), 693–722.

Harbaugh, W. T., Mayr, U., & Burghart, D. R. (2007). Neural responses to taxation and voluntary giving reveal motives for charitable donations. *Science, 316*(5831), 1622–1625.

Harvey, P. H., Martin, R. D. & Clutton-Brock, T. H. (1987). Life histories in comparative perspective. In B. B. Smuts, D. L. Cheney, R. M. Seyfarth, R. W. Wrangham, & T. T. Struhsaker (eds.), *Primate Societies*, pp. 181–196. University of Chicago Press.

Haxby, J. V., & Gobbini, M. I. (2011). Distributed neural systems for face perception. In A. J. Calder, G. Rhodes, M. H. Johnson, & J. V. Haxby (eds.), *Handbook of Face Perception*, pp. 93–110. Oxford University Press.

Healey, M. L., & Grossman, M. (2018). Cognitive and affective perspective-taking: Evidence for shared and dissociable anatomical substrates. *Frontiers in Neurology*, *9*, 491.
Hein, G., Silani, G., Preuschoff, K., Batson, C. D., & Singer, T. (2010). Neural responses to ingroup and outgroup members' suffering predict individual differences in costly helping. *Neuron*, *68*(1), 149–160.
Hein, G., & Singer, T. (2008). I feel how you feel but not always: The empathic brain and its modulation. *Current Opinion in Neurobiology*, *18*, 153–158.
Heller, A. S., van Reekum, C. M., Schaefer, S. M., Lapate, R. C., Radler, B. T., Ryff, C. D., & Davidson, R. J. (2013). Sustained striatal activity predicts eudaimonic well-being and cortisol output. *Psychological Science*, *24*(11), 2191–2200.
Herrmann, E., Call, J., Hernández-Lloreda, M. V., Hare, B., & Tomasello, M. (2007). Humans have evolved specialized skills of social cognition: The cultural intelligence hypothesis. *Science*, *317*(5843), 1360–1366.
Herrmann, E., Hernández-Lloreda, M. V., Call, J., Hare, B., & Tomasello, M. (2010). The structure of individual differences in the cognitive abilities of children and chimpanzees. *Psychological Science*, *21*(1), 102–110.
Heyes, C., & Catmur, C. (2021). What Happened to Mirror Neurons? *Perspectives on Psychological Science*, *17*(1), 153–168. https://doi.org/10.1177/1745691621990638
Hill, R. A., & Dunbar, R. I. (2003). Social network size in humans. *Human Nature*, *14*(1), 53–72.
Holekamp, K. E. (2007). Questioning the social intelligence hypothesis. *Trends in Cognitive Sciences*, *11*(2), 65–69.
House, J. S., Landis, K. R., & Umberson, D. (1988). Social relationships and health. *Science*, *241*(4865), 540–545.
Humphrey, N. K. (1976) The social function of intellect. In P. Bateson & R. Hinde (eds.), *Growing Points in Ethology*, pp. 303–317. Cambridge University Press.
Hynes, C. A., Baird, A. A., & Grafton, S. T. (2006). Differential role of the orbital frontal lobe in emotional versus cognitive perspective-taking. *Neuropsychologia*, *44*(3), 374–383.
Iacoboni, M., & Dapretto, M. (2006). The mirror neuron system and the consequences of its dysfunction. *Nature Reviews Neuroscience*, *7*(12), 942–951.
Insel, T. R., & Fernald, R. D. (2004). How the brain processes social information: searching for the social brain. *Annual Review of Neuroscience*, *27*, 697–722.
Izuma, K., Saito, D. N., & Sadato, N. (2008). Processing of social and monetary rewards in the human striatum. *Neuron*, *58*(2), 284 294.
   (2010). Processing of the incentive for social approval in the ventral striatum during charitable donation. *Journal of Cognitive Neuroscience*, *22*(4), 621–631.
Jackson, P., Meltzoff, A., & Decety, J. (2005). How do we perceive the pain of others? A window into the neural processes involved in empathy. *NeuroImage*, *24*, 771–779.

Johnson-Ulrich, L. (2017). The Social Intelligence Hypothesis. In T. Shackelford & V. Weekes-Shackelford (eds.), *Encyclopedia of Evolutionary Psychological Science*, pp. 1–7.

Kamil, A. C. (2004). Sociality and the evolution of intelligence. *Trends in Cognitive Sciences, 8*(5), 195–197.

Kang, P., Lee, J., Sul, S., & Kim, H. (2013). Dorsomedial prefrontal cortex activity predicts the accuracy in estimating others' preferences. *Frontiers in Human Neuroscience, 7*, 686.

Kanwisher, N., & Yovel, G. (2006). The fusiform face area: A cortical region specialized for the perception of faces. *Philosophical Transactions of the Royal Society B: Biological Sciences, 361*(1476), 2109–2128.

Kim, S. A., Hamann, S., & Kim, S. H. (2021). Neurocognitive mechanisms underlying improvement of prosocial responses by a novel implicit compassion promotion task. *NeuroImage, 240*, 118333.

Kingsbury, L., & Hong, W. (2020). A multi-brain framework for social interaction. *Trends in Neurosciences, 43*(9), 651–666.

Kliemann, D., & Adolphs, R. (2018). The social neuroscience of mentalizing: Challenges and recommendations. *Current Opinion in Psychology, 24*, 1–6.

Klucharev, V., Hytönen, K., Rijpkema, M., Smidts, A., & Fernández, G. (2009). Reinforcement learning signal predicts social conformity. *Neuron, 61*(1), 140–151.

Kross, E., Berman, M. G., Mischel, W., Smith, E. E., & Wager, T. D. (2011). Social rejection shares somatosensory representations with physical pain. *Proceedings of the National Academy of Sciences, 108*(15), 6270–6275.

Kross, E., Egner, T., Ochsner, K., Hirsch, J., & Downey, G. (2007). Neural dynamics of rejection sensitivity. *Journal of Cognitive Neuroscience, 19*(6), 945–956.

Kudo, H., & Dunbar, R. I. (2001). Neocortex size and social network size in primates. *Animal Behaviour, 62*(4), 711–722.

Kudo, H., Lowen, S., & Dunbar, R. (1999). Neocortex size as a constraint on grooming clique size in primates. *Behaviour*.

Kwak, S., Joo, W. T., Youm, Y., & Chey, J. (2018). Social brain volume is associated with in-degree social network size among older adults. *Proceedings of the Royal Society B: Biological Sciences, 285*(1871), 20172708.

Lamm, C., Batson, C. D., & Decety, J. (2007). The neural substrate of human empathy: Effects of perspective-taking and cognitive appraisal. *Journal of Cognitive Neuroscience, 19*(1), 42–58.

Lamm, C., Rütgen, M., & Wagner, I. C. (2019). Imaging empathy and prosocial emotions. *Neuroscience Letters, 693*, 49–53.

Lansford, J. E., Sherman, A. M., & Antonucci, T. C. (1998). Satisfaction with social networks: An examination of socioemotional selectivity theory across cohorts. *Psychology and Aging, 13*(4), 544–552.

Leary, M. R. (2003). Commentary on self-esteem as an interpersonal monitor: The sociometer hypothesis (1995). *Psychological Inquiry, 14*(3–4), 270–274.

Lecce, S., Ceccato, I., Bianco, F., Rosi, A., Bottiroli, S., & Cavallini, E. (2017). Theory of Mind and social relationships in older adults: The role of social motivation. *Aging & Mental Health*, *21*(3), 253–258.

Lewis, K. P. (2000). A comparative study of primate play behaviour: Implications for the study of cognition. *Folia Primatologica*, *71*(6), 417–421.

Lewis, P. A., Rezaie, R., Brown, R., Roberts, N., & Dunbar, R. I. (2011). Ventromedial prefrontal volume predicts understanding of others and social network size. *Neuroimage*, *57*(4), 1624–1629.

Lieberman, M. D., Straccia, M. A., Meyer, M. L., Du, M., & Tan, K. M. (2019). Social, self, (situational), and affective processes in medial prefrontal cortex (MPFC): Causal, multivariate, and reverse inference evidence. *Neuroscience & Biobehavioral Reviews*, *99*, 311–328.

Lockwood, P. L., Apps, M. A., Valton, V., Viding, E., & Roiser, J. P. (2016). Neurocomputational mechanisms of prosocial learning and links to empathy. *Proceedings of the National Academy of Sciences*, *113*(35), 9763–9768.

Lucas, R. E., & Diener, E. (2001). Understanding extraverts' enjoyment of social situations: The importance of pleasantness. *Journal of Personality and Social Psychology*, *81*(2), 343–356.

Luo, Y., Qi, S., Chen, X., You, X., Huang, X., & Yang, Z. (2017). Pleasure attainment or self-realization: The balance between two forms of well-beings are encoded in default mode network. *Social Cognitive and Affective Neuroscience*, *12*(10), 1678–1686.

Luyten, P., Campbell, C., Allison, E., & Fonagy, P. (2020). The mentalizing approach to psychopathology: State of the art and future directions. *Annual Review of Clinical Psychology*, *16*, 297–325.

Maslow, A. H. (1968). *Toward a Psychology of Being*, 2nd ed. D. Van Nostrand.

Masten, C. L., Morelli, S. A., & Eisenberger, N. I. (2011). An fMRI investigation of empathy for "social pain" and subsequent prosocial behavior. *Neuroimage*, *55*(1), 381–388.

Mather, M., & Carstensen, L. L. (2005). Aging and motivated cognition: The positivity effect in attention and memory. *Trends in Cognitive Sciences*, *9*(10), 496–502.

Mende-Siedlecki, P., Said, C. P., & Todorov, A. (2013). The social evaluation of faces: A meta-analysis of functional neuroimaging studies. *Social Cognitive and Affective Neuroscience*, *8*(3), 285–299.

Mennin, D. S., Holaway, R. M., Fresco, D. M., Moore, M. T., & Heimberg, R. G. (2007). Delineating components of emotion and its dysregulation in anxiety and mood psychopathology. *Behavior Therapy*, *38*(3), 284–302.

Meyer-Lindenberg, A., Mervis, C. B., & Berman, K. F. (2006). Neural mechanisms in Williams syndrome: A unique window to genetic influences on cognition and behaviour. *Nature Reviews Neuroscience*, *7*(5), 380–393.

Mitchell, J. P., Macrae, C. N., & Banaji, M. R. (2006). Dissociable medial prefrontal contributions to judgments of similar and dissimilar others. *Neuron*, *50*(4), 655–663.

Molapour, T., Hagan, C. C., Silston, B., Wu, H., Ramstead, M., Friston, K., & Mobbs, D. (2021). Seven computations of the social brain. *Social Cognitive and Affective Neuroscience*, *16*(8), 745–760.

Moll, H. (2018). The transformative cultural intelligence hypothesis: Evidence from young children's problem-solving. *Review of Philosophy and Psychology*, *9*(1), 161–175.

Moran, J. M., Jolly, E., & Mitchell, J. P. (2012). Social-cognitive deficits in normal aging. *Journal of Neuroscience*, *32*(16), 5553–5561.

Morelli, S. A., Sacchet, M. D., & Zaki, J. (2015). Common and distinct neural correlates of personal and vicarious reward: A quantitative meta-analysis. *NeuroImage*, *112*, 244–253.

Morris, J. S., Frith, C. D., Perrett, D. I., Rowland, D., Young, A. W., Calder, A. J., & Dolan, R. J. (1996). A differential neural response in the human amygdala to fearful and happy facial expressions. *Nature*, *383*(6603), 812–815.

Moynihan, D. P., DeLeire, T., & Enami, K. (2015). A life worth living: Evidence on the relationship between prosocial values and happiness. *The American Review of Public Administration*, *45*(3), 311–326.

Nashiro, K., Sakaki, M., & Mather, M. (2012). Age differences in brain activity during emotion processing: Reflections of age-related decline or increased emotion regulation. *Gerontology*, *58*(2), 156–163.

Noonan, M. P., Mars, R. B., Sallet, J., Dunbar, R. I. M., & Fellows, L. K. (2018). The structural and functional brain networks that support human social networks. *Behavioural Brain Research*, *355*, 12–23.

Novembre, G., Zanon, M., & Silani, G. (2015). Empathy for social exclusion involves the sensory-discriminative component of pain: A within-subject fMRI study. *Social Cognitive and Affective Neuroscience*, *10*(2), 153–164.

Ochsner, K. N., Knierim, K., Ludlow, D. H., Hanelin, J., Ramachandran, T., Glover, G., & Mackey, S. C. (2004). Reflecting upon feelings: An fMRI study of neural systems supporting the attribution of emotion to self and other. *Journal of Cognitive Neuroscience*, *16*(10), 1746–1772.

Onoda, K., Okamoto, Y., Nakashima, K. I., Nittono, H., Yoshimura, S., Yamawaki, S., Yamaguchi, S., & Ura, M. (2010). Does low self-esteem enhance social pain? The relationship between trait self-esteem and anterior cingulate cortex activation induced by ostracism. *Social Cognitive and Affective Neuroscience*, *5*(4), 385–391.

Park, S. A., Sestito, M., Boorman, E. D., & Dreher, J. C. (2019). Neural computations underlying strategic social decision-making in groups. *Nature Communications*, *10*(1), 1–12.

Park, S. Q., Kahnt, T., Dogan, A., Strang, S., Fehr, E., & Tobler, P. N. (2017). A neural link between generosity and happiness. *Nature Communications*, *8*(1), 1–10.

Parkinson, C., & Wheatley, T. (2015). The repurposed social brain. *Trends in Cognitive Sciences*, *19*(3), 133–141.

Perini, I., Gustafsson, P. A., Hamilton, J. P., Kämpe, R., Zetterqvist, M., & Heilig, M. (2018). The salience of self, not social pain, is encoded by dorsal anterior cingulate and insula. *Scientific Reports*, *8*(1), 1–9.

Perry, A., & Shamay-Tsoory, S. (2013). Understanding emotional and cognitive empathy: A neuropsychological perspective. In S. Baron-Cohen, H. Tager-Flusberg, & M. V. Lombardo (eds.), *Understanding Other Minds: Perspectives from Developmental Social Neuroscience*, pp. 178–194. Oxford University Press.

Phillips, L. H., Bull, R., Allen, R., Insch, P., Burr, K., & Ogg, W. (2011). Lifespan aging and belief reasoning: Influences of executive function and social cue decoding. *Cognition*, *120*(2), 236–247.

Pitcher, D., & Ungerleider, L. G. (2021). Evidence for a third visual pathway specialized for social perception. *Trends in Cognitive Sciences*, *25*(2), 100–110.

Post, S. G. (2005). Altruism, happiness, and health: It's good to be good. *International Journal of Behavioral Medicine*, *12*(2), 66–77.

Powell, J., Lewis, P. A., Roberts, N., Garcia-Finana, M., & Dunbar, R. I. (2012). Orbital prefrontal cortex volume predicts social network size: An imaging study of individual differences in humans. *Proceedings of the Royal Society B: Biological Sciences*, *279*(1736), 2157–2162.

Reader, S. M., & Laland, K. N. (2002). Social intelligence, innovation, and enhanced brain size in primates. *Proceedings of the National Academy of Sciences*, *99*(7), 4436–4441.

Rizzolatti, G., Fadiga, L., Gallese, V., & Fogassi, L. (1996). Premotor cortex and the recognition of motor actions. *Cognitive Brain Research*, *3*(2), 131–141.

Roberts, S. G., Dunbar, R. I., Pollet, T. V., & Kuppens, T. (2009). Exploring variation in active network size: Constraints and ego characteristics. *Social Networks*, *31*(2), 138–146.

Rosati, A. G. (2017). Foraging cognition: Reviving the ecological intelligence hypothesis. *Trends in Cognitive Sciences*, *21*(9), 691–702.

Sawaguchi, T., & Kudo, H. (1990). Neocortical development and social structure in primates. *Primates*, *31*(2), 283–289.

Saxe, R., & Kanwisher, N. (2003). People thinking about thinking people: The role of the temporo-parietal junction in "theory of mind". *Neuroimage*, *19*(4), 1835–1842.

Saxe, R., & Powell, L. J. (2006). It's the thought that counts: Specific brain regions for one component of theory of mind. *Psychological Science*, *17*(8), 692–699.

Schmidt, S. N., Fenske, S. C., Kirsch, P., & Mier, D. (2019). Nucleus accumbens activation is linked to salience in social decision making. *European Archives of Psychiatry and Clinical Neuroscience*, *269*(6), 701–712.

Schurz, M., Radua, J., Aichhorn, M., Richlan, F., & Perner, J. (2014). Fractionating theory of mind: A meta-analysis of functional brain imaging studies. *Neuroscience & Biobehavioral Reviews*, *42*, 9–34.

Seyfarth, R. M., & Cheney, D. L. (2015). Social cognition. *Animal Behaviour, 103*, 191–202.

Shanafelt, T. D., West, C., Zhao, X., Novotny, P., Kolars, J., Habermann, T., & Sloan, J. (2005). Relationship between increased personal well-being and enhanced empathy among internal medicine residents. *Journal of General Internal Medicine, 20*(7), 559–564.

Singer, T., Seymour, B., O'doherty, J., Kaube, H., Dolan, R. J., & Frith, C. D. (2004). Empathy for pain involves the affective but not sensory components of pain. *Science, 303*(5661), 1157–1162.

Singer, T., Seymour, B., O'Doherty, J. P., Stephan, K. E., Dolan, R. J., & Frith, C. D. (2006). Empathic neural responses are modulated by the perceived fairness of others. *Nature, 439*(7075), 466–469.

Slaughter, V., Imuta, K., Peterson, C. C., & Henry, J. D. (2015). Meta-analysis of theory of mind and peer popularity in the preschool and early school years. *Child Development, 86*(4), 1159–1174.

Somerville, L. H., Heatherton, T. F., & Kelley, W. M. (2006). Anterior cingulate cortex responds differentially to expectancy violation and social rejection. *Nature Neuroscience, 9*(8), 1007–1008.

Sparrow, E. P., Swirsky, L. T., Kudus, F., & Spaniol, J. (2021). Aging and altruism: A meta-analysis. *Psychology and Aging, 36*(1), 49–56.

Sul, S., Kim, J., & Choi, I. (2013). Subjective well-being and hedonic editing: How happy people maximize joint outcomes of loss and gain. *Journal of Happiness Studies, 14*(4), 1409–1430.

(2016). Subjective well-being, social buffering and hedonic editing in the quotidian. *Cognition and Emotion, 30*(6), 1063–1080.

Sul, S., Tobler, P. N., Hein, G., Leiberg, S., Jung, D., Fehr, E., & Kim, H. (2015). Spatial gradient in value representation along the medial prefrontal cortex reflects individual differences in prosociality. *Proceedings of the National Academy of Sciences, 112*(25), 7851–7856.

Sullivan, S., & Ruffman, T. (2004). Social understanding: How does it fare with advancing years? *British Journal of Psychology, 95*(1), 1–18.

Sutcliffe, A., Dunbar, R., Binder, J., & Arrow, H. (2012). Relationships and the social brain: Integrating psychological and evolutionary perspectives. *British Journal of Psychology, 103*(2), 149–168.

Takeuchi, H., Taki, Y., Nouchi, R., Hashizume, H., Sassa, Y., Sekiguchi, A., Kotozaki, Y., Nakagawa, S., Nagase, T., Miyauchi, C. M., & Kawashima, R. (2014). Anatomical correlates of quality of life: Evidence from voxel-based morphometry. *Human Brain Mapping, 35*(5), 1834–1846.

Thornton, M. A., Weaverdyck, M. E., & Tamir, D. I. (2019). The social brain automatically predicts others' future mental states. *Journal of Neuroscience, 39*(1), 140–148.

Todorov, A., & Engell, A. D. (2008). The role of the amygdala in implicit evaluation of emotionally neutral faces. *Social Cognitive and Affective Neuroscience, 3*(4), 303–312.

Tomasello, M., & Moll, H. (2013). Why don't apes understand false beliefs?. In M. R. Banaji & S. A. Gelman (eds.), *Navigating the Social World: What Infants, Children, and Other Species Can Teach Us*, pp. 81–88. Oxford University Press.

Tusche, A., Böckler, A., Kanske, P., Trautwein, F. M., & Singer, T. (2016). Decoding the charitable brain: Empathy, perspective taking, and attention shifts differentially predict altruistic giving. *Journal of Neuroscience, 36*(17), 4719–4732.

Van Overwalle, F. (2011). A dissociation between social mentalizing and general reasoning. *Neuroimage, 54*(2), 1589–1599.

van Reekum, C. M., Urry, H. L., Johnstone, T., Thurow, M. E., Frye, C. J., Jackson, C. A., Schaefer, H. S., Alexander, A. L., & Davidson, R. J. (2007). Individual differences in amygdala and ventromedial prefrontal cortex activity are associated with evaluation speed and psychological well-being. *Journal of Cognitive Neuroscience, 19*(2), 237–248.

Vinayak, S., & Judge, J. (2018). Resilience and empathy as predictors of psychological wellbeing among adolescents. *International Journal of Health Sciences and Research, 8*(4), 192–200.

Von Der Heide, R., Vyas, G., & Olson, I. R. (2014). The social network-network: Size is predicted by brain structure and function in the amygdala and paralimbic regions. *Social Cognitive and Affective Neuroscience, 9*(12), 1962–1972.

Wang, Y., Metoki, A., Xia, Y., Zang, Y., He, Y., & Olson, I. R. (2021). A large-scale structural and functional connectome of social mentalizing. *NeuroImage, 236*, 118115.

Wei, M., Liao, K. Y. H., Ku, T. Y., & Shaffer, P. A. (2011). Attachment, self-compassion, empathy, and subjective well-being among college students and community adults. *Journal of Personality, 79*(1), 191–221.

Weinstein, N., & Ryan, R. M. (2010). When helping helps: Autonomous motivation for prosocial behavior and its influence on well-being for the helper and recipient. *Journal of Personality and Social Psychology, 98*(2), 222–244.

Wheeler, J. A., Gorey, K. M., & Greenblatt, B. (1998). The beneficial effects of volunteering for older volunteers and the people they serve: A meta-analysis. *The International Journal of Aging and Human Development, 47*(1), 69–79.

Whiten, A., & Byrne, R. W. (1988). The Machiavellian intelligence hypotheses: Editorial. In R. W. Byrne & A. Whiten (eds.), *Machiavellian intelligence: Social Expertise and the Evolution of Intellect in Monkeys, Apes, and Humans*, pp. 1–9. Clarendon Press/Oxford University Press.

Woo, C. W., Koban, L., Kross, E., Lindquist, M. A., Banich, M. T., Ruzic, L., Andrews-Hanna, J. R., & Wager, T. D. (2014). Separate neural representations for physical pain and social rejection. *Nature Communications, 5*(1), 1–12.

Wrzus, C., Hänel, M., Wagner, J., & Neyer, F. J. (2013). Social network changes and life events across the life span: A meta-analysis. *Psychological Bulletin, 139* (1), 53–80.

Wu, H., Luo, Y., & Feng, C. (2016). Neural signatures of social conformity: A coordinate-based activation likelihood estimation meta-analysis of functional brain imaging studies. *Neuroscience & Biobehavioral Reviews, 71,* 101–111.

Xie, H., Karipidis, I. I., Howell, A., Schreier, M., Sheau, K. E., Manchanda, M. K., Ayub, R., Glover, G. H., Jung, M., Reiss, A. L., & Saggar, M. (2020). Finding the neural correlates of collaboration using a three-person fMRI hyperscanning paradigm. *Proceedings of the National Academy of Sciences, 117* (37), 23066–23072.

Younger, J., Aron, A., Parke, S., Chatterjee, N., & Mackey, S. (2010). Viewing pictures of a romantic partner reduces experimental pain: Involvement of neural reward systems. *PLoS ONE, 5*(10), e13309.

Zink, C. F., Tong, Y., Chen, Q., Bassett, D. S., Stein, J. L., & Meyer-Lindenberg, A. (2008). Know your place: Neural processing of social hierarchy in humans. *Neuron, 58*(2), 273–283.

CHAPTER 4

The Genomics of Cognitive Aging in Social Isolation

Sung-Ha Lee and Seyul Kwak

4.1 Introduction

Genes, physical and functional units of heredity, carry the information that lays the foundation for the development of physical appearance, such as height and weight, as well as mental characteristics, including cognitive function and personality. Due to the rapid advancement of genome sequencing techniques and high-performance computing and bioinformatic skills in recent decades, there has been a steep increase in studies searching for genetic factors related to psychosocial and cognitive functions. Among those findings, this section aims to introduce recent genomic findings related to social isolation and cognitive decline. In more detail, this chapter covers the evidence from structural genomics (e.g., genetic variants, single nucleotide polymorphism) to functional genomics (e.g., transcriptional profiles, gene expression) related to social interaction and cognitive function. Protein molecules, such as signaling hormones and neurotransmitters encoded from genes involved in social life and cognitive aging, will be introduced later in the book (see Chapter 7).

4.2 The Genomics of Social Relationships

4.2.1 Evidence of Genetic Influence on Forming Friendships

People tend to make friends with people who are similar to themselves. Increasing evidence points to significant similarities between friends sharing common dimensions, including race, gender, religion, education, or social class, compared to random ties (Kandel, 1978; McPherson et al., 2001). Would this phenomenon of homophily (i.e., "birds of a feather flock together") also be detected at the DNA level as well? A pioneering study

This research was supported by the National Research Foundation of Korea, funded by the Ministry of Education, Science and Technology (NRF-2019R1A2C1087833).

answered this question using a classic twin study design; this study revealed that social network attributes such as in-degree (i.e., the number of social ties), transitivity (i.e., the likelihood that two person's contacts are connected), and centrality are heritable (Fowler et al., 2009). A follow-up study further investigated the genetic influence of friendship networks (Fowler et al., 2011) utilizing real genotype data to examine the genetic similarity between friends. The study found that the genetic variant from Dopamine Receptor D2 (DRD2) exhibits significant homophily, whereas that of Cytochrome P450 2A6 (CYP2A6) exhibits heterophily. More recently, as genomics techniques have developed, genome-wide analysis has revealed that there are two types of gene clusters – heterophilic and homophilic genes (Christakis & Fowler, 2014); the homophilic genes exhibited significant genetic similarities, whereas a certain set of genes involved in immune response were found to be heterophilic between friends compared to random pairs. Such specific genetic patterns found in social networks imply that there is a designated driving force to form social networks and even to be prone to sociability. Future research is necessary to further elucidate the exact function and potential roles of genetic variants in forming social connection.

4.2.2 Genes Associated with Loneliness

As forming social relationships is somewhat determined by genetic predisposition, we can hypothesize that lack of social connection can be also explained by genetic influence. In fact, there is evidence suggesting that a lack of social embeddedness is a heritable trait that interplays with genes and environment to determine the degree of loneliness. The tendency to feel lonely comes from genetic predispositions that preset a vulnerability or sensitivity to negative social events through the course of life that may regulate its incidence.

Loneliness is one of the complex polygenic human behaviors in which many genes contribute to determine the phenotype. Evidence from traditional twin and family-based studies indicated that the heritability of loneliness is up to 55% (Boomsma et al., 2005; Waaktaar & Torgersen, 2012). Recent genomics studies have also started to elucidate the genetic contribution to loneliness using a genome-wide approach. For example, Gao et al. (2017) used genotypic and phenotypic data from 10,760 individuals from the Health and Retirement Study to 1) examine genetic variants of loneliness by a genome-wide approach and 2) replicate the results from previously published associations between loneliness and candidate variates, such as rs2254298 in the oxytocin receptor (OXTR) gene, rs7412 in the apolipoprotein (APO) E2 gene, and rs1800497 in DRD2. In spite of the pioneering attempt to investigate a genome-wide association study of loneliness, no associations reached genome-wide significance and further replications were not successful. However, the study revealed strong genetic correlations between loneliness and neuroticism, suggesting the role of negative affectivity shared by both traits.

Recent genome-wide association studies (GWASs), have examined the genetic factors related to loneliness by scanning several hundred thousand genetic variants, or single nucleotide polymorphism (SNP). Such approaches enable the calculation of the beta estimate and its significance (p value) of the association of each SNP with a certain clinical phenotype. Also, based on the estimated effect of many genetic variants, polygenic scores (or polygenic risk scores) can be calculated by summing up the genetic effects of the significant SNPs. One recent study attempted to construct the polygenic score related to loneliness and compared it with other polygenic scores for twenty-seven traits related to loneliness, such as depression, neuroticism, autism, and alcohol use (Abdellaoui et al., 2018). Among the polygenic scores of the behavioral traits related to loneliness, the polygenic scores for depression, neuroticism, and schizophrenia significantly predicted loneliness, which means these traits could inform the genetic predisposition to loneliness. Moreover, a recent meta-genomics analysis involving over 500,000 subjects confirms nineteen genetic variants associated with loneliness (Abdellaoui et al., 2019). This study further investigated the shared genetic correlates of loneliness to other physical and mental health indices; it found that genetic variants of loneliness are not only linked to depression and neuroticism, but also the level of triglycerides and high-density lipoprotein (HDL). In that elevated triglycerides and reduced HDL are strongly linked to heart disease, these findings imply that the association between loneliness and cardiovascular health can be partly explained by their shared genetic predisposition.

4.2.3 *Gene Expression Patterns Regulated by Social Conditions*

Among the 20,000 genes (i.e., protein coding DNA sequences) in the human species, a subset of about 100 are "socially" regulated in response to adverse social environmental cues, such as social threats (Cole et al., 2007; Cole, 2014, 2019). The "social signal transduction pathway" has hypothesized adverse environmental factors that regulate the expression of certain genes (Cole, 2014, 2019). The transcriptional profiles of genes are measured by the level of ribonucleic acid (RNA), molecules coded from DNA via a process called "transcription," which further facilitate the production of proteins such as hormones and neurotransmitters.

Social genomics, pioneered by Dr. Cole and his colleagues, provides molecular evidence of how environmental factors regulate peripheral gene expression patterns. In one of their earlier studies, they explored the difference in gene expression patterns between the groups of people who are chronically lonely versus those who have been consistently integrated socially, and found that there are about 200 genes that were differentially regulated across the two groups (Cole et al., 2007). Further studies confirmed recurrent patterns of such gene expression under adverse social conditions, characterized by increased expression of genes involved in inflammation (e.g., IL-1B, IL-6, IL-8, and TNF-α) and decreased expression of genes involved in Type I interferon-mediated antiviral responses, which has been called a conserved transcriptional response to adversity (CTRA) (Cole, 2014, 2019; Slavich & Cole, 2013). This increase in CTRA gene expression has been observed across various adverse social conditions, such as low socioeconomic status, post-traumatic stress disorder, social discrimination, and chronic loneliness (Cole et al., 2015; Kim et al., 2021 Kohrt et al., 2016; Murray et al., 2019; Sloan et al., 2007; Thames et al., 2019). The social signals are believed to initiate neurocognitive processes by evaluation of the adverse social conditions (Cole, 2014, 2019). A lack of desired social contacts, or loneliness, is perceived by the brain and "taps into" the alarm system that responds to survival threats, activating sympathetic nervous systems and beta adrenergic receptors, and further activating transcriptional factors and regulating CTRA gene expression (Cole, 2014, 2019). Increased CTRA patterns in response to adverse social conditions provide empirical evidence of how the environment can regulate molecular signals inside the cells.

4.3 The Genomics of Cognitive Aging

4.3.1 Genes Associated with Cognitive Aging

Just as height is a physical phenotype, educational attainment has been widely tested as a psychosocial phenotype in GWASs. A recent GWAS with a million individuals (n = 1,131,881) identified 1,271 surrogate genetic markers significantly associated with educational attainment; the number of years of schooling that individuals had completed explained about 11% of the variance (Lee et al., 2018). Interestingly, the significant SNPs associated with educational attainment exhibited especially high expression in the prenatal brain. Moreover, neurophysiological functions of these SNPs are involved in neurotransmitter secretion, more specifically, the activation of ion channels.

The heritability of Alzheimer's disease (AD) is much higher than that of educational attainment – showing up to 70–80% based on concordance for AD among parent–offspring pairs (Wingo et al., 2012). Among the various genetic variants, the strongest genetic risk factor for AD is the apolipoprotein E (APOE) gene; the APOE ε4 allele reduces β-amyloid(Aβ) clearance and increases a person's risk for AD (Apostolova et al., 2018). To expand the genomic research from educational attainment to cognitive decline, the GWAS approach has identified the lead SNPs associated with AD. For example, one recent study using over 17,000 cases of AD from the International Genomics of Alzheimer's Project found over 1,000 SNPs associated with AD in addition to APOE ε4 alleles (Desikan et al., 2017). Based on these AD-associated SNPs, the researchers developed a polygenic hazard score to predict the age-specific risk for AD pathogenesis. Another GWAS investigated the genetic variants associated with the AD-related endophenotypes, such as hippocampal volume, logical memory performance, and cerebrospinal fluid, amyloid, and tau (Chung et al., 2018). So far, most of the genetic variants associated with AD are involved in neuronal functions such as neuronal development and signaling.

It is noteworthy that AD pathology overlaps with non-Alzheimer's pathologies or other nonspecific pathologies that occur in late life (Jack et al., 2018). In other words, various brain changes related to aging converge into the clinical outcomes of dementia risks that result from reduced neural resources and cognitive impairment. In addition to variants of the APOE ε4 allele, other genetic variants also note the neurobiological basis of the cognitive aging process. For example, the polymorphisms of dopaminergic metabolism (e.g., catechol-O-methyltransferase) and neural development (e.g., brain-derived neurotrophic factor Val66Met) have been recognized as influencing the lifelong process of cognitive aging, which significantly explains the individual difference in late-life episodic memory and executive function (Lin et al., 2017; Raz & Lustig, 2014). In spite of the significant associations between such genetic variants and neural pathologies, a small number of polymorphisms cannot explain the complex cognitive aging process sufficiently. Rather, various mediating lifestyle factors modulate cerebrovascular risks and how an individual undergoes cognitive aging (Jiang et al., 2021). Conscientious management of harmful behaviors, such as consumption of alcohol or smoking, and engagement in cognitively and physically stimulating activities are associated risk and protective factors, respectively, that increase or decrease all causes of dementia rather than affecting a specific pathological process (Ferencz et al., 2014).

By examining genetic correlations, however, we can infer which neurobiological mechanisms mediate the complex outcome of cognitive aging. Educational attainment, one of the prominent factors that explain cognitive ability in late life, has been examined in terms of genetic heritability and biological correlations (Okbay et al., 2016). Intracranial volume, development of neural capacity, and major vascular risk factors were also found as correlates of educational attainment. This representative study suggests that lifestyle factors of cognitive aging are not confined within psychosocial factors. Thus, individuals who have certain genotypes associated with lower risk of dementia will nonspecifically benefit from higher education, lower socioeconomic stress, and more conscientious health-seeking behavior.

4.3.2 Gene vs. Environment in Cognitive Function

Cognitive functions are complex human phenotypes that are determined by the interplay of genes, lifestyle, and environment. Using the polygenic score, which summarizes the estimate effect of the putative alleles associated with a certain human trait, researchers can examine the effect of nature vs. nurture, as well as the interplay between them. For example, although education and cognitive function has been consistently suggested as an inherited psychosocial trait (Branigan et al., 2013; Lee et al., 2018; Mukherjee et al., 2020), there is still a wide range of variances where social and environmental factors contribute to education and cognitive functions. One of the moderators that can modify the genetic influence on cognitive function is adverse social conditions, including lower socioeconomic status (SES). Turkheimer and colleagues once suggested that genetic penetrance is much higher in those who are socially advantaged compared to those in the low end of SES distribution using the twin model; that is, socially enriched environments ensure that individuals with higher SES can reach their full "genetic potential" (Turkheimer et al., 2003). Another study also demonstrated that the prediction power of polygenic scores can be moderated by age and gender in addition to SES (Mostafavi et al., 2020). This study questioned why the prediction accuracy differs across genome-wide studies and demonstrated that the accuracy of polygenic scores associated with estimating human phenotypes can be moderated by environmental factors. Thus, a growing number of genomic studies are investigating the interaction between the genotype and environment in cognitive aging. Even though some recent studies identified the effect of the polygenic scores on human complex traits, future studies investigating the exact environmental conditions and to what extent they can affect the phenotypes will be needed to address the complexities of interpreting traits of a social or behavioral nature.

4.4 Protective Factors against Adverse Gene Expression Patterns

Gene expression patterns regulated by the environment (i.e., altered immune gene expression) are "reversible." Recent evidence indicates that prosocial behavior or volunteering activity efficiently reduced proinflammatory gene expression and increased antiviral activity; in other words, they reduced CTRA gene expression profiles (Nelson-Coffey et al., 2017; Seeman et al., 2019). Moreover, leading meaningful and fulfilling lives or having optimism also helped people to have favorable immune gene expression patterns (Fredrickson et al., 2013; Lee et al., 2020; Uchida et al., 2018). Indeed, one study showed that higher purpose in life decreased the risk of AD as well as mild cognitive impairment, suggesting one possibility in behavioral intervention to prevent AD pathology (Boyle et al., 2010).

4.5 Future Directions and Conclusions

An important caveat of the GWAS findings on cognitive aging is that the vast majority of GWASs have involved people of European descent, and the application of these findings to calculate the polygenic score (PGS) in other racial populations remains inconclusive. In that non-Europeans differ from Europeans in their genetic architectures (e.g., minor allele frequency, linkage disequilibrium), the predictive power of GWAS findings may be diminished, in terms of accuracy and portability of PGS, by the genetic distance from European ancestry. For example, the PGS of height estimated from the U.K. Biobank can increase the prediction accuracy of real height by up to 11% in the U.K. population but by only 3% in Japan (Martin et al., 2017). Similarly, the PGS of educational attainment based on the European population shows about seven times more accuracy when used to predict the educational attainment of European Americans than with African Americans (Lee et al., 2018).

In addition to the genetic architecture itself, other socio-environmental factors can also make it difficult to separate genetic vs. non-genetic factors and to calculate the exact interaction of genes and environment. If we can understand to what extent environmental or cultural variability could differ between GWAS and prediction groups, we can estimate the proportion of the variance explained by PGSs on certain phenotypes. The PGS for some traits, especially social behavior, loneliness, and educational attainment, may include environmental and cultural confounding factors, and these hidden factors can change prediction accuracy. Increasing attention has been paid to PGS recently in that the score can be used to estimate genetic influence on complex phenotypes. Among such genomic studies, educational attainment is one of the most studied human traits that involves the environment–gene interaction.

Genomic research is in need of more data, especially those of non-European populations. More specifically, the validation and application of PGS in diverse populations is necessary in that not only genes but social factors, such as education, are different in developing countries, the majority of which are composed of non-European citizens. One of the efficient approaches is to add genomic information to a preexisting longitudinal dataset (e.g., KSHAP), not only to connect social relationship to its genetic bases but also to generalize the findings from European-ancestry populations to other racial groups.

Recent advances in genomics have enabled us to incorporate human genetic variation into investigating human behavior. In fact, recent genomics studies using candidate SNPs to polygenic scores have investigated the genetic influence of human behavior, such as perceived loneliness and cognitive function. Other genomics studies have attempted to reveal genetic predispositions associated with social isolation and cognitive impairment. Ongoing GWASs have identified several genetic risk loci linked to age-related cognitive decline, as well as neuropathological conditions. In addition to the genetic factors, social genomic research suggests adverse social conditions, such as loneliness, alter gene expression patterns in white blood cells. These genomics studies not only suggest that loneliness and neuropathological processes are heritable traits but also that genetic variants interact with environmental factors regulating gene expressions. More studies will be needed to investigate the interaction between genetic and environmental factors to elucidate the determinants of complex human behavior.

Box 4.1 Mini dictionary of terms (modified from genome.gov)

SNP (single nucleotide polymorphism): a type of polymorphism involving variation of a single base pair in the human genome.

GWAS (genome-wide association studies): an approach used in genetics research to associate specific genetic variations with particular diseases. The method involves scanning the whole genome and looking for genetic markers that can be used to predict the presence of a disease.

PGS (polygenic score): the estimated score of how the collection of a person's genetic variants affect the risk for a certain disease.

Allele: the word that we use to describe the alternative form or versions of a gene.

Transcription: the process of making an RNA copy of a gene sequence. This copy, called a messenger RNA (mRNA) molecule, further synthesizes the protein, which it encodes.

REFERENCES

Abdellaoui, A., Nivard, M. G., Hottenga, J. J., Fedko, I., Verweij, K. J. H., Baselmans, B. M. L., Ehli, E. A., Davies, G. E., Bartels, M., Boomsma, D. I., & Cacioppo, J. T. (2018). Predicting loneliness with polygenic scores of social, psychological and psychiatric traits. *Genes, Brain and Behavior*, *17*(6). https://doi.org/10.1111/gbb.12472

Abdellaoui, A., Sanchez-Roige, S., Sealock, J., Treur, J. L., Dennis, J., Fontanillas, P., Elson, S., The 23andme Research Team, Nivard, M. G., Ip, H. F., van der Zee, M., Baselmans, B. M. L., Hottenga, J. J., Willemsen, G., Mosing, M., Lu, Y., Pedersen, N. L., Denys, D., Amin, N., ... Boomsma, D. I. (2019). Phenome-wide investigation of health outcomes associated with genetic predisposition to loneliness. *Human Molecular Genetics*, *28*(22), 3853–3865. https://doi:10.1093/hmg/ddz219

Apostolova, L. G., Risacher, S. L., Duran, T., Stage, E. C., Goukasian, N., West, J. D., Do, T. M., Grotts, J., Wilhalme, H., Nho, K., Phillips, M., Elashoff, D., & Saykin, A. J. (2018). Associations of the top 20 Alzheimer disease risk variants with brain amyloidosis. *JAMA Neurology*, *75*(3), 328–341. https://doi.org/10.1001/jamaneurol.2017.4198

Boomsma, D. I., Willemsen, G., Dolan, C. V., Hawkley, L. C., & Cacioppo, J. T. (2005). Genetic and environmental contributions to loneliness in adults: The Netherlands Twin Register study. *Behavior Genetics*, *35*(6), 745–752. https://doi.org/10.1007/s10519-005-6040-8

Boyle, P. A., Buchman, A. S., Barnes, L. L., & Bennett, D. A. (2010). Effect of a purpose in life on risk of incident Alzheimer disease and mild cognitive impairment in community-dwelling older persons. *Archives of General Psychiatry*, *67*(3), 304–310.

Branigan, A. R., McCallum, K. J., & Freese, J. (2013). Variation in the heritability of educational attainment: An international meta-analysis. *Social Forces*, *92*(1), 109–140. https://doi.org/10.1093/sf/sot076

Christakis, N. A., & Fowler, J. H. (2014). Friendship and natural selection. *PNAS*, *111* (supplement_3), 10796–10801.

Chung, J., Wang, X., Maruyama, T., Ma, Y., Zhang, X., Mez, J., Sherva, R., Takeyama, H., Lunetta, K. L., Farrer, L. A., & Jun, G. R. (2018). Genome-wide association study of Alzheimer's disease endophenotypes at prediagnosis stages. *Alzheimer's and Dementia*, *14*(5), 623–633. https://doi.org/10.1016/j.jalz.2017.11.006

Cole, S. W. (2014). Human Social Genomics. *PLoS Genetics*, *10*(8). https://doi.org/10.1371/journal.pgen.1004601

(2019). The Conserved transcriptional response to adversity. *Current Opinion in Behavioral Sciences*, *28*, 31–37. https://doi.org/10.1016/j.cobeha.2019.01.008

Cole, S. W., Hawkley, L. C., Arevalo, J. M., Sung, C. Y., Rose, R. M., & Cacioppo, J. T. (2007). Social regulation of gene expression in human leukocytes. *Genome Biology*, *8*(9), R189. https://doi.org/10.1186/gb-2007-8-9-r189

Cole, S. W., Levine, M. E., Arevalo, J. M. G., Ma, J., Weir, D. R., & Crimmins, E. M. (2015). Loneliness, eudaimonia, and the human conserved transcriptional response to adversity. *Psychoneuroendocrinology*, *62*, 11–17. https://doi.org/10.1016/j.psyneuen.2015.07.001

Deary, I. J., & Johnson, W. (2010). Intelligence and education: Causal perceptions drive analytic processes and therefore conclusions. *International Journal of Epidemiology*, *39*(5), 1362–1369. https://doi.org/10.1093/ije/dyq072

Desikan, R. S., Fan, C.-C., Wang, Y., Schork, A. J., Cabral, H. J., Cupples, L. A., Thompson, W. K., Besser, L., Kukull, W. A., Holland, D., Chen, C.-H., Brewer, J. B., Karow, D. S., Kauppi, K., Witoelar, A., Karch, C. M., Bonham, L. W., Yokoyama, J. S., Rosen, H. J., ... Dale, A. M. (2017). Genetic assessment of age-associated Alzheimer disease risk: Development and validation of a polygenic hazard score. *PLoS Medicine*, *14*(3), e1002258.

Ferencz, B., Laukka, E. J., Welmer, A. K., Kalpouzos, G., Angleman, S., Keller, L., Graff, C., Lövdén, M., & Bäckman, L. (2014). The benefits of staying active in old age: Physical activity counteracts the negative influence of PICALM, BIN1, and CLU risk alleles on episodic memory functioning. *Psychology and Aging*, *29*(2), 440–449. https://doi.org/10.1037/a0035465

Fowler, J. H., Dawes, C. T., & Christakis, N. A. (2009). Model of genetic variation in human social networks. *Proceedings of the National Academy of Sciences*, *106*(6), 1720–1724. https://doi.org/10.1073/pnas.0806746106

Fowler, J. H., Settle, J. E., & Christakis, N. A. (2011). Correlated genotypes in friendship networks. *Proceedings of the National Academy of Sciences*, *108*(5), 1993–1997. https://doi.org/10.1073/pnas.1011687108

Fredrickson, B. L., Grewen, K. M., Coffey, K. A., Algoe, S. B., Firestine, A. M., Arevalo, J. M. G., & Cole, S. W. (2013). A functional genomic perspective on human well-being. *Proceedings of the National Academy of Sciences*, *110*(33), 13684–13689. https://doi.org/10.1073/pnas.1305419110

Gao, J., Davis, L. K., Hart, A. B., Sanchez-Roige, S., Han, L., Cacioppo, J. T., & Palmer, A. A. (2017). Genome-wide association study of loneliness demonstrates a role for common variation. *Neuropsychopharmacology*, *42*(4), 811–821. https://doi.org/10.1038/npp.2016.197

Jack, C. R., Bennett, D. A., Blennow, K., Carrillo, M. C., Dunn, B., Haeberlein, S. B., Holtzman, D. M., Jagust, W., Jessen, F., Karlawish, J., Liu, E., Molinuevo, J. L., Montine, T., Phelps, C., Rankin, K. P., Rowe, C. C., Scheltens, P., Siemers, E., Snyder, H. M., ... Silverberg, N. (2018). NIA-AA Research Framework: Toward a biological definition of Alzheimer's disease. *Alzheimer's and Dementia*, *14*(4), 535–562. https://doi.org/10.1016/j.jalz.2018.02.018

Jiang, Y., Cui, M., Tian, W., Zhu, S., Chen, J., Suo, C., Liu, Z., Lu, M., Xu, K., Fan, M., Wang, J., Dong, Q., Ye, W., Jin, L., & Chen, X. (2021). Lifestyle, multi-omics features, and preclinical dementia among Chinese: The Taizhou Imaging Study. *Alzheimer's and Dementia*. https://doi.org/10.1002/alz.12171

Kandel, D. B. (1978). Homophily, selection, and socialization in adolescent friendships. *American Journal of Sociology*, *84*(2), 427–436. https://doi.org/10.1086/226792

Kim, Y., Cole, S. W., Carver, C. S., Antoni, M. H., & Penedo, F. J. (2021). Only the lonely: Expression of proinflammatory genes through family cancer caregiving experiences. *Psychosomatic Medicine, 83*(2), 149–156. https://doi.org/10.1097/PSY.0000000000000897

Kohrt, B. A., Worthman, C. M., Adhikari, R. P., Luitel, N. P., Arevalo, J. M. G., Ma, J., McCreath, H., Seeman, T. E., Crimmins, E. M., & Cole, S. W. (2016). Psychological resilience and the gene regulatory impact of posttraumatic stress in Nepali child soldiers. *Proceedings of the National Academy of Sciences, 113*(29), 8156–8161. https://doi.org/10.1073/pnas.1601301113

Lee, J. J., Wedow, R., Okbay, A., Kong, E., Maghzian, O., Zacher, M., Nguyen-Viet, T. A., Bowers, P., Sidorenko, J., Karlsson Linnér, R., Fontana, M. A., Kundu, T., Lee, C., Li, H., Li, R., Royer, R., Timshel, P. N., Walters, R. K., Willoughby, E. A., ... Cesarini, D. (2018). Gene discovery and polygenic prediction from a genome-wide association study of educational attainment in 1.1 million individuals. *Nature Genetics, 50*(8), 1112–1121.

Lee, S. H., Choi, I., Choi, E., Lee, M., Kwon, Y., Oh, B., & Cole, S. W. (2020). Psychological well-being and gene expression in Korean adults: The role of age. *Psychoneuroendocrinology, 120*, 104785. https://doi.org/10.1016/j.psyneuen.2020.104785

Lin, C.-H., Lin, E., and Lane, H.-Y., (2017) Genetic Biomarkers on age-related cognitive decline. *Frontiers in Psychiatry 8*. https://doi.org/10.3389/fpsyt.2017.00247

Martin, A. R., Gignoux, C. R., Walters, R. K., Wojcik, G. L., Neale, B. M., Gravel, S., Daly, M. J., Bustamante, C. D., & Kenny, E. E. (2017). Human demographic history impacts genetic risk prediction across diverse populations. *American Journal of Human Genetics, 100*(4), 635–649. https://doi.org/10.1016/j.ajhg.2017.03.004

McPherson, M., Smith-Lovin, L., & Cook, J. M. (2001). Birds of a feather: Homophily in social networks. *Annual Review of Sociology, 27*, 415–444.

Mostafavi, H., Harpak, A., Agarwal, I., Conley, D., Pritchard, J. K., & Przeworski, M. (2020). Variable prediction accuracy of polygenic scores within an ancestry group. *ELife, 9*, e48376 https://doi.org/10.7554/eLife.48376

Mukherjee, S., Mez, J., Trittschuh, E., Saykin, A. J., Gibbons, L. E., Fardon, D. W., Wessels, M., Bauman, J., Moore, M., Choi, S.-E., Gross, A. L., Rich, J., Louden, D. K. N., Sanders, R. E., Grabowski, T. J., Bird, T. J., McCurry, S. M., Snitz, B. E., Kamboh, M. I., ... Crane, P. K. (2020). Genetic data and cognitively defined late-onset Alzheimer's disease subgroups. *Molecular Psychiatry 25*, 2942–2951. https://doi.org/10.1038/s41380-018-0298-8

Murray, D. R., Haselton, M. G., Fales, M., & Cole, S. W. (2019). Subjective social status and inflammatory gene expression. *Health Psychology, 38*(2), 182–186. https://doi.org/10.1037/hea0000705

Nelson-Coffey, S. K., Fritz, M. M., Lyubomirsky, S., & Cole, S. W. (2017). Kindness in the blood: A randomized controlled trial of the gene regulatory impact of prosocial behavior. *Psychoneuroendocrinology, 81*, 8–13.

Okbay, A., Beauchamp, J. P., Fontana, M. A., Lee, J. J., Pers, T. H., Rietveld, C. A., Turley, P., Chen, G. B., Emilsson, V., Meddens, S. F. W., Oskarsson, S., Pickrell, J. K., Thom, K., Timshel, P., De Vlaming, R., Abdellaoui, A., Ahluwalia, T. S., Bacelis, J., Baumbach, C., ... Benjamin, D. J. (2016). Genome-wide association study identifies 74 loci associated with educational attainment. *Nature*, *533*, 539–542. https://doi.org/10.1038/nature17671

Raz, N., & Lustig, C. (2014). Genetic variants and cognitive aging: Destiny or a nudge? *Psychology and Aging*, *29*(2), 359–362. https://doi.org/10.1037/a0036893

Seeman, T., Merkin, S. S., Goldwater, D., & Cole, S. W. (2019). Intergenerational mentoring, eudaimonic well-being and gene regulation in older adults: A pilot study. *Psychoneuroendocrinology*, *111*, 104468.

Slavich, G. M., & Cole, S. W. (2013). The emerging field of human social genomics. *Clinical Psychological Science*, *1*(3), 331–348. https://doi.org/10.1177/2167702613478594

Sloan, E. K., Capitanio, J. P., Tarara, R. P., Mendoza, S. P., Mason, W. A., & Cole, S. W. (2007). Social stress enhances sympathetic innervation of primate lymph nodes: Mechanisms and implications for viral pathogenesis. *Journal of Neuroscience*, *27*(33), 8857–8865. https://doi.org/10.1523/JNEUROSCI.1247-07.2007

Thames, A. D., Irwin, M. R., Breen, E. C., & Cole, S. W. (2019). Experienced discrimination and racial differences in leukocyte gene expression. *Psychoneuroendocrinology*, *106*, 277–283. https://doi.org/10.1016/j.psyneuen.2019.04.016

Turkheimer, E., Haley, A., Waldron, M., D'Onofrio, B., & Gottesman, I. I. (2003). Socioeconomic status modifies heritability of IQ in young children. *Psychological Science*, *14*(6), 623–628. https://doi.org/10.1046/j.0956-7976.2003.psci_1475.x

Uchida, Y., Kitayama, S., Akutsu, S., Park, J., & Cole, S. W. (2018). Optimism and the conserved transcriptional response to adversity. *Health Psychology*, *37*(11), 1077–1080.

Waaktaar, T., & Torgersen, S. (2012). Genetic and environmental causes of variation in perceived loneliness in young people. *American Journal of Medical Genetics, Part B: Neuropsychiatric Genetics*, *159*B(5), 580–588. https://doi.org/10.1002/ajmg.b.32064

Wingo, T. S., Lah, J. J., Levey, A. I., & Cutler, D. J. (2012). Autosomal recessive causes likely in early-onset Alzheimer disease. *Archives of Neurology*, *69*(1), 59–64. https://doi.org/10.1001/archneurol.2011.221

PART II

Society Interacting with Brain, Cognition, and Health in Late Life

CHAPTER 5

The Life Course Approach to Cognitive Aging and Dementia

Jeanyung Chey and Seyul Kwak

5.1 Introduction

In 1988 a team of neuroscientists at UCSD led by Robert Katzman reported a finding of ten women, who had lived at a nursing home with functional and cognitive performance in the upper quintile of the norm, showing significant neuropathology of Alzheimer's disease (AD). These included "neocortical plaques," more specifically referred to as amyloid beta plaques, discovered in the postmortem neuropathological examination (Katzman et al., 1988). This "unexpected finding" of the discrepancy between the brain pathology and the clinical manifestation puzzled many researchers, since until then dementia had been regarded as a purely biological condition due to brain pathology. After finding that these asymptomatic older adults with the plaques had significantly large brain size, Katzman et al. (1988) proposed that these older adults had AD that did not manifest due to the greater reserve of their brain.

Later, this intriguing phenomenon has been found in other studies, such as the famous "nun study" of the members of the School Sisters of the Notre Dame congregation (Snowdon, 2003), in which 58 and 32% of nuns who lived to their older adulthood without memory impairment were found to have mild to moderate level of neurofibrillary tangles, respectively, a pathognomonic marker of AD according to the Braak and Braak staging of brain autopsy (Riley et al., 2002). Moreover, they found 8% of nuns who demonstrated the severe stage of Alzheimer's pathology upon autopsy but did not show any clinical manifestation of the disease, with a few nuns who were cognitively acute until the very end.

Other important data the study revealed were the essays submitted by the nuns in their youth, when they joined the school. This provided a rare opportunity for researchers to assess the baseline cognitive functioning during early adulthood, which could be compared with that in later life. The essays were assessed in terms of thought density and linguistic ability, which reflected the development of higher cognitive functions (Snowdon et al., 1996). It was found that older adults whose cognitive and daily functions had been well maintained until death but who showed significant neuropathology at the autopsy were those who showed well developed higher cognition in early adulthood.

The observed resistance or resilience toward neurodegenerative diseases were couched in the term "reserve," initially describing brain size or neuronal counts/density that could delay the manifestation of dementia (Katzman et al., 1988; Satz, 1993). It was, however, Yaakov Stern at Columbia University who elaborated the concept to involve two components, the brain and cognitive reserve, that would have different mechanisms and implications for the onset of dementia (Stern, 2002). Initially, brain reserve was characterized as the passive component that can be viewed as the degree of development of normal brain structure and function. Cognitive reserve, the active component, has been proposed as a measure of the brain's capacity to cope with or compensate for pathology, which could moderate the effects of brain diseases and injuries, possibly in terms of efficient utilization of brain networks or an enhanced ability to utilize alternate networks as needed. Both components of the reserve accumulate from early years. Brain reserve, often estimated from the size of the brain or the number of neurons, is thought to be formed early in the fetal stage and continues until late puberty or early adulthood, when brain maturation is usually completed. It is likely to be formed by genetic expression, nutrition, social support, intellectual stimulation, and education. It could also be affected by perinatal exposure to viruses, toxins, or brain injuries. Yet, maintenance of the reserve throughout adulthood can vary greatly between individuals; hence, it should not be assumed to be static from early adulthood (Nyberg & Pudas, 2019). It is known that regional brain volumes can increase in middle-aged adults from intensive training or experience, such as taxi driving in the narrow and complex roads of London (Maguire et al., 2000). Moreover, despite controversy (Duque et al., 2022; Kempermann et al., 2018) and conflicting evidence (Sorrells et al., 2018), recent studies have repeatedly reported evidence of adult neurogenesis in humans (Boldrini et al., 2018; Eriksson et al., 1998; Moreno-Jiménez et al., 2021; Spalding et al., 2013), which is assumed to allow greater neuroplasticity in adulthood.

Cognitive reserve accumulates with stimulating environments and formal education from childhood to youth, and also with occupational experience in adulthood (Stern, 2012). It can be measured most accurately only when brain damage or pathology insults the brain, to which it would adapt effectively by utilizing its networks more efficiently or employing alternative networks to perform the task at hand (Stern, 2002).

The proposal that an earlier development or experience can modify or moderate the effects of the neuropathology of dementias in later life has been regarded as a great opportunity to mitigate the risk of dementia in an individual and lower the incidence and prevalence of dementia in a group or a society (Stern, 2002, 2012; Stern et al., 2019). Further, a recent trend in dementia research has employed the concepts of reserve and resilience in the context of a lifespan to develop the life course approach, which integrates the risks of dementia and provides prevention strategies throughout a person's lifespan (Livingston et al., 2017, 2020; Thomas & Gutchess, 2020; Whalley et al., 2006). This reflects the current understanding of the etiology and clinical manifestation of dementias, which recognize the multifactorial nature of the risks and resilience that continue to interact throughout a person's life.

In this chapter, we will begin by introducing the life course approach to understanding dementia, which is a scientific discipline based on human development that includes input from biology, psychology, and the social sciences within a single integrated causal structure that provides a framework to organize the multifactorial processes involved in human brain aging and dementia (Whalley et al., 2006). The chapter introduces the concept of cognitive reserve (CR), which has been one of the most influential theoretical frameworks to understand the resilience or resistance that individuals show in the face of brain aging and disease. Key studies validating the protective effects of CR, intricately related to education, will be introduced to help understand the moderating effects of early life experiences, which will be helpful for readers in understanding the remaining chapters in Part II. Brain maintenance, another important component in understanding the resistance to brain aging and neurodegenerative diseases, is introduced and discussed, offering another avenue to prevent dementia. Lastly, a hypothetical pathway model is proposed to help understand the complex interaction between social connection and the neural resources underlying moderation that could reduce the risks of dementia.

5.2 Modifiable Dementia Risks throughout the Life Course

It has been over a century since Alois Alzheimer first found the biomarkers of the disease that bears his name (Hippius & Neundorfer, 2003; Wilkins & Brody, 1969), which is the number one cause of dementia around the world. For many decades, research has focused on the search to find the biological etiology of dementias as well as the mechanisms of how the neuropathology of AD, such as amyloid-ß plaques and tau tangles, are formed in some but not others as people age (Jack & Holtzman, 2013). Significant progress has been made in terms of genetics and neurophysiology, yet the etiology of AD has been elusive. Dominant genes have been found to be involved in the early-onset familial forms of the disease, which affects up to 5% of AD patients, while APOE4 has been found to be associated with significantly increased risk of AD in 30-50% of the cases (Strittmatter et al., 1993; Tanzi, 2012). A significant number of AD patients, however, do not carry these genes, and a large proportion of the heritability of AD continues to remain unexplained by the currently known disease genes (Bertram et al., 2010).

Neurofibrillary tangles formed from abnormal tau have been found in postmortem studies to start from the limbic regions and to spread to adjacent regions, including the association cortex (Braak & Braak, 1991; Hyman et al., 2012). These are intracellular pathologies that are associated with neurodegeneration and tend to correlate better with the clinical manifestations of AD, such as the decline of memory and cognitive function (Jack & Holtzman, 2013). On the other hand, senile or neuritic plaques from the amyloid-ß deposits are formed extracellularly, something that has been extensively studied in the past decade with the advancement of the neuroimaging technology of the amyloid positron emission tomography (PET) (Jagust, 2018; Klunk et al., 2004). Although the presence of both peptides associated with AD modestly predicted cognitive decline years later in individuals aged 60 and older who were initially cognitively intact (Jack et al., 2019), it has been repeatedly observed that the relationship between the neuropathology and clinical manifestation of dementia is quite dynamic. It has been proposed that the presence of plaques and tangles appears to be necessary but not sufficient to cause the clinical outcomes of dementia (Borenstein & Mortimer, 2016).

Interestingly, education and other socioeconomic factors have also been found for decades to be associated with the risk of dementia (Katzman, 1993). Further, longitudinal studies examining cardiovascular diseases (Elias et al., 1993), diabetes (Ott et al., 1999), hearing loss (Deal et al., 2017), and depression (Fuhrer et al., 2003) in mid- to late adulthood found that these seemingly unrelated factors were associated with increased risk. Considering that dementia incidence rises with age, especially after 65 years old, and that these factors were what an individual would experience throughout his/her life, it was sensible to summarize the multifactorial findings on a life course. More importantly, however, life course models have been effective in explaining and understanding human behavior, and the research could benefit from the rich array of studies of cognitive and brain development. According to Whalley and his colleagues, who proposed the fetal-origin adult disease model to be applied to dementias, the life course approach provides opportunities to identify the nature and timing of environmental contributions to brain diseases (Richards et al., 2019; Whalley et al., 2006). During the course of life, interaction between genetic and environmental factors concerning brain and cognitive development culminates in late life cognitive trajectories, which could in some cases result in dementia.

The practical attractiveness of the life course model is that the experiences identified as a risk for dementia can be modified to a certain degree, unlike the genes. Potential modifiability has significant implications for prevention of dementia amidst the so-called "dementia epidemic." The Lancet Commission on Dementia, Prevention, Intervention, and Care led by Gil Livingston found nine (2017) and later twelve (2020) modifiable factors that accounted for worldwide dementia cases. Utilizing a population-attributable fraction, the committee identified impoverished *education* in childhood; *hearing loss, hypertension, and obesity* in midlife; and *smoking, depression, physical inactivity, social isolation, and diabetes* in late life as the potentially modifiable risk factors that account for 35% of dementia. In 2020, the commission was able to find evidence for three more risk factors, namely, *traumatic brain injury* and *excessive alcohol consumption* in midlife and *air pollution* in late life to additionally account for 5% of dementias, especially in the low- to middle-income countries, making up 40% in total. These findings have major implications not only for individuals but also for countries and international health agencies to make policies and agendas to remove or reduce the aforementioned modifiable risks and create guidelines for dementia prevention. As a matter of fact, at the Global Dementia Observatory, a WHO platform that offers easy access to dementia data and knowledge for its member states, the first overarching principle of its dementia action plan is the life course approach. Among the Lancet Commission's twelve modifiable risk factors, the role of education during early development, lifestyles and injuries that could be harmful to brain health (especially during midlife), and social isolation in late life are discussed in more detail in the chapters of this volume as they relate to social infrastructure and activities.

5.3 Reserve, Resilience, and Resistance in Cognitive Aging and Dementia

Like many insults, humans cope with brain diseases by resisting the negative outcome and showing resilience, abilities that are probably dependent on the individual's reserve to maintain his/her functions. A host of conceptual frameworks have been proposed to explain the reserve, resilience, and resistance observed in one's ability to cope with brain damage and disease, many of which share common assumptions but also have subtle and significant differences. Several attempts have been made to reach a consensus across the research community on the operational definition of these terms; the white paper from a workgroup established under the auspices of the Alzheimer's Association (Stern et al., 2020) and the Collaboratory on Reserve and Resilience supported by the NIA are the latest, which have produced working definitions for three key concepts: CR, brain maintenance, and brain reserve (Stern et al., 2022). The following discussions in this chapter involve these concepts, focusing on CR, which is an important concept not only in understanding the individual differences in the trajectories of cognitive and brain aging in general but also in investigating the role of social connection in cognitive aging and age-associated brain changes, which have received increased attention in recent years. Studies on the neural correlates of cognitive and brain reserve as well as brain maintenance are reviewed with the goal of better understanding the moderation processes associated with education and social connection.

5.3.1 Cognitive Reserve: The Moderator

When CR theory was proposed by Yaakov Stern in 2002, it provided a much-needed hypothesis that could be tested and used to explore the complex nature of the discrepancy observed between brain damage and its clinical manifestation (Stern, 2002). It also clarified some of the decades-old controversy about the relationship between life experience, such as education, and the prevalence of dementia (Stern, 2012). According to the first paper to define it, CR is the ability to maximize performance through differential recruitment of brain networks, which perhaps reflects the use of alternate cognitive strategies (Stern, 2002). In contrast to brain reserve, which has been characterized as the hardware of the brain, such as brain size, CR was described as the software or function of the brain,

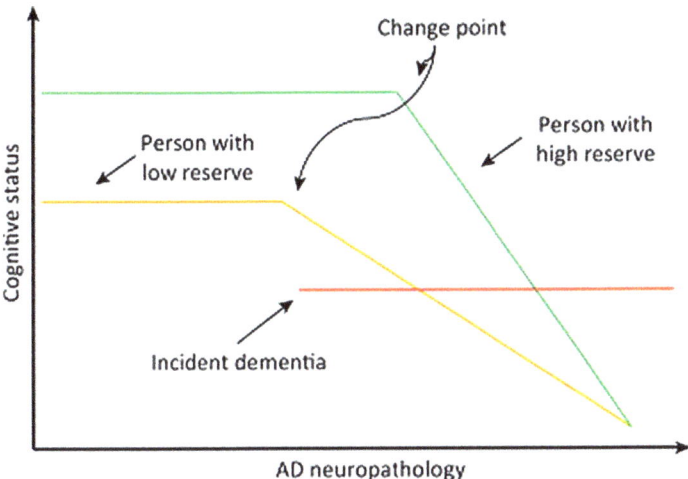

Figure 5.1 Representation of the cognitive reserve hypothesis (permission from Barulli & Stern, 2013). The figure illustrates how CR may moderate the effects of AD pathology on its clinical expression based on epidemiological and imaging studies. The x-axis represents AD pathology, slowly increasing over time. The y-axis represents cognitive function. It assumes that AD pathology increases over time at the same rate in two individuals with high and low reserve. The amount of pathology needed before cognitive function is affected is greater with higher CR, leading to a later change point. It follows that more pathology will be needed for the person with higher CR to meet clinical diagnostic criteria for AD, thus delaying the onset of the disease. Also, at any level of cognitive performance, AD pathology will be more severe in the individual with higher CR. Once cognitive decline begins, it is more rapid in the person with higher CR.

which is very much dependent on the experience and environment of an individual.

As illustrated on the famous CR figure (Barulli & Stern, 2013), neuropathology could accumulate over many years before dementia or significant cognitive decline manifests itself in individuals with high CR, while it could be evident very soon in individuals with low CR (see Figure 5.1). Cognitive reserve could act as a moderator between pathology and clinical manifestation and result in individual differences regarding when cognitive decline occurs or dementia manifests itself.

Although CR would manifest itself after brain damage, it was assumed that it accumulates during an individual's lifetime before damage occurs. The CR of a person, therefore, cannot be measured directly, as its effects can be observed only after a brain disease or injury takes place and only the proxies of CR are available for measurement (Stern et al., 2020).

Education has been the most frequently tested and utilized proxy of CR that could postpone the clinical manifestation of dementia for several decades (Amieva et al., 2014; Hall et al., 2007). Indeed, low education and related features, such as illiteracy and unskilled occupation, have been associated with increased risk for dementia worldwide (He et al., 2000; Langa et al., 2008; Ott et al., 1999; Rentería et al., 2019; Shin, Chey & Lee, "Is low cognitive performance a risk for dementia in elderly people who lack formal education?" Unpublished manuscript; Zhang et al., 1998). As a matter of fact, education during childhood and youth has been found to be one of the most significant modifiable social risk factors, accounting for 8% of worldwide dementia cases (Livingston et al., 2020).

Numerous associative studies investigating the prevalence of dementia in older adults with CR proxies, such as education, intelligence, occupation, or complex mental activity in late life, have found moderating effects of the proxies in the relationship between brain pathology/aging and dementia/ cognitive decline over decades (see Valenzuela & Sachdev, 2006, for review). Lifestyle factors, such as leisure activities, speaking a second language, and participation in cognitively stimulating activities, have also demonstrated moderating effects buffering the effects of aging and neurodegeneration, adding evidence as proxies that can be implemented in mid- to late life (Opdebeeck et al., 2016; Perani & Abutelabi, 2015). Older adults with rich lifelong cognitive activity are more resistant to the neurodegeneration of AD or cognitive decline in the long run (Scarmeas & Stern, 2003; Wilson et al., 2013). While such lifestyle activities may not directly reduce the pathophysiological process of specific dementias (Vemuri et al., 2012), such factors increase the coping resources of cognition, suggesting various manifestations of the CR. Surprisingly, more recent studies have found a host of social factors moderating the effects of brain and cognitive aging, which will be discussed in the following chapters.

5.3.2 *Moderating Brain or Brain Maintained?*

Initially, brain characteristics, such as whole brain size, were found to moderate the impact of neuropathology on clinical manifestation and were conceptualized as brain reserve (Katzman et al., 1988; Mortimer, 1997; Satz, 1993). According to Stern (2002), brain reserve is a static measure based on a passive or threshold model that cannot reflect the life experiences of an individual, whereas the neural mechanisms involved in CR, a theoretical construct that considers life experience conducive to cognitive development, could moderate the effects of brain injury and delay the manifestation of dementia with reserve acquired from the social environment.

Despite its elusiveness, the neural substrates of CR have been investigated with different approaches as they would have wider implications for prevention than brain size or density. Stern's group conducted a series of neuroimaging studies exploring task-invariant neural networks that would function as the neural implementation of CR (Stern et al., 2008, 2018). The networks would be active across multiple cognitive tasks, which consisted of three vocabulary tasks, three perceptual speed tasks, three fluid intelligence tasks, and three episodic memory tasks (detailed in Stern et al., 2014). The individual differences are typically observed in the extent to which neural activity pattern was expressed across tasks. Consistent with the CR hypothesis, the extent of activity pattern expression was not only associated with premorbid cognitive ability but also attenuated the deleterious effect of cortical thinning on cognitive performance (Stern et al., 2018). The network encompassed a wide brain area, which had robust loadings of bilateral cerebellum, bilateral medial frontal gyrus and anterior cingulate (BA9, 32), and bilateral superior temporal gyrus (BA22). The moderating effect of the neural network has been proposed to play a general role in various real-world activities and not confined to specific task processing. On the other hand, the global connectivity of the left frontal cortex (BA6/44) to other cortical regions during resting-state fMRI were found to attenuate poor episodic memory, which was associated with higher concentration of tau PET (Neitzel et al., 2019) and hypometabolism in the precuneus (Franzmeier et al., 2018).

It has been argued that the distinction between cognitive and brain reserve is artificial, since cognition depends on the brain (Cabeza et al., 2018). Reserve is defined as a cumulative improvement in neural resources due to genetic and/or environmental factors that mitigate the effects of neural decline caused by aging or age-related diseases in the cognitive neuroscience approach, which focuses more on healthy older adults (Cabeza et al., 2016). A glimpse of how reserve is manifested in the brains of relatively normal older adults comes from a series of studies that examined the neural correlates of CR proxies, such as education and general cognitive functioning, of community-residing older Koreans with a broad range of education. In a resting-state PET study that compared older women with less than six years of education and those with more than twelve years, marked differences were found between the two education groups (Kim et al., 2015). At first glance the two groups differed in the peak regions of the brain where glucose is metabolized during a resting state, that is, the regional cerebral glucose metabolism rates (rCMRglcs; see Figure 5.2a for details). The high education group (HEG) showed significantly higher metabolism in the ventral cerebral regions, especially in the left hemisphere, such as the left middle temporal gyrus, the left fusiform gyrus, and the left superior temporal gyrus, which have been associated with memory, language, and neurogenesis, while the low education group (LEG) revealed higher metabolism in apical areas that have been regarded as motor and somatosensory areas, such as the right supplementary motor area and the postcentral gyri, with less laterality. The results were consistent with the brain regions associated with mental and physical activities that probably reflect the everyday activities of the HEG and LEG older adults, respectively, over the course of their lives.

More interesting differences emerged as the study analyzed the functional correlation between the regions utilizing graph theoretical analysis (see Figure 5.2b). Overall, the HEG women showed more efficient

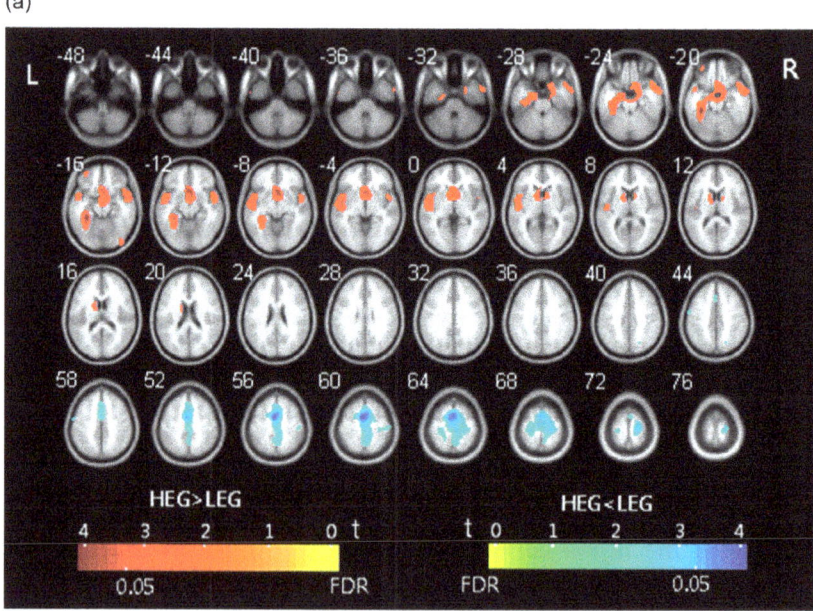

Figure 5.2 Comparison of the brain metabolism (a) and network characteristics of the low and high education groups of women, utilizing graph theoretical analysis. (b) (Kim et al., 2015).

(b)

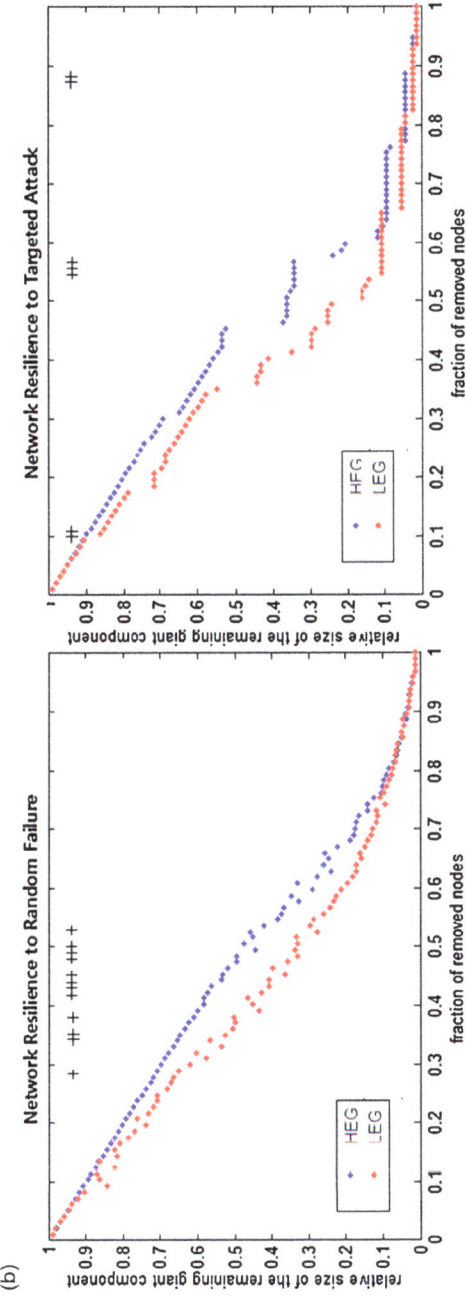

Figure 5.2 (cont.)

functional connectivity, characterized by small-worldness, consistent with the CR theory, and a hub in the left hippocampus, an essential structure for episodic memory. The hubs of LEG women's brains were situated in the pallidum, superior temporal pole, and the pons, which have been associated with motor and sensory functions. Dense short-distance connectivity within local areas and less long-distance connectivity demonstrated the low small-worldness of the LEG women, which would make them vulnerable to both random and targeted attacks. In contrast, the greater resilience observed in the simulated attacks of both kinds found in the HEG women was consistent with the resilient feature of the highly educated individuals observed during neurodegeneration or after focal ischemic injuries (see Figure 5.2b for detail). This was consistent with another study examining the reserve with task-based fMRI and graph analysis that found that global connectivity of a hub in the left frontal cortex, involving the default-mode network and dorsal attention network, mediated the association between education and small-worldness in the global network (Franzmeier et al., 2018).

Premorbid intelligence or cognitive status has been suggested as the more accurate measure of CR or reserve than education, since there is a wide variance in cognitive functioning within an education bracket (Albert & Teresi, 1999; Alexander et al., 1997). Indeed, in the previous standardization study of the Korean Dementia Rating Scale, which was introduced in Chapter 1, the authors found significantly large variance in cognitive performance among older adults with the same education level, especially in those with no or minimal education (Chey et al., 1998). In a subsequent study investigating the nature of very low cognitive performance in uneducated elderly women utilizing the regional optimized voxel-based morphometry, it was found that the structural cortical hubs, such as precuneus and prefrontal cortex, and their connectivity were associated with premorbid general cognitive ability (Chey et al., 2016). Although the definitive neural mechanisms of CR or reserve are still elusive, association cortices in the frontal, parietal, and temporal areas have been found to take part in attenuating the effects of brain aging and pathology, especially in the medial, frontal, and parietal areas. Considering that the association areas have distant connection or connectivity with one another to support cognitive control, inhibition, and working memory(Marek & Dosenbach, 2018) as well as episodic memory (Metzler-Baddeley et al., 2011), which tend to decline prominently during aging (Campbell et al., 2012; Metzler-Baddeley et al., 2011; Yao et al., 2020), it may be that individuals who have developed greater reserve in these areas or the relevant cognitive functions throughout their life may be more apt to attenuate the effects of aging. Moreover, these association areas overlap with regions vulnerable to neurodegeneration in late life (Fjell et al., 2014).

A better maintained brain characterized by relative absence of change in neural integrity throughout one's life, according to Nyberg et al. (2012), is the primary determinant of successful cognitive aging in late life. Brain maintenance (BM), a very important complementary concept to the reserve, focuses on the relative preservation of the brain, while the latter refers to sustaining cognitive function in the face of brain injuries or degeneration. Multiple levels of brain imaging data provide evidence supporting the BM theory (Nyberg et al., 2012, Nyberg & Pudas, 2019). Moreover, a number of identified modifiable risks of dementia in the life course approach (Livingston et al., 2017, 2020) have been associated with conditions that cause brain damage or pathology. For instance, hypertension and cardiovascular conditions have long been recognized as an important contributing factor for neurodegenerative processes (Lockhart & DeCarli, 2014; Vemuri et al., 2017) and excessive drinking or alcoholism has been consistently found to be associated with brain atrophy, cognitive impairment, and risk for various dementias (Rehm et al., 2019). When population-attributable fractions of traumatic brain injury (3%), a direct insult to brain integrity, are added to the indirect factors that are associated with less favorable BM, such as hypertension (2%), excess alcohol consumption (1%), and obesity during midlife (1%), and smoking (5%), air pollution (2%), and physical inactivity (1%) in later life, they account for 15% of dementia cases worldwide (see Livingston et al., 2020 for details). More cautious interpretations are necessary, however, since it is not certain that all portions of the fractions would be mediated by BM. Moreover, the numbers should not be interpreted as risks for any particular individual, especially to give advice for dementia prevention. The study may have controlled for correlation between the variables in the population data; however, they could be related in a person, such as physical inactivity and obesity. Further, there are individual differences in CR, brain and other health, and socioeconomic factors that would add interactions between the variables, making simple prediction or interpretation misleading. Nonetheless, BM and CR are important variables in which social connection (or lack thereof) would exert its effects in the development of clinical dementia.

5.4 A Hypothetical Model of the Pathways Linking Social Connection and Cognitive Health in Late Life

Lack of social connection has been associated with various health problems including brain health, especially in late life (Bang et al., 2019; Kim et al., 2022; Shankar et al., 2011; Steptoe et al., 2013). Yet the mechanisms or pathways underlying the association between social connection and brain health have not been clear. This may have been due to the complex nature of human social behavior and the complexity of brain structures and functions, which requires multidisciplinary investigation that could examine various factors utilizing multilevel analysis of multilayered observations.

In order to better understand the complex array of studies and findings, we introduce a schematic model that integrates the findings of how social connection interacts with neural resources that are undergoing aging through three pathways (see details in Figure 5.3). The first involves the neuroinflammatory response, which is found to be mitigated by social support provided by social relationships (yellow arrows). The second pathway involves the neural resources that can be facilitated by social connection, such as CR and the social brain network, which moderate the effects of neuropathology associated with aging and dementia (green arrows). The third pathway involves health promoted by information and support provided by social connection, which protects the integrity of the

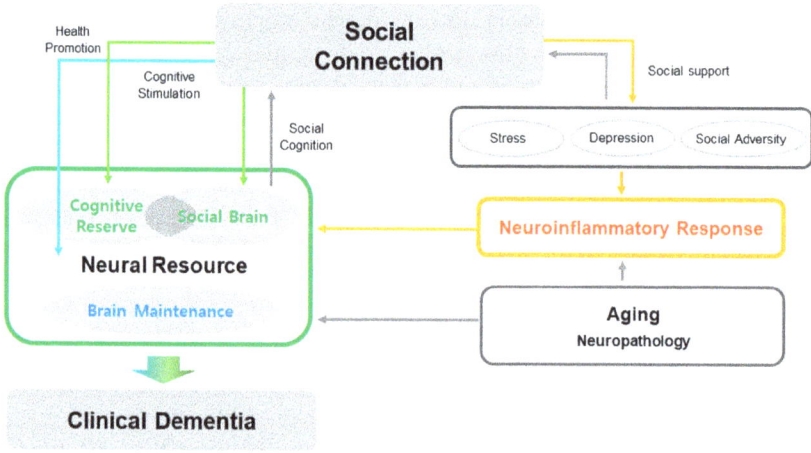

Figure 5.3 A schematic model of how social connection interacts with neural resource undergoing aging to modulate the manifestation of clinical dementia.

brain's structure and function at various levels, especially preventing cardiovascular diseases and brain injuries (blue arrows).

Consistent with the social brain hypothesis, studies have found that older adults with greater social brain capacity have larger social connections and are likely to receive more social support. The psychological effects of social support on brain health appear to be mediated through an attenuated neuroinflammatory response, which protects brain microstructures to prevent dementia. Moreover, social connection involving active interaction and social activities provide cognitive stimulation to older adults, which would facilitate their CR. On the other hand, being socially connected provides information and support for maintaining healthy behaviors and therefore healthy brains.

The following two chapters review findings of the key neural mechanisms of these pathways. While the dynamic bidirectional pathways linking social connection and neural resources (the left side of the schema in Figure 5.3) are reviewed and discussed extensively in Chapter 6, the neuroinflammatory response from stress or aging and its mitigation from social support are reviewed and discussed in Chapter 7. The latter introduces a relatively new field, psychoneuroimmunology, which provides evidence for social and psychological influence on the immune system that appears to affect the brain health of older adults who are also experiencing increased inflammation (i.e., "inflammageing"). A closer look at the psychological toll of loneliness in late life, frequently from social isolation, and its relevant factors are reviewed and discussed in Chapter 8 due to its importance in posing a health risk, including the risk of dementia, in late life. Chapter 9 provides an overview of the various aspects of social life that have been found to influence cognitive aging and details the aspects of social relationships whose effects are mediated through psychological benefits and its associated mitigation of the neuroinflammatory response. It also depicts a more complex nature of human social connection that could aid finer and possibly more accurate interpretation of study results examining social connection and cognitive aging.

5.5 Conclusion

The discrepancy observed between the amount of neuropathology in the brain and the clinical manifestation of dementia is one of the most fascinating findings in dementia research. Although this has been considered a major challenge for accurate dementia diagnosis, it is also the manifestation of the human brain's resilience in the face of neurodegeneration and provides an opportunity for preventive interventions. In this chapter, we introduced the concepts of CR and brain reserve that explicate this discrepancy, observed in the process of cognitive aging and clinical manifestation of dementia. The moderating effect of the reserve, which is developed continuously throughout life, provides a conceptual framework for the life course approach to understanding and integrating the risks and protective factors of dementia. This approach is also supported by the BM hypothesis, which suggests that the best way to prevent dementia is to protect the brain from changes and insults from aging and age-related diseases.

REFERENCES

Albert, S. M., & Teresi, J. A. (1999). Reading ability, education, and cognitive status assessment among older adults in Harlem, New York City. *American Journal of Public Health, 89*(1), 95–97.

Alexander, G. E., Furey, M. L., Grady, C. L., Pietrini, P., Brady, D. R., Mentis, M. J., & Schapiro, M. B. (1997). Association of premorbid intellectual function with cerebral metabolism in Alzheimer's disease: Implications for the cognitive reserve hypothesis. *American Journal of Psychiatry, 154*, 165–172.

Amieva, H., Mokri, H., Le Goff, M., Meillon, C., Jacqmin-Gadda, H., Foubert-Samier, A., Orgogozo, J.-M., Stern, Y., & Dartigues, J. F. (2014). Compensatory mechanisms in higher-educated subjects with Alzheimer's disease: A study of 20 years of cognitive decline. *Brain, 137*(4), 1167–1175.

Bang, M., Kim, J., An, S. K., Youm, Y., Chey, J., Kim, H. C., Park, K., Namkoong, E., & Lee, E. (2019). Associations of systemic inflammation with frontotemporal functional network connectivity and out-degree social-network size in community-dwelling older adults. *Brain, Behavior, and Immunity, 79*, 309–313.

Barulli, D., & Stern, Y. (2013). Efficiency, capacity, compensation, maintenance, plasticity: Emerging concepts in cognitive reserve. *Trends in Cognitive Sciences, 17*(10), 502–509.

Bertram, L., Lill, C. M., & Tanzi, R. E. (2010). The genetics of Alzheimer disease: Back to the future. *Neuron, 68*(2), 270–281.

Boldrini, M., Fulmore, C. A., Tartt, A. N., Simeon, L. R., Pavlova, I., Poposka, V., Rosloklija, G. B., Stankov, A., Arango, V., Dwork, A. J., Hen, R., & Mann, J. J. (2018). Human hippocampal neurogenesis persists throughout aging. *Cell Stem Cell, 22*(4), 589–599.

Borenstein, A., & Mortimer, J. (eds.). (2016). *Alzheimer's disease: Life Course Perspectives on Risk Reduction*. Academic Press.

Braak, H., & Braak, E. (1991). Neuropathological stageing of Alzheimer-related changes. *Acta Neuropathologica, 82*(4), 239–259.

Cabeza, R., Albert, M., Belleville, S., Craik, F. I., Duarte, A., Grady, C. L., Lindenberger, U., Nyberg, L., Park, D. C., Reuter-Lorenz, P. A., Rugg, M. D., Steffener, J., & Rajah, M. N. (2018). Maintenance, reserve and compensation: The cognitive neuroscience of healthy ageing. *Nature Reviews Neuroscience*, *19*(11), 701–710.

Cabeza, R., Nyberg, L., & Park, D. C. (eds.). (2016). *Cognitive Neuroscience of Aging: Linking Cognitive and Cerebral Aging*. Oxford University Press.

Campbell, K. L., Grady, C. L., Ng, C., & Hasher, L. (2012). Age differences in the frontoparietal cognitive control network: Implications for distractibility. *Neuropsychologia*, *50*(9), 2212–2223.

Chey J, Kim MJ, Stern Y, Shin M, Byun HS, et al. (2016) Neural Substrates of Reserve Observed in a Non-Demented Aging Population. *J Alzheimers Dis Parkinsonism*, *7*(294), 1–9.

Chey, J., Na, D. R., Park, S. H., & Park, E. H. (1998). The validity and reliability of the Korean dementia rating scale. *Korean Journal of Clinical Psychology*, *17*(1), 247–58.

Deal, J. A., Betz, J., Yaffe, K., Harris, T., Purchase-Helzner, E., Satterfield, S., Pratt, S., Govil, N., Simonsick, E. M., Lin, F. R., & Health ABC Study Group. (2017). Hearing impairment and incident dementia and cognitive decline in older adults: The health ABC study. *Journals of Gerontology Series A: Biomedical Sciences and Medical Sciences*, *72*(5), 703–709.

Duque, A., Arellano, J. I., & Rakic, P. (2022). An assessment of the existence of adult neurogenesis in humans and value of its rodent models for neuropsychiatric diseases. *Molecular Psychiatry*, *27*(1), 377–382.

Elias, M. F., Wolf, P. A., D'Agostino, R. B., Cobb, J., & White, L. R. (1993). Untreated blood pressure level is inversely related to cognitive functioning: The Framingham Study. *American Journal of Epidemiology*, *138*(6), 353–364.

Eriksson, P. S., Perfilieva, E., Björk-Eriksson, T., Alborn, A. M., Nordborg, C., Peterson, D. A., & Gage, F. H. (1998). Neurogenesis in the adult human hippocampus. *Nature Medicine*, *4*(11), 1313–1317.

Fjell, A. M., McEvoy, L., Holland, D., Dale, A. M., Walhovd, K. B., & Alzheimer's Disease Neuroimaging Initiative. (2014). What is normal in normal aging? Effects of aging, amyloid and Alzheimer's disease on the cerebral cortex and the hippocampus. *Progress in Neurobiology*, *117*, 20–40.

Franzmeier, N., Hartmann, J., Taylor, A. N., Araque-Caballero, M. Á., Simon-Vermot, L., Kambeitz-Ilankovic, L., Bürger, K., Catak, C., Janowitz, D., Müller, C., Ertl-Wagner, B., Stahl, R., Dichgans, M., Duering, M., & Ewers, M. (2018). The left frontal cortex supports reserve in aging by enhancing functional network efficiency. *Alzheimer's Research & Therapy*, *10*(1), 1–12.

Fuhrer, R., Dufouil, C., & Dartigues, J. F. (2003). Exploring sex differences in the relationship between depressive symptoms and dementia incidence: Prospective results from the PAQUID Study. *Journal of the American Geriatrics Society*, *51*(8), 1055–1063.

Hall, C. B., Derby, C., LeValley, A., Katz, M. J., Verghese, J., & Lipton, R. B. (2007). Education delays accelerated decline on a memory test in persons who develop dementia. *Neurology, 69*(17), 1657–1664.

He, Y. L., Zhang, X. K., & Zhang, M. Y. (2000). Psychosocial risk factors for Alzheimer's disease. *Hong Kong Journal of Psychiatry, 10*(2), 2–8.

Hippius, H., & Neundörfer, G. (2003). The discovery of Alzheimer's disease. *Dialogues in Clinical Neuroscience, 5*(1), 101–108.

Hyman, B. T., Phelps, C. H., Beach, T. G., Bigio, E. H., Cairns, N. J., Carrillo, M. C., Dickson, D. W., Duyckaerts, C., Frosch, M. P., Masliah, E., Mirra, S. S., Nelson, P. T., Schneider, J. A., Thal, D. R., Thies, B., Trojanowski, J. Q., Vinters, H. V., & Montine, T. J. (2012). National Institute on Aging–Alzheimer's Association guidelines for the neuropathologic assessment of Alzheimer's disease. *Alzheimer's & dementia, 8*(1), 1–13.

Jack Jr, C. R., & Holtzman, D. M. (2013). Biomarker modeling of Alzheimer's disease. *Neuron, 80*(6), 1347–1358.

Jack Jr, C. R., Wiste, H. J., Therneau, T. M., Weigand, S. D., Knopman, D. S., Mielke, M. M., Lowe, V. J., Vemuri, P., Machulda, M. M., Schwarz, C. G., Gunter, J. L., Senjem, M. L., Graff-Radford, J., Jones, D. T., Roberts, R. O., Rocca, W. A., & Petersen, R. C. (2019). Associations of amyloid, tau, and neurodegeneration biomarker profiles with rates of memory decline among individuals without dementia. *Journal of the American Medical Association, 321*(23), 2316–2325.

Jagust, W. (2018). Imaging the evolution and pathophysiology of Alzheimer disease. *Nature Reviews Neuroscience, 19*(11), 687–700.

Katzman, R. (1993). Education and the prevalence of dementia and Alzheimer's disease. *Neurology. 43*(1), 13–20.

Katzman, R., Terry, R., DeTeresa, R., Brown, T., Davies, P., Fuld, P., Renbing, X., & Peck, A. (1988). Clinical, pathological, and neurochemical changes in dementia: A subgroup with preserved mental status and numerous neocortical plaques. *Annals of Neurology, 23*(2), 138–144.

Kempermann, G., Gage, F. H., Aigner, L., Song, H., Curtis, M. A., Thuret, S., Kuhn, H. G., Jessberger, S., Frankland, P. W., Cameron, H. A., Gould, E., Hen, R., Abrous, D. N., Toni, N., Schinder, A. F., Zhao, X., Lucassen, P. J., & Frisén, J. (2018). Human adult neurogenesis: Evidence and remaining questions. *Cell Stem Cell, 23*(1), 25–30.

Kim, J., Chey, J., Kim, S. E., & Kim, H. (2015). The effect of education on regional brain metabolism and its functional connectivity in an aged population utilizing positron emission tomography. *Neuroscience Research, 94*, 50–61.

Kim, H., Kwak, S., Youm, Y., & Chey, J. (2022). Social network characteristics predict loneliness in older adults. *Gerontology, 68*(3), 309–320.

Klunk, W. E., Engler, H., Nordberg, A., Wang, Y., Blomqvist, G., Holt, D. P., Bergström, M., Savitcheva, I., Huang, G. F., Estrada, S., Ausén, B., Debnath, M. L., Barletta, J., Price, J. C., Sandell, J., Lopresti, B. J., Wall, A., Koivisto, P., Antoni, G., ... Långström, B. (2004). Imaging brain

amyloid in Alzheimer's disease with Pittsburgh Compound-B. *Annals of Neurology*, *55*(3), 306–319.
Langa, K. M., Larson, E. B., Karlawish, J. H., Cutler, D. M., Kabeto, M. U., Kim, S. Y., & Rosen, A. B. (2008). Trends in the prevalence and mortality of cognitive impairment in the United States: Is there evidence of a compression of cognitive morbidity? *Alzheimer's & Dementia*, *4*(2), 134–144.
Livingston, G., Huntley, J., Sommerlad, A., Ames, D., Ballard, C., Banerjee, S., Brayne, C., Burns, A., Cohen-Mansfield, J., Cooper, C., Costafreda, S. G., Dias, A., Fox, N., Gitlin, L. N., Howard, R., Kales, H. C., Kivimäki, M., Larson, E. B., Ogunniyi, A., ... Mukadam, N. (2020). Dementia prevention, intervention, and care: 2020 report of the Lancet Commission. *The Lancet*, *396*(10248), 413–446.
Livingston, G., Sommerlad, A., Orgeta, V., Costafreda, S. G., Huntley, J., Ames, D., Ballard, C., Banerjee, S., Burns, A., Cohen-Mansfield, J., Cooper, C., Fox, N., Gitlin, L. N., Howard R., Kales, H. C., Larson, E. B., Ritchie, K., Rockwood, K., Sampson, E. L., ... Mukadam, N. (2017). Dementia prevention, intervention, and care. *The Lancet*, *390*(10113), 2673–2734.
Lockhart, S. N., & DeCarli, C. (2014). Structural imaging measures of brain aging. *Neuropsychology Review*, *24*(3), 271–289.
Maguire, E. A., Gadian, D. G., Johnsrude, I. S., Good, C. D., Ashburner, J., Frackowiak, R. S., & Frith, C. D. (2000). Navigation-related structural change in the hippocampi of taxi drivers. *Proceedings of the National Academy of Sciences*, *97*(8), 4398–4403.
Marek, S., & Dosenbach, N. U. (2018). The frontoparietal network: Function, electrophysiology, and importance of individual precision mapping. *Dialogues in Clinical Neuroscience*, *20*(2), 133–141.
Metzler-Baddeley, C., Jones, D. K., Belaroussi, B., Aggleton, J. P., & O'Sullivan, M. J. (2011). Frontotemporal connections in episodic memory and aging: A diffusion MRI tractography study. *Journal of Neuroscience*, *31*(37), 13236–13245.
Moreno-Jiménez, E. P., Terreros-Roncal, J., Flor-García, M., Rábano, A., & Llorens-Martín, M. (2021). Evidences for adult hippocampal neurogenesis in humans. *Journal of Neuroscience*, *41*(12), 2541–2553.
Mortimer, J. A. (1997). Brain reserve and the clinical expression of Alzheimer's disease. *Geriatrics*, *52*, S50–S53.
Neitzel, J., Franzmeier, N., Rubinski, A., Ewers, M., & Alzheimer's Disease Neuroimaging Initiative (ADNI). (2019). Left frontal connectivity attenuates the adverse effect of entorhinal tau pathology on memory. *Neurology*, *93*(4), e347–e357.
Nyberg, L., Lövdén, M., Riklund, K., Lindenberger, U., & Bäckman, L. (2012). Memory aging and brain maintenance. *Trends in Cognitive Sciences*, *16*(5), 292–305.
Nyberg, L., & Pudas, S. (2019). Successful memory aging. *Annual Review of Psychology*, *70*, 219–243.

Opdebeeck, C., Martyr, A., & Clare, L. (2016). Cognitive reserve and cognitive function in healthy older people: A meta-analysis. *Aging, Neuropsychology, and Cognition, 23*(1), 40–60.

Ott, A., Stolk, R. P., van Harskamp, F., Pols, H. A. P., Hofman, A., & Breteler, M. M. B. (1999). Diabetes mellitus and the risk of dementia: The Rotterdam Study. *Neurology, 53*(9), 1937–1937.

Ott, A., Van Rossum, C. T. M., van Harskamp, F., Van de Mheen, H., Hofman, A., & Breteler, M. M. B. (1999). Education and the incidence of dementia in a large population-based study: The Rotterdam Study. *Neurology, 52*(3), 663–666.

Perani, D., & Abutalebi, J. (2015). Bilingualism, dementia, cognitive and neural reserve. *Current Opinion in Neurology, 28*(6), 618–625.

Rehm, J., Hasan, O. S., Black, S. E., Shield, K. D., & Schwarzinger, M. (2019). Alcohol use and dementia: A systematic scoping review. *Alzheimer's Research & Therapy, 11*(1), 1–11.

Rentería, M. A., Vonk, J. M., Felix, G., Avila, J. F., Zahodne, L. B., Dalchand, E., Frazer, K. M., Martinez, M. N., Shouel, H. L., & Manly, J. J. (2019). Illiteracy, dementia risk, and cognitive trajectories among older adults with low education. *Neurology, 93*(24), e2247–e2256.

Richards, M., James, S. N., Sizer, A., Sharma, N., Rawle, M., Davis, D. H., & Kuh, D. (2019). Identifying the lifetime cognitive and socioeconomic antecedents of cognitive state: Seven decades of follow-up in a British birth cohort study. *BMJ Open, 9*(4), e024404.

Riley, K. P., Snowdon, D. A., & Markesbery, W. R. (2002). Alzheimer's neurofibrillary pathology and the spectrum of cognitive function: Findings from the nun study. *Annals of Neurology, 51*(5), 567–577.

Satz, P. (1993). Brain reserve capacity on symptom onset after brain injury: A formulation and review of evidence for threshold theory. *Neuropsychology, 7*(3), 273.

Scarmeas, N., & Stern, Y. (2003). Cognitive reserve and lifestyle. *Journal of Clinical and Experimental Neuropsychology, 25*(5), 625–633.

Shankar, A., McMunn, A., Banks, J., & Steptoe, A. (2011). Loneliness, social isolation, and behavioral and biological health indicators in older adults. *Health Psychology, 30*(4), 377.

Snowdon, D. A. (2003). Healthy aging and dementia: Findings from the nun study. *Annals of Internal Medicine, 139*(5), 450–454.

Snowdon, D. A., Kemper, S. J., Mortimer, J. A., Greiner, L. H., Wekstein, D. R., & Markesbery, W. R. (1996). Linguistic ability in early life and cognitive function and Alzheimer's disease in late life: Findings from the nun study. *Journal of the American Medical Association, 275*(7), 528–532.

Sorrells, S. F., Paredes, M. F., Cebrian-Silla, A., Sandoval, K., Qi D., Kelley, K. W., James, D., Mayer, S., Chang, J., Auguste, K. I., Chang, E. F., Gutierrez, A. J., Kriegstein, A. R., Mathern, G. W., Oldham, M. C., Huang, E. J., Garcia-Verdugo, J. M., Yang, Z., & Alvarez-Buylla, A. (2018). Human hippocampal neurogenesis drops sharply in children to undetectable levels in adults. *Nature. 555,* 377–381.

Spalding, K. L., Bergmann, O., Alkass, K., Bernard, S., Salehpour, M., Huttner, H. B., Boström, E., Westerlund, I., Vial, C., Buchholz, B. A., Possnert, G., Mash, D. C., Druid, H., & Frisén, J. (2013). Dynamics of hippocampal neurogenesis in adult humans. *Cell, 153*(6), 1219–1227.

Steptoe, A., Shankar, A., Demakakos, P., & Wardle, J. (2013). Social isolation, loneliness, and all-cause mortality in older men and women. *Proceedings of the National Academy of Sciences, 110*(15), 5797–5801.

Stern, Y. (2002). What is cognitive reserve? Theory and research application of the reserve concept. *Journal of the International Neuropsychological Society, 8*(3), 448–460.

(2012). Cognitive reserve in ageing and Alzheimer's disease. *The Lancet Neurology, 11*(11), 1006–1012.

Stern, Y., Albert, M., Barnes, C., Cabeza, R., Pascual-Leone, A., & Rapp, P. (2022). *Framework for Terms Used in Research of Reserve and Resilience.* Collaboratory on Research Definitions for Reserve and Resilience in Cognitive Aging and Dementia. https://reserveandresilience.com/framework/

Stern, Y., Arenaza-Urquijo, E. M., Bartrés-Faz, D., Belleville, S., Cantilon, M., Chetelat, G., Ewers, M., Franzmeier, N., Kempermann, G., Kremen, W. S., Okonkwo, O., Scarmeas, N., Soldan, A., Udeh-Momoh, C., Valenzuela, M., Vemuri, P., Vuoksimaa, E., & Reserve, Resilience and Protective Factors PIA Empirical Definitions and Conceptual Frameworks Workgroup. (2020). Whitepaper: Defining and investigating cognitive reserve, brain reserve, and brain maintenance. *Alzheimers Dementia, 16*(9), 1305–1311.

Stern, Y., Barnes, C. A., Grady, C., Jones, R. N., & Raz, N. (2019). Brain reserve, cognitive reserve, compensation, and maintenance: Operationalization, validity, and mechanisms of cognitive resilience. *Neurobiology of Aging, 83,* 124–129.

Stern, Y., Gazes, Y., Razlighi, Q., Steffener, J., & Habeck, C. (2018). A task-invariant cognitive reserve network. *Neuroimage, 178,* 36–45.

Stern, Y., Habeck, C., Steffener, J., Barulli, D., Gazes, Y., Razlighi, Q., Shaked, D., & Salthouse, T. (2014). The Reference Ability Neural Network Study: Motivation, design, and initial feasibility analyses. *Neuroimage, 103,* 139–151.

Stern, Y., Zarahn, E., Habeck, C., Holtzer, R., Rakitin, B. C., Kumar, A., Flynn, J., Steffener, J., & Brown, T. (2008). A common neural network for cognitive reserve in verbal and object working memory in young but not old. *Cerebral Cortex, 18*(4), 959–967.

Strittmatter, W. J., Saunders, A. M., Schmechel, D., Pericak-Vance, M., Enghild, J., Salvesen, G. S., & Roses, A. D. (1993). Apolipoprotein E: High-avidity binding to beta-amyloid and increased frequency of type 4 allele in late-onset

familial Alzheimer disease. *Proceedings of the National Academy of Sciences, 90* (5), 1977–1981.
Tanzi, R. E. (2012). The genetics of Alzheimer disease. *Cold Spring Harbor Perspectives in Medicine, 2*(10).
Thomas, A. K. & Gutchess, A. (eds.). (2020). *The Cambridge Handbook of Cognitive Aging: A Life Course Perspective*. Cambridge University Press.
Valenzuela, M. J., & Sachdev, P. (2006). Brain reserve and dementia: A systematic review. *Psychological Medicine, 36*(4), 441–454.
Vemuri, P., Lesnick, T. G., Przybelski, S. A., Knopman, D. S., Lowe, V. J., Graff-Radford, J., Roberts, R. O., Mielke, M. M., Machulda, M. M., Petersen, R. C., & Jack Jr, C. R. (2017). Age, vascular health, and Alzheimer disease biomarkers in an elderly sample. *Annals of Neurology, 82*(5), 706–718.
Vemuri, P., Lesnick, T. G., Przybelski, S. A., Knopman, D. S., Roberts, R. O., Lowe, V. J., Kantarci, K., Senjem, M. L., Gunter, J. L., Boeve, B. F., Petersen, R. C., & Jack Jr, C. R. (2012). Effect of lifestyle activities on Alzheimer disease biomarkers and cognition. *Annals of Neurology, 72*(5), 730–738.
Whalley, L. J., Dick, F. D., & McNeill, G. (2006). A life-course approach to the aetiology of late-onset dementias. *The Lancet Neurology, 5*(1), 87–96.
Wilkins, R. H., & Brody, I. A. (1969). Alzheimers disease. *Archives of Neurology, 21*(1), 109.
Wilson, R. S., Boyle, P. A., Yu, L., Barnes, L. L., Schneider, J. A., & Bennett, D. A. (2013). Life-span cognitive activity, neuropathologic burden, and cognitive aging. *Neurology, 81*(4), 314–321.
Yao, Z. F., Yang, M. H., Hwang, K., & Hsieh, S. (2020). Frontoparietal structural properties mediate adult life span differences in executive function. *Scientific Reports, 10*(1), 1–14.
Zhang, M., Katzman, R., Yu, E., Liu, W., Xiao, S. F., & Yan, H. (1998). A preliminary analysis of incidence of dementia in Shanghai, China. *Psychiatry and Clinical Neurosciences, 52*, S291–S294.

CHAPTER 6

Enriched Social Connectedness and Brain Function

Seyul Kwak, Jeanyung Chey, and Yoosik Youm

Social scientists are now able to investigate the underlying neurobiology of complex human mind and behavior with the advances in brain imaging techniques and the increasing interdisciplinary research in the field. The integration of multiple levels of analysis provides an in-depth illustration of the psychosocial phenomenon of social connectedness with a broader perspective. In this chapter, we first review various neural correlates of social connectedness in neuroimaging studies and their implications in describing late-life cognitive and brain health. We also discuss how cognitive stimulation and inflammation underlie the association between brain and social connectedness. Lastly, we will discuss the possible underlying mechanism of the associations we have reviewed and how dynamic interaction between individual and social surroundings leaves traces in brain structures and functions. A schema with three possible pathways of how social connection and brain characteristics influence one another, a crucial aspect of the schematic model illustrating the pathways between social connection and clinical dementia that has been proposed in Chapter 5, will be discussed in detail.

6.1 Indicators of Brain Health

6.1.1 Cerebrovascular Bases of Brain Health

The brain consumes more than one fifth of the energy of the human metabolism, even when it is not engaged in a particular task. There is a support system that supplies blood to the brain through major arteries and granular small vessels that sustain the ecology of the brain's deep structures. It is thus not surprising to hear that "What is good for the heart is good for the brain" (Barnes, 2011). Functional changes in the brain typically occur when these major support systems are affected by vascular conditions. On the other hand, extensive research has demonstrated that poor social relationships or psychosocial stress cause the body to respond to them as threats, and that chronic persistence of these "adaptive" stress responses may significantly harm one's physical health. We will go further here to examine how these changes are related to brain health by introducing a representative brain imaging indicator called magnetic resonance imaging (MRI).

6.1.2 Structural Indicators of Brain Health

As brain imaging methods became easily accessible in medical or research settings, many people now easily acquire neural information in vivo. The easiest and most commonly used neuroimaging technique is to look at the structural properties of the brain. While observation of more fundamental biological units, such as neurons and synapses, is preferable, quantifications of the brain structures are commonly accessible with existing methods that capture the neural characteristics with enough sensitivity without invading the brain. In MRI, the molecular properties of the brain's tissues typically lead to differences in the timing of absorbing and releasing of the radio-frequency signal pulses. These properties can be used to visualize what certain tissue structures in the brain look like with relatively fine resolution. Diffusion tensor imaging (DTI) also shows how circuit fibers that connect distal brain areas are well integrated. By quantifying the volumes of regional brain structures or the integrity of a bundle of nerve fibers, we can make indirect estimates of how large the neural resources of the brain structure are and how well they have been maintained.

Brain structural measures indicate diverse neural resources. The volume or thickness of the gray matter that consists of neurons tends to shrink in the process of aging, especially with cardiovascular conditions (Fjell et al., 2014; Lockhart & DeCarli, 2014). It is well documented that the increased risk of cardiovascular disease mediates the changes that degrade the brain or deteriorate its function in aging (Vemuri et al., 2017). On the other hand, neurodevelopmental differences are also reflected in the structural measures of the brain (Kanai & Rees, 2011). Both preexisting neural capacity and ongoing maintenance of cerebrovascular health are converged in the image-based measures of brain structures.

6.1.3 Functional Indicators of Brain Health

Brain functioning can be typically measured with subtle changes in oxygenated blood flow, which are expressed in functional MRI. The brain function is not independent of its structure, and the properties of morphological volumes, cortical thickness, and fiber tract account for a significant amount of its functional properties (Davis et al., 2012; Reuter-Lorenz & Park, 2014; Steffener et al., 2016). The aforementioned brain structural measures are relatively stable indicators of brain health or neural resources. However, in the end, it becomes important how well the brain can be "utilized" during and after the process of brain degeneration and damage, respectively. It has been found that even with similar structural measures, such as brain volumes, individuals may exhibit different functional processes. As with the hardware–software analogy, functional indicators can also reveal brain health that would otherwise not be observable with structural indicators. Brain functional differences may be a reflection of microcellular synaptic properties that are not apparent in the structures (Kalpouzos et al., 2012), or may be a result of differences in how a given neural resource is "utilized" (Shine, 2019; Suárez et al., 2020). In the absence of external tasks, intrinsic and spontaneous fluctuations of brain signals reflect how regional brains are utilized at rest (Tavor et al., 2016). It has been found that individual differences in such functional activation and their synchrony (i.e., functional connectivity) reflect the age-related neural decline or compensatory reorganizations (Meunier et al., 2009, 2014). Such functional measures of the brain also reflect differences in circuitries specialized for certain cognitive processes or neural pathways that recruit resources to integrate long-distance brain regions (Wang & Olson, 2018).

According to the concept of cognitive reserve (see Chapter 5 for a detailed discussion of cognitive reserve), the neurobiological process of aging and pathological changes in the brain typically decrease the amount of neural and computational resources, but large individual differences in the resilience to cope with the pathology exist as well (Barulli & Stern, 2013). Lifelong exposure to a cognitively stimulating environment may lead to a larger neural capacity to cope with challenges, possibly through more efficient use of a given network or operating an additional compensatory network (Steffener & Stern, 2012). Though a direct observation of such neural mechanisms is not easy, especially before the onset of dementia, brain structural studies indirectly indicate that such software aspects of neural capacity should be factored in the full assessment of older adults' cognitive health (Habeck et al., 2016; Reed et al., 2010). More recently, the possibility of abundant social relationships playing an important role in developing rich neural resources has been proposed.

6.2 Brain Correlates of Social Connectedness

6.2.1 Amygdala Network

Distinct brain regions anchored in the amygdala have been identified as one of the most important brain networks and crucial in understanding the brain basis of social connectedness. We first introduce major association studies that indicate how brain structural and functional features are associated with social network characteristics and whether the findings are meaningfully converged. According to several studies, brain structural and functional indicators are associated with enriched social engagement, levels of social connectedness, and the quality of social relationships. One of the most representative studies showed that the structural volume of the amygdala was positively correlated with the number of frequently contacting social relationships and the diversity of those relationships (Bickart et al., 2011). The researchers have extended this finding by identifying that the subnuclei of the amygdala were functionally connected to temporal and orbitofrontal cortices, and the strength of such connectivity was associated with the size of the social network (Bickart et al., 2012; Bickart, Dickerson, et al., 2014; see Figure 6.1). Other neuroimaging studies of social network converge to the finding that the volumes of the amygdala and its closely related cortical areas (i.e., orbitofrontal cortex) were associated with the social network size (Lewis et al., 2011; Von der Heide et al., 2013). Not surprisingly, the amygdala–orbitofrontal cortex connectivity also showed a positive correlation with the size of social networks (Hampton et al., 2016; Wang & Olson, 2018; Zou et al., 2016).

6.2.2 Mentalizing Network

Another critical social module in the brain has been recognized. A group of brain regions identified as the mentalizing network governs inference of other people's traits and represents other agents' states of mind (Schurz et al., 2014). There are several commonly activated brain regions that process social information, including the dorsomedial prefrontal cortex, superior temporal sulcus, and temporo-parietal junction. More importantly, individual differences in the levels of activation, amount of structural volume, or integrity of fiber tracts are consistently correlated with the size of social networks. When individuals functionally utilized these brain areas, including the dorsomedial prefrontal cortex, they were able to retain multiple traits of one's social acquaintances so that they can utilize the

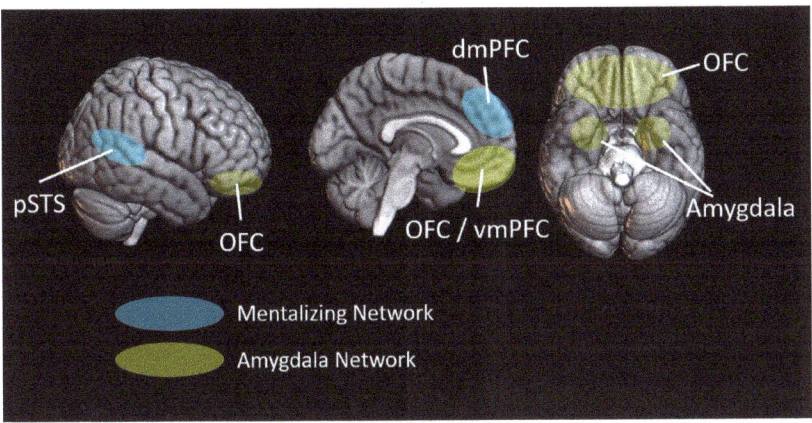

Figure 6.1 Brain regional correlates of social connectedness and their corresponding social brain system.
OFC: orbitofrontal cortex; vmPFC: ventromedial prefrontal cortex; dmPFC: dorsomedial prefrontal cortex; pSTS: posterior superior temporal sulcus

mentalized information at hand (Krol et al., 2018; Meyer et al., 2012). Likewise, functional activation was observed in the posterior superior temporal sulcus when observing the movements of biological agents (Dziura & Thompson, 2014; Kirby et al., 2018; see Figure 6.1). Moreover, the levels of activity in this posterior region of the mentalizing network were also positively correlated with the size of the social network. These results imply that active social engagement and exerting efforts to infer other people's states of mind are reflected in the functional regional activation in the mentalizing network, and individual differences in this responsivity may lead to differences in making social relationships. Moreover, brain structural studies also indicate that larger or smaller gray matter volume in the dorsomedial prefrontal cortex and posterior superior temporal sulcus accounts for the size of an individual's late-life social network (Kwak et al., 2018) or the presence of behavioral impairment in social interactions (i.e., autism spectrum disorder), respectively (Sato et al., 2017).

6.2.3 *Domain-General Brain Regions*

As the domain-specific social brain is not exclusive, studies have suggested that brain structures other than the social brain (i.e., the amygdala and mentalizing network) are also involved in making and maintaining social relationships. This association was particularly evident when correlational studies examined older adults, who frequently experience brain volumetric decrease. In older adults, larger striatum and hippocampus were associated with larger social connections, which were measured by the total number of regular contacts that a person maintains (Bickart et al., 2011; Blumen & Verghese, 2019; Ospina et al., 2019). A similar result was observed when social connectedness was measured with a subjective rating of social support (Kim et al., 2020). As larger gray matter volume indicates abundance of neural resources, it was positively associated with better cognitive test performances as well (Blumen & Verghese, 2019; Kim et al., 2020). Moreover, in a functional imaging study, connectivity of the frontoparietal network was positively associated with the quantity and quality of social networks in older adults (Pillemer et al., 2016). It is noteworthy that individual differences in these brain structures and how they are affected during aging seem to be related to executive function, episodic memory and learning, and motivation in older adults. These systems appear to promote or are promoted by social interactions and engagement.

In a functional brain imaging study that examined the social connections of the entire village, it was found that a pattern of rich social networks was associated with less age-related brain changes (Joo et al., 2017). Functional brain activation while older adults lay in a resting state assessed brain connectivity patterns across the brain regions, while social network analysis examined whether individuals had social connections within a cohesive and deeply embedded position within the larger village network. Interestingly, individuals who maintained embedded and cohesive social networks showed brain network patterns similar to the younger population, which was characterized by stronger connectivity between distal brain areas compared to that of proximal areas, as brain connectivity across long distances tends to decrease while connectivity within adjacent regions tends to increase as people age (Marques et al., 2015; Tomasi & Volkow, 2012).

While the brain imaging evidence offers insights into how enriched social connectedness provides or gains benefit from neurocognitive function, more evidence is needed for a fuller understanding of the relationship between social connectedness and the brain. The neural basis of social connectedness may be more distributed and less focal than expected (Lin et al., 2020). Further, differences in brain regions that are correlated with social connectedness can be affected by the very characteristics of the target population (e.g., age range, clinical state) or the measurements of social network (Liu et al., 2018), thus requiring caution in interpreting the brain process in correlational studies (Genon et al., 2018).

6.3 Mediating Neurobiological Processes Underlying Enriched Social Network

Many studies have shown that a rich social network was associated with specific brain structures or neural resources. Researchers have described several distinct explanatory pathways in how these correlations emerge across the lifespan by combining critical experimental studies and physiological evidence. We will examine how cognitive stimulation and the inflammatory reactions can affect brain functioning, especially in late life.

6.3.1 Cognitive Stimulation

For decades, researchers have acknowledged the importance of a cognitively stimulating environment for optimal neural development (Rosenzweig et al., 1972). Even at a later stage of development, exposure to different environments results in the difference in brain microstructural proficiency (Kolb et al., 2003). The gap between environmental demand and the extent of available neuronal resources stimulates ongoing plastic changes across a person's lifespan (Lövdén et al., 2010). Individuals are required to maintain complex and diverse social relationships. These demands include constructing an accurate representation of other people's mental traits and making accurate predictions of behavioral consequences within a social group. If an individual is not affiliated with a social group, these kinds of computational demands are not necessary for an individual's well-being, leading to lower demands in developing the corresponding social brain resources (Dunbar, 2014).

One of the most representative experimental studies was conducted by Sallet et al. (2011), who examined how enriched social networks result in brain changes in macaque monkeys. The macaques were bred across a differing number of housemates, and researchers examined whether this group difference led to brain structural and functional differences. Researchers hypothesized that living with a larger number of social networking members would promote long-term changes in brain development. Since the researcher's decision on the group assignment was unaffected by the individual characteristics of macaques, researchers were able to preclude the possibility that the observed brain characteristics were mainly due to the group assignment effect. Interestingly, the study showed that the size of the assigned social network was positively correlated with the gray matter volume of brain regions, including the amygdala, superior temporal sulcus, and the rostral prefrontal cortex. These brain regions are major components of the amygdala and mentalizing networks, which are important for processing socio-emotional signals (Adolphs et al., 2002), mental states of other agents via biological motions (Van Overwalle, 2009), and high-order social inference (Badre & D'Esposito, 2009). Moreover, larger regional volume and stronger brain connectivity were also associated with the animals' success and competence within the social group. It seems that stronger demands for social inference promote constant stimulation of brain functions relevant to precise and adaptive social behavior, leading to an extended neural resource in the corresponding area.

Similar findings were shown in experimental studies with rodents. The animals bred within larger or stimulating social groups showed more facilitated microcellular neurodevelopment in the orbitofrontal cortex (Bell et al., 2010; Kolb et al., 2012; Pellis et al., 2006). It is possible that mammals learn to interact with the uncertain social environment with repetitive trial and testing of others' social representation. The richness of social networks may provide opportunities to develop certain types of cognitive efficiency and gain operant efficacy toward the environment.

Unsurprisingly, experimental studies and randomized controlled trials of human social networks are scarce, and the evidence of social network's effects on brain function is largely indirect. Social networking, however, can be one of many forms of activities that can stimulate cognitive processes. One study showed that mentally active older adults showed a slower rate of atrophy rate in hippocampal structures (Valenzuela et al., 2008). In a recent neuroimaging study, more attendance in social activities was associated with larger gray matter volume of the orbitofrontal cortex (Conti et al., 2021). Active engagement in cognitively stimulating activities promotes neurogenesis and synaptic plastic change, leading to reduced risk of dementia (Valenzuela et al., 2007, 2011). The beneficial effect seems to be the result of a lifespan rather than short-term engagement. A socially integrated lifestyle may accumulate neural resources necessary for coping with late-life cognitive decline and constantly promote neuronal plastic changes.

Skepticism, however, remains in interpreting the beneficial effects of social activity. When examining the brain structural correlation with specific lifestyle activities, the unique beneficial effect of activities other than educational attainment is unclear (Foubert-Samier et al., 2012). Moreover, randomized control trials on intervention effects of various cognitively stimulating activities have found that adding socializing activity had minimal effect on the brain functional activity during the cognitive task (McDonough et al., 2015). On the contrary, older adults who participated in activities with significant challenges that required active learning showed significant brain functional changes. It seems that ordinary social activity may not be sufficient for inducing short-term neural changes. As observed in the animal experimental studies, the neural changes may be an outcome of the accumulation of long-term effects, and the causal effects of social networking on brain functioning may require challenging and long-term exposure to induce beneficial outcomes that are commensurate with the extent of effects observed in animal experiments.

6.3.2 Inflammatory Response

Inflammatory reactions are one of the inherent biological mechanisms to cope with socially threatening situations. This responsiveness has played a critical role in attenuating the spread of infection in the face of physical injury (Slavich & Cole, 2013). In modern society, social threats typically do not lead to physical injury, yet our inherent response system still plays a role when situated in social isolation or faced with unfavorable evaluation. Based on this hypothesis, the inflammatory response has been a logical target in examining the neurophysiological underpinnings of social connectedness and isolation. In response to socially stressful and threatening cues, the brain operates one of the physiological alerting systems (Gianaros & Wager, 2015; Slavich et al., 2010). In socially disconnected situations, stressful and isolated experiences can be chronically prolonged due to lack of social support and a secure base, and may harm our physical health (Hackett et al., 2012; Jaremka et al., 2013). The studies have pointed out that such an abnormally prolonged alarm system in response to social stress may exacerbate normally functioning cerebrovascular health (Gianaros et al., 2014, 2020).

An adequate experimental design is necessary in order to examine how inflammatory mechanisms play a causal role in social network and brain functioning. However, it is almost impossible to assign and induce real-life social adversities or constrain social networks of human individuals randomly. Thus, researchers have investigated animal behavior by experimentally manipulating social networking and stress. Rodents, like other mammals, have a habit of forming groups, sharing scarce resources with other members, and developing supportive systems through group life. A recent study examined whether or not the differences in social network size affected memory function, brain function, and inflammatory response in mice (Smith et al., 2018). The mice were randomly assigned between two different environments of social network sizes (pair or seven mice). After three months of housing, behavioral and biological outcomes were assessed. As hypothesized, the group-housed mice with seven members showed lower neuroinflammatory markers in the hippocampus, which is a brain structure essential for building and consolidating memories. They also demonstrated better memory function on new targets and places.

Early effects of social isolation on the brain were found to be significant and irreversible in mice, as the thinning of prefrontal myelination and the dysfunction developed in youth lasted until adulthood (Makinodan et al., 2012). Moreover, socially isolated animals showed an increased pro-inflammatory cytokine, such as interleukin-6 (IL-6), which has been associated with changes in the white matter microstructure (Hermes et al., 2006; Karelina et al., 2009). These findings indicate that a socially isolating environment not only induces pro-inflammatory responses but also degrades neural resources that are involved in organizing long-term plans, memory consolidation, and efficient information processing.

With the recent advancement of DTI techniques, it became possible to examine the subtle changes in white matter microstructural integrity in humans, and studies have examined how social connectedness is associated with both inflammatory markers and brain functioning. According to recent studies, lower socioeconomic position and lower diversity of social relationships were associated not only with elevated IL-6 but also with poorer white matter integrity (Gianaros et al., 2013; Molesworth et al., 2014). Molesworth and colleagues specifically showed that individuals connected with diverse types of relationships and maintaining multiple social roles showed lower inflammation markers and higher microstructural integrity. A functional neuroimaging study of older adults found that systemic inflammation indicated by C-reactive protein (CRP) was associated with both smaller social connections and weaker functional integrity of the frontotemporal network (Bang et al., 2019). Although cross-sectional association studies in humans remain insufficient for inferring causal mechanisms, converging evidence from animal studies cautiously links adverse outcomes of inflammation and white matter integrity due to social isolation. Even in humans, therefore, it appears that less integrated social relationships would result in both pathophysiological stress response and brain health.

Prolonged and chronically high inflammatory response plays a critical role in the process of accelerated brain aging. Elevated peripheral levels of IL-6 and CRP, a relatively stable marker of systemic inflammation, have been shown to be negatively associated with hippocampal gray matter volume (Marsland et al., 2008). Consistent findings were also reported in a larger population of midlife adults, showing that higher peripheral inflammation was negatively correlated with the whole gray matter volume, the whole white matter volume, and the cortical surface area (Marsland et al., 2015). Moreover, these associations also extended to variations in neurocognitive functions, indicating inflammatory response as an important accelerating factor of cognitive aging and risk for dementia. In a functional imaging study, elevated markers of inflammation (IL-6 and CRP) were associated with longitudinal changes in cerebral blood flow in the medial occipital, prefrontal, and hippocampal regions (Warren et al., 2018). In other words, older adults with elevated inflammation showed a more accelerated brain aging process when the inflammatory response was chronically elevated. It should be noted, however, that these studies did not directly examine the relevance to social life and the multiple age-related biological processes that may play a role in the elevation of inflammatory response.

Elevation in inflammatory markers is often observed in the progression of normal aging and Alzheimer's dementia pathology (Rosano et al., 2012). These markers characterize specific trajectories of cognitive decline in later life (Casaletto et al., 2019), while the elevated inflammatory response seems to exacerbate the ongoing pathophysiology of late-life neurodegeneration (Glass et al., 2010). Researchers are now taking pieces of these puzzles to draw a picture that social isolation or the richness of social connection is critical in moderating the stress response (Blevins et al., 2017; Uchino et al., 2015). These chronic changes are harmful not only to physical health but also neuronal functioning by interrupting neurogenesis, synaptic reorganization, white matter maintenance, and neurovascular health. These conditions of degradation may also lead to cognitive decline and reduced capacity to cope with the neuropathological burden.

6.4 Neural Resource Maintains Social Network in Return

The social brain hypothesis suggests that the number of possible social relationships is limited by the capacity of the social brain (Dunbar, 2014). The amount of cognitive resource is differentially constrained across individuals (Dávid-Barrett & Dunbar, 2013; Stiller & Dunbar, 2007), and the amount of neural resource (i.e., regional activation, brain volume, and white matter integrity) in the brain regions, especially those involved in processing social information or hierarchical structures of values, accounts for the differences in socio-cognitive abilities and propensities to maintain meaningful social relationships (Hampton et al., 2016; Kanai et al., 2012; Lewis et al., 2011; Meyer et al., 2012; Sato et al., 2016). Specific symptoms of neurological conditions also support the hypothesis that difference in the social brain leads to diverse social functioning. In older adults with frontotemporal dementia, the amount of neural loss (i.e., gray matter atrophy) within the amygdala network accounts for the severity of socio-emotional dysfunction, which is assessed with lack of attention to social cues, socio-emotional detachment, and inappropriate social behaviors (Bickart, Brickhouse, et al., 2014). Even in the relatively normal functioning population, predispositions emerging from genetic and developmental factors can affect differences in regional brain volumes or white matter microstructures of the regions especially involved in adaptive social behavior (Kanai & Rees, 2011; Wang & Olson, 2018). Therefore, it can be said that the preexisting brain resource enables larger social networking, and the variations of the social network, in turn, also proliferate or diminish the brain's structural or functional resources. The interplay between preexisting neural resources and an ongoing social influence may be more intricate than a simple causal explanation. Ehlers and colleagues conducted an intervention study that attempted to reduce perceived loneliness via group-based exercise training (Ehlers et al., 2017). They found that the older adults with larger amygdala and prefrontal cortex volumes gained more significant benefit in stress reduction and perceived more social support. The results suggest that neural resources play both roles: as a causal factor and an outcome of social connectedness.

6.5 Conclusions

This chapter has reviewed experimental and correlational studies and interpreted the results depending on their conceptual causal hypothesis. It should be noted, however, that each piece of pathway assumes a unidirectional explanation. It is more likely that the benefit of social connectedness on physical and cognitive health would result from multiple instantiations of possible causal effects. We propose a conceptual model in explaining how the positive association emerges across the lifespan in Figure 6.2.

In this schematic model, each pathway represents findings from the reviewed studies. First, as the social brain hypothesis suggests, the number of possible social relationships results from the available neural and cognitive capacity in the social brain (A). On the other hand, those with a rich

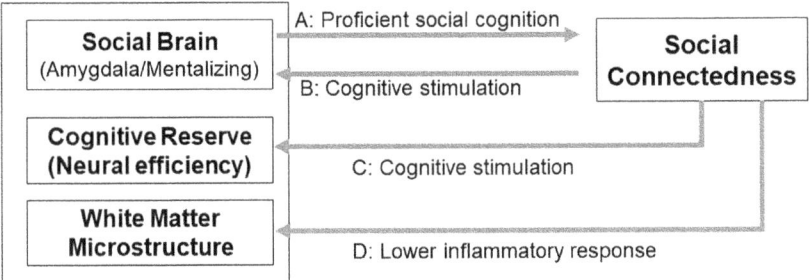

Figure 6.2 Possible pathways of how social connectedness and brain characteristics influence one another.

social network will develop increasing neural resources of social brain structures (B). The positive correlation between the capacity of the social brain and the size of social connection can emerge from the dynamic bidirectional interplay of the two causal mechanisms (A, B).

Other associations are based on more domain-general effects. The social network could affect cognitive health through domain-general neural bases. Socially engaged activities typically induce cognitive stimulation that increases neuronal resources. The intervention studies conducted in older adults showed that cognitively stimulating social activity may enhance brain functioning if the activity is challenging enough (C). Furthermore, social connectedness typically lowers excessive inflammatory response, and such mechanisms may protect the brain from the detrimental effects of stress and aging. Therefore, a larger integrated social network may modulate social stress, attenuate prolonged inflammatory response, and protect against harmful changes in white matter microstructure in the brain (D).

These intricate pathways suggest that the positive effects of social connectedness are not merely conveyed from exogenous factors. Cautious interpretation is warranted in the observed cross-sectional correlations as a single causal pathway, and short-term changes in social life would not directly lead to immediate and dramatic effects in cognitive or brain health. Rather, we highlight that the long-term interplay of the bidirectional relationship between social connectedness and neural resources will ultimately lead to psychologically and physically healthier living. Ongoing investment of cognitive and socio-emotional efforts is also critical in constructing external settings that, in turn, benefit the individual.

Integrating the findings from experimental studies and correlational studies is quite challenging. However, a number of converging threads of evidence suggest multiple benefits of having enriched social connections. We have especially reviewed neural evidence and brain imaging studies that support the argument, especially in the context of aging. Making social bridges, feeling connected, and diligently devoting to social connection are likely to provide us with better health today and later in life.

REFERENCES

Adolphs, R., Baron-Cohen, S., & Tranel, D. (2002). Impaired recognition of social emotions following amygdala damage. *Journal of Cognitive Neuroscience, 14*(8), 1264–1274. https://doi.org/10.1162/089892902760807258

Badre, D., & D'Esposito, M. (2009). Is the rostro-caudal axis of the frontal lobe hierarchical? *Nature Reviews Neuroscience, 10*(9), 659–669. https://doi.org/10.1038/nrn2667

Bang, M., Kim, J., An, S. K., Youm, Y., Chey, J., Kim, H. C., Park, K., Namkoong, K., & Lee, E. (2019). Associations of systemic inflammation with frontotemporal functional network connectivity and out-degree social-network size in community-dwelling older adults. *Brain, Behavior, and Immunity, 79*, 309–313. https://doi.org/10.1016/j.bbi.2019.01.025

Barnes, D. E. (2011). The Mediterranean diet: Good for the heart = good for the brain? *Annals of Neurology, 69*(2), 226–228. https://doi.org/10.1002/ana.22376

Barulli, D., & Stern, Y. (2013). Efficiency, capacity, compensation, maintenance, plasticity: Emerging concepts in cognitive reserve. *Trends in Cognitive Sciences, 17*(10), 502–509. https://doi.org/10.1016/j.tics.2013.08.012

Bell, H. C., Pellis, S. M., & Kolb, B. (2010). Juvenile peer play experience and the development of the orbitofrontal and medial prefrontal cortices. *Behavioural Brain Research, 207*(1), 7–13. https://doi.org/10.1016/j.bbr.2009.09.029

Bickart, K. C., Brickhouse, M., Negreira, A., Sapolsky, D., Barrett, L. F., & Dickerson, B. C. (2014). Atrophy in distinct corticolimbic networks in frontotemporal dementia relates to social impairments measured using the Social Impairment Rating Scale. *Journal of Neurology, Neurosurgery & Psychiatry, 85*(4), 438–448. https://doi.org/10.1136/jnnp-2012-304656

Bickart, K. C., Dickerson, B. C., Barrett, L. F., & Feldman Barrett, L. (2014). The amygdala as a hub in brain networks that support social life. *Neuropsychologia, 63*, 235–248. https://doi.org/10.1016/j.neuropsychologia.2014.08.013

Bickart, K. C., Hollenbeck, M. C., Barrett, L. F., & Dickerson, B. C. (2012). Intrinsic Amygdala – Cortical Functional Connectivity Predicts Social Network Size in Humans. *Journal of Neuroscience, 32*(42), 14729–14741. https://doi.org/10.1523/JNEUROSCI.1599-12.2012

Bickart, K. C., Wright, C. I., Dautoff, R. J., Dickerson, B. C., & Barrett, L. F. (2011). Amygdala volume and social network size in humans. *Nature Neuroscience, 14*(2), 163–164. https://doi.org/10.1038/nn.2724

Blevins, C. L., Sagui, S. J., & Bennett, J. M. (2017). Inflammation and positive affect: Examining the stress-buffering hypothesis with data from the National Longitudinal Study of Adolescent to Adult Health. *Brain, Behavior, and Immunity, 61*, 21–26. https://doi.org/10.1016/j.bbi.2016.07.149

Blumen, H. M., & Verghese, J. (2019). Gray matter volume covariance networks associated with social networks in older adults. *Social Neuroscience, 14*(5), 559–570. https://doi.org/10.1080/17470919.2018.1535999

Casaletto, K. B., Elahi, F. M., Staffaroni, A. M., Walters, S., Contreras, W. R., Wolf, A., Dubal, D., Miller, B., Yaffe, K., & Kramer, J. H. (2019). Cognitive aging is not created equally: Differentiating unique cognitive phenotypes in "normal" adults. *Neurobiology of Aging, 77*, 13–19. https://doi.org/10.1016/j.neurobiolaging.2019.01.007

Conti, L., Riccitelli, G. C., Preziosa, P., Vizzino, C., Marchesi, O., Rocca, M. A., & Filippi, M. (2021). Effect of cognitive reserve on structural and functional MRI measures in healthy subjects: A multiparametric assessment. *Journal of Neurology, 268*(5), 1780–1791. https://doi.org/10.1007/s00415-020-10331-6

Dávid-Barrett, T., & Dunbar, R. I. M. (2013). Processing power limits social group size: Computational evidence for the cognitive costs of sociality. *Proceedings of the Royal Society B: Biological Sciences, 280*(1765), 20131151. https://doi.org/10.1098/rspb.2013.1151

Davis, S. W., Kragel, J. E., Madden, D. J., & Cabeza, R. (2012). The architecture of cross-hemispheric communication in the aging brain: Linking behavior to functional and structural connectivity. *Cerebral Cortex, 22*(1), 232–242. https://doi.org/10.1093/cercor/bhr123

Dunbar, R. I. M. (2014). The social brain: Psychological underpinnings and implications for the structure of organizations. *Current Directions in Psychological Science, 23*(2), 109–114. https://doi.org/10.1177/0963721414135171118

Dziura, S. L., & Thompson, J. C. (2014). Social-network complexity in humans is associated with the neural response to social information. *Psychological Science, 25*(11), 2095–2101. https://doi.org/10.1177/0956797614549209

Ehlers, D. K., Daugherty, A. M., Burzynska, A. Z., Fanning, J., Awick, E. A., Chaddock-Heyman, L., Kramer, A. F., & McAuley, E. (2017). Regional brain volumes moderate, but do not mediate, the effects of group-based exercise training on reductions in loneliness in older adults. *Frontiers in Aging Neuroscience, 9*(APR). https://doi.org/10.3389/fnagi.2017.00110

Fjell, A. M., McEvoy, L., Holland, D., Dale, A. M., Walhovd, K. B., & Alzheimer's Disease Neuroimaging Initiative. (2014). What is normal in normal aging? Effects of aging, amyloid and Alzheimer's disease on the cerebral cortex and the hippocampus. *Progress in Neurobiology, 117*(2014), 20–40. https://doi.org/10.1016/j.pneurobio.2014.02.004

Foubert-Samier, A., Catheline, G., Amieva, H., Dilharreguy, B., Helmer, C., Allard, M., & Dartigues, J.-F. (2012). Education, occupation, leisure activities, and brain reserve: A population-based study. *Neurobiology of Aging*, *33*(2), 423. e15–423.e25. https://doi.org/10.1016/j.neurobiolaging.2010.09.023

Genon, S., Reid, A., Langner, R., Amunts, K., & Eickhoff, S. B. (2018). How to characterize the function of a brain region. *Trends in Cognitive Sciences*, *22* (4), 350–364. https://doi.org/10.1016/j.tics.2018.01.010

Gianaros, P. J., Kraynak, T. E., Kuan, D. C. H., Gross, J. J., McRae, K., Hariri, A. R., Manuck, S. B., Rasero, J., & Verstynen, T. D. (2020). Affective brain patterns as multivariate neural correlates of cardiovascular disease risk. *Social Cognitive and Affective Neuroscience*, *15*(10), 1034–1045. https://doi.org/10.1093/scan/nsaa050

Gianaros, P. J., Marsland, A. L., Kuan, D. C. H., Schirda, B. L., Jennings, J. R., Sheu, L. K., Hariri, A. R., Gross, J. J., & Manuck, S. B. (2014). An inflammatory pathway links atherosclerotic cardiovascular disease risk to neural activity evoked by the cognitive regulation of emotion. *Biological Psychiatry*, *75*(9), 738–745. https://doi.org/10.1016/j.biopsych.2013.10.012

Gianaros, P. J., Marsland, A. L., Sheu, L. K., Erickson, K. I., & Verstynen, T. D. (2013). Inflammatory pathways link socioeconomic inequalities to white matter architecture. *Cerebral Cortex*, *23*(9), 2058–2071. https://doi.org/10.1093/cercor/bhs191

Gianaros, P. J., & Wager, T. D. (2015). Brain-body pathways linking psychological stress and physical health. *Current Directions in Psychological Science*, *24*(4), 313–321. https://doi.org/10.1177/0963721415581476

Glass, C. K., Saijo, K., Winner, B., Marchetto, M. C., & Gage, F. H. (2010). Mechanisms underlying inflammation in neurodegeneration. *Cell*, *140*(6), 918–934. https://doi.org/10.1016/j.cell.2010.02.016

Habeck, C., Razlighi, Q., Gazes, Y., Barulli, D., Steffener, J., & Stern, Y. (2016). Cognitive reserve and brain maintenance: Orthogonal concepts in theory and practice. *Cerebral Cortex*, 1–8. https://doi.org/10.1093/cercor/bhw208

Hackett, R. A., Hamer, M., Endrighi, R., Brydon, L., & Steptoe, A. (2012). Loneliness and stress-related inflammatory and neuroendocrine responses in older men and women. *Psychoneuroendocrinology*, *37*(11), 1801–1809. https://doi.org/10.1016/j.psyneuen.2012.03.016

Hampton, W. H., Unger, A., Von Der Heide, R. J., & Olson, I. R. (2016). Neural connections foster social connections: A diffusion-weighted imaging study of social networks. *Social Cognitive and Affective Neuroscience*, *11*(5), 721–727. https://doi.org/10.1093/scan/nsv153

Hermes, G. L., Rosenthal, L., Montag, A., & McClintock, M. K. (2006). Social isolation and the inflammatory response: Sex differences in the enduring effects of a prior stressor. *American Journal of Physiology: Regulatory, Integrative and Comparative Physiology*, *290*(2), R273–R282. https://doi.org/10.1152/ajpregu.00368.2005

Jaremka, L. M., Fagundes, C. P., Peng, J., Bennett, J. M., Glaser, R., Malarkey, W. B., & Kiecolt-Glaser, J. K. (2013). Loneliness promotes inflammation during acute stress. *Psychological Science*, *24*(7), 1089–1097. https://doi.org/10.1177/0956797612464059

Joo, W., Kwak, S., Youm, Y., & Chey, J. (2017). Brain functional connectivity difference in the complete network of an entire village: The role of social network size and embeddedness. *Scientific Reports*, *7*(1), 4465. https://doi.org/10.1038/s41598-017-04904-1

Kalpouzos, G., Persson, J., & Nyberg, L. (2012). Local brain atrophy accounts for functional activity differences in normal aging. *Neurobiology of Aging*, *33*(3), 623.e1–623.e13. https://doi.org/10.1016/j.neurobiolaging.2011.02.021

Kanai, R., Bahrami, B., Duchaine, B., Janik, A., Banissy, M. J., & Rees, G. (2012). Brain structure links loneliness to social perception. *Current Biology*, *22*(20), 1975–1979. https://doi.org/10.1016/j.cub.2012.08.045

Kanai, R., & Rees, G. (2011). The structural basis of inter-individual differences in human behaviour and cognition. *Nature Reviews. Neuroscience*, *12*(4), 231–242. https://doi.org/10.1038/nrn3000

Karelina, K., Norman, G. J., Zhang, N., Morris, J. S., Peng, H., & DeVries, A. C. (2009). Social isolation alters neuroinflammatory response to stroke. *Proceedings of the National Academy of Sciences*, *106*(14), 5895–5900. https://doi.org/10.1073/pnas.0810737106

Kim, G. E., Han, J. W., Kim, T. H., Suh, S. W., Bae, J. Bin, Kim, J. H., & Kim, K. W. (2020). Hippocampus mediates the effect of emotional support on cognitive function in older adults. *The Journals of Gerontology: Series A*, *75*(8), 1502–1507. https://doi.org/10.1093/gerona/glz183

Kirby, L. A., Moraczewski, D., Warnell, K., Velnoskey, K., & Redcay, E. (2018). Social network size relates to developmental neural sensitivity to biological motion. *Developmental Cognitive Neuroscience*, *30*(March), 169–177. https://doi.org/10.1016/j.dcn.2018.02.012

Kolb, B., Gibb, R., & Gorny, G. (2003). Experience-dependent changes in dendritic arbor and spine density in neocortex vary qualitatively with age and sex. *Neurobiology of Learning and Memory*, *79*(1), 1–10. https://doi.org/10.1016/S1074-7427(02)00021-7

Kolb, B., Mychasiuk, R., Muhammad, A., Li, Y., Frost, D. O., & Gibb, R. (2012). Experience and the developing prefrontal cortex. *Proceedings of the National Academy of Sciences*, *109*, 17186–17193. https://doi.org/10.1073/pnas.1121251109

Krol, S. A., Meyer, M. L., Lieberman, M. D., & Bartz, J. A. (2018). Social working memory predicts social network size in humans. *Adaptive Human Behavior and Physiology*, *4*(4), 387–399. https://doi.org/10.1007/s40750-018-0100-9

Kwak, S., Joo, W., Youm, Y., & Chey, J. (2018). Social brain volume is associated with in-degree social network size among older adults. *Proceedings of the Royal Society B: Biological Sciences*, *285*(1871), 20172708. https://doi.org/10.1098/rspb.2017.2708

Lewis, P. A., Rezaie, R., Brown, R., Roberts, N., & Dunbar, R. I. M. (2011). Ventromedial prefrontal volume predicts understanding of others and social network size. *NeuroImage*, *57*(4), 1624–1629. https://doi.org/10.1016/j.neuroimage.2011.05.030

Lin, C., Keles, U., Tyszka, J. M., Gallo, M., Paul, L., & Adolphs, R. (2020). No strong evidence that social network index is associated with gray matter volume from a data-driven investigation. *Cortex, 125*, 307–317. https://doi.org/10.1016/j.cortex.2020.01.021

Liu, X., Liu, S., Huang, R., Chen, X., Xie, Y., Ma, R., Luo, Y., Bu, J., & Zhang, X. (2018). Neuroimaging studies reveal the subtle difference among social network size measurements and shed light on new directions. *Frontiers in Neuroscience, 12*. https://doi.org/10.3389/fnins.2018.00461

Lockhart, S. N., & DeCarli, C. (2014). Structural imaging measures of brain aging. *Neuropsychology Review, 24*(3), 271–289. https://doi.org/10.1007/s11065-014-9268-3

Lövdén, M., Bäckman, L., Lindenberger, U., Schaefer, S., & Schmiedek, F. (2010). A theoretical framework for the study of adult cognitive plasticity. *Psychological Bulletin, 136*(4), 659–676. https://doi.org/10.1037/a0020080

Makinodan, M., Rosen, K. M., Ito, S., & Corfas, G. (2012). A Critical period for social experience-dependent oligodendrocyte maturation and myelination. *Science, 337*(6100), 1357–1360. https://doi.org/10.1126/science.1220845

Marques, P., Soares, J. M., Magalhães, R., Santos, N. C., & Sousa, N. (2015). The bounds of education in the human brain connectome. *Scientific Reports, 5*, 12812. https://doi.org/10.1038/srep12812

Marsland, A. L., Gianaros, P. J., Abramowitch, S. M., Manuck, S. B., & Hariri, A. R. (2008). Interleukin-6 covaries inversely with hippocampal grey matter volume in middle-aged adults. *Biological Psychiatry, 64*(6), 484–490. https://doi.org/10.1016/j.biopsych.2008.04.016

Marsland, A. L., Gianaros, P. J., Kuan, D. C. H., Sheu, L. K., Krajina, K., & Manuck, S. B. (2015). Brain morphology links systemic inflammation to cognitive function in midlife adults. *Brain, Behavior, and Immunity, 48*, 195–204. https://doi.org/10.1016/j.bbi.2015.03.015

McDonough, I. M., Haber, S., Bischof, G. N., & Park, D. C. (2015). The Synapse Project: Engagement in mentally challenging activities enhances neural efficiency. *Restorative Neurology and Neuroscience, 33*(6), 865–882. https://doi.org/10.3233/RNN-150533

Meunier, D., Lambiotte, R., Fornito, A., Ersche, K. D., & Bullmore, E. T. (2009). Hierarchical modularity in human brain functional networks. *Frontiers in Human Neuroscience, 3*(October), 1–12. https://doi.org/10.3389/neuro.11.037.2009

Meunier, D., Stamatakis, E. A., & Tyler, L. K. (2014). Age-related functional reorganization, structural changes, and preserved cognition. *Neurobiology of Aging, 35*(1), 42–54. https://doi.org/10.1016/j.neurobiolaging.2013.07.003

Meyer, M. L., Spunt, R. P., Berkman, E. T., Taylor, S. E., & Lieberman, M. D. (2012). Evidence for social working memory from a parametric functional MRI study. *Proceedings of the National Academy of Sciences, 109*(6), 1883–1888. https://doi.org/10.1073/pnas.1121077109

Molesworth, T., Sheu, L. K., Cohen, S., Gianaros, P. J., & Verstynen, T. D. (2014). Social network diversity and white matter microstructural integrity in humans. *Social Cognitive and Affective Neuroscience, 10*(9), 1169–1176. https://doi.org/10.1093/scan/nsv001

Ospina, J. P., Larson, A. G., Jalilianhasanpour, R., Williams, B., Diez, I., Dhand, A., Dickerson, B. C., & Perez, D. L. (2019). Individual differences in social network size linked to nucleus accumbens and hippocampal volumes in functional neurological disorder: A pilot study. *Journal of Affective Disorders, 258*, 50–54. https://doi.org/10.1016/j.jad.2019.07.061

Pellis, S. M., Hastings, E., Shimizu, T., Kamitakahara, H., Komorowska, J., Forgie, M. L., & Kolb, B. (2006). The effects of orbital frontal cortex damage on the modulation of defensive responses by rats in playful and nonplayful social contexts. *Behavioral Neuroscience, 120*(1), 72–84. https://doi.org/10.1037/0735-7044.120.1.72

Pillemer, S., Holtzer, R., & Blumen, H. M. (2016). Functional connectivity associated with social networks in older adults: A resting-state fMRI study. *Social Neuroscience, 12*(3), 242–252. https://doi.org/10.1080/17470919.2016.1176599

Reed, B. R., Mungas, D., Farias, S. T., Harvey, D., Beckett, L., Widaman, K., Hinton, L., & DeCarli, C. (2010). Measuring cognitive reserve based on the decomposition of episodic memory variance. *Brain, 133*(8), 2196–2209. https://doi.org/10.1093/brain/awq154

Reuter-Lorenz, P. A., & Park, D. C. (2014). How does it STAC up? Revisiting the scaffolding theory of aging and cognition. *Neuropsychology Review, 24*(3), 355–370. https://doi.org/10.1007/s11065-014-9270-9

Rosano, C., Marsland, A. L., & Gianaros, P. J. (2012). Maintaining brain health by monitoring inflammatory processes: A mechanism to promote successful aging. *Aging and Disease, 3*(1), 16–33. http://www.ncbi.nlm.nih.gov/pubmed/22500269

Rosenzweig, M. R., Bennett, E. L., & Diamond, M. C. (1972). Brain changes in response to experience. *Scientific American, 226*(2), 22–29. https://doi.org/10.1038/scientificamerican0272-22

Sallet, J., Mars, R. B., Noonan, M. P., Andersson, J. L., O'Reilly, J. X., Jbabdi, S., Croxson, P. L., Jenkinson, M., Miller, K. L., & Rushworth, M. F. S. (2011). Social network size affects neural circuits in macaques. *Science, 334*(6056), 697–700. https://doi.org/10.1126/science.1210027

Sato, W., Kochiyama, T., Uono, S., Sawada, R., Kubota, Y., Yoshimura, S., & Toichi, M. (2016). Structural neural substrates of reading the mind in the eyes. *Frontiers in Human Neuroscience, 10*(April), 151. https://doi.org/10.3389/fnhum.2016.00151

Sato, W., Kochiyama, T., Uono, S., Yoshimura, S., Kubota, Y., Sawada, R., Sakihama, M., & Toichi, M. (2017). Reduced Gray matter volume in the social brain network in adults with autism spectrum disorder. *Frontiers in Human Neuroscience, 11*. https://doi.org/10.3389/fnhum.2017.00395

Schurz, M., Radua, J., Aichhorn, M., Richlan, F., & Perner, J. (2014). Fractionating theory of mind: A meta-analysis of functional brain imaging studies. *Neuroscience and Biobehavioral Reviews, 42*, 9–34. https://doi.org/10.1016/j.neubiorev.2014.01.009

Shine, J. M. (2019). Neuromodulatory influences on integration and segregation in the brain. *Trends in Cognitive Sciences*, *23*(7), 572–583. https://doi.org/10.1016/j.tics.2019.04.002

Slavich, G. M., & Cole, S. W. (2013). The emerging field of human social genomics. *Clinical Psychological Science*, *1*(3), 331–348. https://doi.org/10.1177/2167702613478594

Slavich, G. M., Way, B. M., Eisenberger, N. I., & Taylor, S. E. (2010). Neural sensitivity to social rejection is associated with inflammatory responses to social stress. *Proceedings of the National Academy of Sciences*, *107*(33), 14817–14822. https://doi.org/10.1073/pnas.1009164107

Smith, B. M., Yao, X., Chen, K. S., & Kirby, E. D. (2018). A Larger social network enhances novel object location memory and reduces hippocampal microgliosis in aged mice. *Frontiers in Aging Neuroscience*, *10*(May), 142. https://doi.org/10.3389/fnagi.2018.00142

Steffener, J., Gazes, Y., Habeck, C., & Stern, Y. (2016). The indirect effect of age group on switch costs via gray matter volume and task-related brain activity. *Frontiers in Aging Neuroscience*, *8*(JUN), 1–11. https://doi.org/10.3389/fnagi.2016.00162

Steffener, J., & Stern, Y. (2012). Exploring the neural basis of cognitive reserve in aging. *Biochimica et Biophysica Acta (BBA) – Molecular Basis of Disease*, *1822*(3), 467–473. https://doi.org/10.1016/j.bbadis.2011.09.012

Stiller, J., & Dunbar, R. I. M. (2007). Perspective-taking and memory capacity predict social network size. *Social Networks*, *29*(1), 93–104. https://doi.org/10.1016/j.socnet.2006.04.001

Suárez, L. E., Markello, R. D., Betzel, R. F., & Misic, B. (2020). Linking structure and function in macroscale brain networks. *Trends in Cognitive Sciences*, *24*(4), 302–315. https://doi.org/10.1016/j.tics.2020.01.008

Tavor, I., Jones, O. P., Mars, R. B., Smith, S. M., Behrens, T. E., & Jbabdi, S. (2016). Task-free MRI predicts individual differences in brain activity during task performance. *Science*, *352*(6282), 216–220. https://doi.org/10.1126/science.aad8127

Tomasi, D., & Volkow, N. D. (2012). Aging and functional brain networks. *Molecular Psychiatry*, *17*(5), 549–558. https://doi.org/10.1038/mp.2011.81

Uchino, B. N., Ruiz, J. M., Smith, T. W., Smyth, J. M., Taylor, D. J., Allison, M., & Ahn, C. (2015). The strength of family ties: Perceptions of network relationship quality and levels of C-reactive proteins in the North Texas Heart Study. *Annals of Behavioral Medicine*, *49*(5), 776–781. https://doi.org/10.1007/s12160-015-9699-y

Valenzuela, M. J., Brayne, C., Sachdev, P., Wilcock, G., & Matthews, F. (2011). Cognitive lifestyle and long-term risk of dementia and survival after diagnosis in a multicenter population-based cohort. *American Journal of Epidemiology*, *173*(9), 1004–1012. https://doi.org/10.1093/aje/kwq476

Valenzuela, M. J., Breakspear, M., & Sachdev, P. (2007). Complex mental activity and the aging brain: Molecular, cellular and cortical network mechanisms. *Brain Research Reviews*, *56*(1), 198–213. https://doi.org/10.1016/j.brainresrev.2007.07.007

Valenzuela, M. J., Sachdev, P., Wen, W., Chen, X., & Brodaty, H. (2008). Lifespan mental activity predicts diminished rate of hippocampal atrophy. *PLoS ONE*, *3*(7), 1–6. https://doi.org/10.1371/journal.pone.0002598

Van Overwalle, F. (2009). Social cognition and the brain: A meta-analysis. *Human Brain Mapping*, *30*(3), 829–858. https://doi.org/10.1002/hbm.20547

Vemuri, P., Lesnick, T. G., Przybelski, S. A., Knopman, D. S., Lowe, V. J., Graff-Radford, J., Roberts, R. O., Mielke, M. M., Machulda, M. M., Petersen, R. C., & Jack, C. R. (2017). Age, vascular health, and Alzheimer disease biomarkers in an elderly sample. *Annals of Neurology*, *82*(5), 706–718. https://doi.org/10.1002/ana.25071

Von der Heide, R., Vyas, G., & Olson, I. R. (2013). The social network-network: Size is predicted by brain structure and function in the amygdala and paralimbic regions. *Social Cognitive and Affective Neuroscience*, *9*(12), 1962–1972. https://doi.org/10.1093/scan/nsu009

Wang, Y., & Olson, I. R. (2018). The original social network: White matter and social cognition. *Trends in Cognitive Sciences*, *22*(6), 504–516. https://doi.org/10.1016/j.tics.2018.03.005

Warren, K. N., Beason-Held, L. L., Carlson, O., Egan, J. M., An, Y., Doshi, J., Davatzikos, C., Ferrucci, L., & Resnick, S. M. (2018). Elevated markers of inflammation are associated with longitudinal changes in brain function in older adults. *The Journals of Gerontology: Series A*, *73*(6), 770–778. https://doi.org/10.1093/gerona/glx199

Zou, L., Yang, Z., Wang, Y., Lui, S. S. Y., Chen, A., Cheung, E. F. C., & Chan, R. C. K. (2016). What does the nose know? Olfactory function predicts social network size in human. *Scientific Reports*, *6*, 25026. https://doi.org/10.1038/srep25026

CHAPTER 7

Psychoneuroimmunology Linking Social Isolation with Cognitive Aging

Sung-Ha Lee

7.1 Introduction

Considerable evidence indicates that social relationships are important for human survival and well-being. According to the human evolutionary point of view, a lack of social connections is linked to increased vulnerability to physical attack, leading to wounds and death (Leschak & Eisenberger, 2019). Among the biological mechanisms linking social relationships and health outcomes, inflammatory responses have emerged as key processes given their influence across the pathology of various diseases (Uchino, 2006). Moreover, recent evidence indicates that inflammatory response also alters human social behavior, suggesting bi-directional communication between social relationships and the immune system (Eisenberger, 2013; Moieni & Eisenberger, 2018). This chapter first introduces inflammatory processes and studies identifying social isolation and aging as important factors related to increased inflammatory response, and then discusses the protective factors that can mitigate inflammatory response under these conditions.

7.2 Conditions Associated with Elevated Inflammation

The main role of the immune system is to distinguish "self" and "non-self," to look out for the "invader" to protect ourselves from pathogens. Once it detects pathogens such as exogenous viruses and toxins, our body recruits the members of the immune system to maintain homeostasis. For example, the white blood cells, also called leukocytes, take charge of such detection and removal of the strangers by recruiting various kinds of signaling molecules to act as messengers to facilitate the immune processes. Cytokines, the signaling molecules involved in such immune processes, regulate cell proliferation and other functions that help the body's inflammatory response against tissue damage (Salvador et al., 2021). Considering the crucial roles of cytokines, the levels of cytokines such as interleukin (IL)-1B, IL-6, and tumor necrosis factor (TNF)-α have been used to estimate the inflammatory response; the levels of such pro-inflammatory markers from peripheral samples such as blood and saliva are often used as the representative markers of the inflammatory response after statistically controlling for the confounding factors, such as body mass index, smoking, and alcohol consumption.

Immune systems are "intertwined" with multilevel factors that can form a physiological nexus through which social, environmental, cognitive, and psychological factors exert their effects. To understand this process, one needs to distinguish *acute* inflammation from *chronic* inflammation processes. Inflammation is usually accompanied by fever, wound, and redness, as the origin of the word "inflammation" comes from the Latin word for "setting on fire." These conditions actually indicate *acute* inflammatory response, characterized by five cardinal signs: pain, redness, immobility (loss of function), swelling, and heat. Moreover, there is usually explainable stimulus, such as viruses or physical wounds, before the acute inflammation, and the response does not last long after the primary purpose of the inflammation (i.e., to repair tissues and restore homeostasis).

Relatively, much less is known about *chronic* inflammation, whether its cause or the mechanism. Chronic systemic inflammation usually differs from acute inflammation in that it 1) is fever free, 2) does not necessarily accompany physical wounds, and 3) has been associated with various social conditions. Adverse psychosocial conditions, such as chronic stress, childhood adversity, and depression, have been implicated in increased chronic systemic inflammation (Del Giudice & Gangestad, 2018; Kuhlman et al., 2017; Miller et al., 2011). Accordingly, it is not surprising that such chronic systemic inflammation emerges as one of the "social-to-biological transitions" or "the biological embodiment of social environments," where psychosocial factors and biological processes interact with each other (Blane et al., 2013). Due to increased levels of pro-inflammatory cytokines, people with chronic systemic inflammation experience frequent fatigue, emotional disturbance, anhedonia and increased sensitivity to pain, together called "sickness behavior" (Dantzer et al., 2008). However, in that the inflammatory markers are involved in multifaceted functions to maintain somatic homeostasis (Del Giudice & Gangestad, 2018), we need to be cautious when interpreting the psychosocial and environmental factors associated with increased inflammatory markers. This section will review the factors that are known to increase chronic low-grade systemic inflammation.

7.2.1 Aging and Cognitive Decline

The aging process is one of the main factors that increase pro-inflammatory markers, which has been conceptualized as "inflammageing" (Calder et al., 2017; Franceschi et al., 2000). One of the physiological changes people confront as they age is the altered immune system, also known as "immunosenescence." Such an altered immune system usually accompanies elevated levels of chronic low inflammation (Calder et al., 2017; Piber et al., 2019; Puzianowska-Kuźnicka et al., 2016). This dysregulation in the immune system may increase susceptibility to infection linked to higher morbidity and mortality in older adults.

Generally, the aging process is associated with systemic low-grade inflammation measured by elevated pro-inflammatory markers such as C-reactive protein (CRP), IL-1B, and IL-6. For example, one recent study found that IL-6 and CRP levels chronically increased with age in healthy elderly populations (Puzianowska-Kuźnicka et al., 2016). Another study also found that age is associated with increased levels of IL-6, TNF response, and signal transducer and activator of transcription activation (Piber et al., 2019). Although inflammatory markers are increased in an age-dependent manner, higher IL-6 and CRP levels were associated with poorer physical and cognitive performance, even in the same age group (Puzianowska-Kuźnicka et al., 2016). Moreover, older adults with multi-morbidity as well as higher baseline pro-inflammatory markers show steeper increases of IL-6 over time (Fabbri et al., 2015), suggesting that the level of pro-inflammatory markers can be an accelerating factor for the pathological aging process.

Chronic systemic inflammation has been positively associated with cognitive decline as well as brain changes related to Alzheimer's disease (AD; Beydoun et al., 2019; Corlier et al., 2018). Among the various pro-inflammatory markers, a recent study found a significant link between IL-6 and a faster decline in verbal memory, and between IL-18 and poorer performance in attention tests (Beydoun et al., 2019). There are also studies suggesting that the regulatory variants of inflammatory markers contribute to brain aging through regulating the expression of those markers. For example, the common variant of IL-6R (rs2228145), primarily expressed in microglia, was significantly associated with IL-6 levels in the brains of AD patients (Haddick et al., 2017). Efforts to develop therapeutic agents using anti-inflammatory drugs to reduce the clinical symptoms of AD also support the links between pro-inflammatory processes and cognitive dysfunction (Wyss-Coray & Rogers, 2012). However, there are still mixed results on the efficacy of anti-inflammatory treatments; for example, a recent study involving randomized trials with the tetracycline antibiotic minocycline failed to delay the progress of mild AD (Gyengesi & Münch, 2020; Howard et al., 2020). Future studies of candidate drugs with more specific targets and appropriate doses will be needed to validate the use of anti-inflammatory agents for curing cognitive decline.

7.2.2 Adverse Social Conditions

Social isolation and exclusion pose a serious threat to survival and well-being in humans (Cacioppo et al., 2002; Holt-Lunstad, 2018). It is also well established that adverse social conditions, including social isolation and exclusion, are associated with increased risk for diseases and mental disorders. Recent studies have found potential mechanisms underlying the association between adverse social conditions and health outcomes by measuring various systemic inflammation markers (Muscatell et al., 2020). From an evolutionary point of view, social isolation is likely to increase physical wounds and, thus, the body is more readily able to induce pro-inflammatory responses (Leschak & Eisenberger, 2019). However, social integration increases the chance of exposure to pathogens through human-to-human infection, making the body more prepared to induce antibody production. Social genomics studies that link social environments to leukocyte gene expression have revealed the significant association between altered immune gene expression patterns and loneliness at the transcriptional levels (Cole et al., 2007, 2015). More specifically, chronically lonely individuals showed significantly higher-level expression of genes called conserved transcriptional response to adversity, characterized by up-regulation of pro-inflammatory genes and down-regulation of antiviral responses.

At protein or hormone level, there are still mixed results on the elevation of immune response through loneliness or social isolation. One study using middle-aged American adults revealed the positive association between loneliness and CRP, IL-6, and fibrinogen (Nersesian et al., 2018). Another study also showed that loneliness significantly increases CRP levels and, interestingly, this change in CRP was worse in older adults (Shiovitz-Ezra & Parag, 2019). A recent meta-analysis, however, indicates that the findings could vary with different methodological approaches (Smith et al., 2020); loneliness was associated with elevation of IL-6 in studies using most adjusted sensitivity analyses, whereas social isolation was associated with CRP and fibrinogen in studies using certain sensitivity analyses but not others. Even though there is some evidence suggesting links between loneliness and inflammatory markers, the associations are still not robust enough to be conclusive. More research using consistent measurements and analysis is needed to draw firm conclusions.

7.3 Alternative Marker for Inflammation: Gut Microbiome

The gut microbiome has recently emerged as an alternative inflammatory marker since it has been found that the microbiota plays a significant role in the function of the host immune system (Belkaid & Hand, 2014). With an estimated 100 trillion cells, which is about ten times the number of host cells in humans, commensal microbiota is involved in multiple hosts' physiological processes, including immune function. The neuronal and hormonal connections between the gut and the brain and immune function implies the role of the gut microbiome in psychiatric and inflammatory diseases (Dinan et al., 2015; Dinan & Cryan, 2017). One of the characteristics of the gut microbiome that has been consistently reported in many pathological conditions is a lack of microbiota diversity, the index of intestinal dysbiosis (Badal et al., 2020; Mosca et al., 2016). Recent evidence suggests significant links between gut microbiome diversity and loneliness and cognitive impairment. For example, one exploratory study found that higher levels of loneliness and a lower level of social support were associated with decreased diversity in the gut microbiome (Nguyen et al., 2021). Moreover, lower microbial diversity was strongly linked to poor cognitive functions, such as verbal fluency and memory, in community-dwelling older adults (Verdi et al., 2018). Interestingly, increasing evidence indicates that abnormal function of gut microbiota contributes to the pathogenesis of AD, since gut microbiota is the source of a large amount of amyloid and regulates the permeability of the gut barrier, which further impacts neuroinflammation (Kowalski & Mulak, 2019; Sochocka et al., 2019; Vogt et al., 2017).

7.4 Protective Factors against Elevated Inflammation

As adverse social conditions have been consistently associated with inflammatory responses, more studies are investigating favorable psychosocial factors that can protect physiological health against increased levels of pro-inflammation. Here, we summarize a few psychological and lifestyle factors that have been associated with reduced inflammation.

7.4.1 Social Support

The immune response emerges as one of the biological and physiological processes linking social connection or isolation and physical health (Leschak & Eisenberger, 2019). One recent meta-study of 73,037 participants from 47 studies confirmed the significant link between social support, social integration, and levels of inflammatory cytokines including IL-6, TNF-α, CRP, and fibrinogen (Uchino et al., 2018), finding that higher levels of social support and integration were associated with lower levels of inflammatory cytokines. The results indicate that positive social relationships with greater social support and connection can work as a protective factor, which can lower inflammation and other disease pathology. Given that positive and supportive social relationships have been linked to lower rates of morbidity and mortality in later life, a recent meta-study even suggested that social support is related to higher antibody responses after vaccination (Uchino et al., 2020). Even though the biological mechanisms mediating social support and health outcomes are still under investigation, the immune system can be one of the pathways through which social support can influence biological reactions.

7.4.2 Having a Sense of Purpose in Life

Recently, mounting evidence has pointed to the fact that purpose in life (beliefs that give individuals a sense of purpose and meaning) has a positive influence on mental as well as physical health outcomes. For example, having a higher sense of purpose in life is significantly associated with reduced levels of all-cause mortality and cardiovascular events (Cohen et al., 2016; Kim et al., 2021; Shiba et al., 2021). Moreover, higher levels of purpose in life have been linked to better cognitive functioning in older adults as well as a reduced risk for AD (Boyle et al., 2010). A sense of purpose has also been observed to reduce the risk of cerebral infarcts in community-dwelling older adults (Yu et al., 2015) and the risk of stroke (Kim et al., 2013), which would in turn mitigate the risk of vascular dementia. Moreover, older adults with a higher sense of purpose in life demonstrated reduced inflammatory response (see Ryff et al., 2016, for a comprehensive review).

In that social relationship significantly impacts one's sense of meaning in life, it is not surprising that social integration can also protect against adverse inflammatory responses. In fact, one study suggests that meaning in life and loneliness are negatively correlated with one another in terms of brain measures of functional connectivity (Mwilambwe-Tshilobo et al., 2019), implying that one's perspective on life and social relations are intrinsically intertwined in neural signaling patterns. More research on the relationship between loneliness, cognitive function, and purpose in life can advance our knowledge of how these factors can protect our immune system from lack of social connection and cognitive impairment.

Even though many recent studies point out the importance of having a sense of direction and goals associated with health outcomes, the associations still remain inconclusive, partly because most of the findings are based on Western, educated older adults. The relationships need to be examined in other cultures and extended to diverse populations, such as less-educated older adults, to generalize the findings. For example, when researchers from the Korean Social life, Health, and Aging Project (KSHAP) assessed purpose in life using the Ryff scale in the subsamples of KSHAP participants, the Cronbach's alpha was too low, (i.e., less than 0.5) to further investigate the link between health outcomes such as inflammatory markers and brain imaging with purpose in life measures. This was partly due to the difficulty in understanding the concepts of "purpose" and "goal" because the words were too abstract and may be far from the everyday experience of older Koreans living in a rural area with low educational attainment. It might be necessary to customize or develop reliable scales to measure the sense of purpose in life familiar to older Koreans.

7.4.3 *Healthy Lifestyle: Diet*

Effective interventions that help to reduce an age-induced rise in inflammation have focused on improving and maintaining healthy lifestyles in older adults. Reducing chronic low-grade pro-inflammatory conditions may be one of the ways to prevent or reduce the severity of age-related diseases including AD (Valentini et al., 2015). To alleviate "inflammageing" conditions in older adults, several recent studies have examined the impact of diet and nutrition supplements. The recently coined term "psychobiotics" also implies the potential impact of gut microbes and mental health (Bermúdez-Humarán et al., 2019). Psychobiotics includes a family of beneficial bacteria, as well as dietary soluble fibers, which stimulate the growth of "good" bacteria that enhance psychological well-being. Again, given the high comorbidity present between AD and disrupted gut microbiome diversity, it is plausible that the modification of microbial ecology via an intake of psychobiotics could improve an individual's mental health. In fact, one randomized controlled trial in healthy older adults demonstrated that psychobiotics increase "good microbiota" (bifidobacteria), especially in subjects with enhanced inflammatory markers (Valentini et al., 2015). This study also found that eight weeks of dietary intervention with psychobiotics could improve other health-related parameters, like cholesterol and glucose in the elderly population. Moreover, a higher intake of whole grain, fruit, vegetables, and fish was significantly associated with lower inflammation in individuals who were overweight and obese (Calder et al., 2011). As emerging evidence points to the effect of altering microbiota on mental health, more research will be needed to develop dietary intervention programs to counter age-related symptoms.

7.5 Conclusions

Increasing amounts of evidence indicate that social disconnectedness and cognitive aging are associated with disrupted immune function, which may in turn link to morbidity and mortality. Among various biological pathways linked to social behavior and cognitive function, this chapter has focused on inflammatory markers, especially those indicating chronic systemic inflammation, that have been found to be important in both prolonged social stress situations and aging. Future research needs to extend and integrate the previous findings regarding inflammatory responses to other aspects of health, such as cardiovascular and neuroendocrine functions, as they are relevant for understanding the dynamic interactions between social isolation and cognitive functions in the context of aging. Furthermore, more clinical studies will be needed to validate the beneficial effects of psychosocial factors that could delay cognitive aging.

REFERENCES

Badal, V. D., Vaccariello, E. D., Murray, E. R., Yu, K. E., Knight, R., Jeste, D. V., & Nguyen, T. T. (2020). The gut microbiome, aging, and longevity: A systematic review. *Nutrients*, *12*(12), 3759. https://doi.org/10.3390/nu12123759

Belkaid, Y., & Hand, T. W. (2014). Role of the microbiota in immunity and inflammation. *Cell*, *157*(1), 121–141. https://doi.org/10.1016/j.cell.2014.03.011

Beydoun, M. A., Weiss, J., Obhi, H. K., Beydoun, H. A., Dore, G. A., Liang, H., Evans, M. K., & Zonderman, A. B. (2019). Cytokines are associated with longitudinal changes in cognitive performance among urban adults. *Brain,*

Behavior, and Immunity, 80, 474–487. https://doi.org/10.1016/j.bbi.2019.04.027

Bermúdez-Humarán, L. G., Salinas, E., Ortiz, G. G., Ramirez-Jirano, L. J., Morales, J. A., & Bitzer-Quintero, O. K. (2019). From probiotics to psychobiotics: Live beneficial bacteria which act on the brain–gut axis. *Nutrients, 11*(4), 890. https://doi.org/10.3390/nu11040890

Blane, D., Kelly-Irving, M., & Bartley, M. (2013). Social-biological transitions: How does the social become biological? *Longitudinal and Life Course Studies, 4*(2), 136–146. https://doi.org/10.14301/llcs.v4i2.236

Boyle, P. A., Buchman, A. S., Barnes, L. L., & Bennett, D. A. (2010). Effect of a purpose in life on risk of incident alzheimer disease and mild cognitive impairment in community-dwelling older persons. *Archives of General Psychiatry, 67*(3), 304–310. http://archpsyc.jamanetwork.com/article.aspx?doi=10.1001/archgenpsychiatry.2009.208

Cacioppo, J. T., Hawkley, L. C., Crawford, L. E., Ernst, J. M., Burleson, M. H., Kowalewski, R. B., Malarkey, W. B., Van Cauter, E., & Berntson, G. G. (2002). Loneliness and health: Potential mechanisms. *Psychosomatic Medicine, 64*(3), 407–417. https://doi.org/10.1097/00006842-200205000-00005

Calder, P. C., Ahluwalia, N., Brouns, F., Buetler, T., Clement, K., Cunningham, K., Esposito, K., Jönsson, L. S., Kolb, H., Lansink, M., Marcos, A., Margioris, A., Matusheski, N., Nordmann, H., O'Brien, J., Pugliese, G., Rizkalla, S., Schalkwijk, C., Tuomilehto, J., ... Winklhofer-Roob, B. M. (2011). Dietary factors and low-grade inflammation in relation to overweight and obesity. *British Journal of Nutrition, 106*(Suppl. 3), S1–S78. https://doi.org/10.1017/s0007114511005460

Calder, P. C., Bosco, N., Bourdet-Sicard, R., Capuron, L., Delzenne, N., Doré, J., Franceschi, C., Lehtinen, M. J., Recker, T., Salvioli, S., & Visioli, F. (2017). Health relevance of the modification of low grade inflammation in ageing (inflammageing) and the role of nutrition. *Ageing Research Reviews, 40*, 95–119. https://doi.org/10.1016/j.arr.2017.09.001

Cohen, R., Bavishi, C., & Rozanski, A. (2016). Purpose in life and its relationship to all-cause mortality and cardiovascular events: A meta-analysis. *Psychosomatic Medicine, 78*(2), 122–133. https://doi.org/10.1097/PSY.0000000000000274

Cole, S. W., Hawkley, L. C., Arevalo, J. M., Sung, C. Y., Rose, R. M., & Cacioppo, J. T. (2007). Social regulation of gene expression in human leukocytes. *Genome Biology, 8*(9), R189. https://doi.org/10.1186/gb-2007-8-9-r189

Cole, S. W., Levine, M. E., Arevalo, J. M. G., Ma, J., Weir, D. R., & Crimmins, E. M. (2015). Loneliness, eudaimonia, and the human conserved transcriptional response to adversity. *Psychoneuroendocrinology, 62*, 11–17. https://doi.org/10.1016/j.psyneuen.2015.07.001

Corlier, F., Hafzalla, G., Faskowitz, J., Kuller, L. H., Becker, J. T., Lopez, O. L., Thompson, P. M., & Braskie, M. N. (2018). Systemic inflammation as a predictor of brain aging: Contributions of physical activity, metabolic risk, and genetic risk. *NeuroImage*, *172*, 118–129. https://doi.org/10.1016/j.neuroimage.2017.12.027

Dantzer, R., O'Connor, J. C., Freund, G. G., Johnson, R. W., & Kelley, K. W. (2008). From inflammation to sickness and depression: When the immune system subjugates the brain. *Nature Reviews Neuroscience*, *9*(1), 46–56. https://doi.org/10.1038/nrn2297

Del Giudice, M., & Gangestad, S. W. (2018). Rethinking IL-6 and CRP: Why they are more than inflammatory biomarkers, and why it matters. *Brain, Behavior, and Immunity*, *70*, 61–75. https://doi.org/10.1016/j.bbi.2018.02.013

Dinan, T. G., & Cryan, J. F. (2017). Brain–gut–microbiota axis and mental health. *Psychosomatic Medicine*, *79*(8), 920–926. http://eutils.ncbi.nlm.nih.gov/entrez/eutils/elink.fcgi?dbfrom=pubmed&id=28806201&retmode=ref&cmd=prlinks

Dinan, T. G., Stilling, R. M., Stanton, C., & Cryan, J. F. (2015). Collective unconscious: How gut microbes shape human behavior. In *Journal of Psychiatric Research*, *63*, 1–9. https://doi.org/10.1016/j.jpsychires.2015.02.021

Eisenberger, N. I. (2013). Social ties and health: A social neuroscience perspective. *Current Opinion in Neurobiology*, *23*(3), 407–413. https://doi.org/10.1016/j.conb.2013.01.006

Fabbri, E., An, Y., Zoli, M., Simonsick, E. M., Guralnik, J. M., Bandinelli, S., Boyd, C. M., & Ferrucci, L. (2015). Aging and the burden of multimorbidity: Associations with inflammatory and anabolic hormonal biomarkers. *Journals of Gerontology: Series A, Biological Sciences and Medical Sciences*, *70*(1), 63–70. https://doi.org/10.1093/gerona/glu127

Franceschi, C., Bonafè, M., Valensin, S., Olivieri, F., De Luca, M., Ottaviani, E., & De Benedictis, G. (2000). Inflamm-aging. An evolutionary perspective on immunosenescence. *Annals of the New York Academy of Sciences*, *908*, 244–254. https://doi.org/10.1111/j.1749-6632.2000.tb06651.x

Gyengesi, E., & Münch, G. (2020). In search of an anti-inflammatory drug for Alzheimer disease. *Nature Reviews Neurology*, *16*(3), 131–132. https://doi.org/10.1038/s41582-019-0307-9

Haddick, P. C. G., Larson, J. L., Rathore, N., Bhangale, T. R., Phung, Q. T., Srinivasan, K., Hansen, D. V., Lill, J. R., Pericak-Vance, M. A., Haines, J., Farrer, L. A., Kauwe, J. S., Schellenberg, G. D., Cruchaga, C., Goate, A. M., Behrens, T. W., Watts, R. J., Graham, R. R., Kaminker, J. S., & Van Der Brug, M. (2017). A common variant of IL-6R is associated with elevated IL-6 pathway activity in Alzheimer's disease brains. *Journal of Alzheimer's Disease*, *56*(3), 1037–1054. https://doi.org/10.3233/JAD-160524

Holt-Lunstad J. (2018). Why Social relationships are important for physical health: A systems approach to understanding and modifying risk and protection. *Annual Review of Psychology*, *69*, 437–458. https://doi.org/10.1146/annurev-psych-122216-011902

Howard, R., Zubko, O., Bradley, R., Harper, E., Pank, L., O'Brien, J., Fox, C., Tabet, N., Livingston, G., Bentham, P., McShane, R., Burns, A., Ritchie, C., Reeves, S., Lovestone, S., Ballard, C., Noble, W., Nilforooshan, R., Wilcock, G., & Gray, R. (2020). Minocycline at 2 different dosages vs placebo for patients with mild Alzheimer disease: A randomized clinical trial. *JAMA Neurology, 77*(2), 164–174. https://doi.org/10.1001/jamaneurol.2019.3762

Kim, E. S., Sun, J. K., Park, N., & Peterson, C. (2013). Purpose in life and reduced incidence of stroke in older adults: "The Health and Retirement Study." *Journal of Psychosomatic Research, 74*(5), 427–432. https://linkinghub.elsevier.com/retrieve/pii/S0022399913000391

Kim, E. S., Chen, Y., Nakamura, J. S., Ryff, C. D., & VanderWeele, T. J. (2021). Sense of purpose in life and subsequent physical, behavioral, and psychosocial health: An outcome-wide approach. *American Journal of Health Promotion, 36*(1):137–147. https://doi.org/10.1177/08901171211038545

Kowalski, K., & Mulak, A. (2019). Brain–gut–microbiota axis in Alzheimer's disease. *Journal of Neurogastroenterology and Motility, 25*(1), 48–60. https://doi.org/10.5056/jnm18087

Kuhlman, K. R., Chiang, J. J., Horn, S., & Bower, J. E. (2017). Developmental psychoneuroendocrine and psychoneuroimmune pathways from childhood adversity to disease. *Neuroscience and Biobehavioral Reviews, 80*(April), 166–184. https://doi.org/10.1016/j.neubiorev.2017.05.020

Leschak, C. J., & Eisenberger, N. I. (2019). Two distinct immune pathways linking social relationships with health: Inflammatory and antiviral processes. *Psychosomatic Medicine, 81*(8), 711–719. https://doi.org/10.1097/PSY.0000000000000685

Miller, G. E., Lachman, M. E., Chen, E., Gruenewald, T. L., Karlamangla, A. S., & Seeman, T. E. (2011). Pathways to resilience: Maternal nurturance as a buffer against the effects of childhood poverty on metabolic syndrome at midlife. *Psychological Science, 22*(12), 1591–1599. http://journals.sagepub.com/doi/10.1177/0956797611419170

Moieni, M., & Eisenberger, N. I. (2018). Effects of inflammation on social processes and implications for health. *Annals of the New York Academy of Sciences, 1428*(1), 5–13. https://doi.org/10.1111/nyas.13864

Mosca, A., Leclerc, M., & Hugot, J. P. (2016). Gut Microbiota diversity and human diseases: Should we reintroduce key predators in our ecosystem? *Frontiers in Microbiology, 7*(1182), 842. http://journal.frontiersin.org/Article/10.3389/fmicb.2016.00455/abstract

Muscatell, K. A., Brosso, S. N., & Humphreys, K. L. Socioeconomic status and inflammation: A meta-analysis. *Molecular Psychiatry* 25, 2189–2199 (2020). https://doi.org/10.1038/s41380-018-0259-2

Mwilambwe-Tshilobo, L., Ge, T., Chong, M., Ferguson, M. A., Misic, B., Burrow, A. L., Leahy, R. M., & Spreng, R. N. (2019). Loneliness and meaning in life are reflected in the intrinsic network architecture of the brain. *Social Cognitive and Affective Neuroscience, 14*(4), 423–433. https://doi.org/10.1093/scan/nsz021

Nersesian, P. V, Han, H.-R., Yenokyan, G., Blumenthal, R. S., Nolan, M. T., Hladek, M. D., & Szanton, S. L. (2018). Loneliness in middle age and biomarkers of systemic inflammation: Findings from midlife in the United States. *Social Science & Medicine (1982), 209*, 174–181. https://linkinghub.elsevier.com/retrieve/pii/S0277953618301667

Nguyen, T. T., Zhang, X., Wu, T. C., Liu, J., Le, C., Tu, X. M., Knight, R., & Jeste, D. V. (2021). Association of loneliness and wisdom with gut microbial diversity and composition: An exploratory study. *Frontiers in Psychiatry, 12* (March), 1–8. https://doi.org/10.3389/fpsyt.2021.648475

Piber, D., Olmstead, R., Cho, J. H. J., Witarama, T., Perez, C., Dietz, N., Seeman, T. E., Breen, E. C., Cole, S. W., & Irwin, M. R. (2019). Inflammaging: Age and systemic, cellular, and nuclear inflammatory biology in older adults. *Journals of Gerontology: Series A, Biological Sciences and Medical Sciences, 74*(11), 1716–1724. https://doi.org/10.1093/gerona/glz130

Puzianowska-Kuźnicka, M., Owczarz, M., Wieczorowska-Tobis, K., Nadrowski, P., Chudek, J., Slusarczyk, P., Skalska, A., Jonas, M., Franek, E., & Mossakowska, M. (2016). Interleukin-6 and C-reactive protein, successful aging, and mortality: The PolSenior study. *Immunity and Ageing, 13*(1). https://doi.org/10.1186/s12979-016-0076-x

Ryff, C. D., Heller, A. S., Schaefer, S. M., van Reekum, C., & Davidson, R. J. (2016). Purposeful engagement, healthy aging, and the brain. *Current Behavioral Neuroscience Reports, 3*(4), 318–327. https://doi.org/10.1007/s40473-016-0096-z

Salvador, A. F., de Lima, K. A. & Kipnis, J. Neuromodulation by the immune system: a focus on cytokines. *Nat Rev Immunol* 21, 526–541 (2021). https://doi.org/10.1038/s41577-021-00508-z

Shiba, K., Kubzansky, L. D., Williams, D. R., VanderWeele, T. J., & Kim, E. S. (2021). Associations between purpose in life and mortality by SES. *American Journal of Preventive Medicine, 61*(2), e53–e61. https://doi.org/10.1016/j.amepre.2021.02.011

Shiovitz-Ezra, S., & Parag, O. (2019). Does loneliness "get under the skin"? Associations of loneliness with subsequent change in inflammatory and metabolic markers. *Aging and Mental Health, 23*(10), 1358–1366. https://doi.org/10.1080/13607863.2018.1488942

Smith, K. J., Gavey, S., Riddell, N. E., Kontari, P., & Victor, C. (2020). The association between loneliness, social isolation and inflammation: A systematic review and meta-analysis. *Neuroscience and Biobehavioral Reviews, 112*, 519–541. https://doi.org/10.1016/j.neubiorev.2020.02.002

Sochocka, M., Donskow-Łysoniewska, K., Diniz, B. S., Kurpas, D., Brzozowska, E., & Leszek, J. (2019). The gut microbiome alterations and inflammation-driven pathogenesis of alzheimer's disease – A critical review. *Molecular Neurobiology, 56*(3), 1841–1851. https://doi.org/10.1007/s12035-018-1188-4

Uchino, B. N. (2006). Social support and health: A review of physiological processes potentially underlying links to disease outcomes. *Journal of*

Behavioral Medicine, 29(4), 377–387. https://doi.org/10.1007/s10865-006-9056-5

Uchino, B. N., Landvatter, J., Zee, K., & Bolger, N. (2020). Social support and antibody responses to vaccination: A meta-analysis. *Annals of Behavioral Medicine, 54*(8), 567–574. https://doi.org/10.1093/abm/kaaa029

Uchino, B. N., Trettevik, R., Kent de Grey, R. G., Cronan, S., Hogan, J., & Baucom, B. R. W. (2018). Social support, social integration, and inflammatory cytokines: A meta-analysis. *Health Psychology, 37*(5), 462–471. https://doi.org/10.1037/hea0000594

Valentini, L., Pinto, A., Bourdel-Marchasson, I., Ostan, R., Brigidi, P., Turroni, S., Hrelia, S., Hrelia, P., Bereswill, S., Fischer, A., Leoncini, E., Malaguti, M., Blanc-Bisson, C., Durrieu, J., Spazzafumo, L., Buccolini, F., Pryen, F., Donini, L. M., Franceschi, C., & Lochs, H. (2015). Impact of personalized diet and probiotic supplementation on inflammation, nutritional parameters and intestinal microbiota – The "RISTOMED project": Randomized controlled trial in healthy older people. *Clinical Nutrition, 34*(4), 593–602. https://doi.org/10.1016/j.clnu.2014.09.023

Verdi, S., Jackson, M. A., Beaumont, M., Bowyer, R. C. E., Bell, J. T., Spector, T. D., & Steves, C. J. (2018). An Investigation into physical frailty as a link between the gut microbiome and cognitive health. *Frontiers in Aging Neuroscience, 10*. https://doi.org/10.3389/fnagi.2018.00398

Vogt, N. M., Kerby, R. L., Dill-McFarland, K. A., Harding, S. J., Merluzzi, A. P., Johnson, S. C., Carlsson, C. M., Asthana, S., Zetterberg, H., Blennow, K., Bendlin, B. B., & Rey, F. E. (2017). Gut microbiome alterations in Alzheimer's disease. *Scientific Reports, 7*(1), 1–11. https://doi.org/10.1038/s41598-017-13601-y

Wyss-Coray, T., & Rogers, J. (2012). Inflammation in Alzheimer disease – A brief review of the basic science and clinical literature. *Cold Spring Harbor Perspectives in Medicine, 2*(1), a006346–a006346. https://doi.org/10.1101/cshperspect.a006346

Yu, L., Boyle, P. A., Wilson, R. S., Levine, S. R., Schneider, J. A., & Bennett, D. A. (2015). Purpose in life and cerebral infarcts in community-dwelling older people. *Stroke, 46*(4), 1071–1076. https://doi.org/10.1161/STROKEAHA.114.008010

CHAPTER 8

Loneliness and Psychological Health in Late Life
Hairin Kim and Jeanyung Chey

8.1 Loneliness in Late Life

8.1.1 Definition of Loneliness

Loneliness is a distressing emotion accompanied by the perception that actual social relationships fail to satisfy social needs (S. Cacioppo et al., 2015). Loneliness can be developed when individuals feel they have insufficient social ties because they have fewer relationships than they need or the quality of their relationships is inadequate (Victor et al., 2018). In contemporary society, loneliness is drawing more attention because social isolation has become more prevalent and severe than in the past. Holt-Lunstad et al. (2015) reported that loneliness increases the likelihood of mortality by 1.26 times when other risk factors for health are considered. As a result, loneliness has been compared to well-known risk factors for death, such as drinking and smoking. Even if loneliness has gained prominence in recent years, humanity has been aware of it for a very long time. The renowned Maslow (1943) stated that one of the fundamental human desires is a sense of belonging. He argued that when the urge to connect with others is not realized, humans have developed strategies to deal with the situation through various physical reactions, including negative emotions.

Loneliness needs to be distinguished from solitude since solitude is a psychological detachment from society for the purpose of cultivating the inner world of the self (Hollenhorst & Jones, 2001). Throughout history, a number of people, including philosophers, spiritual leaders, and artists, have demonstrated the benefits of solitude. For instance, many writers crave solitude and emphasize its importance in their creative process (Long & Averill, 2003). While loneliness refers to the negative emotions associated with isolation, solitude stresses the psychological and spiritual advantages of time alone (Long & Averill, 2003; Peplau & Perlman, 1982). This chapter will differentiate between loneliness and solitude and focus on the former.

8.1.2 Prevalence of Loneliness in Late Life

Prevalence statistics indicate that nearly one in every three older adults in the United States reports loneliness (Perissinotto et al., 2012). Older adults aged 80 years and older appear to have comparatively high rates of loneliness – by some estimates, 40–50% report being frequently lonely (Dykstra, 2009). In South Korea, 37% of the people aged 50 years or more reported that they do not have relatives or friends they can count on in times of need (OECD, 2020). Although lack of social support is different from loneliness, it is highly correlated (Chen & Feeley, 2014). With such a high incidence, loneliness in old age is a significant societal concern, but the apparent association between loneliness and age is generally unknown. It has been argued that loneliness in old age is also related to changes in the older adults' life. Younger adults experience new things and extend their social networks, meeting new people. However, social interactions steadily deteriorate in old age due to retirement, death of loved ones, and physical infirmities. Accordingly, individuals become more vulnerable to social isolation and loneliness as they age (Olsen et al., 1991; Penninx et al., 1997; Seeman, 2000; Shiovitz-Ezra & Ayalon, 2010; Thurston & Kubzansky, 2009).

The socio-emotional selectivity theory highlights how people pay less attention to unfavorable aspects late in life (Charles & Carstensen, 2010). It has been hypothesized that older adults are more adept at emotional regulation in social circumstances and report less interpersonal tension and conflict than younger adults (Birditt & Fingerman, 2005). Additionally, they are better at resolving issues that arise in interpersonal relationships than young adults. Experiments examining the view that older adults pay less attention to negative stimuli substantiated this hypothesis (Charles et al., 2003). Carstensen and Mikels (2005) named this phenomenon the *positivity effect*. The characteristics of older adults paying less attention to negative features explain why older adults report less stress in unpleasant social environments than younger adults. Despite the virtues of positivity in later life, older adults' risk factors leading to loneliness have remained and, at times, involve neglecting emotional pain, which could exacerbate loneliness in late life.

8.2 Risk Factors for Loneliness

Intuitively, extrinsic circumstances such as marital status and number of friends influence loneliness. However, there is substantial evidence of a genetic predisposition toward loneliness (Clyde, 2018). Study findings have implied that loneliness could be induced by situations (i.e., state loneliness) or dispositional conditions (i.e., trait loneliness), and these two types of loneliness appear to be different (Cairns et al., 1995). Researchers have hypothesized that loneliness is a state in which an individual has a discrepancy between desired and actual social relationships, but it is also a component of heritable traits (Hector-Taylor & Adams, 1996). Based on this idea, we will review the risk factors for loneliness identified in previous studies in the framework of trait and state loneliness.

8.2.1 Genetic Risk and Loneliness

Genome-wide studies have elucidated the genetic contribution to loneliness. Genes that have been revealed to be associated with loneliness and its possible mechanism were introduced in Chapter 4. Therefore, we will briefly review the representative studies in this chapter. Researchers conducted a meta-analysis of loneliness, including 511,280 subjects in the UK Biobank study, and discovered 19 meaningful genetic variants from 16 loci and 58 significantly associated genes (Abdellaoui et al., 2019). In another study involving 452,302 individuals from the UK Biobank, researchers identified 15 genomic loci for loneliness. They established a possible causal association between adiposity and increased susceptibility to loneliness and depressive symptoms. They also found substantial enrichment for genes expressed in brain regions that control emotional expression and behavior, such as the amygdala (Day et al., 2018).

Meanwhile, the Health and Retirement Study (HRS) investigation reported little relation with loneliness at genome-wide significance when they performed a genome-wide association analysis. However, they identified meaningful genetic correlations between loneliness, neuroticism, and depressive symptoms. As a result, they suggested that loneliness is a modestly heritable trait with a polygenic architecture (Gao et al., 2017).

8.2.2 Social Disconnection and Loneliness

Whereas genetic variation is a critical feature forming trait loneliness, social disconnection contributes to state loneliness. The nationally representative German study (n = 16,132) illustrated an age difference in loneliness from late adolescence to the oldest old age (Luhmann & Hawkley, 2016). The age distribution of loneliness revealed a complex nonlinear trajectory, with higher levels among young adults and older adults but lower in middle age.

While this study established that loneliness rises with age, it explored other variables affecting the relationship between age and loneliness by statistically adjusting for other variables that influence loneliness. Researchers considered gender, socioeconomic level, work status, living arrangement, relationship status, functional limitations, social engagement, and contact frequency as covariates when assessing the connection between age and loneliness. In young and early middle-aged adults, there was minimal change in the relationship between age and loneliness with the addition of a covariate. In other words, covariates explained a minor proportion of loneliness in those age populations. However, research on people aged over 80 has demonstrated that the covariate defines a sizable portion of loneliness. Adjusting for functional restraints decreased the average level of loneliness among older adults from about age 80. Hence, a higher prevalence of functional impairments in this age group partly explains why the oldest people experience such high degrees of loneliness. Among other factors, higher income was related to considerably reduced levels of loneliness across all categories. This connection was particularly remarkable among middle-aged people compared to young adults and older individuals for both comparisons. Work status did not explain average differences in loneliness among older adults, partially due to this age group's low employment rate.

Individuals develop social relationships throughout their lives, and constant reorganizations maintain social relations. Old age frequently involves a natural decline in social interactions due to children's independence, retirement, and bereavement rather than deliberate social connection building. Even though these are frequent experiences in late life, they make older individuals vulnerable to social isolation and lead to the loss of crucial social roles (Ferraro, 1984). Besides, multiple health problems inhibit active social participation as people age, restricting the opportunity to maintain and create relationships (Li & Ferraro, 2006; Thoits & Hewitt, 2001), which is consistent with the findings from the German national study that highlighted the importance of functional limitations in late-life loneliness (Luhmann & Hawkley, 2016). Additionally, Newmyer et al. (2020) reviewed several harmonized studies on aging adults around the world. They found that living alone and being without a spouse, especially in late life, were highly associated with increased degrees of loneliness across 31 countries. It is noteworthy that a very common experience of losing social contacts for various reasons in late life would lead to loneliness in older adults.

Social connectedness is categorized across different levels, from proximal to distal levels. Measures for proximal social connectedness include individual-level social relationships, such as the perceived number of friends or closeness around an individual. However, the measures for distal social connectedness focus on global characteristics of individuals' society, such as the cohesiveness of their community or the social network position of individuals within their community. The proximal and distal social characteristics capture different aspects of social isolation. For instance, the collective aspect of loneliness, which is associated with group identification and cohesion, can be distinguished from the relational part of loneliness, characterized by a feeling of familiarity, closeness, and support (Hawkley et al., 2005).

Numerous studies that have found associations between social disconnectedness and loneliness have concentrated on the proximal features of social networks. Several studies have examined the distal aspects of social networks, most existing approaches involving rating emotions of collective connectedness ("I feel a sense of belonging to a group of friends" and "I truly feel a sense of belonging to this area") or assessing the number of social relationships using respondent-centered methods due to practical limitations in examining the outermost layer of social disconnection (Russell et al., 1980). The operational definition and objective measurement of such disconnectedness have been a challenging issue.

Such methodological difficulties can be partly resolved by mapping the complete social connections and utilizing social network analysis (SNA) (Burt et al., 2013; Smith & Christakis, 2008). While individual-level measures indicate one's perception of proximal social connectedness, SNA provides measures of distal social connection from a globally mapped social network by evaluating one's social network position or location in a broader community. In contrast to respondent-centered information about social relationships, the global network method evaluates the structural properties of social connectedness. It is less reliant on endogenous personal factors while reflecting one's distal or objective social network characteristics.

Among various global social network features, two major indicators (brokerage and embeddedness) depict whether an individual benefits from connecting with diverse network members or staying within a cohesive network group, respectively. These structural aspects of social networks also represent the outermost layer of one's social network that can contribute to an individual's loneliness. The literature suggests that external social events influence loneliness via proximal determinants, with significant changes in social roles crucially related to late-life loneliness (Hawkley et al., 2008). The fact that older adults' social networks eventually go

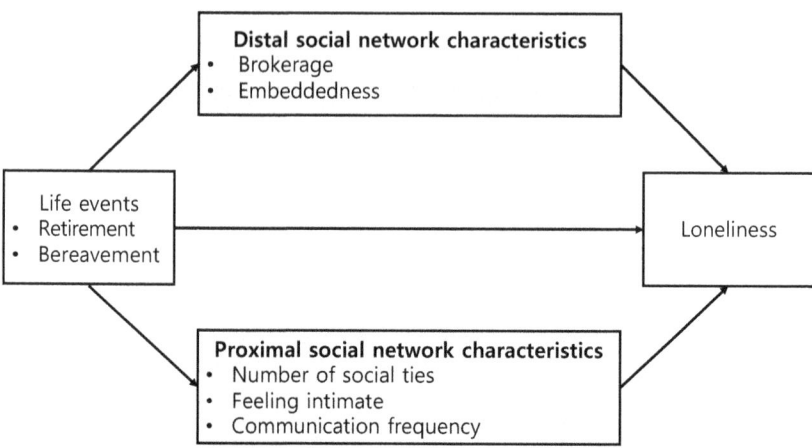

Figure 8.1 Path model of the proximal and distal characteristics of the social network

through numerous transitions in size and composition raises concerns about their mental and physical health (Wrzus et al., 2013). Thus, late-life situational factors appear to influence various dimensions of older individuals' social networks (Antonucci et al., 2014). It is mostly unknown how external aspects of life events, such as marital status changes and retirement, reorganize social networks' size, strength, and structural properties.

A study examining the Korean Social Life, Health, and Aging Project (KSHAP) data (n = 1,724) evaluated how the proximal and distal aspects of social networks predicted loneliness using a hierarchical linear regression model (Kim et al., 2021). As Figure 8.1 describes, the cross-sectional mediation analysis also investigated whether the major loss of social roles (marital and working status) affects perceived loneliness through social networks' proximal and distal characteristics. The study found that the distal aspects (i.e., brokerage and embeddedness) of social networks in addition to the proximal measures (i.e., subjective number of connections) explained the frequency of loneliness. Moreover, the distal characteristic of social networks mediated the relationship between loss of late-life social roles (marital and working status) and loneliness. The findings imply that the proximal and distal aspects of social networks are social predictors of late-life loneliness. They demonstrate that bridging and cohesive positions within community networks may be critical for psychosocial transition following marital and work status changes.

In addition to social connectedness, researchers noticed the importance of place of residence as a socially constructed phenomenon in late-life loneliness. According to the literature, older adults living in long-term care facilities have higher rates of loneliness than community-dwelling older adults because they have a greater number of chronic health conditions and limited ability to engage in daily activities (Pinquart & Sörensen, 2000; Prieto-Flores et al., 2011). However, it has been revealed that a sense of belonging also affects loneliness among older adults living across different residential environments. Prieto-Flores and colleagues found that residential satisfaction was negatively associated with loneliness in both community and residential care facilities. Also, they presented that sense of belonging acted as a mediating factor in this relationship. They concluded that residential satisfaction and a sense of belonging appeared to protect against loneliness.

8.2.3 *Gender Difference in Loneliness*

Gender differences also exist regarding the adverse effects of loneliness at a later age. It has been suggested that men who are socially isolated and feel lonely are more susceptible to disease and death than women (House et al., 1988). In addition, a recent study suggests that white matter lesion may be a possible neurological mechanism underlying loneliness-related memory dysfunction in late life, and that the influence of loneliness on memory dysfunction through white matter hyperintensities was stronger for men than women (Park, Youm, & Chey, The impact of loneliness and white matter hyperintensities on memory function in older adults: Moderating effects of gender. Unpublished manuscript). Indeed, men and women receive social support through different types of social interactions and may experience different discomfort within the same social context. For instance, women get diverse social support through their multifaceted and dense networks. As a result of social isolation, when individuals face a social loss, they can substitute other connections for the lost connection or cope with caregiving from other ties (Yang et al., 2013). Meanwhile, men are likely to seek social contact in public spaces that tend to provide less social support than women (Zebhauser et al., 2014).

Older women report more loneliness than men (Beal, 2006). However, due to women's longer life expectancy, characteristics related to loneliness, such as older age and a higher risk of being widowed, are all more prevalent in women, which can confound the findings that loneliness is more common in women (Luanaigh & Lawlor, 2008). Furthermore, it should be acknowledged that social connections may not function the same way for men and women. For example, women whose network members have excessive needs are less likely to obtain social support through social relationships since they frequently have a more challenging time responding to those needs (Kawachi & Berkman, 2001). In addition, it should be noted that these social interactions may operate as a psychological burden rather than a source of social support for women in some social contexts (Kim et al., 2019; Shumaker & Hill, 1991; Umberson, 1992).

8.2.4 Socioeconomic Status and Loneliness

Socioeconomic status has been identified as important in individual differences in loneliness (Pinquart & Sörensen, 2000). Sufficient financial resources are inextricably linked to people's possibilities to participate in social activities connected to active social engagement (Hawkley et al., 2008). Thus, it has been considered that financial difficulties in old age contribute to loneliness and that lower income is significantly associated with more severe loneliness (Cohen-Mansfield et al., 2016; Pinquart & Sörensen, 2000). Assuming that financial resources affect loneliness, one of the most critical aspects to examine is whether economic resources influence loneliness by mediating more active social activities or health conditions. According to a cross-sectional study, however, economic levels were correlated with loneliness even though the effects of social network size, health, and life events were controlled (Cohen-Mansfield et al., 2009; Cohen-Mansfield & Parpura-Gill, 2007). Therefore, the underlying mechanisms and pathways are still unclear. Further research should be conducted to elucidate the process involved in the relationship between socioeconomic status and loneliness (Macdonald et al., 2018; Szabo et al., 2019).

8.3 Loneliness and Late-Life Psychological Health

8.3.1 Loneliness and Stress Response

Humans perceive isolation as a threatening social situation (S. Cacioppo et al., 2015). Additionally, isolation and dissatisfaction with one's social relationships can be a substantial source of stress. Activation of the hypothalamic–pituitary–adrenal axis (HPA axis) has been recognized as the most common physiological response to threats. When the brain perceives the threat, the HPA axis is activated, directly affecting the body, behavior, and health (Hostinar, 2015; McEwen & Gianaros, 2011), for example, by stimulating the release of hormones such as cortisol, which increases blood pressure and heart rate and prepares our bodies to respond to stress. While an acute stress response is necessary for human survival, chronic activation of the HPA axis results in an excessive inflammatory reaction, such as an elevated C-reactive protein level, an indicator of coronary artery disease (Hänsel et al., 2010).

Researchers investigating stress have categorized loneliness into two types: transient and chronic (Shiovitz-Ezra & Ayalon, 2010). Transient loneliness occurs after experiencing stressful life events such as parting from friends due to retirement or losing one's spouse or family members. Even if transient loneliness entails emotional and social difficulties, the individual who experiences it typically overcomes these obstacles and recovers. On the other hand, chronic loneliness is more stable and induces chronic immunological dysfunction (Smith & Vale, 2006). Based on the distinction between transient and chronic loneliness, Shiovitz-Ezra and Ayalon (2010) found that chronic loneliness slightly increased mortality risk in people over 50. Moreover, the chronicity of loneliness played a role in the incidence of psychiatric disorders such as late-life major depression. For instance, people suffering chronic loneliness were at markedly higher risk of presenting major depression (odds ratio = 6.11; 95% confidence interval = 2.62, 14.22) than people experiencing transient loneliness (odds ratio = 2.22; 95% confidence interval = 1.19, 4.14) (Martín-María et al., 2021).

While both chronic and transient loneliness have been connected to adverse health effects, previous studies highlight that continuous stimulation of the HPA axis promotes overall morbidity and mortality by disrupting brain and body functions in such ways as sleep disorders, decreased metabolism, increased cognitive load, and poor executive functioning (Aisa et al., 2007; Silverman & Sternberg, 2012). An association between loneliness and HPA axis activity has been observed in both young and older adults. In a diary study of young adults, loneliness ratings over one week were associated with higher morning and nighttime salivary cortisol levels, indicating that lonely individuals have a more activated HPA axis than those who did not report loneliness (Pressman et al., 2005). In a healthy sample of middle-aged adults (47–59 years), loneliness was related to greater cortisol response to awakening (Steptoe et al., 2004). Moreover, in the participants of 50- to 68-year-olds, loneliness as reported in end-of-day diaries predicted a higher cortisol response upon awakening each subsequent day (Adam et al., 2006). Although the HPA regulation impairment is harmful to both young and older adults, HPA regulation impairments may accelerate the age-related decline in physiological resilience by breaking down the typical feedback system in which increases in cortisol levels inhibit the production of further cortisol.

8.3.2 Loneliness and Dementia

Increasing evidence supports the role of inflammation in the development of dementia (Simone & Tan, 2011). Lonely older adults had a higher amyloid burden in their brains (associated with dementia) than non-lonely older adults. A cross-sectional study of 79 community-dwelling older adults revealed that a considerably greater amyloid load was associated with more frequent feelings of isolation, independent of sociodemographic factors, objective measures of a social network, or depressive or anxiety symptoms (Donovan et al., 2016). Moreover, in a study of 117 cognitively normal older adults, researchers discovered that higher tau pathology in the right entorhinal cortex was associated with greater loneliness after adjusting for age, gender, and apolipoprotein e (APOe), a genetic marker connected with an increased risk of Alzheimer's disease. This association remained significant even after further adjustment for socioeconomic status, social network, depression and anxiety scores, and memory performance (d'Oleire Uquillas et al., 2018).

Alzheimer's disease (AD) is one of the most common diseases to elicit dementia. It is a progressive neurodegenerative illness characterized by cognitive impairment and the presence of amyloid plaques and neurofibrillary tangles. In the last decade, the involvement of a prolonged immunological response in the brain has been postulated and examined as a possible etiological pathogenesis of AD (Kinney et al., 2018). The most representative mechanism by which loneliness impairs health is increased inflammatory reactions mediated by the HPA axis. Accordingly, constant loneliness in older persons has been hypothesized to influence the development of dementia via immunological dysfunction. Also, numerous studies have established a consistent association between loneliness and cognitive deficiencies in several domains, including memory, attention, executive function, and an increased risk of dementia (Donovan et al., 2017; Hawkley & Cacioppo, 2010; Tilvis et al., 2004).

The community-based cognitive aging study has disclosed an association between loneliness and dementia in older people. The English Longitudinal Study of Ageing (ELSA) examined 6,677 dementia-free individuals at baseline, and the research group investigated the relationship between loneliness and dementia incidents over 6.25 years. It was discovered that dementia risk was positively correlated with increased loneliness (hazard ratio 1.40, 95% confidence interval 1.09–1.80, p = 0.008) and inversely associated with several intimate relationships and marriage in multivariable correlations (Rafnsson et al., 2020). Another research group examined the frequency and determinants of loneliness in 1,547 adults with mild to severe dementia using data from the baseline wave of the Improving the Experience of Dementia and Enhancing Active Life (IDEAL) cohort study (Victor et al., 2020). Around 30.2% of dementia patients reported experiencing mild loneliness, while 5.2% reported experiencing severe loneliness. Mild and severe loneliness were both correlated with depressive symptoms. Individuals who lived alone were more likely to experience loneliness than those with a lower quality of life measured by the overall ability for daily living, including physical condition, mood, interpersonal relationship, ability to participate in meaningful activities, and financial situation.

The condition of one's physical health also affects loneliness, as physical infirmity hinders participation in social activities, leaving the older individual vulnerable to social isolation and loneliness. Longitudinal studies have shown that self-rated ill-health and functional limitations predict higher levels of loneliness (Cohen-Mansfield et al., 2009; Dykstra et al., 2005; Jylhä, 2004). In addition to physical health, loneliness is related to various mental health issues in old age. For instance, depressed older adults are more likely to feel lonely. Adam and her colleagues (2006) expected a strong association between loneliness and depression among older persons. According to their observations, loneliness and depressive symptoms work synergistically to impair the well-being of middle-aged and older adults. Additionally, in a five-year longitudinal study conducted in Chicago, older adults demonstrated that loneliness predicted a subsequent increase in depressive symptoms, but not the reverse (J. T. Cacioppo et al., 2010).

8.4 Conclusions

This chapter has reviewed the risk factors for loneliness and its detrimental effects on late-life psychological health. Accumulating studies have revealed that older adults' social relationships gradually decrease due to retirement, the death of loved ones, and physical disabilities (Olsen et al., 1991; Penninx et al., 1997; Seeman, 2000; Shiovitz-Ezra & Ayalon, 2010; Thurston & Kubzansky, 2009). Thus, people in their late life may be more susceptible to social isolation and loneliness.

Multiple risk factors contribute to loneliness, which can be described in terms of trait and state loneliness. While genetic variation acts as a predisposed vulnerability, social isolation or separation is considered a direct trigger of loneliness. It should also be noted that stable aspects of loneliness, such as personality and behavioral pattern (i.e., trait loneliness), and other features of loneliness such as social disconnection (i.e., state loneliness) have a reciprocal relationship. Consequently, we assume that the risk factors we have reviewed are dependent on each other.

Loneliness in older adults is a serious issue in societies with a rapidly aging population, and a growing body of research is exploring the impact of loneliness on older adults' physical and mental health (Deniro, 1995; Hawkley, 2007; Neeleman & Power, 1994; Richman & Sokolove, 1992; Youm et al., 2014).

REFERENCES

Abdellaoui, A., Sanchez-Roige, S., Sealock, J., Treur, J. L., Dennis, J., Fontanillas, P., Elson, S., Nivard, M. G., Ip, H. F., Van Der Zee, M., Baselmans, B. M. L., Hottenga, J. J., Willemsen, G., Mosing, M., Lu, Y., Pedersen, N. L., Denys, D., Amin, N., M Van Duijn, C., Szilagyi, I., ... Boomsma, D. I. (2019). Phenome-wide investigation of health outcomes associated with genetic predisposition to loneliness. *Human Molecular Genetics*, *28*(22), 3853–3865. https://doi.org/10.1093/hmg/ddz219

Adam, E. K., Hawkley, L. C., Kudielka, B. M., & Cacioppo, J. T. (2006). Day-to-day dynamics of experience-cortisol associations in a population-based sample of older adults. *Proceedings of the National Academy of Sciences*, *103*(45), 17058–17063. https://doi.org/10.1073/pnas.0605053103

Aisa, B., Tordera, R., Lasheras, B., Del Río, J., & Ramírez, M. J. (2007). Cognitive impairment associated to HPA axis hyperactivity after maternal separation in rats. *Psychoneuroendocrinology*, *32*(3), 256–266. https://doi.org/10.1016/j.psyneuen.2006.12.013

Antonucci, T. C., Ajrouch, K. J., & Birditt, K. S. (2014). The convoy model: Explaining social relations from a multidisciplinary perspective. *Gerontologist*, *54*(1), 82–92. https://doi.org/10.1093/geront/gnt118

Beal, C. (2006). Loneliness in older women: A review of the literature. *Issues in Mental Health Nursing*, *27*(7), 795–813. https://doi.org/10.1080/01612840600781196

Birditt, K. S., & Fingerman, K. L. (2005). Do we get better at picking our battles? Age group differences in descriptions of behavioral reactions to interpersonal tensions. *Journals of Gerontology: Series B, Psychological Sciences and Social Sciences*, *60*(3), P121–P128. https://doi.org/10.1093/geronb/60.3.P121

Burt, R. S., Kilduff, M., & Tasselli, S. (2013). Social network analysis: Foundations and frontiers on advantage. *Annual Review of Psychology*, *64* (January 2013), 527–547. https://doi.org/10.1146/annurev-psych-113011-143828

Cacioppo, J. T., Hawkley, L. C., & Thisted, R. A. (2010). Perceived social isolation makes me sad: 5-year cross-lagged analyses of loneliness and depressive symptomatology in the Chicago Health, Aging, and Social Relations Study. *Psychology and Aging*, *25*(2), 453–463. https://doi.org/10.1037/a0017216

Cacioppo, S., Grippo, A. J., London, S., Goossens, L., & Cacioppo, J. T. (2015). Loneliness: Clinical Import and Interventions. *Perspectives on Psychological Science*, *10*(2), 238–249. https://doi.org/10.1177/1745691615570616

Cairns, R. B., Leung, M.-C., Buchanan, L., & Cairns, B. D. (1995). Friendships and social networks in childhood and adolescence: Fluidity, reliability, and interrelations. *Child Development*, *66*(5), 1330–1345. https://doi.org/10.2307/1131650

Carstensen, L. L., & Mikels, J. A. (2005). At the intersection of emotion and cognition: Aging and the positivity effect. *Current Directions in Psychological Science*, *14*(3), 117–121.

Charles, S. T., & Carstensen, L. L. (2010). Social and emotional aging. *Annual Review of Psychology*, *61*, 383–409. https://doi.org/10.1146/annurev.psych.093008.100448

Charles, S. T., Mather, M., & Carstensen, L. L. (2003). Aging and emotional memory: The forgettable nature of negative images for older adults. *Journal of Experimental Psychology: General*, *132*(2), 310–324. https://doi.org/10.1037/0096-3445.132.2.310

Chen, Y., & Feeley, T. H. (2014). Social support, social strain, loneliness, and well-being among older adults: An analysis of the Health and Retirement Study. *Journal of Social and Personal Relationships*, *31*(2), 141–161.

Clyde, D. (2018). The genetics of loneliness. *Nature Reviews Genetics*, *19*(9), 532–533. https://doi.org/10.1038/s41576-018-0036-8

Cohen-Mansfield, J., Hazan, H., Lerman, Y., & Shalom, V. (2016). Correlates and predictors of loneliness in older-adults: A review of quantitative results informed by qualitative insights. *International Psychogeriatrics*, *28*(4), 557–576. https://doi.org/10.1017/S1041610215001532

Cohen-Mansfield, J., & Parpura-Gill, A. (2007). Loneliness in older persons: A theoretical model and empirical findings. *International Psychogeriatrics*, *19*(2), 279–294. https://doi.org/10.1017/S1041610206004200

Cohen-Mansfield, J., Shmotkin, D., & Goldberg, S. (2009). Loneliness in old age: Longitudinal changes and their determinants in an Israeli sample. *International Psychogeriatrics*, *21*(6), 1160–1170. https://doi.org/10.1017/S1041610209990974

d'Oleire Uquillas, F., Jacobs, H. I. L., Biddle, K. D., Properzi, M., Hanseeuw, B., Schultz, A. P., Rentz, D. M., Johnson, K. A., Sperling, R. A., & Donovan, N. J. (2018). Regional tau pathology and loneliness in cognitively normal older adults. *Translational Psychiatry*, *8*(1), 282. https://doi.org/10.1038/s41398-018-0345-x

Day, F. R., Ong, K. K., & Perry, J. R. B. (2018). Elucidating the genetic basis of social interaction and isolation. *Nature Communications*, *9*(1), 2457. https://doi.org/10.1038/s41467-018-04930-1

Deniro, D. A. (1995). Perceived alienation in individuals with residual-type schizophrenia. *Issues in Mental Health Nursing*, *16*(3), 185–200.

Donovan, N. J., Okereke, O. I., Vannini, P., Amariglio, R. E., Rentz, D. M., Marshall, G. A., Johnson, K. A., & Sperling, R. A. (2016). Association of higher cortical amyloid burden with loneliness in cognitively normal older adults. *JAMA Psychiatry*, *73*(12), 1230–1237. https://doi.org/10.1001/jamapsychiatry.2016.2657

Donovan, N. J., Wu, Q., Rentz, D. M., Sperling, R. A., Marshall, G. A., & Glymour, M. M. (2017). Loneliness, depression and cognitive function in older US adults. *International Journal of Geriatric Psychiatry*, *32*(5), 564–573. https://doi.org/10.1002/gps.4495

Dykstra, P. A. (2009). Older adult loneliness: Myths and realities. *European Journal of Ageing*, *6*(2), 91–100. https://doi.org/10.1007/s10433-009-0110-3

Dykstra, P. A., Van Tilburg, T. G., & Gierveld, J. D. J. (2005). Changes in older adult loneliness: Results from a seven-year longitudinal study. *Research on Aging*, *27*(6), 725–747. https://doi.org/10.1177/0164027505279712

Ferraro, K. F. (1984). Widowhood and Social Participation in Later Life: Isolation or Compensation? *Research on Aging*, *6*(4), 451–468. https://doi.org/10.1177/0164027584006004001

Gao, J., Davis, L. K., Hart, A. B., Sanchez-Roige, S., Han, L., Cacioppo, J. T., & Palmer, A. A. (2017). Genome-wide association study of loneliness demonstrates a role for common variation. *Neuropsychopharmacology*, *42*, 811–821. https://doi.org/10.1038/npp.2016.197

Hänsel, A., Hong, S., Cámara, R. J. A., & von Känel, R. (2010). Inflammation as a psychophysiological biomarker in chronic psychosocial stress. *Neuroscience and Biobehavioral Reviews*, *35*(1), 115–121. https://doi.org/10.1016/j.neubiorev.2009.12.012

Hawkley, L. C. (2007). Aging and loneliness: Downhill quickly? *Current Directions in Psychological Science*, *16*(4), 187–191. https://doi.org/10.1111/j.1467-8721.2007.00501.x

Hawkley, L. C., Browne, M. W., & Cacioppo, J. T. (2005). How can I connect with thee? Let me count the ways. *Psychological Science*, *16*(10), 798–804.

Hawkley, L. C., & Cacioppo, J. T. (2010). Loneliness matters: A theoretical and empirical review of consequences and mechanisms. *Annals of Behavioral Medicine*, *40*(2), 218–227. https://doi.org/10.1007/s12160-010-9210-8

Hawkley, L. C., Hughes, M. E., Waite, L. J., Masi, C. M., Thisted, R. A., & Cacioppo, J. T. (2008). From social structural factors to perceptions of relationship quality and loneliness: The Chicago Health, Aging, and Social Relations Study. *The Journals of Gerontology. Series B, Psychological Sciences and Social Sciences*, *63*(6), S375–S384. https://doi.org/10.1093/geronb/63.6.S375

Hector-Taylor, L., & Adams, P. (1996). State versus trait loneliness in elderly New Zealanders. *Psychological Reports*, *78*(3_suppl), 1329–1330. https://doi.org/10.2466/pr0.1996.78.3c.1329

Hollenhorst, S. J., & Jones, C. D. (2001). Wilderness solitude: Beyond the social-spatial perspective. In W. A. Freimund, D. N. Cole, comps. *Visitor Use*

Density and Wilderness Experience: Proceedings 13 June 2000, Missoula, MT. Proceedings RMRS-P-20, Ogden, UT. US Department of Agriculture, Forest Service, Rocky Mountain Research Station, 20, 56–61.

Holt-Lunstad, J., Smith, T. B., Baker, M., Harris, T., & Stephenson, D. (2015). Loneliness and social isolation as risk factors for mortality. *Perspectives on Psychological Science*, *10*(2), 227–237. https://doi.org/10.1177/1745691614568352

Hostinar, C. E. (2015). Recent developments in the study of social relationships, stress responses, and physical health. *Current Opinion in Psychology*, *5*, 90–95. https://doi.org/10.1016/j.copsyc.2015.05.004

House, J. S., Landis, K. R., & Umberson, D. (1988). Social relationships and health. *Science*, *241*(4865), 540–545.

Jylhä, M. (2004). Old age and loneliness: Cross-sectional and longitudinal analyses in the Tampere longitudinal study on aging. *Canadian Journal on Aging/La Revue Canadienne Du Vieillissement*, *23*(2), 157–168. https://doi.org/10.1353/cja.2004.0023

Kawachi, I., & Berkman, L. F. (2001). Social ties and mental health. *Journal of Urban Health*, *78*(3), 458–467. https://doi.org/10.1093/jurban/78.3.458

Kim, H., Kwak, S., Kim, J., Youm, Y., & Chey, J. (2019). Social network position moderates the relationship between late-life depressive symptoms and memory differently in men and women. *Scientific Reports*, *9*(1), 1–10. https://doi.org/10.1038/s41598-019-42388-3

Kim, H., Kwak, S., Youm, Y., & Chey, J. (2021). Social network characteristics predict loneliness in older adults. *Gerontology*, *68*(3), 309–320. https://doi.org/10.1159/000516226

Kinney, J. W., Bemiller, S. M., Murtishaw, A. S., Leisgang, A. M., Salazar, A. M., & Lamb, B. T. (2018). Inflammation as a central mechanism in Alzheimer's disease. *Alzheimer's and Dementia: Translational Research and Clinical Interventions*, *4*(1), 575–590. https://doi.org/10.1016/j.trci.2018.06.014

Li, Y., & Ferraro, K. F. (2006). Volunteering in middle and later life: Is health a benefit, barrier or both? *Social Forces*, *85*(1), 497–519. https://doi.org/10.1353/sof.2006.0132

Long, C. R., & Averill, J. R. (2003). Solitude: An exploration of benefits of being alone. *Journal for the Theory of Social Behaviour*, *33*(1), 21–44. https://doi.org/10.1111/1468-5914.00204

Luanaigh, C. Ó., & Lawlor, B. A. (2008). Loneliness and the health of older people. *International Journal of Geriatric Psychiatry*, *23*(12), 1213–1221. https://doi.org/10.1002/gps.2054

Luhmann, M., & Hawkley, L. C. (2016). Age differences in loneliness from late adolescence to oldest old age. *Developmental Psychology*, *52*(6), 943–959. https://doi.org/10.1037/dev0000117

Macdonald, S. J., Nixon, J., & Deacon, L. (2018). "Loneliness in the city": Examining socio-economics, loneliness and poor health in the North East of England. *Public Health*, *165*, 88–94. https://doi.org/10.1016/j.puhe.2018.09.003

Martín-María, N., Caballero, F. F., Lara, E., Domènech-Abella, J., Haro, J. M., Olaya, B., Ayuso-Mateos, J. L., & Miret, M. (2021). Effects of transient and chronic loneliness on major depression in older adults: A longitudinal study. *International Journal of Geriatric Psychiatry*, *36*(1), 76–85. https://doi.org/10.1002/gps.5397

Maslow, A. H. (1943). A theory of human motivation. *Psychological Review*, *50*(4), 370.

McEwen, B. S., & Gianaros, P. J. (2011). Stress- and allostasis-induced brain plasticity. *Annual Review of Medicine*, *62*(1), 431–445. https://doi.org/10.1146/annurev-med-052209-100430

Neeleman, J., & Power, M. J. (1994). Social support and depression in three groups of psychiatric patients and a group of medical controls. *Social Psychiatry and Psychiatric Epidemiology*, *29*(1), 46–51. https://doi.org/10.1007/BF00796448

Newmyer, L., Verdery, A. M., Margolis, R., & Pessin, L. (2020). Measuring older adult loneliness across countries. *The Journals of Gerontology: Series B*, *76*(7), 1408–1414. https://doi.org/10.1093/geronb/gbaa109

OECD (2020), Social Connections. In *How's Life? 2020: Measuring Well-Being*, Paris: OECD Publishing. https://doi.org/10.1787/b2090ea8-en

Olsen, R. B., Olsen, J., Gunner-Svensson, F., & Waldstrøm, B. (1991). Social networks and longevity. A 14 year follow-up study among elderly in Denmark. *Social Science & Medicine*, *33*(10), 1189–1195.

Penninx, B. W. J. H., Van Tilburg, T., Kriegsman, D. M. W., Deeg, D. J. H., Boeke, A. J. P., & Van Eijk, J. T. M. (1997). Effects of social support and personal coping resources on mortality in older age: The Longitudinal Aging Study Amsterdam. *American Journal of Epidemiology*, *146*(6), 510–519.

Peplau, L. A., & Perlman, D. (1982). Perspectives on Loneliness. In *Loneliness: A Sourcebook of Current Theory, Research and Therapy*. John Wiley & Sons.

Perissinotto, C. M., Stijacic Cenzer, I., & Covinsky, K. E. (2012). Loneliness in older persons: A predictor of functional decline and death. *Archives of Internal Medicine*, *172*(14):1078–1084. https://doi.org/10.1001/archinternmed.2012.1993

Pinquart, M., & Sörensen, S. (2000). Influences of socioeconomic status, social network, and competence on subjective well-being in later life: A meta-analysis. *Psychology and Aging*, *15*(2), 187–224. https://doi.org/10.1037/0882-7974.15.2.187

Pressman, S. D., Cohen, S., Miller, G. E., Barkin, A., Rabin, B. S., & Treanor, J. J. (2005). Loneliness, social network size, and immune response to influenza vaccination in college freshmen. *Health Psychology*, *24*(3), 297–306. https://doi.org/10.1037/0278-6133.24.3.297

Rafnsson, S. B., Orrell, M., D'Orsi, E., Hogervorst, E., & Steptoe, A. (2020). Loneliness, social integration, and incident dementia over 6 years: Prospective findings from the English Longitudinal Study of Ageing. *Journals of Gerontology: Series B, Psychological Sciences and Social Sciences*, *75*(1), 114–124. https://doi.org/10.1093/geronb/gbx087

Richman, N. E., & Sokolove, R. L. (1992). The experience of aloneness, object representation, and evocative memory in borderline and neurotic patients. *Psychoanalytic Psychology, 9*(1), 77.

Prieto-Flores, M. E., Fernandez-Mayoralas, G., Forjaz, M. J., Rojo-Perez, F., & Martinez-Martin, P. (2011). Residential satisfaction, sense of belonging and loneliness among older adults living in the community and in care facilities. *Health & Place, 17*(6), 1183–1190.

Russell, D., Peplau, L. A., & Cutrona, C. E. (1980). The revised UCLA Loneliness Scale: Concurrent and Discriminant validity evidence. *Journal of Personality and Social Psychology, 39*(3), 472–480. https://doi.org/10.1037//0022-3514.39.3.472

Seeman, T. E. (2000). Health promoting effects of friends and family on health outcomes in older adults. *American Journal of Health Promotion, 14*(6), 362–370.

Shiovitz-Ezra, S., & Ayalon, L. (2010). Situational versus chronic loneliness as risk factors for all-cause mortality. *International Psychogeriatrics, 22*(3), 455–462. https://doi.org/10.1017/S1041610209991426

Shumaker, S. A., & Hill, D. R. (1991). Gender differences in social support and physical health. *Health Psychology, 10*(2), 102–111. https://doi.org/10.1037/0278-6133.10.2.102

Silverman, M. N., & Sternberg, E. M. (2012). Glucocorticoid regulation of inflammation and its functional correlates: From HPA axis to glucocorticoid receptor dysfunction. *Annals of the New York Academy of Sciences, 1261*(1), 55–63. https://doi.org/10.1111/j.1749-6632.2012.06633.x

Simone, M. J., & Tan, Z. S. (2011). The role of inflammation in the pathogenesis of delirium and dementia in older adults: A review. *CNS Neuroscience and Therapeutics, 17*(5), 506–513. https://doi.org/10.1111/j.1755-5949.2010.00173.x

Smith, K. P., & Christakis, N. A. (2008). Social networks and health. *Annual Review of Sociology, 34*, 405–429. http://dx.doi.org/10.1146/annurev.soc.34.040507.134601

Smith, S. M., & Vale, W. W. (2006). The role of the hypothalamic-pituitary-adrenal axis in neuroendocrine responses to stress. *Dialogues in Clinical Neuroscience, 8*(4), 383–395. https://doi.org/10.31887/dcns.2006.8.4/ssmith

Steptoe, A., Owen, N., Kunz-Ebrecht, S. R., & Brydon, L. (2004). Loneliness and neuroendocrine, cardiovascular, and inflammatory stress responses in middle-aged men and women. *Psychoneuroendocrinology, 29*(5), 593–611. https://doi.org/10.1016/S0306-4530(03)00086-6

Szabo, A., Allen, J., Alpass, F., & Stephens, C. (2019). Loneliness, socioeconomic status and quality of life in old age: The moderating role of housing tenure. *Ageing and Society, 39*(5), 998–1021. https://doi.org/10.1017/S0144686X17001362

Thoits, P. A., & Hewitt, L. N. (2001). Volunteer work and well-being. *Journal of Health and Social Behavior, 42*(2), 115–131. https://doi.org/10.2307/3090173

Thurston, R. C., & Kubzansky, L. D. (2009). Women, loneliness, and incident coronary heart disease. *Psychosomatic Medicine*, *71*(8), 836–842. https://doi.org/10.1097/PSY.0b013e3181b40efc

Tilvis, R. S., Ka, M. H., Jolkkonen, J., Valvanne, J., Pitkala, K. H., & Strandberg, T. E. (2004). Predictors of cognitive decline and mortality of aged people over a 10-year period. *The Journals of Gerontology. Series A, Biological Sciences and Medical Sciences*, *59*(3), 268–274.

Umberson, D. (1992). Gender, marital status and the social control of health behavior. *Social Science and Medicine*, *34*(8), 907–917. https://doi.org/10.1016/0277-9536(92)90259-S

Victor, C., Mansfield, L., Kay, T., Daykim, N., Lane, J., Duffy, L. G., Tomlinsom, A., & Meads, C. (2018). *An Overview of Reviews: The Effectiveness of Interventions to Address Loneliness at All Stages of the Life-Course*. What Works Centre for Wellbeing.

Victor, C. R., Rippon, I., Nelis, S. M., Martyr, A., Litherland, R., Pickett, J., Hart, N., Henley, J., Matthews, F., & Clare, L. (2020). Prevalence and determinants of loneliness in people living with dementia: Findings from the IDEAL programme. *International Journal of Geriatric Psychiatry*, *35*(8), 851–858. https://doi.org/10.1002/gps.5305

Wrzus, C., Hänel, M., Wagner, J., & Neyer, F. J. (2013). Social network changes and life events across the life span: A meta-analysis. *Psychological Bulletin*, *139*(1), 53–80. https://doi.org/10.1037/a0028601

Yang, Y. C., McClintock, M. K., Kozloski, M., & Li, T. (2013). Social Isolation and adult mortality: The role of chronic inflammation and sex differences. *Journal of Health and Social Behavior*, *54*(2), 183–203. https://doi.org/10.1177/0022146513485244

Youm, Y., Laumann, E. O., Ferraro, K. F., Waite, L. J., Kim, H. C., Park, Y.-R., Chu, S. H., Joo, W.-T., & Lee, J. A. (2014). Social network properties and self-rated health in later life: Comparisons from the Korean social life, health, and aging project and the national social life, health and aging project. *BMC Geriatrics*, *14*(102), 1–15. https://doi.org/10.1186/1471-2318-14-102

Zebhauser, A., Baumert, J., Häfner, S., Lacruz, M. E., Emeny, R. T., Döring, A., & Grill, E. (2014). How much does it hurt to be lonely? Mental and physical differences between older men and women in the KORA-Age Study. *Geriatric Psychiatry*, *29*(3), 245–252. https://doi.org/10.1002/gps.3998

PART III

An Individual's Cognitive Aging with Others: Key Findings, Issues, and Implications

CHAPTER 9

Social Relationships and Cognitive Function in Older Adults

Hoyoung Kim

9.1 Introduction

As the human lifespan increases and the duration of late life extends, there is a growing interest in prolonging the health span and maintaining or enhancing the quality of life across the lifespan. This interest has led to various efforts to identify the determinants of successful aging. Rowe and Kahn (1987) noted that maintaining physical and cognitive functioning, a disease-free state, and engaging in productive activities are the key components of successful aging. Among these components, cognitive health is essential to maintaining physical health, managing diseases common to late life, and independently maintaining social activities and daily life. Older adults, however, have an increasing risk of developing neurocognitive disorders with age, which could undermine their and their families' quality of life. The Cognitive and Emotional Health Project of the National Institutes of Health has defined cognitive health, especially in late life, as the following (Hendrie et al., 2006):

> not just as the absence of disease, but rather as the development and preservation of the multidimensional cognitive structure that allows the older adult to maintain social connectedness, an ongoing sense of purpose, and the abilities to function independently, to permit functional recovery from illness or injury, and to cope with residual functional deficits. (p. 13)

Despite playing a vital role in determining the quality of life and functional independence in older adults, cognitive health has garnered less attention than physical health and disease prevention in the field of successful aging.

Cognitive decline in old age is typical, but there is substantial individual difference in the rate of decline. Some determinants of cognitive health, including genetic influences, gender, and early life experiences, such as educational opportunity and socioeconomic adversity (Polidori et al., 2010), are difficult, if not impossible, to modify in late life. In contrast, lifestyle factors, such as cognitive stimulation, social engagement, and health behaviors (Anstey et al., 2013), are potentially modifiable, even in late life. Moreover, cognitive functioning is somewhat plastic, even in old age, is responsive to environmental stimulation (Hertzog et al., 2008), and could be enhanced by a protective lifestyle.

This chapter highlights the influence of social relationships on cognitive function in old age. Social relationships are a determinant of healthy aging and have been proposed as a modifiable protective factor against dementia. First, the chapter provides a description of the characteristics of cognitive decline and social relationships in late life. Second, it reviews the evidence of the effects of structural and functional aspects of social relationships on cognitive function. Finally, it elaborates on the factors that mediate or modulate the relationship between social relationships and cognitive function.

9.2 Age-Associated Changes in Cognitive Function and Social Relationships

Studies on cognitive aging have shown that age-associated cognitive changes vary by cognitive domain (Hedden & Gabrieli, 2004; Salthouse, 2010). Hedden and Gabrieli (2004) classified three descriptive patterns of age-associated cognitive changes based on research findings. Lifelong decline areas, where cognitive decline begins in early adulthood and accelerates during old age, include processing speed, working memory, episodic memory, spatial ability, reasoning, and executive function. Late-life decline areas, including short-term memory, vocabulary, and semantic knowledge, are maintained relatively well until very late in life. Lastly, autobiographical memory, implicit memory, and emotional processing belong to areas that seem to remain relatively unchanged throughout life.

Memory decline is the most common complaint among older adults. However, memory is a multifaceted function, and each aspect has a differential vulnerability to cognitive aging (Nyberg et al., 2012). In late life, there is a pronounced decline in working memory (maintaining and manipulating the necessary information to perform a task) (Park et al., 2002) and prospective memory (remembering to perform planned actions at an appropriate time or event) (Henry et al., 2004). The decline in episodic memory for new information or sources of information is also prominent and may be the most noticeable. However, semantic memory (such as lexical and historical knowledge), implicit memory (such as skills and habits), and autobiographical memory are well maintained throughout life (Hedden & Gabrieli, 2004; Nyberg et al., 2012; Park et al., 2002). The executive function and processing speed are also vulnerable to aging (Fisk & Sharp, 2004; Park et al., 2002). Older adults are particularly susceptible to interference due to the decline in inhibitory control (Gazzaley et al., 2005; West & Alain, 2000). They also have difficulties multitasking and adjusting to new environments because of the decline in their set-shifting ability and flexibility (Kray et al., 2002; Wecker et al., 2005). Moreover, the decline in sensation, such as hearing and vision, and slower processing leads to reduced accuracy and agility in coping with environmental demands. Cognitive decline in late life, which may not reach the clinical level of cognitive impairment, causes difficulties in adjusting to new environments and performing the complex activities of daily living. Additionally, age-associated cognitive decline can interfere with social engagement and make it difficult to manage various health-related issues common in old age, such as taking medication, visiting the doctor's office, or following a diet. Thus, cognitive decline may disrupt multiple areas of life and reduce the quality of life among older adults.

Additionally, late life brings changes in social relationships. Older people experience drastic loss and change in social relationships due to children leaving home, retirement, and the death of friends or spouses. The types of social activities that they engage in also change. Studies have shown that social networks become smaller with less frequent contact as people age (Ajrouch et al., 2005; Cornwell et al., 2008). Moreover, the composition of their social networks changes, and the proportion of family members or relatives in the network increases (Cornwell et al., 2008; Pahl & Pevalin, 2005). Older people tend to be more involved in their community compared to younger people. They have more contact with neighbors and participate more in religious activities and volunteering if physical health is maintained (Cornwell et al., 2008).

Age-associated changes in cognitive function and social relationships are a natural part of the aging process. Therefore, an accurate understanding of the interrelationships between the different aspects of age-related changes is essential for identifying the keys to healthy aging. In this chapter, previous studies on the relationship between social relationships and cognitive function in older adults are reviewed to describe the characteristics of social relationships for healthy cognitive aging.

9.3 Two Aspects of Social Relationships and Cognitive Health

Accumulating evidence suggests that social relationships affect cognitive function as well as physical and mental health in older adults. However, since studies define and measure social relationships in various ways, it is difficult to compare the research findings directly to reach a conclusive understanding. To understand the specific mechanisms by which social relationships in late life lead to healthy aging, we need to clarify the terms describing different aspects of social relationships in the literature. Many researchers have classified structure and function as sub-concepts of social relationships (Amieva et al., 2010; Avlund et al., 2004; Kuiper et al., 2016), although there may not be an absolute dichotomy. The structural aspects of social relationships are mostly quantitative features of social networks and social engagement. They are generally studied in terms of the size and diversity of social networks, frequency of social contact, and level of social activity participation. The functional aspects of social relationships are mainly qualitative, that is, they relate to the function of the social network and the purpose of the relationship. Social support, social conflict, loneliness, and satisfaction with social relationships generally represent the functional aspects of social relationships in studies.

However, the structural and functional aspects are not entirely independent of each other. The enriched social network and frequent social engagement can provide more opportunities for positive or negative social exchanges. Some studies on the protective effects of social relationships on cognitive health have focused on social relationships as a source of cognitive stimulation, while others have considered it a protective factor for psychological health. Different aspects of social relationships may affect cognitive function in late life, either independently through different pathways or interactively. The following sections classify social relationships into structure and function to review the empirical evidence on each aspect's influence on cognitive function in older adults.

9.3.1 Structural Aspects of Social Relationships and Cognitive Function

Establishing social relationships with many people, interacting frequently, and participating in various social activities requires cognitive processing to understand a complex social situation and react appropriately. The mental operation underpinning social interaction is called social cognition (Penn et al., 1997), which includes encoding and interpreting social cues, generating and selecting social responses, and enacting social behaviors. Moreover, conversations between people at times require memory, attention, and reasoning abilities. Thus, frequent social interaction with many people and participation in various social activities may offer cognitive stimulation. In general, environments with enriched cognitive stimulation facilitate neural development and contribute to building more cognitive reserve (Hertzog et al., 2008; Scarmeas & Stern, 2003). An enriched environment may increase the efficiency of neural networks and enhance cognitive reserve (see Chapter 5 for more detailed discussion on cognitive reserve). Furthermore, evidence has shown that neural and cognitive plasticity in response to environmental stimulation is retained to some degree, even in old age (Erickson & Kramer, 2009; Nguyen et al., 2019; Park & Bischof, 2013; Rose et al., 2015). An abundance of social relationships, such as large social networks and frequent social engagement in late life, may also enhance cognitive reserve by offering cognitive stimulation, thereby preventing cognitive aging and dementia (Clare et al., 2017).

The Kungsholmen project in Sweden (Fratiglioni et al., 2000) was one of the first studies to explore the relationship between social relationships and cognitive function in old age. The findings of this project have led to many studies on the protective influences of social relationships on cognitive aging and dementia. In this project, Fratiglioni and her colleagues (2000) investigated social relationships as a potential preventive factor for dementia. They assessed the social relationship characteristics, including social network size, frequency of social contact, and satisfaction with the social network, in 1,203 older adults aged 75 and above. They followed up the elderly cohort for three years and examined the incidence of dementia. The results showed that older adults living alone had a 1.5 times higher risk of dementia than those living with others. Another study in the United States (US) also found that a poor social network increased the risk of dementia over a four-year follow-up (Crooks et al., 2008). In the cohort of 2,249 older women without dementia at baseline, a larger social network and daily social contact were associated with a lower risk of dementia, even after adjusting for age, education, depression, and other health conditions. Kuiper et al. (2015) conducted a systematic review and meta-analysis of longitudinal studies on the relationship between social relationships and risk of dementia in the general elderly population that included the two studies mentioned above. The authors found that dementia risk was consistently associated with less frequent social contact but not with a smaller social network size.

Since Fratiglioni et al. (2000) suggested the protective effect of social networks on developing dementia, there have been many studies on the relationship between cognitive function and social relationships in healthy older people, but the conclusions have been inconsistent. Studies that support the beneficial effects of social relationships have reported that a larger social network is associated with better cognitive function and gradual cognitive decline in old age. Zunzunegui et al. (2003) assessed cognitive function and social relationships over four years in community-dwelling people aged 65 and over in Spain. They used social ties and social engagement with children, relatives, and friends to measure social networks. Older adults with more family ties, including children and relatives, showed better cognitive function and slower cognitive decline. This beneficial effect of family ties persisted up to age 80 (Béland et al., 2005). Moreover, having friends was associated with a high cognitive function and maintenance of cognitive function only in women (Béland et al., 2005; Zunzunegui et al., 2003).

Holtzman et al. (2004) investigated the relationship between social networks and cognitive function over twelve years in adults aged 50 and over in the U.S. They measured social network size by the number of family members, relatives, neighbors, and friends and measured general cognitive function using the Mini-Mental State Examination. The results showed that the size and change of social networks affected cognitive function, even after controlling for known factors of cognitive aging in late life, such as demographic variables, mood state, and physical health. In the cross-sectional analysis, a larger social network was associated with higher cognitive function. People with larger social networks at baseline and a lesser decrease in the follow-up period maintained cognitive function longitudinally. A meta-analysis of longitudinal cohort studies (Kuiper et al., 2016) also showed a strong association between smaller social networks and cognitive decline in healthy older adults.

The frequency of social contacts, another quantitative measure of social relationships, also positively affects cognitive function (Seeman et al., 2011; Ybarra et al., 2008) as they protect against dementia incidences (Kuiper et al., 2015). In American cohorts, including young and old adults, people who contacted their relatives, friends, and neighbors more frequently had higher cognitive function (Seeman et al., 2011; Ybarra et al., 2008). Moreover, in longitudinal data, adults with a higher average frequency of social contact across the study's duration and a smaller decrease in that frequency showed better executive function and episodic memory, two key cognitive domains that are vulnerable to cognitive aging, at the ten-year follow-up (Seeman et al., 2011). More recently, Elovainio et al. (2018) examined the influence of social contact frequency and marital status on cognitive aging trajectories over twenty-one years, from midlife to old age, using data from the Whitehall II cohort study in the United Kingdom. They found that more frequent social contact and having a spouse were both associated with a better cognitive aging trajectory over time.

However, not all studies have supported the benefits of social networks and social contact on cognitive function in older adults. Longitudinal studies of American older adults with good cognitive and physical health in three communities (Durham, East Boston, and New Haven) (Seeman et al., 2001) and Taiwanese older adults (Glei et al., 2005) showed that social network size was not associated with cognitive aging. Another longitudinal study of adults aged 18 and over indicated that the longitudinal increase in social contact was related to a decline in episodic memory, suggesting that an increase in social contact might imply an increase in the need for support (Green et al., 2008). These inconsistent results regarding the association between social interaction and cognitive function may be due to differences in sample characteristics, such as health status and educational attainment, and differences in the characteristics of social relationships, such as network composition and function of the relationship.

Participation in social activities, such as religious, political, and recreational group activities, volunteering, and regular visits with others, was also underscored as a protective factor against cognitive decline (Kuiper et al., 2016) and dementia (Kuiper et al., 2015). Since the concept of cognitive reserve has been proposed as a protective factor in the clinical manifestation of dementia, an active lifestyle has been noted as a modifiable aspect of life experiences contributing to cognitive reserve in old age (Clare et al., 2017; Richards & Deary, 2005; Scarmeas & Stern, 2003). An active lifestyle is characterized by active engagement in intellectual, social, and physical activities. Many studies have found positive influences of participation in social activities on cognitive function in older adults. In the aforementioned Kungsholmen project, researchers found that participation in social activities decreased dementia risk at the six-year follow-up even after controlling for the effect of social network size (Wang et al., 2002). Many other studies also reported that older people who actively participated in social activities showed less cognitive decline (Barnes et al., 2004; Bassuk et al., 1999; Ertel et al., 2008; James et al., 2011). Participation in more social activities was associated with better performance and improved general cognition, memory, and executive function (Kelly et al., 2017).

Seeman et al. (2001), however, did not find a significant association between social activity and cognitive function in cross-sectional and longitudinal data. Brown et al. (2012) conducted a coordinated analysis of longitudinal data from four independent studies: the Origins of Variance in the Oldest-Old: Octogenarian Twins Study (Sweden); the Long Beach Longitudinal Study (US); the Seattle Longitudinal Study (US); and the

Victoria Longitudinal Study (Canada) to clarify the longitudinal relationship between social activity and cognitive functions. The researchers were unable to find consistent evidence for the immediate cognitive benefits of social activities. In their study, initial social activity levels did not predict the rate of decline of most cognitive abilities, and social activity changes were not consistently associated with time-varying cognitive function. Moreover, a study examining the temporal relations of social activity changes and cognitive performance across twelve years (Small et al., 2012) suggested that, conversely, cognitive decline may also reduce social activities. Due to these inconsistencies, some experts argue that there is still controversy about whether greater engagement in social activities in old age is a genuine protective factor against cognitive decline and dementia risk (Daviglus et al., 2010).

The benefits of social relationships on cognitive function in older adults may depend on the characteristics of their social networks and activities and the quality of their social relationships. In addition, the association between the structure of social relationships and cognitive function may vary depending on the demographic characteristics of an individual, such as gender, education, and ethnicity. Consecutively, these factors can influence the composition and function of the individual's social networks and lifestyle. Therefore, the characteristics of the study sample and their social networks and the quality of social interactions should be considered when discussing the benefits of social relationships on cognition in older adults.

9.3.2 *Functional Aspects of Social Relationships and Cognitive Function*

Social interactions can also affect psychological health depending on their positive or negative nature. These subjective experiences correspond to the qualitative and functional aspects of social relationships and are proposed as one of the potential mechanisms by which social relationships affect cognitive function. An explanation for why more social relationships protect against cognitive aging and dementia could be related to their potential to buffer stress. Frequent social contact and social activities provide opportunities to engage with others and lead to positive social exchanges and emotional states, and the reduction of loneliness. Positive social exchanges and emotional states may contribute to mitigating the deleterious effects of stress on health (Cohen, 2004; Fratiglioni et al., 2004). However, social engagement can also lead to negative social exchanges, which may be a source of stress. Therefore, some studies on the functional aspects of social relationships have included separate indicators of positive exchanges (e.g., social support) and negative exchanges (e.g., social conflict). Others have investigated the overall quality of social relationships, such as satisfaction with social relationships and loneliness.

According to meta-analyses of longitudinal elderly cohort studies, the functional aspects of social relationships do appear to be associated with cognitive function in late life (Kuiper et al., 2015, 2016). Poor social relationships, such as low social support or loneliness, have been associated with a higher risk of cognitive decline (Kuiper et al., 2016). Lonely older people also had a higher risk of developing dementia than those who were not lonely (Kuiper et al., 2015). Amieva et al. (2010) showed that the quality of social interaction, such as satisfaction with social interaction and social support, rather than the quantity, was protective against developing dementia up to 15 years later. In their study, older adults who felt very satisfied with their social network presented a 23% reduced risk of subsequent dementia. Those who felt that they received more from others than they gave to them also had a 55% reduced risk of incident dementia and a 53% reduced risk of Alzheimer's disease. It should be noted that the association between satisfaction with social networks and dementia risk was not supported in a meta-analysis that included the study of Amieva and her colleagues (Kuiper et al., 2015).

A number of studies on the relationship between cognition and the quality of social interactions assessed both positive and negative social interactions (Choi et al., 2016; Hughes et al., 2008; Seeman et al., 2001, 2011; Windsor et al., 2014). Seeman et al. (2011) hypothesized that the diametrical quality of social relationships would generate different patterns of cognitive–emotional and physiological activation, which could impact cognition differently. It is expected that the cognitive–emotional and physiological activation patterns following positive social interactions will support better cognitive function, while patterns following negative social interactions will negatively impact cognition. As expected, their study found that greater social support was positively associated with both executive function and episodic memory performances, whereas greater social strain or conflict was negatively related to executive function (Seeman et al., 2011). Similarly, older adults with greater social support from their spouses and lower conflicts with neighbors and friends showed higher levels of global cognition in the Korean Social Life, Health, and Aging Project (KSHAP) (Choi et al., 2016). The beneficial effect of positive social interaction on cognitive function has been consistently replicated in other studies (Gow et al., 2013; Hughes et al., 2008;

Seeman et al., 2001; Windsor et al., 2014). However, there is inconclusive evidence on the deleterious effects of negative social interactions. Some studies found that even negative social interaction, especially with friends and family other than a spouse, was associated with better cognitive function (Hughes et al., 2008; Seeman et al., 2001; Windsor et al., 2014). Hughes and her colleagues (2008) explained that this finding might result from negative social interactions that provide a greater level of cognitive stimulation, which benefits cognitive functioning. However, in their study, conflicts with spouses were found to negatively impact working memory. The association between negative social interactions and cognitive function in old age may vary depending on the relationship or interaction type. In terms of the relationship type, negative interactions may be cognitively stimulating only in relationships where cognitive efforts are made to resolve conflicts. In terms of interaction type, a longitudinal study revealed that only a part of the negative interaction adversely affected cognition in old age (Wilson et al., 2015). Wilson and his colleagues (2015) found that frequent negative social interactions were associated with lower general cognitive function, faster cognitive decline, and higher risk of developing mild cognitive impairment. This association was mainly due to neglect and rejection among the various types of negative social interactions. Neglect and rejection are likely to make people feel lonely and isolated. The detrimental effects of social isolation and loneliness have been detailed in Chapters 7 and 8. On the contrary, minor conflicts, such as unwanted intrusions and insensitive behaviors, with people other than co-residents, such as a spouse, may act as a cognitive stimulus during the conflict resolution process, thereby protecting cognitive function in older adults.

Therefore, it can be inferred that the functional aspects of social relationships affect their cognitive function through several pathways, some of which overlap with the structural aspects, while others do not. In addition, the structure and the function of social relationships may influence each other. Social network size and frequency of social contacts may be associated with opportunities for social exchange, and low quality of social relationships may lead to social withdrawal.

9.4 How Do Social Relationships Impact the Cognitive Health of Older Adults?

Even though some controversy remains about which characteristics of social relationships may positively impact cognition, the overall results of previous studies suggest that a socially engaged lifestyle, especially engagement in cognitively stimulating social contacts and activities, and positive social interaction, benefits older adults' cognitive function. Why does having a greater number of social relationships protect against age-associated cognitive decline and dementia in older people? Researchers have proposed multiple pathways that mediate the relationship between social relationships and cognitive function (Fratiglioni et al., 2004; Kuiper et al., 2015, 2016; McHugh Power et al., 2018). Potential mediators in these pathways include cognitive reserve, psychological benefits, cardiovascular health, and health behaviors (see Figure 5.3 for details on neural mechanism of the pathways), which are either positively or negatively associated with the risk of developing dementia.

Lifetime experiences such as education, occupation, and engagement in leisure activities of an intellectual and social nature may be conducive to building cognitive reserve (Stern, 2009; Xu et al., 2019). In particular, early life experiences are a well-known determinant of neurocognitive development. However, midlife intellectual, physical, and social activities (Chan et al., 2018) and late-life social networks (Bennett et al., 2006) also contribute to late-life cognition. Greater active participation in middle age and more extensive social networks in old age mitigate the influence of brain atrophy and pathology on cognition in older adults, which suggests that lifelong experiences may contribute to cognitive reserve. Moreover, Wilson et al. (2005) found that the influence of late-life participation in activities on older adults' cognitive function was stronger than that of activity participation in childhood or middle age. In their study, activity in childhood and middle age contributed to late-life cognitive function mainly through its association with current activity in old age, whereas current activity affected the cognitive function of older adults independent of past activity. Therefore, even in late life, social relationships appear to enhance cognitive reserve, which safeguards against cognitive decline and the development of dementia.

Social relationships may positively impact cognition, partly via psychological benefits that reduce stress and depression as well as loneliness. This pathway may be closely related to the influence of the functional aspect. Of course, active social engagement or a large social network may also contribute to the quality of social relationships by increasing opportunities for greater social support and alleviating loneliness. It has been argued, however, that the influence of functional aspects of social relationships on physical health is related to psychological stress (Cohen, 2004). More specifically, social support may reduce the effects of stressful experiences, while negative interactions may contribute to stress. In other words, the quality of social relationships may affect an individual's psychological stress and mood, resulting in a psychological state that may affect both mental and physical health.

On the other hand, studies have suggested that stress has detrimental effects on brain health, which, in turn, may influence cognitive aging and the development of dementia. Chronic exposure to high concentrations of the stress-related hormone cortisol and chronic psychological stress have been associated with hippocampal atrophy, a decline in learning and memory, and the risk of developing dementia (Lupien et al., 2005; Wilson et al., 2006). The brain's hippocampal region and the cognitive domain (i.e., learning and memory) are most susceptible to aging and Alzheimer's disease. Social interaction may buffer the deleterious impact of physiological and neuroendocrine reactions to stress on the brain and cognitive function (DeVries et al., 2003). A recent study showed that perceived stress mediated the relationship between social activity and cognitive function at the two-year follow-up among Irish adults aged 50 and over (McHugh Power et al., 2018). Meanwhile, loneliness and depression appear to be risk factors for cognitive decline (Donovan et al., 2017) and dementia (Sutin et al., 2020). Empirical evidence suggested that social support, especially emotional support, may protect against cognitive decline by alleviating loneliness and depression in older adults (Ellwardt et al., 2013; Gow et al., 2013). In the China Health and Retirement Longitudinal Study, frequent engagement in social activities and social contact were also associated with higher cognitive function, partially through the mediating effect of alleviating loneliness (Yang et al., 2020). In other words, social relationships may influence cognitive health along with physical health by reducing negative psychological states, such as stress, depression, and loneliness.

Other possible mediators that are noteworthy are cardiovascular functions and health behaviors. Cardiovascular disease and adverse health habits, such as smoking, drinking, and a sedentary lifestyle, are well-known risk factors for dementia (Fratiglioni et al., 2004; Gorelick et al., 2011) and other physical diseases (Cohen, 2004). Both structural and functional aspects of social relationships may influence cardiovascular functions and health behaviors. Social engagement, such as social activities and social contact, often involves physical activities, which have been found to benefit cardiovascular health and cognition (Etnier, 2007). Social support is also associated with an improved cardiovascular function (Uchino et al., 1996). However, a recent study found an insignificant mediating effect of vascular function on the relationship between social activity and cognitive function (McHugh Power et al., 2018). Frequent interactions with others may also promote positive health behaviors and decrease negative health behaviors by lowering psychological stress, increasing access to multiple healthy lifestyles, and providing health-related information.

9.5 What Factors Modulate the Relationship between Social Relationships and Cognition?

In general, social relationships positively impact cognition in old age, but the degree of impact may differ depending on an individual's demographic characteristics and the types of relationships and activities that the individual engages in. Research findings indicate that the beneficial effects of social relationships in old age differ according to demographic characteristics such as age, gender, and education level. For example, researchers found a stronger association between social network size and cognition (Hughes et al., 2008) and between the quality of social relationships and depression (Yim et al., 2016) in young-old adults under 75 years of age, compared to old-old adults aged 75 years and above. In terms of gender, the quality of social relationships (Zunzunegui et al., 2003) and social isolation, especially from friends (Evans et al., 2019; Giles et al., 2012), has a stronger impact on the cognition of older female than male adults. Social relationships, such as social activity, social contact, and loneliness, were more strongly associated with cognitive function in low-educated older adults than in those who were highly educated (Ertel et al., 2008; Ihle et al., 2015; Kang et al., 2016; Shankar et al., 2013). Larger social networks were associated with better cognitive functioning in older adults whose networks comprised a greater proportion of friends than family members (Sharifian et al., 2019). Furthermore, relationship types that comprise an individual's social networks appear to differentially modulate the effects of social interactions on cognition across specific ethnic and gender groups. For example, Sharifian et al. (2019) found that larger social networks were associated with better cognitive functioning only in African Americans whose networks comprise a greater proportion of friends than family members. Liao and Scholes (2017), using data from the English Longitudinal Study of Aging, indicated that gender and relationship type modified the association between functional aspects of social relationships and cognitive aging. For men, higher social support from spouse/partner and lower social conflict with all relationships were associated with higher cognitive function and milder cognitive decline. Among women, higher social support from children and friends, and not spouse/partner and relatives, was positively associated with cognitive function.

As mentioned earlier, empirical evidence has suggested that the benefits of social relationships on cognitive function in older adults differ according to the characteristics of the individuals and social relationships. This may stem from the differential mediating effect sizes that can be obtained from each activity and relationship type, depending on demographic characteristics. In other words, the extent to which social engagement and the quality of social interaction are cognitively stimulating and beneficial to psychological health may differ according to individuals' demographic characteristics, so their effects on cognitive function may also vary.

As research findings have supported that active social engagement in old age enhances emotional and cognitive health, interventions to promote social engagement of older people to maintain or improve cognitive functions have been developed and studied. To understand the effectiveness of social interventions, experts should consider the mediators and modulators between social relationships and cognition based on empirical evidence. Essential components and characteristics of effective social interventions for cognitive health are reviewed in Chapter 12.

9.6 Discussions

Accumulated research findings reinforce the proposition that social engagement in old age contributes to healthier cognitive aging. While some studies investigating the effect of social engagement on cognitive function and dementia risk in older adults have focused on the structural aspects of social relationships (i.e., the quantity), others have focused on its functional aspects (i.e., the quality). As for structural aspects, larger social networks, more frequent social contacts, and participation in various social activities appear to benefit cognition in older adults. However, some studies on the relationship between structural aspects and cognition in late life reported differing results, suggesting that there were no immediate cognitive benefits of social relationships. This inconclusiveness may be related to the heterogeneity of the structural aspects of social relationships as well as the study samples. The structural aspects quantify social relationships but do not represent the detailed characteristics of social relationships, such as the composition of social networks, complexity of social activities, and quality of social interaction. The attributes of an individual may also modulate the influence of social networks and activities. As for the functional aspect of social relationships, positive social interaction and overall satisfaction with social relationships are consistently beneficial to cognitive function. However, the relationship between negative social interactions and cognition seems to be fairly complex, as they usually have deleterious effects on cognitive function, but their effects may vary depending on the relationship and conflict type. It can be concluded from previous studies that social relationships and activities benefit cognitive function in late life when they are cognitively stimulating and beneficial to psychological health.

Although both the quantity and quality of social relationships appear to protect against cognitive aging and dementia, different mechanisms may be involved in the relationship between cognition and each aspect of social relationships. The plausible psychological mechanisms through which social relationships influence cognitive aging are: increased cognitive reserve by stimulating cognition, improving psychological health through positive social interactions, and improving cardiovascular health and health behaviors. These mediating factors modulate the risk of developing dementia. Further, social isolation also appears to bring forth a variety of adverse health outcomes in these factors (Leigh-Hunt et al., 2017).

Additionally, the benefits of social relationships may differ according to personal attributes (e.g., age, gender, education level, occupational experiences), cultural contexts, and the type of relationship. Previous evidence has predicted that the degree to which life experiences affect cognition might depend on an individual's prior experiences and age. The benefits of social relationships seem limited in highly educated people and seniors of late old age when compared to low-educated people and seniors of early old age. Research findings suggest that activities may differentially stimulate cognition and the brain, depending on the amount of novelty and the extent of cognitive challenge (Bielak, 2010; McDonough et al., 2015; Park et al., 2014). Highly educated older people may have participated in various activities with greater cognitive challenges throughout their lifetime. Hence, social engagement in old age may be less novel for them compared to low-educated older people. Moreover, brain and cognitive plasticity decrease with age.

Although social relationships may not be the most influential determinants of cognitive health, there are many benefits to promoting social relationships, and this can be a base for potential strategies to promote healthier cognitive aging and prevent dementia in late life. Social interventions may significantly benefit the cognitive and overall brain health of at-risk older people, such as low-educated and socially isolated older adults, who are at risk for dementia. Moreover, social relationships influence individuals' cognitive and emotional health throughout their lifetimes, whereas social isolation could lead to negative consequences at any developmental stage. Therefore, attention should be focused on socially isolated people of all generations.

In conclusion, social relationships in old age are important factors that result in a wide range of psychological, physical, and cognitive health benefits. Social engagement, which stimulates cognition and provides social support, may be one of the best strategies for healthy cognitive aging and dementia prevention. A well-designed social intervention that considers the societal environment and individual susceptibility may be most effective. In the context of population aging, efforts to prevent social isolation and promote social engagement among older adults would benefit society and individuals.

REFERENCES

Ajrouch, K. J., Blandon, A. Y., & Antonucci, T. C. (2005). Social networks among men and women: The effects of age and socioeconomic status. *The Journals of Gerontology Series B: Psychological Sciences and Social Sciences, 60*(6), S311–S317.

Amieva, H., Stoykova, R., Matharan, F., Helmer, C., Antonucci, T. C., & Dartigues, J.-F. (2010). What aspects of social network are protective for dementia? Not the quantity but the quality of social interactions is protective up to 15 years later. *Psychosomatic Medicine, 72*(9), 905–911.

Anstey, K. J., Cherbuin, N., & Herath, P. M. (2013). Development of a new method for assessing global risk of Alzheimer's disease for use in population health approaches to prevention. *Prevention Science, 14*(4), 411–421.

Avlund, K., Lund, R., Holstein, B. E., Due, P., Sakari-Rantala, R., & Heikkinen, R.-L. (2004). The impact of structural and functional characteristics of social relations as determinants of functional decline. *The Journals of Gerontology Series B: Psychological Sciences and Social Sciences, 59*(1), S44–S51.

Barnes, L. L., De Leon, C. M., Wilson, R. S., Bienias, J. L., & Evans, D. A. (2004). Social resources and cognitive decline in a population of older African Americans and whites. *Neurology, 63*(12), 2322–2326.

Bassuk, S. S., Glass, T. A., & Berkman, L. F. (1999). Social disengagement and incident cognitive decline in community-dwelling elderly persons. *Annals of Internal Medicine, 131*(3), 165–173.

Béland, F., Zunzunegui, M.-V., Alvarado, B., Otero, A., & Del Ser, T. (2005). Trajectories of cognitive decline and social relations. *The Journals of Gerontology Series B: Psychological Sciences and Social Sciences, 60*(6), P320–P330.

Bennett, D. A., Schneider, J. A., Tang, Y., Arnold, S. E., & Wilson, R. S. (2006). The effect of social networks on the relation between Alzheimer's disease pathology and level of cognitive function in old people: A longitudinal cohort study. *The Lancet Neurology, 5*(5), 406–412.

Bielak, A. A. (2010). How can we not "lose it" if we still don't understand how to "use it"? Unanswered questions about the influence of activity participation on cognitive performance in older age – A mini-review. *Gerontology, 56*(5), 507–519.

Brown, C. L., Gibbons, L. E., Kennison, R. F., Robitaille, A., Lindwall, M., Mitchell, M. B., Shirk, S. D., Atri, A., Cimino, C. R., Benitez, A., Macdonald, S. W., Zelinski, E. M., Willis, S. L., Schaie, K. W., Johansson, B., Dixon, R. A., Mungas, D. M., Hofer, S. M., & Piccinin, A. M. (2012). Social activity and cognitive functioning over time: A coordinated analysis of four longitudinal studies. *Journal of Aging Research, 2012*, 287438.

Chan, D., Shafto, M., Kievit, R., Matthews, F., Spink, M., Valenzuela, M., & Henson, R. N. (2018). Lifestyle activities in mid-life contribute to cognitive reserve in late-life, independent of education, occupation, and late-life activities. *Neurobiology of Aging, 70*, 180–183.

Choi, J., Kim, H., & Youm, Y. (2016). Social network, social support, social conflict and mini-mental state examination scores of rural older adults: Differential associations across relationship types. *Journal of Korean Geriatric Psychiatry 20*(2), 8.

Clare, L., Wu, Y.-T., Teale, J. C., MacLeod, C., Matthews, F., Brayne, C., Woods, B., & Team, C.-W. S. (2017). Potentially modifiable lifestyle factors, cognitive reserve, and cognitive function in later life: A cross-sectional study. *PLoS Medicine, 14*(3), e1002259.

Cohen, S. (2004). Social relationships and health. *American Psychologist, 59*(8), 676–684.

Cornwell, B., Laumann, E. O., & Schumm, L. P. (2008). The social connectedness of older adults: A national profile. *American Sociological Review, 73*(2), 185–203.

Crooks, V. C., Lubben, J., Petitti, D. B., Little, D., & Chiu, V. (2008). Social network, cognitive function, and dementia incidence among elderly women. *American Journal of Public Health, 98*(7), 1221–1227.

Daviglus, M. L., Bell, C. C., Berrettini, W., Bowen, P. E., Connolly, E. S., Jr., Cox, N. J., Dunbar-Jacob, J. M., Granieri, E. C., Hunt, G., McGarry, K., Patel, D., Potosky, A. L., Sanders-Bush, E., Silberberg, D., & Trevisan, M. (2010). NIH state-of-the-science conference statement: Preventing Alzheimer's disease and cognitive decline. *NIH consensus and state-of-the-science statements, 27*(4), 1–30.

DeVries, A. C., Glasper, E. R., & Detillion, C. E. (2003). Social modulation of stress responses. *Physiology & Behavior, 79*(3), 399–407.

Donovan, N. J., Wu, Q., Rentz, D. M., Sperling, R. A., Marshall, G. A., & Glymour, M. M. (2017). Loneliness, depression and cognitive function in older U.S. adults. *International Journal of Geriatric Psychiatry, 32*(5), 564–573.

Ellwardt, L., Aartsen, M., Deeg, D., & Steverink, N. (2013). Does loneliness mediate the relation between social support and cognitive functioning in later life? *Social Science & Medicine, 98*, 116–124.

Elovainio, M., Sommerlad, A., Hakulinen, C., Pulkki-Råback, L., Virtanen, M., Kivimäki, M., & Singh-Manoux, A. (2018). Structural social relations and cognitive ageing trajectories: Evidence from the Whitehall II cohort study. *International Journal of Epidemiology, 47*(3), 701–708.

Erickson, K. I., & Kramer, A. F. (2009). Aerobic exercise effects on cognitive and neural plasticity in older adults. *British Journal of Sports Medicine, 43*(1), 22–24.

Ertel, K. A., Glymour, M. M., & Berkman, L. F. (2008). Effects of social integration on preserving memory function in a nationally representative US elderly population. *American Journal of Public Health, 98*(7), 1215–1220.

Etnier, J. (2007). Interrelationships of exercise, mediator variables, and cognition. In W. W. Spirduso, L. W. Poon, & W. J. Chodzko-Zajko (eds.), *Exercise and Its Mediating Effects on Cognition*, vol. 2, pp. 13–30. Human Kinetics.

Evans, I. E., Martyr, A., Collins, R., Brayne, C., & Clare, L. (2019). Social isolation and cognitive function in later life: A systematic review and meta-analysis. *Journal of Alzheimer's Disease, 70*(s1), S119–S144.

Fisk, J. E., & Sharp, C. A. (2004). Age-related impairment in executive functioning: Updating, inhibition, shifting, and access. *Journal of Clinical and Experimental Neuropsychology, 26*(7), 874–890.

Fratiglioni, L., Paillard-Borg, S., & Winblad, B. (2004). An active and socially integrated lifestyle in late life might protect against dementia. *The Lancet Neurology, 3*(6), 343–353.

Fratiglioni, L., Wang, H.-X., Ericsson, K., Maytan, M., & Winblad, B. (2000). Influence of social network on occurrence of dementia: A community-based longitudinal study. *The Lancet, 355*(9212), 1315–1319.

Gazzaley, A., Cooney, J. W., Rissman, J., & D'Esposito, M. (2005). Top-down suppression deficit underlies working memory impairment in normal aging. *Nature Neuroscience, 8(10)*, 1298–1300.

Giles, L. C., Anstey, K. J., Walker, R. B., & Luszcz, M. A. (2012). Social networks and memory over 15 years of followup in a cohort of older Australians: Results from the Australian longitudinal study of ageing. *Journal of Aging Research*, 2012, 856048.

Glei, D. A., Landau, D. A., Goldman, N., Chuang, Y.-L., Rodríguez, G., & Weinstein, M. (2005). Participating in social activities helps preserve cognitive function: An analysis of a longitudinal, population-based study of the elderly. *International Journal of Epidemiology, 34*(4), 864–871.

Gorelick, P. B., Scuteri, A., Black, S. E., DeCarli, C., Greenberg, S. M., Iadecola, C., Launer, L. J., Laurent, S., Lopez, O. L., & Nyenhuis, D. (2011). Vascular contributions to cognitive impairment and dementia: A statement for healthcare professionals from the American Heart Association/American Stroke Association. *Stroke, 42*(9), 2672–2713.

Gow, A. J., Corley, J., Starr, J. M., & Deary, I. J. (2013). Which social network or support factors are associated with cognitive abilities in old age? *Gerontology, 59*(5), 454–463.

Green, A. F., Rebok, G., & Lyketsos, C. G. (2008). Influence of social network characteristics on cognition and functional status with aging. *International Journal of Geriatric Psychiatry, 23*(9), 972–978.

Hedden, T., & Gabrieli, J. D. (2004). Insights into the ageing mind: A view from cognitive neuroscience. *Nature Reviews Neuroscience, 5*(2), 87–96.

Hendrie, H. C., Albert, M. S., Butters, M. A., Gao, S., Knopman, D. S., Launer, L. J., Yaffe, K., Cuthbert, B. N., Edwards, E., & Wagster, M. V. (2006). The NIH Cognitive and Emotional Health Project. *Report of the Critical Evaluation Study Committee. Alzheimer's & Dementia, 2*(1), 12–32.

Henry, J. D., MacLeod, M. S., Phillips, L. H., & Crawford, J. R. (2004). A Meta-analytic review of prospective memory and aging. *Psychology and Aging, 19* (1), 27–39.

Hertzog, C., Kramer, A. F., Wilson, R. S., & Lindenberger, U. (2008). Enrichment effects on adult cognitive development: Can the functional capacity of older adults be preserved and enhanced? *Psychological Science in the Public Interest, 9*(1), 1–65.

Holtzman, R. E., Rebok, G. W., Saczynski, J. S., Kouzis, A. C., Wilcox Doyle, K., & Eaton, W. W. (2004). Social network characteristics and cognition in middle-aged and older adults. *The Journals of Gerontology Series B: Psychological Sciences and Social Sciences, 59*(6), P278–P284.

Hughes, T. F., Andel, R., Small, B. J., Borenstein, A. R., & Mortimer, J. A. (2008). The association between social resources and cognitive change in older adults: Evidence from the Charlotte County Healthy Aging Study. *The Journals of Gerontology Series B: Psychological Sciences and Social Sciences, 63* (4), P241–P244.

Ihle, A., Oris, M., Fagot, D., Baeriswyl, M., Guichard, E., & Kliegel, M. (2015). The association of leisure activities in middle adulthood with cognitive performance in old age: The moderating role of educational level. *Gerontology, 61*(6), 543–550.

James, B. D., Wilson, R. S., Barnes, L. L., & Bennett, D. A. (2011). Late-life social activity and cognitive decline in old age. *Journal of the International Neuropsychological Society, 17*(6), 998–1005.

Kang, S., Kim, H., & Youm, Y. (2016). Influence of social activity on cognitive function in older adults: Moderating effects of education. *Korean Journal of Psychology: General, 35*(4), 525–549.

Kelly, M. E., Duff, H., Kelly, S., McHugh Power, J. E., Brennan, S., Lawlor, B. A., & Loughrey, D. G. (2017). The impact of social activities, social networks, social support and social relationships on the cognitive functioning of healthy older adults: A systematic review. *Systematic Reviews, 6*(1), 259.

Kray, J., Li, K. Z., & Lindenberger, U. (2002). Age-related changes in task-switching components: The role of task uncertainty. *Brain and Cognition, 49* (3), 363–381.

Kuiper, J. S., Zuidersma, M., Oude Voshaar, R. C., Zuidema, S. U., van den Heuvel, E. R., Stolk, R. P., & Smidt, N. (2015). Social relationships and risk of dementia: A systematic review and meta-analysis of longitudinal cohort studies. *Ageing Research Reviews, 22*, 39–57.

Kuiper, J. S., Zuidersma, M., Zuidema, S. U., Burgerhof, J. G., Stolk, R. P., Oude Voshaar, R. C., & Smidt, N. (2016). Social relationships and cognitive decline: A systematic review and meta-analysis of longitudinal cohort studies. *International Journal of Epidemiology, 45*(4), 1169–1206.

Leigh-Hunt, N., Bagguley, D., Bash, K., Turner, V., Turnbull, S., Valtorta, N., & Caan, W. (2017). An overview of systematic reviews on the public health consequences of social isolation and loneliness. *Public Health, 152*, 157–171.

Liao, J., & Scholes, S. (2017). Association of social support and cognitive aging modified by sex and relationship type: A prospective investigation in the English Longitudinal Study of Ageing. *American Journal of Epidemiology, 186*(7), 787–795.

Lupien, S. J., Schwartz, G., Ng, Y. K., Fiocco, A., Wan, N., Pruessner, J. C., Meaney, M. J., & Nair, N. P. (2005). The Douglas Hospital Longitudinal Study of Normal and Pathological Aging: Summary of findings. *Journal of Psychiatry and Neuroscience, 30*(5), 328–334.

McDonough, I. M., Haber, S., Bischof, G. N., & Park, D. C. (2015). The Synapse Project: Engagement in mentally challenging activities enhances neural efficiency. *Restorative Neurology and Neuroscience, 33*(6), 865–882.

McHugh Power, J., Tang, J., Lawlor, B., Kenny, R. A., & Kee, F. (2018). Mediators of the relationship between social activities and cognitive function among older Irish adults: Results from the Irish Longitudinal Study on Ageing. *Aging & Mental Health, 22*(1), 129–134.

Nguyen, L., Murphy, K., & Andrews, G. (2019). Cognitive and neural plasticity in old age: A systematic review of evidence from executive functions cognitive training. *Ageing Research Reviews, 53*, 100912.

Nyberg, L., Lövdén, M., Riklund, K., Lindenberger, U., & Bäckman, L. (2012). Memory aging and brain maintenance. *Trends in Cognitive Sciences, 16*(5), 292–305.

Pahl, R., & Pevalin, D. J. (2005). Between family and friends: A longitudinal study of friendship choice. *The British Journal of Sociology, 56*(3), 433–450.

Park, D. C., & Bischof, G. N. (2013). The aging mind: Neuroplasticity in response to cognitive training. *Dialogues in Clinical Neuroscience, 15*(1), 109–119.

Park, D. C., Lautenschlager, G., Hedden, T., Davidson, N. S., Smith, A. D., & Smith, P. K. (2002). Models of visuospatial and verbal memory across the adult life span. *Psychology and Aging, 17(2)*, 299.

Park, D. C., Lodi-Smith, J., Drew, L., Haber, S., Hebrank, A., Bischof, G. N., & Aamodt, W. (2014). The impact of sustained engagement on cognitive function in older adults: The Synapse Project. *Psychological Science, 25*(1), 103–112.

Penn, D. L., Corrigan, P. W., Bentall, R. P., Racenstein, J. M., & Newman, L. (1997). Social cognition in schizophrenia. *Psychological Bulletin, 121*(1), 114–132.

Polidori, M. C., Nelles, G., & Pientka, L. (2010). Prevention of dementia: Focus on lifestyle. *International Journal of Alzheimer's Disease, 2010*, 393579.

Richards, M., & Deary, I. J. (2005). A life course approach to cognitive reserve: A model for cognitive aging and development? *Annals of Neurology, 58*(4), 617–622.

Rose, N. S., Rendell, P. G., Hering, A., Kliegel, M., Bidelman, G. M., & Craik, F. I. M. (2015). Cognitive and neural plasticity in older adults' prospective memory following training with the Virtual Week computer game. *Frontiers in Human Neuroscience, 9*(592), 1–13.

Rowe, J. W., & Kahn, R. L. (1987). Human aging: Usual and successful. *Science, 237*(4811), 143–149.

Salthouse, T. A. (2010). Selective review of cognitive aging. *Journal of the International Neuropsychological Society, 16*(5), 754–760.

Scarmeas, N., & Stern, Y. (2003). Cognitive reserve and lifestyle. *Journal of Clinical and Experimental Neuropsychology, 25*(5), 625–633.

Seeman, T. E., Lusignolo, T. M., Albert, M., & Berkman, L. (2001). Social relationships, social support, and patterns of cognitive aging in healthy, high-functioning older adults: MacArthur studies of successful aging. *Health Psychology, 20*(4), 243–255.

Seeman, T. E., Miller-Martinez, D. M., Stein Merkin, S., Lachman, M. E., Tun, P. A., & Karlamangla, A. S. (2011). Histories of social engagement and adult cognition: Midlife in the U.S. study. *The Journals of Gerontology Series B: Psychological Sciences and Social Sciences 66* (Suppl 1), i141–i152.

Shankar, A., Hamer, M., McMunn, A., & Steptoe, A. (2013). Social isolation and loneliness: Relationships with cognitive function during 4 years of follow-up in the English Longitudinal Study of Ageing. *Psychosomatic Medicine, 75*(2), 161–170.

Sharifian, N., Manly, J. J., Brickman, A. M., & Zahodne, L. B. (2019). Social network characteristics and cognitive functioning in ethnically diverse older adults: The role of network size and composition. *Neuropsychology, 33*(7), 956–963.

Small, B. J., Dixon, R. A., McArdle, J. J., & Grimm, K. J. (2012). Do changes in lifestyle engagement moderate cognitive decline in normal aging? Evidence from the Victoria Longitudinal Study. *Neuropsychology, 26*(2), 144–155.

Stern, Y. (2009). Cognitive reserve. *Neuropsychologia, 47*(10), 2015–2028.

Sutin, A. R., Stephan, Y., Luchetti, M., & Terracciano, A. (2020). Loneliness and risk of dementia. *The Journals of Gerontology Series B: Psychological Sciences and Social Sciences, 75*(7), 1414–1422.

Uchino, B. N., Cacioppo, J. T., & Kiecolt-Glaser, J. K. (1996). The relationship between social support and physiological processes: A review with emphasis on underlying mechanisms and implications for health. *Psychological Bulletin, 119*(3), 488–531.

Wang, H.-X., Karp, A., Winblad, B., & Fratiglioni, L. (2002). Late-life engagement in social and leisure activities is associated with a decreased risk of dementia: A longitudinal study from the Kungsholmen project. *American Journal of Epidemiology, 155*(12), 1081–1087.

Wecker, N. S., Kramer, J. H., Hallam, B. J., & Delis, D. C. (2005). Mental flexibility: Age effects on switching. *Neuropsychology, 19(3)*, 345–352.
West, R., & Alain, C. (2000). Age-related decline in inhibitory control contributes to the increased Stroop effect observed in older adults. *Psychophysiology, 37(2)*, 179–189.
Wilson, R. S., Arnold, S. E., Schneider, J. A., Kelly, J. F., Tang, Y., & Bennett, D. A. (2006). Chronic psychological distress and risk of Alzheimer's disease in old age. *Neuroepidemiology, 27(3)*, 143–153.
Wilson, R. S., Barnes, L. L., Krueger, K. R., Hoganson, G., Bienias, J. L., & Bennett, D. A. (2005). Early and late life cognitive activity and cognitive systems in old age. *Journal of the International Neuropsychological Society, 11*(4), 400–407.
Wilson, R. S., Boyle, P. A., James, B. D., Leurgans, S. E., Buchman, A. S., & Bennett, D. A. (2015). Negative social interactions and risk of mild cognitive impairment in old age. *Neuropsychology, 29(4)*, 561–570.
Windsor, T. D., Gerstorf, D., Pearson, E., Ryan, L. H., & Anstey, K. J. (2014). Positive and negative social exchanges and cognitive aging in young-old adults: Differential associations across family, friend, and spouse domains. *Psychology and Aging, 29(1)*, 28–43.
Xu, H., Yang, R., Qi, X., Dintica, C., Song, R., Bennett, D. A., & Xu, W. (2019). Association of lifespan cognitive reserve indicator with dementia risk in the presence of brain pathologies. *JAMA Neurology, 76*(10), 1184–1191.
Yang, R., Wang, H., Edelman, L. S., Tracy, E. L., Demiris, G., Sward, K. A., & Donaldson, G. W. (2020). Loneliness as a mediator of the impact of social isolation on cognitive functioning of Chinese older adults. *Age and Ageing, 49*(4), 599–604.
Ybarra, O., Burnstein, E., Winkielman, P., Keller, M. C., Manis, M., Chan, E., & Rodriguez, J. (2008). Mental exercising through simple socializing: Social interaction promotes general cognitive functioning. *Personality and Social Psychology Bulletin, 34*(2), 248–259.
Yim, J., Kim, H., & Youm, Y. (2016). The effect of social support and conflict in different types of relationships on depression and suicidal ideation among the young-old and the old-old. *Korean Journal of Clinical Psychology 35*(3), 645–657.
Zunzunegui, M.-V., Alvarado, B. E., Del Ser, T., & Otero, A. (2003). Social networks, social integration, and social engagement determine cognitive decline in community-dwelling Spanish older adults. *The Journals of Gerontology Series B: Psychological Sciences and Social Sciences, 58*(2), S93–S100.

CHAPTER 10

Social Network and the Brain
Yoosik Youm and Junsol Kim

10.1 Introduction

The "social brain hypothesis" was originally developed by evolutionary psychologists. The hypothesis suggested that the exceptionally large neocortex of human beings evolved to support cognitively demanding social interactions involving social networks (Dunbar & Shultz, 2007). For instance, Dunbar found that between-species differences in the size of social groups was correlated with neocortex size (Dunbar, 1998, 2014). This earlier empirical finding suggested that large neocortex size might enable the cognitive capacity to interact in a large social group, such as mind reading, tactical deception, and coalition formation (Dunbar, 1998, 2014). Although various confounding factors other than social group size may be correlated with the evolution of large brains, species' social group size was robustly associated with between-species differences of social group size even after controlling for diet and ecological variables (Barton, 2001; Dunbar & Shultz, 2017; Lin et al., 2020).

Structural and functional magnetic resonance imaging (MRI) studies have further shown that individual differences in the volume and connectivity of the "social brain," such as the amygdala and the mentalizing network, were positively related to social network size (i.e., the number of relationships one occupies) among human beings (Bickart et al., 2011, 2012; Bickart, Dickerson, et al., 2014; Kwak et al., 2018). However, these empirical findings pose two possibilities regarding the association between social brain and social networks. First, as suggested by the social brain hypothesis, it is possible that the higher information processing capacity of individuals who have larger or highly connected social brains leads to higher social network size. Second, the cognitive challenge of maintaining

---

This work was supported by the Ministry of Education of the Republic of Korea, the National Research Foundation of Korea (NRF-2022S1A3A2A02089737), and the Yonsei Signature Research Cluster Program of 2021 (2022-22-0009).

greater social network size might reversely affect the structure and function of the social brain (Joo et al., 2017).

Although the role of social brains in social networks has been of interest, neural correlates of social network indices other than social network size have rarely been studied. This limits our understanding about the link between the complex social world and our social brain. Also, the causal relationship between social brains and social networks has rarely been examined (Kwak et al., 2018; Lin et al., 2020). The reason is that we lack the brain and social network data that would allow us to utilize a variety of social network indices and investigate the causal relationship (Kwak et al., 2018).

In this chapter, we first review earlier studies on the association between social brain features and social network size. Then, we move on to introduce studies which explore the association between the social brain and a variety of social network indices based on data from the Korean Social Life, Health, and Aging Project (KSHAP). Finally, we discuss the issue regarding the causal relationship between the social brain and social networks.

10.2 The Social Brain and Social Network Size

As already discussed in Chapters 3 and 6, neuroimaging studies have shown that the structure and functional connectivity of "the social brain" is correlated with social network size among human beings (Bickart et al., 2011, 2012; Bickart, Dickerson, et al., 2014; Kwak et al., 2018). The social brain is known to be composed of the amygdala and the mentalizing or theory-of-mind network (Bickart, Dickerson, et al., 2014; Kwak et al., 2018; Van Overwalle, 2009). Although the role of the social brain has already been explored in earlier chapters, we would like to briefly summarize it again before focusing on how the social brain supports complex social networks.

First, the amygdala network is composed of the amygdala and its associated brain regions, such as the orbitofrontal cortex (OFC) (Kwak et al., 2018). Previous studies have found that disrupted amygdala–OFC connectivity leads to social impairment, such as impairment of one's ability to interpret other people's facial expressions, learn social consequences, process social values, and behave appropriately for group affiliation (Adolphs, 2010; Bickart, Brickhouse, et al., 2014; Craig et al., 2009; Klein et al., 2009). Based on these studies, the amygdala was even considered as a "hub" of the social brain network, connecting various

Social Network and the Brain 219

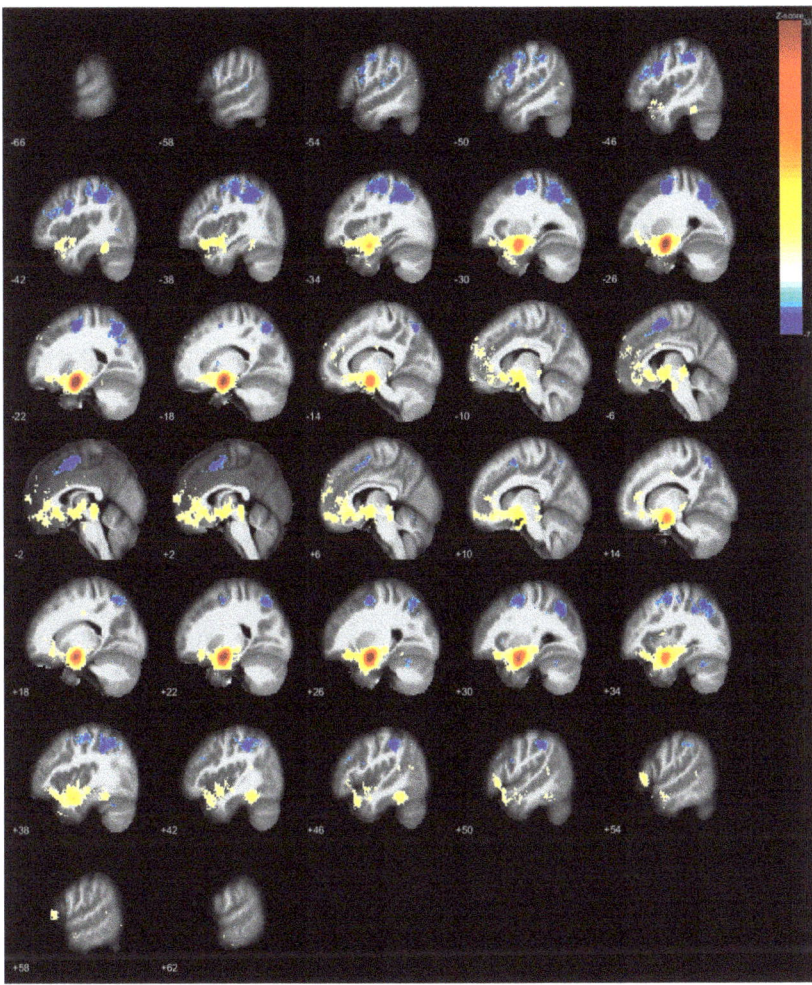

Figure 10.1 Regions of interest in the amygdala network. A Neurosynth (Yarkoni et al., 2011) association map of the term "amygdala" based on 1,579 studies, FDR 0.01 corrected, was used to create this ROI mask. Regions colored red are the frequently activated brain regions in studies including the term "amygdala."

brain regions related to social functioning (Bickart, Dickerson, et al., 2014). These results imply that the amygdala and the OFC regions are likely to contribute to social functioning and larger social network size. Figure 10.1 illustrates the brain regions involved in the amygdala network based on the Neurosynth automated meta-analysis.

The mentalizing or theory-of-mind network consists of the dorsomedial prefrontal cortex (dmPFC), temporo-parietal junction (TPJ) and precuneus. It has been associated with one's ability to simulate and infer the states of other people's minds. Also, the mentalizing network is associated with social network size (Bunner & Rebec, 2016; Dziura & Thompson, 2014; Kanai et al., 2012; Lewis et al., 2011). Figure 10.2 shows brain regions activated in the research papers including the term "mentalizing."

A series of studies has found that the structures of the social brain regions, such as the volume and white matter connectivity between the brain structures, are associated with social network size. First, Bickart et al. (2011) found that the left and right amygdala, along with the right subgenial anterior cingulate cortex (ACC), left caudal superior frontal gyrus (SFG), and left causal inferior temporal sulcus (ITS), were associated with social network size measured by the number of people who interacted with participants at least once every two weeks (Bickart et al. 2011; Bickart, Dickerson, et al., 2014). This result suggests that the role of the amygdala might be expanded to adjacent brain regions, including the ACC, SFG, and ITS, which are densely connected to the amygdala.

Lewis and his colleagues (2011) showed that mentalizing regions, such as the ventromedial frontal cortex, were associated with the number of people who had been in contact with the participants in the previous thirty days (i.e., Dunbar's number). Moreover, Kanai et al. (2012) discovered that the bilateral amygdala, right posterior superior temporal sulcus (STS), right entorhinal cortex, and left middle temporal gyrus were correlated with online social network size measured by participants' Facebook friend counts. Lastly, Bickart and his colleagues (2012) revealed that the resting-state functional connectivity of the ventrolateral amygdala with the OFC, STS, fusiform gyrus, and hippocampus was associated with social network size measured by the total number of people that participants interacted with at least once every two weeks (Bickart et al., 2012).

However, some studies have suggested that social brain regions are not significantly correlated with social network size. Recently, Lin and her colleagues (2020) found that the amygdala network, mentalizing network, and other brain regions were not significantly associated with the social network index when using a relatively large sample of healthy adults (N = 92) and applying multiple comparison corrections (Lin et al., 2020). Similarly, some studies failed to reveal the association between mentalizing regions and social networks (Dziura & Thompson, 2014; Lewis et al., 2011). This may be due to the limitations of the social network measures used in the studies. There are a couple of limitations in the measures that indicate social network size used in previous studies (Kwak et al., 2018).

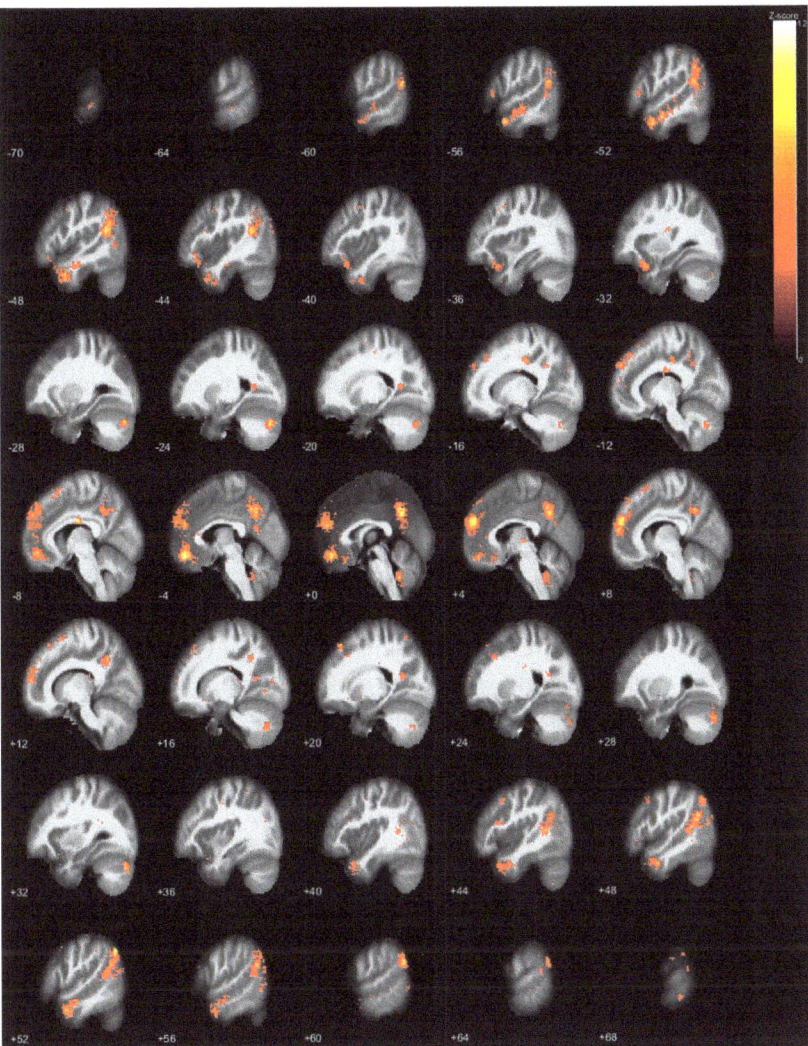

Figure 10.2 Regions of interest in the mentalizing network. A Neurosynth (Yarkoni et al., 2011) association map of the term "mentalizing" based on 151 studies, FDR 0.01 corrected, was used to create this ROI mask. Regions colored red are the frequently activated brain regions in studies including the term "mentalizing."

First, many studies relied on the self-reporting of individuals (e.g., the total number of people that they interacted with at least once every two weeks) to measure their social network sizes. However, respondent-centered measures may not fully capture the interpersonal nature of social relationships.

Social networks are not always symmetrical and reciprocal. Although a person responds that he/she has five friends, it is possible that the number of people who really think that the person is their friend could be more or less than five. Further, social network size captures only a part of the complex nature of human beings' social networks.

As discussed in Chapter 2, there are a variety of social network indices other than the network size, such as closure and brokerage position, which may require different types of cognitive capacity and may be correlated with different kinds of brain regions. Closure position refers to a position in a social network where one's friends are densely connected to each other. In a closure position, an individual is constrained by a homogeneous social norm, sharing similar attitudes with other connected people (Burt, 2005; Cornwell, 2009; Festinger et al., 1950; Krackhardt, 1998). On the other hand, brokerage position refers to a position in a social network where people interact with other people who are strangers to each other. If an individual occupies a brokerage position, he/she can be exposed to other people with diverse social characteristics, such as beliefs, attitudes, information, and ideas. Also, in a brokerage position, one can obtain power to control and moderate diverse and even incompatible attitudes (Burt, 1992, 2005; Cornwell, 2009; Gould & Fernandez, 1989; Granovetter, 1973). These two positions capture different characteristics of our complex social world. Also, they may require different cognitive capacities that involve distinct regions of the social brain. Thus, we would further our understanding about the link between social brain and social networks by examining studies employing both measures.

10.3 In-Degree Social Network Size, Social Network Embeddedness, and Diversity

In this section, we introduce recent studies from the KSHAP that have revealed how social network measures other than social network size are related to our social brain. KSHAP researchers collected social network data from all the residents of a rural village in South Korea, which allowed them to construct a complete map of the social networks of all older adults residing in a township (see Chapter 2). This comprehensive social network data was valuable, in that it shed light on the complexity of social network structures and the limitations of social network size measures based on self-reporting, frequently used in previous studies, while enabling the investigation of different aspects of social networks that could fully capture the complex relationship between intricate social networks and the social brain.

To begin with, Kwak and his colleagues (2018) examined the association between "in-degree social network size" and social brain volume. By doing so, they were able to discuss why there had been mixed findings regarding the association between social brain and social network size. Why did some studies find significant correlation between social brain and social network size while other studies could not? They suggested that there are two kinds of social network size measures: out-degree and in-degree social network size. The out-degree social network size refers to the number of social ties that the respondent claims to have. In other words, out-degree social network size is a respondent-centered measure that captures the perceived social resources one can access. Since it is easy to measure based on traditional survey methods, out-degree social network size has been the most frequently used index in studies examining the social brain's role in social networks (Bickart et al., 2011, 2012; Bickart, Dickerson et al., 2014; Kwak et al., 2018).

On the other hand, in-degree social network size indicates the number of people who cite the respondent as a friend. This can be measured if and only if survey data are collected from the entire population of the community. Based on such data, one can draw a complete map of the social network in a community and quantify in-degree social network size for each individual. Unlike out-degree social network size, which captures the perceived social resources, in-degree social network size is believed to measure one's objective social network size or popularity.

Kwak and his colleagues used the village-level social network data (n = 835) along with the brain MRI data (n = 68) from the KSHAP. Utilizing the both social network size data and voxel-based morphometry (VBM), they investigated how out-degree and in-degree social network size was correlated to social brain regions. The VBM allowed them to figure out which specific regional gray matter densities (rGMD) were associated with each measure of the social network size. They found that the volume or rGMD of social brain regions were correlated to in-degree social network size but not with out-degree. More specifically, after the multiple comparison corrections, they found that the rGMD of right SFG, left OFC, and fusiform gyrus were positively associated with in-degree social network size. On the other hand, they were not able to find the brain regions significantly associated with out-degree network size. These results were found even after sociodemographic variables, including age, gender, and education, as well as self-rated health were controlled for.

The results of this study suggest that one's actual popularity (i.e., in-degree social network size) rather than one's perceived connectedness (i.e., out-degree social network size) is strongly related to the social brain. In short, social network size was associated with the social brain only when the directionality was considered. Hence, caution is warranted before concluding that social networks are not related to social brains solely based on a single measure.

Another study conducted by Joo and his colleagues (2017) found that social network embeddedness, or closure position in a social network, was correlated with long-distance functional connectivity in the human brain (Joo et al., 2017). The study used the village-level social network data from the KSHAP with resting-state functional MRI (fMRI) data to investigate the brain functional connectivity of participants in a subsample (N = 64). If two brain regions are co-activated while the study participant is in resting state, it is assumed that these two regions are functionally connected. Based on this assumption, Joo et al. created a map of brain functional connectivity for each participant and investigated its association with social network embeddedness and sociodemographic factors, such as age and education. They found that social network embeddedness was correlated with functional connectivity between the inferior prefrontal and occipital/parietal lobe (i.e., long-distance connectivity in the brain), even though other sociodemographic covariates and an indicator of general cognitive function, such as age, gender, education, and Mini-Mental State Examination score, were controlled for.

A more recent study conducted by Youm et al. (2021) showed that the attitudinal diversity of social network members was associated with functional connectivity of the mentalizing regions. Why is attitudinal diversity important? Today's society is often described as a small-world society where people are within six degrees of separation (Milgram, 1967). How can this be possible between diverse people having different cultural backgrounds? To achieve small-worldness in a society, people should stay connected with others who have diverse and even incompatible attitudes. Youm and his colleagues examined what kinds of brain functional connectivity are involved in making social connections with diverse others. The study used resting-state fMRI data from 139 people and the complete social networks from two Korean villages, and it identified brain functional connectivity that could predict the attitudinal diversity of social network members. Specifically, connectivity of the mentalizing network with other brain regions was positively associated with attitudinal diversity. For instance, brain regions in the mentalizing network, such as the ventromedial prefrontal cortex (vmPFC), anterior temporal lobe, STS, TPJ, supramarginal gyrus, and posterior cingulate cortex (PCC), were recruited with the dorsolateral prefrontal cortex (dlPFC) and intraparietal sulcus, which are implicated in modulating social values according to context in people who have diverse friends (Strombach et al., 2015). Furthermore, the study found that the association between brain functional connectivity and attitudinal diversity of social network members was moderated by a brokerage position. People whose mentalizing brain connectivity was high and who are in brokerage positions in a social network were most likely to connect with diverse friends. For brain functional connectivity to enable social connections with diverse others, one should be in a brokerage position where there are rich opportunities to face people having diverse attitudes.

These studies have demonstrated the advantage of comprehensive social network data by utilizing a variety of social network measures, such as the in-degree social network size, social network embeddedness, and diversity. These novel measures were able to overcome the methodological issues of the traditional social network size measure, such as its inability to consider the directionality and interpersonal nature of social relationships. Also, the measures allow us to effectively capture how the complex nature of human beings' social world can be explained by our social brains.

10.4 Functional Activity of the Social Brain and Social Networks

The activity of the social brain during social interactions or when processing social contexts has mostly been investigated with fMRI experiments, which have implicated certain social brain regions for the formation, maintenance, and navigation of social networks in humans. Recent studies have employed brain fMRI experiments to show how the social brain is activated during social interactions, and how the patterns of social brain activation explain the individual differences in how human beings are organized in social networks.

Zerubavel et al. (2015), using task-based fMRI and social networks data, discovered that brain regions related to valuation, such as the ventral striatum, vmPFC, and amygdala, were activated when looking at popular others (i.e., other people whose in-degree social network sizes are high). Valuation regions are known to be activated when receiving monetary rewards, implying that our brains estimate social interactions with popular others to be valuable. Also, mentalizing brain regions were activated when looking at popular others. Interestingly, popular individuals' brain regions involved in valuation and mentalizing were sensitively activated when looking at popular others. However, if one's popularity index was low, these brain regions were not activated even when looking at popular others. These results may explain why inequality in popularity and social status occurs in social groups. Our brains reinforce the inequality of popularity by inducing motivations to connect with popular others more strongly in popular individuals.

Parkinson and her colleagues showed how our brains track differences of people's positions in their social networks, such as social distance, popularity, and brokerage position (Parkinson et al., 2017). Social distance was measured by the number of intermediary social ties that are required to connect two individuals. Popularity was measured by eigenvector centrality, indicating whether an individual has many social ties and connects with popular others. Brokerage position was measured by Burt's structural constraint (See Chapter 2). The researchers collected social networks of an academic cohort (N = 275) and a subset of participants' brain fMRI data (n = 21) that tracked the brain regions active while spontaneously looking at other people, a task similar to the study by Zerubavel et al. (2015). The study found that social distance between two people was reflected in the activation of the lateral posterior superior temporal cortex (SPC), the lateral temporal cortex (LTC), and the inferior parietal lobule (IPL), while the difference of popularity between two people was in the activation of the vmPFC and the ventrolateral prefrontal cortex (vlPFC). The difference of brokerage position was encoded in the lateral SPC activation.

These studies suggest that our brains have an intrinsic system that allows us to navigate, form, and maintain social networks around us. As such, growing evidence suggests that our social brain and social networks are intricately related. These studies, however, could not clarify the causality between the two realms, since they simply identified associations.

10.5 Causal Relationship between the Social Brain and Social Networks

Many studies investigating the association between social brain and social networks are based on the social brain hypothesis. The hypothesis claims that our brain enables our social networks, and that the structure and function of our social brain influence the characteristics of those networks. However, it is possible that the reverse causality holds true. It is possible that social networking reversely influences the structure and function of the individual's brain, but only a few studies have examined this possibility. Sallet and his colleagues found that macaques' social group size caused changes in the neural circuits (Sallet et al., 2011). They randomly selected macaques, assigned them to live in a larger social group, and found that their gray matter volume in regions related to processing social signals, such as the rostral prefrontal cortex and amygdala, increased. To our knowledge, few studies have examined such a causal hypothesis using human data.

By contrast, the impact of social networks on general cognitive function has been examined in a large body of studies, particularly using the data of older adults. To examine the causal relationship between social networks and cognition, two potential biases should be controlled for: first, the influences of the social brain on social networks; second, potential confounders that affect both the social brain and social networks and create spurious relationships between the two. By employing longitudinal design, studies have found that social network characteristics, such as larger social network size, positively affect cognitive function among older adults (Christelis & Dobrescu, 2019; Evans et al., 2019; Shankar et al., 2013).

These studies support the use-it-or-lose-it hypothesis (Hultsch et al., 1999), which argues that the cognitively challenging experiences of interacting with other people in social networks buffer cognitive decline. Thus, social networking could potentially affect our social brain and mitigate the negative changes of our social brain in late life. For a better overview with regard to the causal nature of the association between social networks and the social brain, future studies would benefit from longitudinal observations of social networks coupled with causal inference methods.

10.6 Conclusions

Based on the social brain hypothesis, many researchers have been interested in how human beings' large neocortex size supports complex social interactions and enables the formation and maintenance of their social networks (Dunbar & Shultz, 2007). A growing body of studies based on structural and functional MRI has elaborated on how the human brain and social networks are closely related (Bickart et al., 2011, 2012; Bickart, Dickerson et al., 2014; Kwak et al., 2018). By focusing on the two distinct brain regions that constitute the social brain network, which are the amygdala and the mentalizing (theory-of-mind) network, we have introduced earlier empirical studies that investigated the relationship between the social brain and social network size. More recent approaches to this inquiry involving comprehensive social network analysis and fMRI experiments from the KSHAP have revealed how a variety of social network characteristics, such as in-degree social network size, embeddedness, and diversity of social networks, are related to our social brain, utilizing the task-based fMRI that illustrates which brain regions are activated when people develop and navigate their social networks. Despite a large body of studies showing the association between the social brain and social networks, however, few studies have investigated the causal relationship in humans. A few experimental studies with animals marginally support the causal relationship between the two. Still, the field lacks robust evidence, especially from human studies regarding the causal direction, which seriously limits the interpretability of the association between the brain and social networks. We hope that future studies employing longitudinal data analyses and state-of-the-art causal inference methods, such as the counterfactual approach, could better address this issue.

REFERENCES

Adolphs, R. (2010). What does the amygdala contribute to social cognition? *Annals of the New York Academy of Sciences, 1191*(1), 42.

Barton, R. (2001). The evolutionary ecology of the primate brain. In P. Lee (ed.), *Comparative Primate Socioecology*, Cambridge Studies in Biological and Evolutionary Anthropology, pp. 167–203. Cambridge University Press.

Bickart, K. C., Brickhouse, M., Negreira, A., Sapolsky, D., Barrett, L. F., & Dickerson, B. C. (2014). Atrophy in distinct corticolimbic networks in frontotemporal dementia relates to social impairments measured using the Social Impairment Rating Scale. *Journal of Neurology, Neurosurgery & Psychiatry, 85*(4), 438–448.

Bickart, K. C., Dickerson, B. C., & Barrett, L. F. (2014). The amygdala as a hub in brain networks that support social life. *Neuropsychologia, 63*, 235–248.

Bickart, K. C., Hollenbeck, M. C., Barrett, L. F., & Dickerson, B. C. (2012). Intrinsic amygdala–cortical functional connectivity predicts social network size in humans. *Journal of Neuroscience, 32*(42), 14729–14741.

Bickart, K. C., Wright, C. I., Dautoff, R. J., Dickerson, B. C., & Barrett, L. F. (2011). Amygdala volume and social network size in humans. *Nature Neuroscience, 14*(2), 163–164.

Bunner, K. D., & Rebec, G. V. (2016). Corticostriatal dysfunction in Huntington's disease: The basics. *Frontiers in Human Neuroscience, 10*, 317.

Burt, R. S. (1992). *Structural Holes*, Harvard University Press.

 (2005). *Brokerage and Closure: An Introduction to Social Capital*, Oxford University Press.

Christelis, D., & Dobrescu, L. (2019). The causal effect of social activities on cognition: Evidence from 20 European countries. *Social Science & Medicine, 247*, 112783.

Cornwell, B. (2009). Good health and the bridging of structural holes. *Social Networks, 31*(1), 92–103.

Craig, M. C., Catani, M., Deeley, Q., Latham, R., Daly, E., Kanaan, R., Picchioni, M., McGuire, P. K., Fahy, T., & Murphy, D. G. (2009). Altered connections on the road to psychopathy. *Molecular Psychiatry 14*(10), 946–953.

Dunbar, R. I. M. (1998). The social brain hypothesis. *Evolutionary Anthropology: Issues, News, and Reviews, 6*(5), 178–190.

(2014). The social brain: Psychological underpinnings and implications for the structure of organizations. *Current Directions in Psychological Science, 23*(2), 109–114.

Dunbar, R. I. M., & Shultz, S. (2007). Evolution in the social brain. *Science, 317* (5843), 1344–1347.

(2017). Why are there so many explanations for primate brain evolution? *Philosophical Transactions of the Royal Society B: Biological Sciences, 372* (1727), 20160244.

Dziura, S. L., & Thompson, J. C. (2014). Social-network complexity in humans is associated with the neural response to social information. *Psychological Science, 25*(11), 2095–2101.

Evans, I. E. M., Martyr, A., Collins, R., Brayne, C., & Clare, L. (2019). Social isolation and cognitive function in later life: A systematic review and meta-analysis. *Journal of Alzheimer's Disease, 70*(s1), S119–S144.

Festinger, L., Schachter, S., & Back, K. (1950). *Social Pressures in Informal Groups: A Study of Human Factors in Housing.* Harper.

Gould, R. V., & Fernandez, R. M. (1989). Structures of mediation: A formal approach to brokerage in transaction networks. *Sociological Methodology, 19*, 89–126.

Granovetter, M. S. (1973). The strength of weak ties. *American Journal of Sociology, 78*(6), 1360–1380.

Hultsch, D. F., Hertzog, C., Small, B. J., & Dixon, R. A. (1999). Use it or lose it: Engaged lifestyle as a buffer of cognitive decline in aging? *Psychology and Aging, 14*(2), 245.

Joo, W.-t., Kwak, S., Youm, Y., & Chey, J. (2017). Brain functional connectivity difference in the complete network of an entire village: The role of social network size and embeddedness. *Scientific Reports, 7*(1), 1–12.

Kanai, R., Bahrami, B., Roylance, R., & Rees, G. (2012). Online social network size is reflected in human brain structure. *Proceedings of the Royal Society B: Biological Sciences, 279*(1732), 1327–1334.

Klein, J. T., Shepherd, S. V., Platt, M. L. (2009). Social attention and the brain. *Current Biology, 19*(20), R958–R962.

Krackhardt, D. (1998). Super strong and sticky. In R. M. Kramer & M. A. Neale (eds.), *Power and Influence in Organizations.* SAGE Publications.

Kwak, S., Joo, W.-t., Youm, Y., & Chey, J. (2018). Social brain volume is associated with in-degree social network size among older adults. *Proceedings of the Royal Society B: Biological Sciences, 285*(1871), 20172708.

Lewis, P. A., Rezaie, R., Brown, R., Roberts, N., & Dunbar, R. I. M. (2011). Ventromedial prefrontal volume predicts understanding of others and social network size. *Neuroimage, 57*(4), 1624–1629.

Lin, C., Keles, U., Tyszka, J. M., Gallo, M., Paul, L., & Adolphs, R. (2020). No strong evidence that social network index is associated with gray matter volume from a data-driven investigation. *Cortex*, *125*, 307–317.

Milgram, S. (1967). The small world problem. *Psychology Today*, *2*(1). 60–67.

Parkinson, C., Kleinbaum, A., & Wheatley, T. (2017). Spontaneous neural encoding of social network position. *Nature Human Behaviour*, *1*(5), 1–7.

Sallet, J., Mars, R. B., Noonan, M. P., Andersson, J. L., O'Reilly, J. X., Jbabdi, S., Croxson, P. L., Jenkinson, M., Miller, K. L., & Rushworth, M. F. (2011). Social network size affects neural circuits in macaques. *Science*, *334*(6056), 697–700.

Shankar, A., Hamer, M., McMunn, A., & Steptoe, A. (2013). Social isolation and loneliness: Relationships with cognitive function during 4 years of follow-up in the English Longitudinal Study of Ageing. *Psychosomatic Medicine*, *75*(2). 161–170.

Strombach, T., Weber, B., Hangebrauk, Z., Kenning, P., Karipidis, I. I., Tobler, P. N., Kalenscher, T. (2015). Social discounting involves modulation of neural value signals by temporoparietal junction. *Proceedings of the National Academy of Sciences*, *112*(5), 1619–1624. https://doi.org/10.1073/pnas.1414715112

Van Overwalle, F. (2009). Social cognition and the brain: A meta-analysis. *Human Brain Mapping*, *30*(3), 829–858.

Yarkoni, T., Poldrack, R. A., Nichols, T. E., Van Essen, D. C., & Wager, T. D. (2011). Large-scale automated synthesis of human functional neuroimaging data. *Nature Methods*, *8*(8), 665–670.

Youm, Y., Kim, J., Kwak, S., & Chey, J. (2021). Neural and social correlates of attitudinal brokerage: Using the complete social networks of two entire villages. *Proceedings of the Royal Society B*, *288*(1944), 20202866.

Zerubavel, N., Bearman, P. S., Weber, J., & Ochsner, K. N. (2015). Neural mechanisms tracking popularity in real-world social networks. *Proceedings of the National Academy of Sciences*, *112*(49), 15072–15077.

CHAPTER 11

Origins of Individual Differences in Social Behavior and the Social Brain

Isu Cho and Sunhae Sul

11.1 Introduction

Human sociality can be characterized by basic motivation for social bonding and highly demanding computation of social information, which is supported by a unique architecture of the human brain, the so-called social brain. As social beings, we are all alike because we share the species-specific characteristics of human sociality, but at the same time we are all different. In this chapter, we consider the genetic and environmental factors contributing to individual variations in human social behavior and the social brain, a set of brain regions involved in processing information about the social world. Specifically, we review genetic and environmental factors and their interactions, which influence social behaviors encompassing social bonding, socio-cognitive and socio-emotional functions, and antisocial and prosocial behaviors, as well as the social brain (see Figure 11.1). Lastly, we introduce some evidence illustrating that what individuals experience in later life can modulate the effects of early experience on their social behaviors.

11.2 Genetic Influences on Individual Differences in Social Behavior and the Social Brain

Recent advances in behavioral and cognitive genomics have led scientists to investigate the genetic influences on social behavior and the social brain. In this section, we focus on the genetic factors influencing three important neuropeptides and neurotransmitters: oxytocin, arginine-vasopressin, and serotonin (see Table 11.1). These neurochemicals are known to be closely associated with various social phenotypes (i.e., an organism's observable

This work was supported by the Ministry of Education of the Republic of Korea and the National Research Foundation of Korea (NRF-2020S1A3A2A02097375 granted to Sunhae Sul).

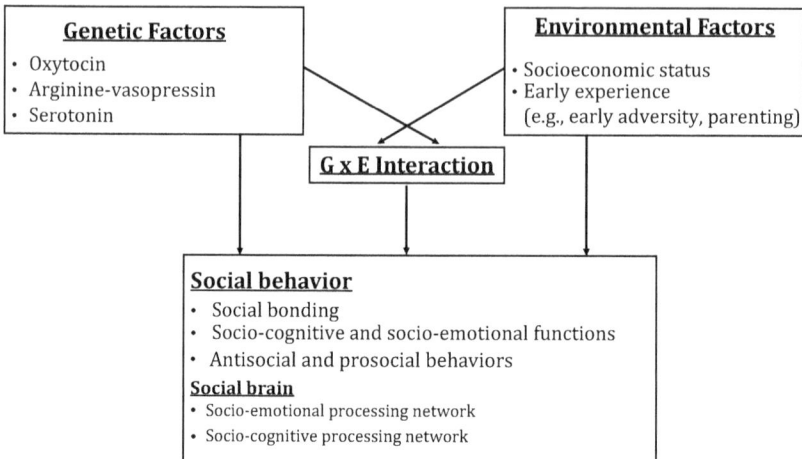

Figure 11.1 The influence of genetic and environmental factors on human social behavior and the social brain

socially behavioral characteristics), such as social bonding (e.g., affiliative behaviors, social network properties), socio-cognitive and socio-emotional functions, and the function and structure of the social brain (see Skuse, 2006; Zink & Meyer-Lindenberg, 2012 for review). To answer the question of whether individual differences in social behaviors and the social brain can be accounted for with genetic variations, researchers collect DNA via saliva or buccal swabs to identify genotypes (i.e., the genetic identity inherited from parents) from hundreds or thousands of people. Then, they look at the DNA and identify variations that people with a certain phenotype (e.g., trait, disease) have but that people without such a phenotype do not have. This analysis shows relationships between the individual variations in genotypes and phenotypes of interest. Studies have suggested that genetic variations in the abovementioned neurochemicals are associated with individual differences in social behavior and the social brain.

Oxytocin is involved in childbirth and childcaring (e.g., contractions of the uterus and lactation) as a hormone. However, when it works as a neuropeptide in the central nervous system, oxytocin is associated with more general social cognition and social behaviors, including processing of important social information and forming of social bonding (e.g., parenting, attachment). For example, in a seminal study (Kosfeld et al., 2005), people who received a dose of oxytocin showed greater trust in a

Table 11.1 *Neurotransmitters, related function, social behavior, genes, and brain regions*

Neurotransmitter	Relevant function	Relevant social behavior	Relevant genes	Relevant brain regions
Oxytocin	Social bonding	– Social bonding – Sociability – Prosocial behavior	Oxytocin receptor genes (e.g., OXTR gene)	– Emotional processing-related regions (e.g., amygdala, inferior frontal cortex) – Social functioning-related regions (e.g., inferior temporal gyrus, superior temporal sulcus, and inferior anterior prefrontal cortex)
Arginine-vasopressin	Anxiety, arousal	– Social bonding – Empathy – Prosocial behavior	Arginine-vasopressin receptor genes (e.g., AVPR1A gene)	– Social functioning-related regions (e.g., inferior anterior PFC)
Serotonin	Mood and sleep regulation, perception, learning and memory	– Social bonding – Emotional processing – Prosocial behavior	Serotonin transporter genes (e.g., 5-HTTLPR in SLC6A4 gene)	– Emotional processing-related region (e.g., amygdala)

social exchange game than people who received a placebo, suggesting oxytocin enhances positive social interaction.

Regarding genetic factors, the oxytocin receptor gene (OXTR) has been intensively studied. The OXTR single nucleotide polymorphism – a variation in a combination of alleles at a specific position in the genome – is known to be related to individual differences in social bonding (e.g., parenting behaviors: Bakermans-Kranenburg & van IJzendoorn, 2008; attachment: Chen et al., 2011; emotional support seeking: Kim et al., 2010; positive social emotion: Algoe et al., 2014). Carrying the G allele of OXTR (i.e., rs53576) has been reported to be positively associated with social bonding behaviors. For example, in one study, individuals with the G allele homozygotes of OXTR (i.e., rs53576-GG) displayed greater levels of sensitive parenting behaviors toward their children compared to individuals with the A allele (i.e., those who have rs53576-AA or -AG genotype: Bakermans-Kranenberg & van IJzendoorn, 2008). Similarly, Americans with the G allele of OXTR (i.e., rs53576-GG or -AG) were more likely to seek emotional support in a distressing situation than Americans with the AA genotype, which, however, was not observed in the Korean population (Kim et al., 2010). These findings suggest that levels of social bonding behaviors can depend on genetic variation in OXTR (e.g., whether individuals carry the G allele of OXTR or the A allele of OXTR) but may be modulated by ethnicity or sociocultural factors.

In addition to the single nucleotide polymorphism, recent studies have paid attention to the relationship between DNA methylation of the genes linked to oxytocin release and the oxytocin receptors and social behaviors. DNA methylation is a process of adding methyl groups to the DNA molecule that influences gene expression. Even with the same gene sequence, the expression of relevant phenotype can depend on this process of epigenetic modification. Typically, methylation represses gene expression. In other words, lower DNA methylation is associated with greater gene expression. Regarding the oxytocin and OXTR genes, individuals with lower DNA methylation showed greater secure attachment (Haas et al., 2016), less insecure attachment (e.g., anxiety attachment: Ebner et al., 2019; avoidant attachment: Ein-Dor et al., 2018), and lower levels of anxiety in response to others' distress (Hiraoka et al., 2021) compared to individuals with higher levels of DNA methylation. In other words, individuals who have lower DNA methylation are likely to have greater oxytocin gene expression, thereby showing greater positive social bonding behaviors.

Genetic variations in OXTR also appear to be linked to diverse sociocognitive and socio-emotional functions (Laursen et al., 2014; Rodrigues et al., 2009; Smith et al., 2014; Wade et al., 2014). Li et al. (2015) conducted a meta-analysis to investigate whether individual differences in OXTR genes are related to general sociability – how people generally respond to others, including friends, caregivers, partners, children, and even strangers. To that end, they combined the results of eighteen relevant existing studies and analyzed the effects of individual differences in OXTR (i.e., rs53576, one of the OXTR single nucleotide polymorphisms) on general sociability. Results showed that individuals with the G allele homozygotes of the rs53576 (i.e., rs53576-GG) tended to be more sociable generally compared to individuals with the A allele carriers (i.e., rs53576-AA or -AG). Such patterns were also found in infants. Babies with more copies of the G allele in rs11131149 in OXTR displayed better socio-cognitive and socio-emotional processes encompassing joint attention, precursors to mentalizing skills, self-recognition, and empathy (Wade et al., 2014).

Prosocial behavior may also differ depending on genetic variation in OXTR (Bernhard et al., 2016; Israel et al., 2009; Kogan et al., 2011; Tost et al., 2010). For instance, in Kogan and his colleagues' (2011) study, naïve observers were asked to watch silenced video clips showing a conversation between participants with varying OXTR (i.e., rs53576) genotypes and their romantic partner when the partner was talking about his or her personal suffering. Then, the observers evaluated the prosociality (i.e., trustworthiness, compassion, and kindness) of the participants in the video clips. Results showed that the naïve observers rated the participants with the G allele homozygotes of the OXTR gene (i.e., rs53576-GG) as more prosocial than participants with the A allele. In addition, the participants carrying the G allele homozygotes were evaluated as showing greater affiliative nonverbal cues to their romantic partner compared to the participants carrying the A allele. These results suggest that carrying the G allele of OXTR could be related to a greater tendency to show prosocial behavior.

Research linking genes to the brain suggests that genes might influence social bonding, socio-cognitive and socio-emotional functions, and other social behaviors via phenotypic differences in the social brain. Individual differences in OXTR single nucleotide polymorphisms and OXTR DNA methylation levels are associated with the structure and function of the amygdala, the region involved in evaluating social stimuli and emotion processing (see Chapter 3 for details), as well as other socio-cognitive and socio-emotional processing regions, including the inferior frontal cortex (Furman et al., 2011; Inoue et al., 2010; Krol et al., 2019; Tost et al.,

2010), inferior temporal gyrus (Hiraoka et al., 2021), superior temporal sulcus (STS) (Laursen et al., 2014), and inferior anterior prefrontal cortex (PFC) (Nishitani et al., 2017). Studies using magnetic resonance imaging (MRI) data to measure the amygdala volume reported that individuals with OXTR (i.e., rs2254298) G allele homozygotes (i.e., GG) had smaller amygdalae than those with the A allele carriers (i.e., GA: Furman et al., 2011; and AA: Inoue et al., 2010). In another study using functional MRI, it was found that mothers with OXTR rs2254298-GG, compared to mothers with A carriers, showed greater neural activation in the right inferior anterior PFC in response to watching their own child smiling relative to an unfamiliar child (Nishitani et al., 2017). Similarly, lower levels of OXTR DNA methylation (i.e., higher OXT gene expression) were related to increased neural activation in the STS during social cognitive tasks and greater gray matter volume in the fusiform gyrus (Haas et al., 2016). An infant study reported consistent results that lower levels of OXTR DNA methylation were associated with reduced neural responses to emotionally negative stimuli (e.g., angry and fearful faces) and greater responses to emotionally positive stimuli (e.g., happy faces) in the right inferior frontal cortex (Krol et al., 2019). These results suggest that individuals with more copies of the G allele or individuals with higher oxytocin gene expression seem to display a larger structure and greater neural activation in brain regions related to social functioning (e.g., inferior anterior PFC, STS, fusiform gyrus) but have a smaller structure of the brain region (i.e., amygdala) related to processing negative stimuli.

Arginine-vasopressin is another neuropeptide that plays an important role in social behaviors. Contrary to oxytocin, arginine-vasopressin is associated with anxiety and arousal in social interactions. Similar to the oxytocin-related genes, genetic variation in the arginine-vasopressin receptor (e.g., AVPR1A) appears to contribute to individual differences in social behaviors including social bonding (Avinun et al., 2012; Leerkes et al., 2017; Nishitani et al., 2017; Walum et al., 2008), socio-cognitive and socio-emotional functions (e.g., cognitive empathy: Uzefovsky et al., 2015; response to social stress: Moons et al., 2014), as well as prosociality (e.g., prosocial decision-making: Avinun et al., 2011; Knafo et al., 2008; reciprocity: Nishina et al., 2019). For instance, in humans, one of the most extensively studied AVPR1A polymorphic DNA sequences in relation to social behavior is AVPR1A repeat polymorphisms RS3, which appears to be related to social bonding. Specifically, men carrying the RS3 allele 334 reported lower perceived partner bonding and greater marital problems compared to men without the allele 334 (Walum et al., 2008).

Likewise, mothers with a long form of RS3 displayed less social bonding behaviors toward their children than mothers with a short form of RS3 (Avinun et al., 2012). Regarding socio-cognitive and socio-emotional functions as well as prosocial behaviors, possessing the RS3 327 allele is associated with lower cognitive empathy in young adults (Uzefovsky et al., 2015). Similar patterns were found in children, such that children with the RS3 327 repeat allele showed less altruistic behaviors during a distribution game than children without the RS3 327 repeat allele (Avinun et al., 2011). These findings suggest that carriers of AVPR1A repeat polymorphisms show weaker social bonding, decreased socio-emotional functions, and less prosocial behavior compared to individuals without such an allele.

Studies on the gene–brain association suggest that genetic variation in AVPR1A is related to the function of the social brain. In a functional MRI (fMRI) study, activation in the amygdala during the processing of emotional stimuli differed depending on the variants of AVPR1A RS3 (Meyer-Lindenberg et al., 2009). Specifically, individuals with the RS3 334 allele displayed higher activation in the amygdala while processing negative facial stimuli (i.e., angry and fearful faces) than individuals with all other alleles. In addition, individuals with long allele lengths of RS3 showed greater activation in the amygdala compared to individuals with short alleles. Similar to the aforementioned finding on the association between possessing the RS3 allele 334 and lower social bonding in men (Walum et al., 2008), fathers without the RS3 334 allele showed greater activation in the left inferior anterior PFC in response to their child's smile compared to an unfamiliar child's smile, whereas fathers with the RS3 334 allele did not show such a difference (Nishitani et al., 2017). Also, the higher activation in the left inferior anterior PFC of fathers without the 334 allele was positively correlated with bonding with their children, whereas such a correlation was not found among fathers with the 334 allele. Results suggest that the left inferior anterior PFC might be relevant to positive parental bonding, which can be found only in fathers without the 334 allele.

A neurotransmitter serotonin is known to contribute to a wide range of human psychology and behavior including mood and sleep regulation, cognition and perception, learning and memory, and social cognition and behaviors. In terms of social phenotype, variations in the serotonin-related genes are linked to social bonding (Bakermans-Kranenburg & van IJzendoorn, 2008), socio-emotional processes, including emotional processing (Pérez-Edgar et al., 2010; Pergamin-Hight et al., 2012) and emotional resilience (i.e., the ability to have sustained psychological functioning:

Stein et al., 2009), as well as prosociality (Enge et al., 2017; Gärtner et al., 2018; Stoltenberg et al., 2013). For instance, mothers homozygous for the short allele of the serotonin transporter genes (5-HTTLPR in the SLC6A4 gene) (i.e., 5-HTT ss) displayed lower parental sensitivity than did mothers with the 5-HTT long allele (i.e., 5-HTT sl or ll: Bakermans-Kranenburg & van IJzendoorn, 2008). Regarding socio-emotional function, Pergamin-Hight and colleagues (2012) conducted a meta-analysis by integrating the results from ten existing studies to analyze the genetic variation in the serotonin transporter gene (5-HTTLPR) and emotional processing. Results suggested that individuals with the genotype of low serotonin transmission efficacy (e.g., short allele), but not individuals with the genotype of intermediate and high efficacy (e.g., long allele), tended to be vigilantly attentive to emotionally negative stimuli (e.g., threatening stimuli). In addition, individuals with the short allele of 5-HTTLPR were less likely to help others (Stoltenberg et al., 2013) and displayed a weaker tendency to punish individuals who violate social norms (i.e., people who suggest unfair offers: Enge et al., 2017) compared to individuals with the long allele. These findings suggest that individuals with the short form of the serotonin polymorphisms appear to show less social bonding and less prosocial behavior but more sensitivity to negative stimuli.

Genetic variations in the serotonin systems and transporter have been also linked to the social brain function, especially socio-emotional processing (see Hariri & Holmes, 2006 for review). For example, in response to negative emotional stimuli (e.g., fearful faces, aversive pictures), individuals with a short allele of the serotonin transporter (i.e., 5-HTTLPR in the SLC6A4 gene), compared to individuals with the long allele, showed greater activation in the amygdala (Hariri et al., 2002; Heinz et al., 2005) and greater coupling between the amygdala and the prefrontal cortex (Heinz et al., 2005).

Taken together, genetic variations in the neurochemicals that are critically involved in social bonding as well as socio-cognitive and socio-emotional functions are associated with individual differences in a broader domain of social behaviors and the functions and structure of the social brain. However, it is important to note that the aforementioned neurochemicals do not always have consistent effects. The effects can depend on situational and individual differences (see Bartz et al., 2011 for a review). For instance, although we looked at the study where oxytocin is associated with greater trust in social interaction (Kosfeld et al., 2005), there is also evidence that oxytocin is related to more parochial altruism, that is, greater trust toward the in-group and an increased defensive attitude toward the out-group (De Dreu et al., 2010), and that oxytocin is associated with decreases of positive social interaction (e.g., cooperation) in individuals with borderline personality disorder (Bartz et al., 2011). It is also noteworthy that genes interact with environmental factors, as we discuss in the following section, and that genes can influence human behaviors differently depending on ethnicity or culture (Chen et al., 2011; Kim et al., 2010). In the next section, we will look at how environmental factors shape social behavior and the social brain.

11.3 Environmental Influences on Individual Differences in Social Behavior and the Social Brain

In this section, we will review socioeconomic status (SES) and early experience as environmental factors associated with individual differences in social behavior and the social brain. First, SES has been one of the most extensively studied factors influencing social behavior and the social brain. It is often measured as a combination of income, education level, occupation, and wealth, namely objective SES, and it is known to reflect the amount of economic and social resources an individual or a group possesses in relation to others (Saegert et al., 2006). Although the components of the objective SES tend to be correlated, they do not always correspond to each other (Ensminger & Fothergill, 2003; Shavers, 2007). For example, people who have lower education levels can have higher income than people with higher education levels. Also, individuals' perceived position in social hierarchies compared to others in their world, namely subjective SES, is an important factor that should be considered differently from their objective SES (Adler et al., 2000; Anderson et al., 2012). Both the objective and subjective measures of SES are widely used in research. Early poverty is also addressed because poverty is mainly related to economic status, one of the SES components. Second, early childhood experience is another topic that has been broadly studied in relation to social behavior and the social brain. What one experiences at the early life stage, especially the social environment, appears to influence how one interprets the world (Crawford et al., 2022; Germine et al., 2015). We will look at the effects of early adversity (e.g., maltreatment, institutionalization) and interaction with caregivers (e.g., parenting) on social behavior and the social brain.

11.3.1 Socioeconomic Status (SES)

Individuals or groups with higher SES are regarded as having greater advantages in obtaining material and social capital. Affluent capital due to higher SES allows individuals to have easier and better access to information, human resources, and opportunities that they seek, possibly leading to greater psychological and social resources. Here, we will review how SES is linked to these resources, centering on social network structures, social relationship qualities, and socio-cognitive and socio-emotional functions.

Empirically, it has been well documented that the structure of social networks varies depending on a person's SES. To be specific, individuals with higher SES are likely to have larger social networks (e.g., having more friends, being involved in more social groups), whereas individuals with lower SES tend to report smaller social networks (e.g., being involved in less social groups, a higher divorce rate) (Fischer, 1982; House et al., 1988; Van Groenou & Van Tilburg, 2003; Veroff et al., 1981). A more recent study found similar patterns. Within a sample of middle-aged and older adults, education predicted the size of social network (Ajrouch et al., 2005). Specifically, individuals who received more than high school education had larger social networks than individuals who received less than high school education. The quality of social resources also differs depending on the SES, such that lower SES is associated with less positive and greater negative flow of social exchange. For instance, women of lower occupational status reported higher social strain (Gallo et al., 2005) and men with lower occupational status reported less emotional support and more negative features of close relationship (e.g., conflicts) (Stringhini et al., 2012). Such influences of SES on the social network structure and function can be found in diverse stages of life, extending from childhood (Samuelsson, 1997) and adolescence (e.g., Arias et al., 2018) to old age (Bielderman et al., 2015).

Studies comparing social support from kin and non-kin relationships suggest that social networks serve differently among individuals with high SES and low SES (Krause & Borawski-Clark 1995; Van Groenou & Van Tilburg, 2003). For instance, older adults with high SES (e.g., educational and occupational status) tend to have a larger network than older adults with lower SES. Interestingly, the types and providers of social support were different depending on the SES. Older adults with high SES received greater social support from non-kin relationships, compared to older adults with lower SES. The forms of social support that the high SES individuals received from non-kin relationship were both instrumental (e.g., material or practical assistance) and emotional (e.g., trust, caring, love). On the other hand, older adults with lower SES reported to have received greater instrumental social support from kin relationships than older adults with higher SES, while there was no SES-related difference in emotional support from kin relationships (Van Groenou & Van Tilburg, 2003). It seems that individuals of high SES have more diverse and wider non-kin relationships through benefits offered by their higher education or occupation levels, enabling them to have greater social resources that they can access when necessary. On the contrary, individuals of lower SES have narrower non-kin relationships, leading them to seek for assistance mainly from kin relationships.

SES has also been known to be related to individual differences in socio-cognitive and socio-emotional functions. Conceptually, it has been suggested that SES should influence one's development of such social functions both directly and indirectly. It can directly influence development of socio-cognitive and socio-emotional abilities through family investment, for example, by providing resources such as books and extracurricular activities (see Conger & Donnellan, 2007 for review). The indirect effects of SES could be found in family stressors and low self-efficacy experienced by individuals in the lower SES class. Family stressors negatively influence development of the necessary social skills (Conger et al., 2002) and self-efficacy, one's belief and ability to have control over a situation (Mazur et al., 2014), which can ultimately influence socio-cognitive and socio-emotional functions and interpersonal skills (Bandura, 1993). Empirical evidence supports these connections. Lower family SES was linked to decreased self-regulation skills, including emotion regulation (Crandall et al. 2017; Farley & Kim-Spoon, 2017; Herd et al., 2020), less accuracy in mentalizing tasks (Cutting & Dunn, 1999; Pears & Moses, 2003; Shatz et al., 2003), and slower development of mentalizing (Ebert et al., 2017) in childhood and adolescence.

Given that SES contributes to individual variations in social behaviors (e.g., social bonding, socio-cognitive and socio-emotional functions), it would be natural to ask whether SES would also influence the structure and function of the social brain. The answer seems positive, but more converging evidence is needed. Some studies report positive correlations between SES and the gray matter density and volume of the social brain regions. For instance, lower SES (e.g., family income: Hanson et al., 2013; parental education and occupation levels: Raizada et al., 2008) is associated with lower gray matter volumes in the frontal regions in children, which are known to be involved in mentalizing abilities. Moreover, children with lower SES have reduced hippocampal gray matter density (e.g., family income: Hanson et al., 2011) and reduced hippocampal volumes (e.g., income-to-needs: Noble et al., 2012; both subjective and objective parental SES: Yu et al., 2018). Though the hippocampus is not often included among the social brain regions, it is one of the core structures of the limbic system, along with the amygdala, which processes socio-emotional information (Montagrin et al., 2018). Objective SES was also found to be associated with children's amygdala volume, such that children who had greater poverty (i.e., lower income-to-needs ratio) had smaller amygdala volume (Luby et al., 2013).

SES appears to be linked to social brain structures in adulthood as well. For example, adults who reported current financial hardship had smaller volumes in the amygdala and hippocampus than adults who did not report financial hardship (Butterworth et al., 2012). Adults with lower subjective SES had reduced gray matter volume in the perigenual area of the anterior cingulate cortex, the region associated with regulating emotions and reaction to stress (Gianaros et al., 2007). However, there are other studies reporting nonsignificant correlations or even negative correlations between SES and volumes of social brain structures, including the amygdala (Hanson et al., 2011; Noble et al., 2012) and the hippocampus (Lawson et al., 2017). The variations in the ways of measuring SES (e.g., income or education), the ways of quantifying brain structures (e.g., cortical volume or thickness), different age spans of the participants (e.g., children, adolescents, adults), and the timing of socioeconomic adversity were proposed as possibilities underlying such inconsistent findings (see Brito & Noble, 2014 for review). Further investigation is necessary to elucidate how SES is linked to the variation in structures of the social brain.

Though the evidence is still preliminary, SES has been associated with functional differences in the social brain regions as well. For instance, functional brain imaging studies suggest that individuals of lower SES may face greater challenges in regulating emotions during stressful interpersonal situations. In a functional near-infrared spectroscopy (fNIRS) study, young adults with lower perceived SES during childhood reported greater social stress when they were excluded during an online ball-tossing game, while showing lower activity in the ventrolateral prefrontal cortex (vlPFC), a region related to self-regulation (Yanagisawa et al., 2013). In fMRI studies using facial expression stimuli, adults' retrospective SES during their childhood was found to be negatively associated with neural activation in the amygdala (Gianaros et al., 2008; Javanbakht, et al., 2015). For example, young adults who perceived their parental social standing (e.g., income, occupation, education levels) during their childhood and adolescence as lower displayed greater amygdala activation in response to threatening (i.e., angry) faces compared to their counterparts who perceived their parental social status as higher (Gianaros et al., 2008). These findings imply that SES can influence individuals' socio-emotional experiences, which are mediated by differences in the neural activity of relevant brain regions.

Extremely low economic status in childhood (i.e., childhood poverty) appears to influence neural systems for emotion regulation, even later in life. For example, in an fMRI study using a task requiring emotion regulation skills, young adults exposed to poverty in childhood showed reduced activation in the dorsolateral prefrontal cortex (dlPFC), a region related to emotion regulation, during the task than young adults who had not been exposed to early poverty (Liberzon et al., 2015). In one study (Javanbakht et al., 2015) with a subset of participants in a larger longitudinal project, researchers investigated differences in brain activity in response to emotional faces between young adults who grew up in lower-income households during childhood (i.e., at age 9) and those from middle-income households. Results showed that childhood poverty was associated with greater reactivity in the amygdala to fearful faces, lesser reactivity in the amygdala to happy faces, and greater reactivity in the medial PFC (mPFC) in response to angry faces. The results suggest that individuals of lower childhood family income possess greater sensitivity to social threat than social reward, while the opposite might be the case for those of higher childhood family income. In the same study, individuals of lower childhood family income also showed decreased functional connectivity between the amygdala and PFC in response to an angry face than with a happy face, indicating a possibility of inefficient neural circuits for regulating negative emotions.

Similarly, another study where participants were from the same longitudinal project as Javanbakht et al. (2015) found that during emotional reappraisal, one of effective cognitive strategies for emotion regulation, young adults who experienced greater poverty at the age of nine showed decreased activity in the dlPFC and vlPFC and increased activity in the amygdala (Kim et al., 2013). Also, when examining the functional connectivity between the amygdala and vlPFC during emotional reappraisal, a negative amygdala–vlPFC connectivity (e.g., reduced amygdala activity associated with greater vlPFC activity) was observed in the individuals of higher childhood family income, whereas a positive amygdala–vlPFC functional connectivity (e.g., greater amygdala activity associated with greater vlPFC activity) was found in the individuals of lower childhood family income. The researchers interpreted these results to indicate that the vlPFC of the higher SES individuals might be effective in regulating the amygdala, leading to their lower amygdala activation during emotion regulation, whereas the vlPFC of the lower SES individuals might be less effective in regulating the amygdala, leading to their higher amygdala activity. Overall, early poverty seems to exert influence on the functional changes in brain regions involved in emotion regulation. The factors underlying such long-term effects of early poverty may include chronic stress (Kim et al., 2013; Liberzon et al., 2015), in that childhood poverty exposes individuals to greater chronic stressors associated with emotional distress and dysregulation.

On the other hand, individuals of lower SES may display socially adaptive behaviors in other domains, such as mentalizing and prosociality. Kraus and colleagues (2012) proposed that individuals of lower social status are more likely to focus on external and environmental factors than internal factors and show greater interdependence in social relationships because their life outcomes tend to rely on external contexts relative to individuals of higher social status. Thus, compared to individuals with higher SES, individuals with low SES are more sensitive to other people's emotions and external factors that build the emotions (see Manstead, 2018 for review). Studies showed that lower SES is associated with higher empathy levels (Kraus et al., 2010; Stellar et al., 2012), greater willingness to help others in need (e.g., Miller et al., 2015), and less tendency to make unethical decisions (Piff et al., 2010, 2012). For instance, in one study, researchers examined the effect of SES on empathic responses and found that individuals with low SES exhibited higher self-reported dispositional compassion and showed stronger physiological response (i.e., heart rate deceleration) than those with high SES while watching a video of others suffering (Stellar et al., 2012).

Findings from neuroimaging research are consistent with the behavioral evidence that individuals with lower SES exhibit greater empathy and prosociality. Muscatell and her colleagues (2012) examined the effects of perceived SES on neural activity in the mentalizing network while participants performed a mentalizing task. They found that young adults with lower perceived SES displayed greater activation in the mentalizing network, including dmPFC, mPFC, and precuneus/posterior cingulate cortex (PCC) than their counterparts with higher perceived SES. Taken together, although lower SES has been regarded as related to a smaller social network and lower socio-emotional functions (e.g., emotion regulation), there has been evidence that lower SES does not negatively impact all aspects of social functioning. Lower SES can lead individuals to be more sensitive to others' minds. To better understand the seemingly inconsistent relationships between SES and social functioning, a more integrated investigation across diverse social functioning would be necessary.

11.3.2 Early Childhood Experience

Early childhood environment plays a key role in social development. What one experiences in early childhood is closely related to family environment (e.g., maltreatment, parents' marital conflict, and relationship with caregivers). For example, parents can be a social role model by directly and indirectly providing guidance on how to adapt to society. There are findings that children whose parents have marital conflict are more likely to show aggressive behaviors to peers or siblings (see Cummings & Zahn-Waxler, 1992) and have lower social competence in peer relationships (Finger et al., 2010). Abused children were also reported to show more aggressive and less positive social behaviors (Salzinger et al., 1993; Trickett & Kuczynski, 1986). Likewise, children with insecure attachment seem to be more likely to receive negative social evaluation (e.g., aggressive, less competent) from peers and teachers (Cohn, 1990) and negative reactions from peers even when they show positive behaviors (Fagot, 1997). Children who had more secure attachment with their parents tend to have a larger social network and greater social competence (Bost et al., 1998) and higher quality of peer relationships (Coleman, 2003; Main & Weton, 1981; Suess et al., 1992; Youngblade & Belsky, 1992) and to be more popular and accepted by peers (Verschueren & Marcoen, 1999). In other words, how children form social networks can differ by their relationship with their caregivers. It is noteworthy, however, that there is a possibility that parents' social networks may influence the relationship between attachment and children's social behaviors given that maternal social networks are related to both child–mother attachment and children's social functions. For example, infants whose mothers have greater satisfaction with the quality of their social network are likely to have more secure attachment (Huth-Bocks et al., 2004), and children whose mothers have greater social network size tend to have larger social networks themselves (Prinstein & La Greca, 1999).

Early childhood experience seems to be associated with individual differences in the structure and function of social networks in later life as well (see Ladd & Pettit, 2002 for review). For example, in a cross-sectional study (Ford et al., 2011), adults who reported that they had experienced physical abuse in childhood were more likely to have negative social experiences (e.g., stress, worries) from their close relationships at midlife, and adults who reported parental divorce in childhood had a higher likelihood of having smaller social networks. Likewise, in another cross-sectional study (Melkman, 2017), adults who reported adversity in childhood (e.g., adverse family conditions, maltreatment) had a smaller network size, less satisfaction with their social networks, and less frequently received emotional and instrumental social support. In a longitudinal study (Seibert & Kerns, 2015), child–mother attachment in early childhood predicted peer relationships at grades 3 and 5. In particular, children who had secure attachment with their mothers in early life (i.e., at age three) were rated by parents and teachers to be less excluded by peers, whereas children with insecure attachment at an early stage were reported to be more asocial (e.g., children with avoidant attachment) or less prosocial (e.g., children with disorganized attachment), suggesting the effect of early experience on later social relationships.

As SES is associated with one's socio-cognitive and socio-emotional functions, adverse early childhood experience may also be related to one's social functioning. A negative environment (e.g., maltreatment, poor parenting) can lead children to imitate and learn socially negative behaviors that they observe from their caregivers, and it can deprive children of opportunities to learn and develop their social abilities (see Morris et al., 2007 for review). A review study encompassing fifty-one empirical studies (Luke & Banerjee, 2013) suggests that physical abuse and neglect in childhood are negatively associated with various socio-cognitive and socio-emotional functions, including emotion recognition, emotion understanding, and mentalizing. Specifically, such negative associations were stronger for more complex levels of social functions (e.g., emotion understanding) than for less complex ones (e.g., emotion recognition). Another study (Germine et al., 2015) found similar patterns. Retrospectively reported early adversity, especially experience of physical abuse, was closely associated with poor higher-level social functions, such as mentalizing abilities, social motivation to pursue social interaction, and perceived social support in adulthood. Basic-level functions like facial processing, however, were not related to early adversity. These results suggest that early adversity is powerfully linked to poor higher-level social functions such as emotion understanding and mentalizing, which requires analysis and inference, rather than basic social functions such as emotion recognition, which requires low-level detection.

Child–parent interaction, such as parental talk focused on each other's mental state and child–parent attachment, is also known to influence the development of socio-cognitive and socio-emotional functions (Dunn et al., 1991; Ensor & Hughes, 2008; Ensor et al., 2011; Meins et al., 2002). To be specific, mothers' more frequent use of mental state terms during the child–mother interaction at age 2 (Ensor & Hughes, 2008) and a secure parent–child attachment at 11 or 13 months (Meins et al., 1998) predicted children's performance on social understanding tasks that measure mentalizing and emotion understanding abilities later (i.e., at age 3 or 4). Child–parent interaction is also related to emotion regulation skills. For instance, maternal responsiveness and support are associated with children's emotion regulation skills (Hardy et al., 1993). Negative maternal parenting, such as scolding, expressing anger to children, or physical or verbal control over children, is linked to a child's lower-level emotional regulation (Calkins et al., 1998).

Early childhood experience is also closely related to antisocial and prosocial behaviors. For example, children whose parents showed aggressive and hostile behaviors or children whose parents were less responsive and unsupportive were more likely to display antisocial behaviors (see Repetti et al., 2002 for review). On the other hand, children who had greater levels of mother-child mutuality (e.g., mother's responsiveness to child, child's responsiveness to mother, and reciprocity) at age 2 showed greater prosocial behavior at age 4 (Ensor et al., 2011). This implies that children's experience with their mother at early age influences their later prosociality. Furthermore, a recent meta study analyzing 123 previous articles revealed that stress in early life, such as childhood abuse or trauma, was related to less prosociality (Wu et al., 2020).

Regarding the effects of early childhood experiences on the social brain, although most of the previous studies involved animals (see Sandi & Haller, 2015 for review), several studies on humans suggest that early exposure to stress is associated with change in social brain structures and functions. First, when examining the structure of the social brain, children who experienced maltreatment (Kelly et al., 2013) and who were raised in institutions (McLaughlin et al., 2014) displayed reduced cortical thickness in extended prefrontal brain regions, including the orbitofrontal cortex (OFC) and the superior frontal gyrus. Hippocampal volume also seems to be influenced by childhood maltreatment, such that adults who reported childhood maltreatment had reduced hippocampal volume (Lawson et al., 2017). Amygdala volume has also been related to early childhood experiences, but there are mixed findings. For example, some studies showed that children exposed to institutional rearing had greater amygdala volume (Mehta et al., 2009; Tottenham et al., 2010). However, in other studies with different measures of childhood stress, this association was reversed (physical abuse: Hanson et al., 2015) or disappeared (negative parenting: Kok et al., 2015). More evidence is needed to delineate the effects of various childhood experiences on the development of the social brain.

Parenting style is one of the important factors influencing childhood experiences, which has also been associated with individual differences in various structures of the social brain. For example, positive parenting style using praise was positively linked to children's gray matter volume in the posterior insula cortex, a brain region involved in processing emotions (Matsudaira et al., 2016), whereas negative parenting style using punishment was positively associated with adolescents' larger volume in reward processing-related regions, such as the dorsal ACC and OFC (Whittle et al., 2009). In a longitudinal study (Whittle et al., 2014), adolescents whose mothers showed more frequent positive behaviors, such as warm and supportive behaviors, toward them during early adolescence displayed a lesser increase in amygdala volume and greater cortical thinning in OFC from early- to mid-adolescence, compared to those whose mothers showed fewer positive behaviors. Considering that the adolescent brain is characterized by cortical pruning, it suggests that positive parenting behaviors may yield children's optimal prefrontal–amygdala balance, which could lower reactivity to emotionally salient stimuli and support a higher level of emotion regulation skills. On the other hand, male adolescents whose mothers displayed more frequent negative parenting, like being aggressive toward them during early adolescence, were more likely to have greater increases in cortical thickness in some brain regions involved in emotion regulation, such as the superior frontal gyrus, superior parietal lobe, and supramarginal gyrus, compared to male adolescents whose mothers displayed less frequent negative parenting (Whittle et al., 2016). Again, given that cortical thinning in adolescence is considered as brain maturation, this suggests that negative parenting is associated with delayed maturation of brain regions related to emotion regulation.

Early experience seems to influence social brain functions as well, mostly in the regions related to emotion processing. First, when looking at the effects of early adversity, including institutionalization and maltreatment, individuals with early adversity seem to have different functional patterns in the social brain. For example, Moulson and her colleagues (2009) measured neural responses during facial emotion processing (e.g., angry, happy, fearful, and sad faces) using event-related potentials (ERPs) from three groups of children with different early experiences: an institutionalized group, a foster group who had previously been institutionalized but got foster care later, and a control group who had never been institutionalized. The ERPs were obtained at three different age points: baseline (5–31 months), 30 months, and 42 months. In general, all three groups displayed different patterns of neural processing in the frontocentral components in response to facial emotions. However, the institutionalized group displayed reduced amplitude and longer latencies in the occipital components compared to the foster group and the control group. Likewise, when examining neural response during passive processing of positive and negative stimuli and active emotional regulation via cognitive appraisal, adolescents exposed to physical or sexual abuse showed increased neural responses in the amygdala, putamen, and anterior insula in response to negative stimuli (relative to neutral stimuli) and greater neural activity in the superior frontal gyrus, dorsal anterior cingulate cortex, and frontal pole when regulating emotions (relative to passive processing; McLaughlin et al., 2015). The result suggests that early maltreatment could be associated with greater responses to negative emotional stimuli and greater effort to regulate negative emotions.

Family environment, such as parenting and family conflicts, also seems to be related to individual differences in the functioning of the social brain, especially of the brain regions involved in processing emotions and reward. Although inconsistencies may be observed (e.g., Romund et al., 2016), studies found that reporting a positive family environment, such as greater emotional responsiveness during adolescence (Farber et al., 2018) and less family conflicts during childhood (Taylor et al., 2006), was associated with greater neural activation in the amygdala in response to emotionally threatening stimuli (e.g., angry, fearful faces) in adolescence (Farber et al., 2018) and early adulthood (Taylor et al., 2006). The results may reflect that individuals with more positive family environments are sensitive to emotionally threatening stimuli, possibly leading to greater activation in the amygdala, compared to individuals with less positive family environments who could be accustomed to such emotionally negative stimuli. Importantly, the evidence suggests that parenting may be related to long-term neural alterations during emotion perception and reward processing. In a longitudinal study (Kopala-Sibley et al., 2020), 10-year-old children who had experienced hostile maternal parenting, measured at age 3, showed greater negative functional connectivity between the amygdala and frontal/parietal regions when perceiving emotionally negative stimuli relative to neutral stimuli. Hostile parenting was also associated with increased negative functional connectivity between the ventral striatal and posterior orbital frontal cortex/inferior frontal gyrus in response to monetary reward, suggesting the influence of parenting on emotion- and reward-related neural circuits. Interestingly, individual differences in the function of the social brain depending on family environment seem to be found at an early age. For instance, using electroencephalogram (EEG) readings, maternal depression appears to impact the child's brain's function as well. Dawson and her colleagues (1992) examined infants' brain activity when interacting with their mothers, comparing infants whose mothers reported depressive symptoms to those whose mothers did not. Results showed that infants of depressed mothers displayed reduced activity in the left frontal area, which is known to be associated with positive emotions. Such patterns can even be extended to scenarios when infants positively interacted with nondepressed adult others (i.e., playing peek-a-boo) (Dawson et al., 1999), implying that maternal depression can negatively influence infants' brain activity in a more general situation.

It is noteworthy, however, that adversity in early life does not always lead to negative outcomes (see Gee, 2016 for review), as seen in Section 11.3.1 on SES. For example, children exposed to early life stress (e.g., physical/emotional/sexual neglect and abuse, maternal deprivation) seem to undergo earlier maturation in functional connectivity between the PFC and amygdala (Fan et al., 2014; Gee, Gabard-Durnam et al., 2013). To be specific, children exposed to early adversity, such as institutionalization, showed negative amygdala–PFC connectivity (Gee, Gabard-Durnam, et al., 2013), which usually emerges at a later age as emotion regulation skills develop (Gee, Humphreys, et al., 2013). Also, some findings suggest that children exposed to early adversity show greater sensitivity to emotional stimuli (Tottenham et al., 2011) and have greater amygdala volume (Mehta et al., 2009; Tottenham et al., 2010). The mixed results on the effects of early adversity seem to be because of various factors, including timing of exposure to adversity, the types and severity of adversity, and the presence of supportive friends and adults outside the family (see Cohodes et al., 2021; Gartland et al., 2019 for review). In other words, there are huge individual differences in the developmental responses to early childhood adversity, leading to individual variations in the effects of early childhood adversity.

Importantly, SES and early childhood experience are in a reciprocal relationship, and both factors involve stress (Baum et al., 1999; Gunnar, 2000), which influences social behaviors and well-being and could have a combined impact on one's socio-cognitive abilities. For example, low SES, or poverty, influences childhood experiences, including family violence and parenting practices, which could eventually lead to maladaptive emotion regulation (see Raver, 2004). Longitudinally, adolescents from a higher SES family tend to have a more positive family environment that includes positive parental practices and good quality of relationship between parents and children, which is associated with better emotion regulation skills later in life (Herd et al., 2020).

Thus far, we have separately reviewed the effects of genes and environmental factors (e.g., SES and early childhood adversity) on social behavior and well-being. Which of the two factors, then, is more important in explaining individual differences? As we all know, the textbook answer to the nature versus nurture question is that genes and environment interact (see Ben-Shlomo & Kuh, 2002; Cohen et al., 2010 for review).

11.4 Gene–Environment Interaction in Shaping Social Behavior and Well-Being

Gene–environment interaction can be studied by examining whether the association between genetic (or environmental) factors and social behavior differs depending on environmental (or genetic) factors. Twin studies comparing monozygotic and dizygotic twins can be a good example. Given that monozygotic twins share almost 100% of their DNA whereas dizygotic twins share about 50%, the extents to which genes or heritability, shared environment, and non-shared environment each explain the individual differences in the behavior of interest can be estimated. The interplay between these variables can thereby be examined. One study using this twin design (Rivizzigno et al., 2014) showed that the interaction between genes and environment predicted children's prosocial behavior. Specifically, for children with fewer close friends, genes and environment had similar effects on prosociality, whereas for children with more close friends, the effect of environment on prosociality was greater than the effect of genes. In other words, the effect of genetic predisposition on prosociality decreased in affluent social environments (e.g., having more friends).

Another approach to study the gene–environment interaction is to examine genetic variations and test how environmental factors influence the genotype–phenotype association (see Veenema, 2012 for review). For instance, compared to children who had no experience of maltreatment, children who had experienced maltreatment showed greater DNA methylation of oxytocin receptor (i.e., OXTR CpGs), in other words, less OXTR gene expression, which is negatively associated with gray matter volume in the left OFC (Fujisawa et al., 2019). In addition, the association between the OXTR G allele and positive sociality (e.g., greater social cognitive abilities and prosociality) seems to be modulated by environmental factors. For instance, although the G allele of the OXTR rs53576 is known to be associated with greater sociality, as reviewed earlier, G allele carriers of the OXTR rs53576 who had adverse childhood experience, such as maltreatment or harsh family environment, displayed lower social competence (Bradley et al., 2013; Hostinar et al., 2014; McQuaid et al., 2013). Similar patterns were found in neuroimaging studies. Among the individuals who reported higher levels of childhood maltreatment, the OXTR rs53576-GG carriers, but not the A allele carriers, showed reduced gray matter volume in the ventral striatum, which was associated with lower scores in self-reported prosociality (Dannlowski et al. 2016). These findings imply that environmental factors can change the expression of OXTR genotype as well as the OXTR genotype–phenotype relationship.

The relationship between the genetic variation in vasopressin and social behavior is also known to be influenced by environmental factors. For example, individuals with the long alleles of AVPR1A RS3 (i.e., LL carriers) reported receiving greater social support than individuals with the short allele, while such patterns were observed only among those who had not experienced early adversity (Liu et al., 2015). The gene–environment interaction is also found in studies on the neurotransmitter serotonin (Caspi et al., 2003; Kaufman et al., 2004; Sugden et al., 2010). For instance, it has been proposed that people with the short allele of the serotonin transporter (5-HTTLPR) are more sensitive to the influence of environment compared to those with the long allele. The association between stressful life experiences and self-reported depression symptoms in later life was much stronger for individuals with the short allele of 5-HTTLPR compared to those with the long allele (Caspi et al., 2003), suggesting that the environment–phenotype relationship depends on the genotype. Likewise, the influence of childhood adversity on depression and anxiety was found only among the individuals carrying at least one short allele of 5-HTTLPR (LS/SS), but not among the individuals carrying the homozygous long allele (i.e., LL) (Owens et al., 2012). Taken together, genes and environment interact with each other in shaping the individual differences in social behavior and social brain.

11.5 Moderating Adulthood Experiences

Even though early environment appears to play a critical role in developing social behavior and well-being over time (Ford et al., 2011; Germine et al., 2015; Liu & Lachman, 2019; McCrory et al., 2015; Tani et al., 2016; Tucker-Seeley et al., 2011), there is evidence showing that such effects can largely be modulated by adulthood environment. For example, the relationship between childhood adversity and well-being in later life, including cognitive functions (Greenfield & Moorman, 2019; Liu & Lachman,

2019; Lyu & Burr, 2016), everyday life functioning (Zhong et al., 2017), physical health (Tucker-Seeley et al., 2011; Turner et al., 2016), and overall subjective well-being (Oshio et al., 2013), can be influenced by environmental factors in adulthood (e.g., adulthood SES). Furthermore, a recent study reported that the negative association between adults' retrospective SES during their childhood and the number of chronic conditions in late adulthood disappeared after controlling for adulthood SES (Pavela & Latham, 2016). These results suggest that the effects of early childhood environment on individuals' well-being can be diminished significantly by environmental factors in later life stages.

If adulthood experience can alter the association between early adversity and well-being in later life, then what factors can act as moderators? First, adulthood SES can be a protective factor. For instance, individuals with higher educational attainment are more likely to have preserved cognitive function later in life (Kobayashi et al., 2017; Lyu & Burr, 2016). Adulthood SES measured by one's own education and occupation appears to be more strongly related to social networks (e.g., receiving more support from non-kin, larger social networks) than childhood SES measured by parental education and occupation (Van Groenou & Van Tilburg, 2003). Second, recreational activities in later life also appear to buffer against the negative effects of childhood adversity. For example, the effect of early adversity on cognitive function in late adulthood disappeared after controlling for literacy and late-life recreational activity. The literacy and recreational activity in later stages of life were associated with a slower decline of cognitive function (Brewster et al., 2014). Lastly, social support in adulthood can have a protective function as well (Corcoran & McNulty, 2018; Huxhold et al., 2014). For example, childhood adversity is linked to psychological distress in later life, but social support in adulthood mediated such a relationship (Sheikh, 2018; Sheikh et al., 2016). Similarly, the effects of childhood parenting differentially influence individuals' well-being in late adulthood depending on their current quality of social relationships (Andersson & Stevens, 1993).

11.6 Conclusion

Genetic factors (e.g., whether an individual has the G allele of OXTR rs53576, AVPR1A repeat polymorphisms, short or long allele of 5-HTTLPR, and lower or higher DNA methylation) and early experience (e.g., SES in childhood, early adversity) contribute to a person's social behaviors, including social bonding, socio-cognitive and socio-emotional functions, and prosociality, as well as one's social brain. It is noteworthy, however, that individual experiences in later life can modulate the effects of genetic and early experience factors. Encouraging reports of interventions and strategies to improve individuals' social brain functions and well-being will be discussed in the last chapter of this book.

REFERENCES

Adler, N. E., Epel, E. S., Castellazzo, G., & Ickovics, J. R. (2000). Relationship of subjective and objective social status with psychological and physiological functioning: Preliminary data in healthy white women. *Health Psychology, 19* (6), 586–592.

Ajrouch, K. J., Blandon, A. Y., & Antonucci, T. C. (2005). Social networks among men and women: The effects of age and socioeconomic status. *The Journals of Gerontology Series B: Psychological Sciences and Social Sciences, 60* (6), S311–S317.

Algoe, S. B., & Way, B. M. (2014). Evidence for a role of the oxytocin system, indexed by genetic variation in CD38, in the social bonding effects of expressed gratitude. *Social Cognitive and Affective Neuroscience, 9*(12), 1855–1861.

Anderson, C., Kraus, M. W., Galinsky, A. D., & Keltner, D. (2012). The local-ladder effect: Social status and subjective well-being. *Psychological Science, 23* (7), 764–771.

Andersson, L., & Stevens, N. (1993). Associations between early experiences with parents and well-being in old age. *Journal of Gerontology, 48*(3), P109–P116.

Arias, N., Calvo, M. D., Benítez-Andrades, J. A., Álvarez, M. J., Alonso-Cortés, B., & Benavides, C. (2018). Socioeconomic status in adolescents: A study of its relationship with overweight and obesity and influence on social network configuration. *International Journal of Environmental Research and Public Health, 15*(9), 2014.

Avinun, R., Ebstein, R. P., & Knafo, A. (2012). Human maternal behaviour is associated with arginine vasopressin receptor 1A gene. *Biology Letters, 8*(5), 894–896.

Avinun, R., Israel, S., Shalev, I., Gritsenko, I., Bornstein, G., Ebstein, R. P., & Knafo, A. (2011). AVPR1A variant associated with preschoolers' lower altruistic behavior. *PLoS ONE, 6*(9), e25274.

Bakermans-Kranenburg, M. J., & van IJzendoorn, M. H. (2008). Oxytocin receptor (OXTR) and serotonin transporter (5-HTT) genes associated with observed parenting. *Social Cognitive and Affective Neuroscience, 3*(2), 128–134.

Bandura, A. (1993). Perceived self-efficacy in cognitive development and functioning. *Educational Psychologist, 28*(2), 117–148.

Bartz, J., Simeon, D., Hamilton, H., Kim, S., Crystal, S., Braun, A., Vicens, V., & Hollander, E. (2011). Oxytocin can hinder trust and cooperation in

borderline personality disorder. *Social Cognitive and Affective Neuroscience, 6*(5), 556–563.
Bartz, J. A., Zaki, J., Bolger, N., & Ochsner, K. N. (2011). Social effects of oxytocin in humans: Context and person matter. *Trends in Cognitive Sciences, 15*(7), 301–309.
Baum, A., Garofalo, J. P., & Yali, A. M. (1999). Socioeconomic status and chronic stress: Does stress account for SES effects on health? *Annals of the New York Academy of Sciences, 896*(1), 131–144.
Ben-Shlomo, Y., & Kuh, D. (2002). A life course approach to chronic disease epidemiology: Conceptual models, empirical challenges and interdisciplinary perspectives. *International Journal of Epidemiology, 31*(2), 285–293.
Bernhard, R. M., Chaponis, J., Siburian, R., Gallagher, P., Ransohoff, K., Wikler, D., Perlis, R. H., & Greene, J. D. (2016). Variation in the oxytocin receptor gene (OXTR) is associated with differences in moral judgment. *Social Cognitive and Affective Neuroscience, 11*(12), 1872–1881.
Bielderman, A., de Greef, M. H., Krijnen, W. P., & van der Schans, C. P. (2015). Relationship between socioeconomic status and quality of life in older adults: A path analysis. *Quality of Life Research, 24*(7), 1697–1705.
Bost, K. K., Vaughn, B. E., Washington, W. N., Cielinski, K. L., & Bradbard, M. R. (1998). Social competence, social support, and attachment: Demarcation of construct domains, measurement, and paths of influence for preschool children attending Head Start. *Child Development, 69*(1), 192–218.
Bradley, B., Davis, T. A., Wingo, A. P., Mercer, K. B., & Ressler, K. J. (2013). Family environment and adult resilience: Contributions of positive parenting and the oxytocin receptor gene. *European Journal of Psychotraumatology, 4*(1), 21659.
Brewster, P. W., Melrose, R. J., Marquine, M. J., Johnson, J. K., Napoles, A., MacKay-Brandt, A., Farias, S., Reed, B., Mungas, D. (2014). Life experience and demographic influences on cognitive function in older adults. *Neuropsychology, 28*(6), 846–858.
Brito, N. H., & Noble, K. G. (2014). Socioeconomic status and structural brain development. *Frontiers in Neuroscience, 8*, 276.
Butterworth, P., Cherbuin, N., Sachdev, P., & Anstey, K. J. (2012). The association between financial hardship and amygdala and hippocampal volumes: Results from the PATH through life project. *Social Cognitive and Affective Neuroscience, 7*(5), 548–556.
Calkins, S. D., Smith, C. L., Gill, K. L., & Johnson, M. C. (1998). Maternal interactive style across contexts: Relations to emotional, behavioral and physiological regulation during toddlerhood. *Social Development, 7*(3), 350–369.
Caspi, A., Sugden, K., Moffitt, T. E., Taylor, A., Craig, I. W., Harrington, H., McClay, J., Mill, J., Martin, J., Braithwaite, A., & Poulton, R. (2003). Influence of life stress on depression: Moderation by a polymorphism in the 5-HTT gene. *Science, 301*(5631), 386–389.

Chen, F. S., Barth, M., Johnson, S. L., Gotlib, I. H., & Johnson, S. C. (2011). Oxytocin receptor (OXTR) polymorphisms and attachment in human infants. *Frontiers in Psychology*, *2*, 200.

Cohen, S., Janicki-Deverts, D., Chen, E., & Matthews, K. A. (2010). Childhood socioeconomic status and adult health. *Annals of the New York Academy of Sciences*, *1186*(1), 37–55.

Cohn, D. A. (1990). Child-mother attachment of six-year-olds and social competence at school. *Child Development*, *61*(1), 152–162.

Cohodes, E. M., Kitt, E. R., Baskin-Sommers, A., & Gee, D. G. (2021). Influences of early-life stress on frontolimbic circuitry: Harnessing a dimensional approach to elucidate the effects of heterogeneity in stress exposure. *Developmental Psychobiology*, *63*(2), 153–172.

Coleman, P. K. (2003). Perceptions of parent-child attachment, social self-efficacy, and peer relationships in middle childhood. *Infant and Child Development: An International Journal of Research and Practice*, *12*(4), 351–368.

Conger, R. D., & Donnellan, M. B. (2007). An interactionist perspective on the socioeconomic context of human development. *Annual Review of Psychology*, *58*, 175–199.

Conger, R. D., Wallace, L. E., Sun, Y., Simons, R. L., McLoyd, V. C., & Brody, G. H. (2002). Economic pressure in African American families: A replication and extension of the family stress model. *Developmental Psychology*, *38*(2), 179–193.

Corcoran, M., & McNulty, M. (2018). Examining the role of attachment in the relationship between childhood adversity, psychological distress and subjective well-being. *Child Abuse & Neglect*, *76*, 297–309.

Crandall, A., Magnusson, B. M., Novilla, M. L. B., Novilla, L. K. B., & Dyer, W. J. (2017). Family financial stress and adolescent sexual risk-taking: The role of self-regulation. *Journal of Youth and Adolescence*, *46*(1), 45–62.

Crawford, K. M., Choi, K., Davis, K. A., Zhu, Y., Soare, T. W., Smith, A. D. A. C., Germine, L., & Dunn, E. C. (2022). Exposure to early childhood maltreatment and its effect over time on social cognition. *Development and Psychopathology*, *34*(1), 409–419.

Cummings, E. M., & Zahn-Waxler, C. (1992). Emotions and the socialization of aggression: Adults' angry behavior and children's arousal and aggression. In *Socialization and Aggression*, pp. 61–84. Springer.

Cutting, A. L., & Dunn, J. (1999). Theory of mind, emotion understanding, language, and family background: Individual differences and interrelations. *Child Development*, *70*(4), 853–865.

Dannlowski, U., Kugel, H., Grotegerd, D., Redlich, R., Opel, N., Dohm, K., Zaremba, D., Grögler, A., Schwieren, J., Suslow, T., Ohrmann, P., Bauer, J., Krug, A., Kircher, T., Jansen, A., Domschke, K., Hohoff, C., Zwitserlood, P., Heinrichs, M., ... Baune, B. T. (2016). Disadvantage of social sensitivity: Interaction of oxytocin receptor genotype and child maltreatment on brain structure. *Biological Psychiatry*, *80*(5), 398–405.

Dawson, G., Frey, K., Panagiotides, H., Yamada, E., Hessl, D., & Osterling, J. (1999). Infants of depressed mothers exhibit atypical frontal electrical brain activity during interactions with mother and with a familiar, nondepressed adult. *Child Development, 70*(5), 1058–1066.

Dawson, G., Klinger, L. G., Panagiotides, H., Hill, D., & Spieker, S. (1992). Frontal lobe activity and affective behavior of infants of mothers with depressive symptoms. *Child Development, 63*(3), 725–737.

De Dreu, C. K., Greer, L. L., Handgraaf, M. J., Shalvi, S., Van Kleef, G. A., Baas, M., Ten Velden, F. S., Van Dijk, E., & Feith, S. W. (2010). The neuropeptide oxytocin regulates parochial altruism in intergroup conflict among humans. *Science, 328*(5984), 1408–1411.

Dunn, J., Brown, J., & Beardsall, L. (1991). Family talk about feeling states and children's later understanding of others' emotions. *Developmental Psychology, 27*(3), 448–455.

Ebert, S., Peterson, C., Slaughter, V., & Weinert, S. (2017). Links among parents' mental state language, family socioeconomic status, and preschoolers' theory of mind development. *Cognitive Development, 44*, 32–48.

Ebner, N. C., Lin, T., Muradoglu, M., Weir, D. H., Plasencia, G. M., Lillard, T. S., Pournajafi-Nazarloo, H., Cohen, R. A., Sue Carter, C., & Connelly, J. J. (2019). Associations between oxytocin receptor gene (OXTR) methylation, plasma oxytocin, and attachment across adulthood. *International Journal of Psychophysiology, 136*, 22–32.

Ein-Dor, T., Verbeke, W. J., Mokry, M., & Vrtička, P. (2018). Epigenetic modification of the oxytocin and glucocorticoid receptor genes is linked to attachment avoidance in young adults. *Attachment & Human Development, 20*(4), 439–454.

Enge, S., Mothes, H., Fleischhauer, M., Reif, A., & Strobel, A. (2017). Genetic variation of dopamine and serotonin function modulates the feedback-related negativity during altruistic punishment. *Scientific Reports, 7*(1), 1–12.

Ensminger, M.E., & Fothergill, K.E. (2003). A decade of measuring SES: What it tells us and where to go from here. In M.H. Bornstein & R.H. Bradley (eds.), *Socioeconomic Status, Parenting and Child Development*, pp. 13–2). Lawrence Erlbaum Associates.

Ensor, R., & Hughes, C. (2008). Content or connectedness? Mother–child talk and early social understanding. *Child Development, 79*(1), 201–216.

Ensor, R., Spencer, D., & Hughes, C. (2011). "You feel sad?" Emotion understanding mediates effects of verbal ability and mother–child mutuality on prosocial behaviors: Findings from 2 years to 4 years. *Social Development, 20*(1), 93–110.

Fagot, B. I. (1997). Attachment, parenting, and peer interactions of toddler children. *Developmental Psychology, 33*(3), 489–499.

Fan, Y., Herrera-Melendez, A. L., Pestke, K., Feeser, M., Aust, S., Otte, C., Pruessner, J. C., Böker, H., Bajbouj, M., & Grimm, S. (2014). Early life stress modulates amygdala-prefrontal functional connectivity: Implications for oxytocin effects. *Human Brain Mapping, 35*(10), 5328–5339.

Farber, M. J., Romer, A. L., Kim, M. J., Knodt, A. R., Elsayed, N. M., Williamson, D. E., & Hariri, A. R. (2018). Paradoxical associations between familial affective responsiveness, stress, and amygdala reactivity. *Emotion, 19* (4), 645–654.

Farley, J. P., & Kim-Spoon, J. (2017). Parenting and adolescent self-regulation mediate between family socioeconomic status and adolescent adjustment. *The Journal of Early Adolescence, 37*(4), 502–524.

Finger, B., Eiden, R. D., Edwards, E. P., Leonard, K. E., & Kachadourian, L. (2010). Marital aggression and child peer competence: A comparison of three conceptual models. *Personal Relationships, 17*(3), 357–376.

Fischer, C. S. (1982). *To Dwell Among Friends: Personal Networks in Town and City.* University of Chicago Press.

Ford, E., Clark, C., & Stansfeld, S. A. (2011). The influence of childhood adversity on social relations and mental health at mid-life. *Journal of Affective Disorders, 133*(1–2), 320–327.

Fujisawa, T. X., Nishitani, S., Takiguchi, S., Shimada, K., Smith, A. K., & Tomoda, A. (2019). Oxytocin receptor DNA methylation and alterations of brain volumes in maltreated children. *Neuropsychopharmacology, 44*(12), 2045–2053.

Furman, D. J., Chen, M. C., & Gotlib, I. H. (2011). Variant in oxytocin receptor gene is associated with amygdala volume. *Psychoneuroendocrinology, 36*(6), 891–897.

Gallo, L. C., Bogart, L. M., Vranceanu, A. M., & Matthews, K. A. (2005). Socioeconomic status, resources, psychological experiences, and emotional responses: A test of the reserve capacity model. *Journal of Personality and Social Psychology, 88*(2), 386–399.

Gartland, D., Riggs, E., Muyeen, S., Giallo, R., Afifi, T. O., MacMillan, H., Herrman, H., Bulford, E., & Brown, S. J. (2019). What factors are associated with resilient outcomes in children exposed to social adversity? A systematic review. *BMJ Open, 9*(4), e024870.

Gärtner, A., Strobel, A., Reif, A., Lesch, K. P., & Enge, S. (2018). Genetic variation in serotonin function impacts on altruistic punishment in the ultimatum game: A longitudinal approach. *Brain and Cognition, 125*, 37–44.

Gee, D. G. (2016). Sensitive periods of emotion regulation: Influences of parental care on frontoamygdala circuitry and plasticity. In H. J. V. Rutherford & L. C. Mayes (eds.), *Maternal Brain Plasticity: Preclinical and Human Research and Implications for Intervention,* pp. 87–110. Jossey-Bass/Wiley.

Gee, D. G., Gabard-Durnam, L. J., Flannery, J., Goff, B., Humphreys, K. L., Telzer, E. H., Hare, T. A., Bookheimer, S. Y., & Tottenham, N. (2013). Early developmental emergence of human amygdala–prefrontal connectivity after maternal deprivation. *Proceedings of the National Academy of Sciences, 110*(39), 15638–15643.

Gee, D. G., Humphreys, K. L., Flannery, J., Goff, B., Telzer, E. H., Shapiro, M., Hare, T. A., Bookheimer, S. Y., & Tottenham, N. (2013). A developmental shift from positive to negative connectivity in human amygdala–prefrontal circuitry. *Journal of Neuroscience, 33*(10), 4584–4593.

Germine, L., Dunn, E. C., McLaughlin, K. A., & Smoller, J. W. (2015). Childhood adversity is associated with adult theory of mind and social affiliation, but not face processing. *PLoS ONE, 10*(6), e0129612.

Gianaros, P. J., Horenstein, J. A., Cohen, S., Matthews, K. A., Brown, S. M., Flory, J. D., Critchley, H. D., Manuck, S. B., & Hariri, A. R. (2007). Perigenual anterior cingulate morphology covaries with perceived social standing. *Social Cognitive and Affective Neuroscience, 2*(3), 161–173.

Gianaros, P. J., Horenstein, J. A., Hariri, A. R., Sheu, L. K., Manuck, S. B., Matthews, K. A., & Cohen, S. (2008). Potential neural embedding of parental social standing. *Social Cognitive and Affective Neuroscience, 3*(2), 91–96.

Greenfield, E. A., & Moorman, S. M. (2019). Childhood socioeconomic status and later life cognition: Evidence from the Wisconsin Longitudinal Study. *Journal of Aging and Health, 31*(9), 1589–1615.

Gunnar, M. R. (2000). Early adversity and the development of stress reactivity and regulation. In C. A. Nelson (ed.), *The Minnesota Symposia on Child Psychology, Vol. 31. The Effects of Early Adversity on Neurobehavioral Development* (pp. 163–200). Lawrence Erlbaum Associates.

Haas, B. W., Filkowski, M. M., Cochran, R. N., Denison, L., Ishak, A., Nishitani, S., & Smith, A. K. (2016). Epigenetic modification of OXT and human sociability. *Proceedings of the National Academy of Sciences, 113*(27), E3816–E3823.

Hanson, J. L., Chandra, A., Wolfe, B. L., & Pollak, S. D. (2011). Association between income and the hippocampus. *PLoS ONE, 6*(5), e18712.

Hanson, J. L., Hair, N., Shen, D. G., Shi, F., Gilmore, J. H., Wolfe, B. L., & Pollak, S. D. (2013). Family poverty affects the rate of human infant brain growth. *PLoS ONE, 8*(12), e80954.

Hanson, J. L., Nacewicz, B. M., Sutterer, M. J., Cayo, A. A., Schaefer, S. M., Rudolph, K. D., Shirtcliff, E. A., Pollak, S. D., & Davidson, R. J. (2015). Behavioral problems after early life stress: Contributions of the hippocampus and amygdala. *Biological Psychiatry, 77*(4), 314–323.

Hardy, D. F., Power, T. G., & Jaedicke, S. (1993). Examining the relation of parenting to children's coping with everyday stress. *Child Development, 64*(6), 1829–1841.

Hariri, A. R., & Holmes, A. (2006). Genetics of emotional regulation: The role of the serotonin transporter in neural function. *Trends in Cognitive Sciences, 10*(4), 182–191.

Hariri, A. R., Mattay, V. S., Tessitore, A., Kolachana, B., Fera, F., Goldman, D., Egan, M. F., & Weinberger, D. R. (2002). Serotonin transporter genetic variation and the response of the human amygdala. *Science, 297*(5580), 400–403.

Heinz, A., Braus, D. F., Smolka, M. N., Wrase, J., Puls, I., Hermann, D., Klein, S., Grüsser, S. M., Flor, H., Schumann, G., Mann, K., & Büchel, C. (2005). Amygdala–prefrontal coupling depends on a genetic variation of the serotonin transporter. *Nature Neuroscience, 8*(1), 20–21.

Herd, T., King-Casas, B., & Kim-Spoon, J. (2020). Developmental changes in emotion regulation during adolescence: Associations with socioeconomic risk and family emotional context. *Journal of Youth and Adolescence, 49*(7), 1545–1557.

Hiraoka, D., Nishitani, S., Shimada, K., Kasaba, R., Fujisawa, T. X., & Tomoda, A. (2021). Epigenetic modification of the oxytocin gene is associated with gray matter volume and trait empathy in mothers. *Psychoneuroendocrinology, 123*, 105026.

Hostinar, C. E., Cicchetti, D., & Rogosch, F. A. (2014). Oxytocin receptor gene polymorphism, perceived social support, and psychological symptoms in maltreated adolescents. *Development and Psychopathology, 26*(2), 465–477.

House, J. S., Landis, K. R., & Umberson, D. (1988). Social relationships and health. *Science, 241*(4865), 540–545.

Huth-Bocks, A. C., Levendosky, A. A., Bogat, G. A., & Von Eye, A. (2004). The impact of maternal characteristics and contextual variables on infant–mother attachment. *Child Development, 75*(2), 480–496.

Huxhold, O., Miche, M., & Schüz, B. (2014). Benefits of having friends in older ages: Differential effects of informal social activities on well-being in middle-aged and older adults. *Journals of Gerontology Series B: Psychological Sciences and Social Sciences, 69*(3), 366–375.

Inoue, H., Yamasue, H., Tochigi, M., Abe, O., Liu, X., Kawamura, Y., Takei, K., Suga, M., Yamada, H., Rogers, M. A., Aoki, S., Sasaki, T., & Kasai, K. (2010). Association between the oxytocin receptor gene and amygdalar volume in healthy adults. *Biological Psychiatry, 68*(11), 1066–1072.

Israel, S., Lerer, E., Shalev, I., Uzefovsky, F., Riebold, M., Laiba, E., Bachner-Melman, R., Maril, A., Bornstein, G., Knafo, A., & Ebstein, R. P. (2009). The oxytocin receptor (OXTR) contributes to prosocial fund allocations in the dictator game and the social value orientations task. *PLoS ONE, 4*(5), e5535.

Javanbakht, A., King, A. P., Evans, G. W., Swain, J. E., Angstadt, M., Phan, K. L., & Liberzon, I. (2015). Childhood poverty predicts adult amygdala and frontal activity and connectivity in response to emotional faces. *Frontiers in Behavioral Neuroscience, 9*, 154.

Kaufman, J., Yang, B. Z., Douglas-Palumberi, H., Houshyar, S., Lipschitz, D., Krystal, J. H., & Gelernter, J. (2004). Social supports and serotonin transporter gene moderate depression in maltreated children. *Proceedings of the National Academy of Sciences, 101*(49), 17316–17321.

Kelly, P. A., Viding, E., Wallace, G. L., Schaer, M., De Brito, S. A., Robustelli, B., & McCrory, E. J. (2013). Cortical thickness, surface area, and gyrification abnormalities in children exposed to maltreatment: Neural markers of vulnerability? *Biological Psychiatry, 74*(11), 845–852.

Kim, P., Evans, G. W., Angstadt, M., Ho, S. S., Sripada, C. S., Swain, J. E., Liberzon, I., & Phan, K. L. (2013). Effects of childhood poverty and chronic stress on emotion regulatory brain function in adulthood. *Proceedings of the National Academy of Sciences, 110*(46), 18442–18447.

Kim, H. S., Sherman, D. K., Sasaki, J. Y., Xu, J., Chu, T. Q., Ryu, C., Suh, E. M., Graham, K., & Taylor, S. E. (2010). Culture, distress, and oxytocin receptor polymorphism (OXTR) interact to influence emotional support seeking. *Proceedings of the National Academy of Sciences*, *107*(36), 15717–15721.

Knafo, A., Israel, S., Darvasi, A., Bachner-Melman, R., Uzefovsky, F., Cohen, L., Feldman, E., Lerer, E., Laiba, E., Raz, Y., Nemanov, L., Gritsenko, I., Dina, C., Agam, G., Dean, B., Bornstein, G., & Ebstein, R. P. (2008). Individual differences in allocation of funds in the dictator game associated with length of the arginine vasopressin 1a receptor RS3 promoter region and correlation between RS3 length and hippocampal mRNA. *Genes, Brain and Behavior*, *7*(3), 266–275.

Kobayashi, L. C., Glymour, M. M., Kahn, K., Payne, C. F., Wagner, R. G., Montana, L., Mateen, F. J., Tollman, S. M., & Berkman, L. F. (2017). Childhood deprivation and later-life cognitive function in a population-based study of older rural South Africans. *Social Science & Medicine*, *190*, 20–28.

Kogan, A., Saslow, L. R., Impett, E. A., Oveis, C., Keltner, D., & Saturn, S. R. (2011). Thin-slicing study of the oxytocin receptor (OXTR) gene and the evaluation and expression of the prosocial disposition. *Proceedings of the National Academy of Sciences*, *108*(48), 19189–19192.

Kok, R., Thijssen, S., Bakermans-Kranenburg, M. J., Jaddoe, V. W., Verhulst, F. C., White, T., van IJzendoorn, M. H., & Tiemeier, H. (2015). Normal variation in early parental sensitivity predicts child structural brain development. *Journal of the American Academy of Child & Adolescent Psychiatry*, *54*(10), 824–831.

Kopala-Sibley, D. C., Cyr, M., Finsaas, M. C., Orawe, J., Huang, A., Tottenham, N., & Klein, D. N. (2020). Early childhood parenting predicts late childhood brain functional connectivity during emotion perception and reward processing. *Child Development*, *91*(1), 110–128.

Kosfeld, M., Heinrichs, M., Zak, P. J., Fischbacher, U., & Fehr, E. (2005). Oxytocin increases trust in humans. *Nature*, *435*(7042), 673–676.

Kraus, M. W., Côté, S., & Keltner, D. (2010). Social class, contextualism, and empathic accuracy. *Psychological Science*, *21*(11), 1716–1723.

Kraus, M. W., Piff, P. K., Mendoza-Denton, R., Rheinschmidt, M. L., & Keltner, D. (2012). Social class, solipsism, and contextualism: How the rich are different from the poor. *Psychological Review*, *119*(3), 546–572.

Krause, N., & Borawski-Clark, E. (1995). Social class differences in social support among older adults. *The Gerontologist*, *35*(4), 498–508.

Krol, K. M., Puglia, M. H., Morris, J. P., Connelly, J. J., & Grossmann, T. (2019). Epigenetic modification of the oxytocin receptor gene is associated with emotion processing in the infant brain. *Developmental Cognitive Neuroscience*, *37*, 100648.

Ladd, G. W., & Pettit, G. S. (2002). Parenting and the development of children's peer relationships. In M. H. Bornstein (ed.), *Handbook of Parenting: Practical Issues in Parenting*, pp. 269–309. Lawrence Erlbaum Associates.

Laursen, H. R., Siebner, H. R., Haren, T., Madsen, K., Grønlund, R., Hulme, O., & Henningsson, S. (2014). Variation in the oxytocin receptor gene is associated with behavioral and neural correlates of empathic accuracy. *Frontiers in Behavioral Neuroscience, 8*, 423.

Lawson, G. M., Camins, J. S., Wisse, L., Wu, J., Duda, J. T., Cook, P. A., Gee, J. C., & Farah, M. J. (2017). Childhood socioeconomic status and childhood maltreatment: Distinct associations with brain structure. *PLoS ONE, 12*(4), e0175690.

Leerkes, E. M., Su, J., Calkins, S., Henrich, V. C., & Smolen, A. (2017). Variation in mothers' arginine vasopressin receptor 1a and dopamine receptor D4 genes predicts maternal sensitivity via social cognition. *Genes, Brain and Behavior, 16*(2), 233–240.

Li, J., Zhao, Y., Li, R., Broster, L. S., Zhou, C., & Yang, S. (2015). Association of oxytocin receptor gene (OXTR) rs53576 polymorphism with sociality: A meta-analysis. *PLoS ONE, 10*(6), e0131820.

Liberzon, I., Ma, S. T., Okada, G., Shaun Ho, S., Swain, J. E., & Evans, G. W. (2015). Childhood poverty and recruitment of adult emotion regulatory neurocircuitry. *Social Cognitive and Affective Neuroscience, 10*(11), 1596–1606.

Liu, Y., & Lachman, M. E. (2019). Socioeconomic status and parenting style from childhood: Long-term effects on cognitive function in middle and later adulthood. *The Journals of Gerontology: Series B, 74*(6), e13–e24.

Liu, J. J., Lou, F., Lavebratt, C., & Forsell, Y. (2015). Impact of childhood adversity and vasopressin receptor 1a variation on social interaction in adulthood: A cross-sectional study. *PLoS ONE, 10*(8), e0136436.

Luby, J., Belden, A., Botteron, K., Marrus, N., Harms, M. P., Babb, C., Nishino, T., & Barch, D. (2013). The effects of poverty on childhood brain development: The mediating effect of caregiving and stressful life events. *JAMA pediatrics, 167*(12), 1135–1142.

Luke, N., & Banerjee, R. (2013). Differentiated associations between childhood maltreatment experiences and social understanding: A meta-analysis and systematic review. *Developmental Review, 33*(1), 1–28.

Lyu, J., & Burr, J. A. (2016). Socioeconomic status across the life course and cognitive function among older adults: An examination of the latency, pathways, and accumulation hypotheses. *Journal of Aging and Health, 28*(1), 40–67.

Main, M., & Weston, D. R. (1981). The quality of the toddler's relationship to mother and to father: Related to conflict behavior and the readiness to establish new relationships. *Child Development, 52*(3), 932–940.

Manstead, A. S. (2018). The psychology of social class: How socioeconomic status impacts thought, feelings, and behaviour. *British Journal of Social Psychology, 57*(2), 267–291.

Matsudaira, I., Yokota, S., Hashimoto, T., Takeuchi, H., Asano, K., Asano, M., Sassa, Y., Taki, Y., & Kawashima, R. (2016). Parental praise correlates with posterior insular cortex gray matter volume in children and adolescents. *PLoS ONE, 11*(4), e0154220.

Mazur, J., Malkowska-Szkutnik, A., & Tabak, I. (2014). Changes in family socioeconomic status as predictors of self-efficacy in 13-year-old Polish adolescents. *International Journal of Public Health*, *59*(1), 107–115.

McCrory, C., Dooley, C., Layte, R., & Kenny, R. A. (2015). The lasting legacy of childhood adversity for disease risk in later life. *Health Psychology*, *34*(7), 687–696.

McLaughlin, K. A., Peverill, M., Gold, A. L., Alves, S., & Sheridan, M. A. (2015). Child maltreatment and neural systems underlying emotion regulation. *Journal of the American Academy of Child & Adolescent Psychiatry*, *54*(9), 753–762.

McLaughlin, K. A., Sheridan, M. A., Winter, W., Fox, N. A., Zeanah, C. H., & Nelson, C. A. (2014). Widespread reductions in cortical thickness following severe early-life deprivation: A neurodevelopmental pathway to attention-deficit/hyperactivity disorder. *Biological Psychiatry*, *76*(8), 629–638.

McQuaid, R. J., McInnis, O. A., Stead, J. D., Matheson, K., & Anisman, H. (2013). A paradoxical association of an oxytocin receptor gene polymorphism: Early-life adversity and vulnerability to depression. *Frontiers in Neuroscience*, *7*, 128.

Mehta, M. A., Golembo, N. I., Nosarti, C., Colvert, E., Mota, A., Williams, S. C., Rutter, M., & Sonuga-Barke, E. J. (2009). Amygdala, hippocampal and corpus callosum size following severe early institutional deprivation: The English and Romanian Adoptees study pilot. *Journal of Child Psychology and Psychiatry*, *50*(8), 943–951.

Meins, E., Fernyhough, C., Russell, J., & Clark-Carter, D. (1998). Security of attachment as a predictor of symbolic and mentalising abilities: A longitudinal study. *Social Development*, *7*(1), 1–24.

Meins, E., Fernyhough, C., Wainwright, R., Das Gupta, M., Fradley, E., & Tuckey, M. (2002). Maternal mind–mindedness and attachment security as predictors of theory of mind understanding. *Child Development*, *73*(6), 1715–1726.

Melkman, E. P. (2017). Childhood adversity, social support networks and well-being among youth aging out of care: An exploratory study of mediation. *Child Abuse & Neglect*, *72*, 85–97.

Meyer-Lindenberg, A., Kolachana, B., Gold, B., Olsh, A., Nicodemus, K. K., Mattay, V., Dean, M., & Weinberger, D. R. (2009). Genetic variants in AVPR1A linked to autism predict amygdala activation and personality traits in healthy humans. *Molecular Psychiatry*, *14*(10), 968–975.

Miller, J. G., Kahle, S., & Hastings, P. D. (2015). Roots and benefits of costly giving: Children who are more altruistic have greater autonomic flexibility and less family wealth. *Psychological Science*, *26*(7), 1038–1045.

Montagrin, A., Saiote, C., & Schiller, D. (2018). The social hippocampus. *Hippocampus*, *28*(9), 672–679.

Moons, W. G., Way, B. M., & Taylor, S. E. (2014). Oxytocin and vasopressin receptor polymorphisms interact with circulating neuropeptides to predict human emotional reactions to stress. *Emotion*, *14*(3), 562–572.

Morris, A. S., Silk, J. S., Steinberg, L., Myers, S. S., & Robinson, L. R. (2007). The role of the family context in the development of emotion regulation. *Social Development*, *16*(2), 361–388.

Moulson, M. C., Fox, N. A., Zeanah, C. H., & Nelson, C. A. (2009). Early adverse experiences and the neurobiology of facial emotion processing. *Developmental Psychology*, *45*(1), 17–30.

Muscatell, K. A., Morelli, S. A., Falk, E. B., Way, B. M., Pfeifer, J. H., Galinsky, A. D., Lieberman, M. D., Dapretto, M., & Eisenberger, N. I. (2012). Social status modulates neural activity in the mentalizing network. *Neuroimage*, *60*(3), 1771–1777.

Nishina, K., Takagishi, H., Takahashi, H., Sakagami, M., & Inoue-Murayama, M. (2019). Association of polymorphism of arginine-vasopressin receptor 1A (AVPR1a) gene with trust and reciprocity. *Frontiers in Human Neuroscience*, *13*, 230.

Nishitani, S., Ikematsu, K., Takamura, T., Honda, S., Yoshiura, K. I., & Shinohara, K. (2017). Genetic variants in oxytocin receptor and arginine-vasopressin receptor 1A are associated with the neural correlates of maternal and paternal affection towards their child. *Hormones and Behavior*, *87*, 47–56.

Noble, K. G., Houston, S. M., Kan, E., & Sowell, E. R. (2012). Neural correlates of socioeconomic status in the developing human brain. *Developmental Science*, *15*(4), 516–527.

Oshio, T., Umeda, M., & Kawakami, N. (2013). Childhood adversity and adulthood subjective well-being: Evidence from Japan. *Journal of Happiness Studies*, *14*(3), 843–860.

Owens, M., Goodyer, I. M., Wilkinson, P., Bhardwaj, A., Abbott, R., Croudace, T., Dunn, V., Jones, P. B., Walsh, N. D., Ban, M., & Sahakian, B. J. (2012). 5-HTTLPR and early childhood adversities moderate cognitive and emotional processing in adolescence. *PLoS ONE*, *7*(11), e48482.

Pavela, G., & Latham, K. (2016). Childhood conditions and multimorbidity among older adults. *Journals of Gerontology Series B: Psychological Sciences and Social Sciences*, *71*(5), 889–901.

Pears, K. C., & Moses, L. J. (2003). Demographics, parenting, and theory of mind in preschool children. *Social Development*, *12*(1), 1–20.

Pérez-Edgar, K., Bar-Haim, Y., McDermott, J. M., Gorodetsky, E., Hodgkinson, C. A., Goldman, D., Ernst, M., Pine, D. S., & Fox, N. A. (2010). Variations in the serotonin-transporter gene are associated with attention bias patterns to positive and negative emotion faces. *Biological Psychology*, *83*(3), 269–271.

Pergamin-Hight, L., Bakermans-Kranenburg, M. J., Van Ijzendoorn, M. H., & Bar-Haim, Y. (2012). Variations in the promoter region of the serotonin transporter gene and biased attention for emotional information: A meta-analysis. *Biological Psychiatry*, *71*(4), 373–379.

Piff, P. K., Kraus, M. W., Côté, S., Cheng, B. H., & Keltner, D. (2010). Having less, giving more: The influence of social class on prosocial behavior. *Journal of Personality and Social Psychology*, *99*(5), 771–784.

Piff, P. K., Stancato, D. M., Côté, S., Mendoza-Denton, R., & Keltner, D. (2012). Higher social class predicts increased unethical behavior. *Proceedings of the National Academy of Sciences, 109*(11), 4086–4091.

Prinstein, M. J., & La Greca, A. M. (1999). Links between mothers' and children's social competence and associations with maternal adjustment. *Journal of Clinical Child Psychology, 28*(2), 197–210.

Raizada, R. D., Richards, T. L., Meltzoff, A., & Kuhl, P. K. (2008). Socioeconomic status predicts hemispheric specialisation of the left inferior frontal gyrus in young children. *Neuroimage, 40*(3), 1392–1401.

Raver, C. C. (2004). Placing emotional self-regulation in sociocultural and socioeconomic contexts. *Child Development, 75*(2), 346–353.

Repetti, R. L., Taylor, S. E., & Seeman, T. E. (2002). Risky families: Family social environments and the mental and physical health of offspring. *Psychological Bulletin, 128*(2), 330–366.

Rivizzigno, A. S., Brendgen, M., Feng, B., Vitaro, F., Dionne, G., Tremblay, R. E., & Boivin, M. (2014). Gene–environment interplay between number of friends and prosocial leadership behavior in children. *Merrill-Palmer Quarterly, 60*(2), 110–141.

Rodrigues, S. M., Saslow, L. R., Garcia, N., John, O. P., & Keltner, D. (2009). Oxytocin receptor genetic variation relates to empathy and stress reactivity in humans. *Proceedings of the National Academy of Sciences, 106*(50), 21437–21441.

Romund, L., Raufelder, D., Flemming, E., Lorenz, R. C., Pelz, P., Gleich, T., Heinz, A., & Beck, A. (2016). Maternal parenting behavior and emotion processing in adolescents – An fMRI study. *Biological Psychology, 120*, 120–125.

Saegert, S. C., Adler, N. E., Bullock, H. E., Cauce, A. M., Liu, W. M., & Wyche, K. F. (2006). *Report of the APA Task Force on Socioeconomic Status.* http://www.apa.org/pi/ses/resources/publications/task-force-2006.pdf

Salzinger, S., Feldman, R. S., Hammer, M., & Rosario, M. (1993). The effects of physical abuse on children's social relationships. *Child Development, 64*(1), 169–187.

Samuelsson, M. A. (1997). Social networks of children in single-parent families: Differences according to sex, age, socioeconomic status and housing-type and their associations with behavioural disturbances. *Social Networks, 19*(2), 113–127.

Sandi, C., & Haller, J. (2015). Stress and the social brain: Behavioural effects and neurobiological mechanisms. *Nature Reviews Neuroscience, 16*(5), 290–304.

Seibert, A., & Kerns, K. (2015). Early mother–child attachment: Longitudinal prediction to the quality of peer relationships in middle childhood. *International Journal of Behavioral Development, 39*(2), 130–138.

Shatz, M., Diesendruck, G., Martinez-Beck, I., & Akar, D. (2003). The influence of language and socioeconomic status on children's understanding of false belief. *Developmental Psychology, 39*(4), 717–729.

Shavers, V. L. (2007). Measurement of socioeconomic status in health disparities research. *Journal of the National Medical Association, 99*(9), 1013–1023.

Sheikh, M. A. (2018). The potential protective effect of friendship on the association between childhood adversity and psychological distress in adulthood: A retrospective, preliminary, three-wave population-based study. *Journal of Affective Disorders, 226,* 21–27.

Sheikh, M. A., Abelsen, B., & Olsen, J. A. (2016). Clarifying associations between childhood adversity, social support, behavioral factors, and mental health, health, and well-being in adulthood: A population-based study. *Frontiers in Psychology, 7,* 727.

Skuse, D. (2006). Genetic influences on the neural basis of social cognition. *Philosophical Transactions of the Royal Society B: Biological Sciences, 361*(1476), 2129–2141.

Smith, K. E., Porges, E. C., Norman, G. J., Connelly, J. J., & Decety, J. (2014). Oxytocin receptor gene variation predicts empathic concern and autonomic arousal while perceiving harm to others. *Social Neuroscience, 9*(1), 1–9.

Stein, M. B., Campbell-Sills, L., & Gelernter, J. (2009). Genetic variation in 5HTTLPR is associated with emotional resilience. *American Journal of Medical Genetics Part B: Neuropsychiatric Genetics, 150*(7), 900–906.

Stellar, J. E., Manzo, V. M., Kraus, M. W., & Keltner, D. (2012). Class and compassion: Socioeconomic factors predict responses to suffering. *Emotion, 12*(3), 449–459.

Stoltenberg, S. F., Christ, C. C., & Carlo, G. (2013). Afraid to help: Social anxiety partially mediates the association between 5-HTTLPR triallelic genotype and prosocial behavior. *Social Neuroscience, 8*(5), 400–406.

Stringhini, S., Berkman, L., Dugravot, A., Ferrie, J. E., Marmot, M., Kivimaki, M., & Singh-Manoux, A. (2012). Socioeconomic status, structural and functional measures of social support, and mortality: The British Whitehall II Cohort Study, 1985–2009. *American Journal of Epidemiology, 175*(12), 1275–1283.

Suess, G. J., Grossmann, K. E., & Sroufe, L. A. (1992). Effects of infant attachment to mother and father on quality of adaptation in preschool: From dyadic to individual organisation of self. *International Journal of Behavioral Development, 15*(1), 43–65.

Sugden, K., Arseneault, L., Harrington, H., Moffitt, T. E., Williams, B., & Caspi, A. (2010). Serotonin transporter gene moderates the development of emotional problems among children following bullying victimization. *Journal of the American Academy of Child & Adolescent Psychiatry, 49*(8), 830–840.

Tani, Y., Fujiwara, T., Kondo, N., Noma, H., Sasaki, Y., & Kondo, K. (2016). Childhood socioeconomic status and onset of depression among Japanese older adults: The JAGES prospective cohort study. *The American Journal of Geriatric Psychiatry, 24*(9), 717–726.

Taylor, S. E., Eisenberger, N. I., Saxbe, D., Lehman, B. J., & Lieberman, M. D. (2006). Neural responses to emotional stimuli are associated with childhood family stress. *Biological Psychiatry, 60*(3), 296–301.

Tost, H., Kolachana, B., Hakimi, S., Lemaitre, H., Verchinski, B. A., Mattay, V. S., Weinberger, D. R., & Meyer-Lindenberg, A. (2010). A common allele in the oxytocin receptor gene (OXTR) impacts prosocial temperament and human hypothalamic-limbic structure and function. *Proceedings of the National Academy of Sciences, 107*(31), 13936–13941.

Tottenham, N., Hare, T. A., Millner, A., Gilhooly, T., Zevin, J. D., & Casey, B. J. (2011). Elevated amygdala response to faces following early deprivation. *Developmental Science, 14*(2), 190–204.

Tottenham, N., Hare, T. A., Quinn, B. T., McCarry, T. W., Nurse, M., Gilhooly, T., Millner, A., Galvan, A., Davidson, M. C., Eigsti, I. M., Thomas, K. M., Freed, P. J., Booma, E. S., Gunnar, M. R., Altemus, M., Aronson, J., & Casey, B. J. (2010). Prolonged institutional rearing is associated with atypically large amygdala volume and difficulties in emotion regulation. *Developmental Science, 13*(1), 46–61.

Trickett, P. K., & Kuczynski, L. (1986). Children's misbehaviors and parental discipline strategies in abusive and nonabusive families. *Developmental Psychology, 22*(1), 115–123.

Tucker-Seeley, R. D., Li, Y., Sorensen, G., & Subramanian, S. V. (2011). Lifecourse socioeconomic circumstances and multimorbidity among older adults. *BMC Public Health, 11*(1), 1–9.

Turner, R. J., Thomas, C. S., & Brown, T. H. (2016). Childhood adversity and adult health: Evaluating intervening mechanisms. *Social Science & Medicine, 156*, 114–124.

Uzefovsky, F., Shalev, I., Israel, S., Edelman, S., Raz, Y., Mankuta, D., Knafo-Noam, A., & Ebstein, R. P. (2015). Oxytocin receptor and vasopressin receptor 1a genes are respectively associated with emotional and cognitive empathy. *Hormones and Behavior, 67*, 60–65.

Van Groenou, M. I. B., & Van Tilburg, T. (2003). Network size and support in old age: Differentials by socio-economic status in childhood and adulthood. *Ageing & Society, 23*(5), 625–645.

Veenema, A. H. (2012). Toward understanding how early-life social experiences alter oxytocin-and vasopressin-regulated social behaviors. *Hormones and Behavior, 61*(3), 304–312.

Veroff, J., Douvan, E., & Kulka, R. A. (1981). *The Inner American: A Self-Portrait from 1957 to 1976*. Basic Books.

Verschueren, K., & Marcoen, A. (1999). Representation of self and socioemotional competence in kindergartners: Differential and combined effects of attachment to mother and to father. *Child Development, 70*(1), 183–201.

Wade, M., Hoffmann, T. J., Wigg, K., & Jenkins, J. M. (2014). Association between the oxytocin receptor (OXTR) gene and children's social cognition at 18 months. *Genes, Brain and Behavior, 13*(7), 603–610.

Walum, H., Westberg, L., Henningsson, S., Neiderhiser, J. M., Reiss, D., Igl, W., Ganiban, J. M., Spotts, E. L., Pedersen, N. L., Eriksson, E., & Lichtenstein, P. (2008). Genetic variation in the vasopressin receptor 1a gene (AVPR1A) associates with pair-bonding behavior in humans. *Proceedings of the National Academy of Sciences, 105*(37), 14153–14156.

Whittle, S., Simmons, J. G., Dennison, M., Vijayakumar, N., Schwartz, O., Yap, M. B., Sheeber, L., & Allen, N. B. (2014). Positive parenting predicts the development of adolescent brain structure: A longitudinal study. *Developmental Cognitive Neuroscience, 8*, 7–17.

Whittle, S., Vijayakumar, N., Dennison, M., Schwartz, O., Simmons, J. G., Sheeber, L., & Allen, N. B. (2016). Observed measures of negative parenting predict brain development during adolescence. *PLoS ONE, 11*(1), e0147774.

Whittle, S., Yap, M. B., Yücel, M., Sheeber, L., Simmons, J. G., Pantelis, C., & Allen, N. B. (2009). Maternal responses to adolescent positive affect are associated with adolescents' reward neuroanatomy. *Social Cognitive and Affective Neuroscience, 4*(3), 247–256.

Wu, J., Guo, Z., Gao, X., & Kou, Y. (2020). The relations between early-life stress and risk, time, and prosocial preferences in adulthood: A meta-analytic review. *Evolution and Human Behavior, 41*(6), 557–572.

Yanagisawa, K., Masui, K., Furutani, K., Nomura, M., Yoshida, H., & Ura, M. (2013). Family socioeconomic status modulates the coping-related neural response of offspring. *Social Cognitive and Affective Neuroscience, 8*(6), 617–622.

Youngblade, L. M., & Belsky, J. (1992). Parent-child antecedents of 5-year-olds' close friendships: A longitudinal analysis. *Developmental Psychology, 28*(4), 700–713.

Yu, Q., Daugherty, A. M., Anderson, D. M., Nishimura, M., Brush, D., Hardwick, A., Lacey, W., Raz, S., & Ofen, N. (2018). Socioeconomic status and hippocampal volume in children and young adults. *Developmental Science, 21*(3), e12561.

Zink, C. F., & Meyer-Lindenberg, A. (2012). Human neuroimaging of oxytocin and vasopressin in social cognition. *Hormones and Behavior, 61*(3), 400–409.

Zhong, Y., Wang, J., & Nicholas, S. (2017). Gender, childhood and adult socioeconomic inequalities in functional disability among Chinese older adults. *International Journal for Equity in Health, 16*(1), 1–11.

CHAPTER 12

Preventing Dementia with Social Connection

Jeanyung Chey, Isu Cho, Hairin Kim, Hoyoung Kim, Seyul Kwak, Sunhae Sul, Sung-Ha Lee, and Yoosik Youm

12.1 Introduction

According to cognitive reserve theory, the manifestation of dementia can be delayed for years depending on the capacity of the person's reserve (Stern, 2012). Moreover, it has been found that older adults can maintain a healthy brain that can be much younger than their chronological age (Kwak et al., 2018). This resilience against brain aging and neurodegeneration has been found to be supported by processes characterized as reserve and brain maintenance (Nyberg et al., 2012). Employing the moderating effects of the reserve and resilience to reduce the risk of dementia can be a powerful intervention strategy. People have competing causes of death in late life, as multiple health risks arise as we age. As the risk of dementia doubles every five years after age 65, delaying just five years of its clinical manifestation could result in reducing the dementia incidence by half in an elderly population (Cao et al., 2020; Lopes et al., 2007).

Recently, efforts to mitigate the risk of dementia through social engagement or relieving social isolation are gaining attention, based on the observation that loneliness or social isolation is a major risk for dementia in late life (Kuiper et al., 2015). In the report by the Lancet Commission on Dementia Prevention, Intervention, and Care, social isolation in late life accounted for 4% of the worldwide dementia cases, while low education in youth, a major socioeconomic indicator, accounted for 7%, social factors making up more than one fourth of the total percentage of potentially modifiable risk for dementia of 40% (Livingston et al., 2020; see Chapter 5 for details). In fact, social and intellectual engagement, along with new learning, cognitive training, meditation, and exercise, has been couched in terms of "neural resource enrichment," in the revised Scaffolding Theory of Aging and Cognition (STAC) model, which could enhance brain structure or function dynamically influencing the compensatory scaffolding in late life (Reuter-Lorenz & Park, 2014).

Social isolation and its subjective discomfort of loneliness, however, is on the rise globally. The urbanization that had accompanied industrialization for the past two centuries slowly expanded social disintegration around the world (Scott, 2008), while the recent digital revolution has further exacerbated social isolation in modern societies, a trend that saw its peak during the recent COVID-19 pandemic when social distancing was required or encouraged in most countries (Banerjee & Rai, 2020). Although moving away from your kin and community for work or education has been part of life in industrialized countries for decades, this has challenged many in terms of finding social support and maintaining a sense of belonging. On the other hand, the exodus of residents to urban areas left families and communities in rural areas with looser social networks characterized by weaker social support or integration in countries where abrupt or rapid industrialization took place. Therefore, a sense of belonging has become a vulnerable resource in modern societies, despite being part of a very basic human need (Le Penne, 2017).

Loneliness, social disengagement, and dissolved social integration in late life have been found to carry significant health risks, including for dementia (Luo et al., 2012; Rafnsson et al., 2020). Thus, various efforts have been made to improve social connectedness and reduce loneliness among older people to reduce the risk of dementia in late life. This chapter reviews psychosocial approaches to reduce the risk of dementia in older adults within communities and at societal level in the context of global population aging. First, the importance of maintaining social relationships in late life is discussed as older adults lose social roles and connections. The typical factors contributing to the loss of social relationships in older adults are discussed, such as retirement, death of loved ones, functional impairment, and other factors due to social and cultural conditions (e.g., the estrangement of family members in South Korea). Interventions promoting social engagement, alleviating loneliness, and improving social life and well-being are reviewed successively. Many of these interventions are intricately related to cognitive reserve and brain health, psychologically mediated by cognitive stimulation and psychological well-being, respectively. In addition, more direct intervention strategies to boost cognitive reserve and maintain brain health in social contexts are reviewed. Lastly, we propose social policies and strategies that could improve social integration, alleviate loneliness, and boost the reserve of individuals throughout one's lifetime to lower the risk of dementia in late life.

12.2 Psychosocial Approaches to Mitigate Social Isolation and the Risk of Dementia

12.2.1 Maintaining and Building Social Relationships in Late Life

Social relationships are important in old age and could bring benefits across the range of psychological, physical, and cognitive health. Many studies have demonstrated the benefits of social relationships on cognitive function in older adults, as reviewed in Chapter 9. Notably, social relationships could influence cognitive aging through multiple pathways. Consistent with the effects of education and occupation during youth and early adulthood, midlife social and leisure activities (Chan et al., 2018) as well as late-life social networks (Bennett et al., 2006) and activities (Wilson et al., 2005) have also been found to enhance or maintain cognitive reserve, suggesting that lifelong experience of social stimulation contributes to cognitive reserve, which could delay the clinical manifestation of dementia for years, if not decades. Another important mediation has been found to be the psychological benefits, especially reduction of stress, provided by social relationships (Cohen, 2004), which have been associated with cardiovascular health and brain integrity in late life (Fratiglioni et al., 2004).

Life events in late life, however, such as retirement, death of loved ones, and functional impairment, have been found to make it challenging for many older adults to maintain social networks and relationships. Moreover, stressful events or tension with relatives or friends could lead to further estrangement and loss of close relationships, as resilience and resources to cope with stressful relationships may diminish in vulnerable populations (Diehl et al., 2012). For instance, "family fatigue" has been reported as a frequent and significant source of stress for South Koreans by a sociologist who examined the complex family dynamics of South Korean families, which took a significant role in educating the youth and taking care of the elderly population during the rapid modernization period (Chang, 2009; see Chapter 1 for details). The family-related stress and its associated fatigue intensified during and after a couple of financial crises around the turn of the twenty-first century, as many Korean families shared financial resources and relational duties, leading to the estrangement of family members and contributing to a major increase in the number of older adults without the necessary social support during difficult times (OECD, 2020). Estrangement from family members due to stress, distance, or both, therefore, could be another cause for loss of social relationships in late life in recently industrialized or developing countries. Therefore, older adults from developing countries, who have grown up in traditional communities but now live in an individualized modern society far apart from their family of origin, can be at higher risk of being left with a diminished sense of belonging and smaller social networks.

Complex family dynamics leading to "family fatigue" can also be detrimental for cognitive aging even without estrangement, as it implies a greater possibility of social conflicts and greater risks to cognitive and mental health, since the influence of negative social interaction on an individual could be stronger than that of positive social interaction (Newsom et al., 2005). Notably, relational conflict has been found to be detrimental for cognitive aging when experienced repeatedly (Wilson et al., 2015), especially with spouses (Hughes et al., 2008).

While family therapy and cognitive behavioral therapy have been found to be helpful in engaging family members (Qualls, 2014) and addressing the negative or maladaptive social cognition of the elderly individual to alleviate loneliness (Jarvis et al., 2019; Masi et al., 2011), respectively, access to psychological intervention may not be available to older adults or the public in developing countries (Chey & Lee, 2022). Furthermore, when social relationships with kin are absent or too stressful, the possibility of building social networks with friends needs to be considered even in late life, especially for women, since studies suggest that having friends in social networks could be helpful in maintaining high cognitive function in women (Bélande et al., 2005; Zunzunegui et al., 2003).

12.2.2 *Promoting Social Engagement in Older Adults*

Most studies on social interventions for cognitive health in older people have investigated the effect of social engagement, which is likely to involve cognitive stimulation based on the engagement hypothesis (Bielak, 2010). This predicts that engaging in lifestyle activities would lead to positive changes in cognitive function. Several studies have shown that social interventions that induce participation in social activities can lead to changes in the cognition and brains of older adults (Carlson et al., 2008, 2009; Mortimer et al., 2012; Stine-Morrow et al., 2008). For example, Carlson and colleagues found positive effects of the Experience Corps (EC) program on cognition (Carlson et al., 2008) and brain function (Carlson et al., 2009) in city-dwelling older minority adults without higher education who were marginally normal in cognitive performance. The EC program is an intergenerational volunteer-based program based in the

United States that empowers older adults to help vulnerable children acquire reading ability and cooperative problem-solving skills. Older adults who participated in this program for 15 hours a week during an academic year showed improved episodic memory and executive function (Carlson et al., 2008) and increased brain activity in the prefrontal cortex during the executive control tasks (Carlson et al., 2009). In another study (Mortimer et al., 2012) to promote social interaction, community-dwelling Chinese older adults in Shanghai participated in an hour-long group discussion on varying topics chosen by the participants three times a week for forty weeks, and their changes in cognitive function and brain volume were compared to those of the control group and physical activity groups (e.g., Tai Chi group and walking group). The social interaction group, as well as the Tai Chi group, showed increased brain volume and improved cognitive function compared to the control group.

Cognitive stimulation during social intervention seems more beneficial to older adults' cognition than the social interaction itself. In particular, the amount of novelty provided during an intervention may be the most important component (Bielak, 2010). Another study comparing the effects of different lifestyle activities (McDonough et al., 2015; Park et al., 2014) found that group activities with high cognitive challenge, including learning new skills (e.g., digital photography, quilting), had beneficial effects on episodic memory and brain function. In contrast, the group that participated in social activities mimicking social clubs without much cognitive demand showed only subtle improvement in processing speed when compared to the control group. However, the effects could vary with the target population. For instance, a Finnish study that examined social interventions to stimulate friendship in individuals suffering from loneliness, which did not involve cognitive challenges, found cognitive benefits from social intervention in lonely older adults (Pitkala et al., 2011). Future studies are needed to replicate these findings as well as examine the factors relevant for effectiveness, but social engagement interventions based in neighborhood communities appear to be effective in improving cognitive and brain functions of older adults demonstrated in the EC program carried out in the public elementary schools and the Chinese program provided in and around the neighborhood park. It is possible that participation in these programs developed into social relationships in the community, which could result in more meaningful changes in the cognitive and brain functioning of the older adults. Future community-based studies with longitudinal design are necessary to confirm whether participants developed relationships beyond the program.

As mentioned earlier, empirical evidence has suggested that the benefits of social life on cognitive function in older adults differ according to the characteristics of the individuals and their social relationships. This may stem from the differential mediating effect sizes that can be obtained from each activity and relationship type, depending on demographic characteristics. Furthermore, the timing of the intervention could be important in its effectiveness in reversing or reducing the effects of social isolation or disengagement (Berkman et al., 2011). In other words, the extent to which social engagement and the quality of social interaction are cognitively stimulating and beneficial to psychological health may differ according to individuals' demographic characteristics and the timing of intervention, so their effects on cognitive function may also vary.

12.2.3 Interventions for Alleviating Loneliness in Late Life

Loneliness has emerged as a significant risk factor for cognitive decline and dementia in late life (Tilvis et al., 2000; Wilson et al., 2007). To date, a variety of psychosocial approaches involving various paradigms have been developed to help disadvantaged older adults alleviate depression and loneliness. When it comes to intervention effectiveness, however, one of the most important questions is whether loneliness and social isolation among older adults can be mitigated through psychosocial intervention.

With variable degrees of success, these interventions have sought to develop social skills (e.g., through peer recreation), increase social support (e.g., through mentoring, home visits), increase opportunities for social contact (e.g., through telephone outreach, nonverbal communication), and fix maladaptive social processing (e.g., through telephone outreach, nonverbal communication, and psychological reframing or cognitive behavioral therapy). A study that examined seventeen related strategies aimed at reducing social alienation and loneliness in older people concluded that many intervention strategies were not proven to have sufficient evidence for reducing loneliness (Findlay, 2003).

Masi and colleagues (2011) used meta-analytic approaches to evaluate the effectiveness of loneliness-relieving measures. Among the fifty intervention studies reviewed, twelve were single-group pre-post trials, eighteen nonrandomized, and twenty randomized group comparison studies. Ten of the twenty randomized studies focused on adults aged 60 and up, six on middle-aged adults, three on young adults, and one on children. Meta-analysis of the randomized studies revealed a small effect size (-0.198, 96% CI = -0.32, -0.08) in reducing loneliness. Compared to other interventions, those addressing deficits in social cognition had the largest mean effect (–0.598, 96% CI = –0.96, –0.23). Further analyses with potential moderators, such as gender, age, type of loneliness measure, revealed that only gender had a moderating influence on the effect size (i.e., samples with more men found greater reduction in loneliness).

Questions have been raised as to whether various intervention programs can alleviate loneliness that could lead to protective effects against dementia. Only a few studies have examined whether the improved social relationships had slowed cognitive aging. The aforementioned Finnish study investigated the effects of socially stimulating interventions to promote peer support and friendship in older adults suffering from loneliness (Pitkala et al., 2011; Routasalo et al., 2009). The social intervention and control groups participated in one of the usual group activities, such as writing, exercise, or art, while only the social intervention group participated in an active discussion to enhance interaction and friendships between the participants in order to stimulate them socially. Compared to the control group, the social intervention group did not show a significant difference in loneliness and social network changes but did show more improvement in psychological well-being (Routasalo et al., 2009) and cognitive functioning (Pitkala et al., 2011). Therefore, the cognitive benefits of social intervention might have been the result of improved psychological well-being in older adults.

The findings from the systematic reviews and the comprehensive meta-analyses reviewed above can be cautiously interpreted as encouraging. Psychosocial interventions developed from well-designed loneliness strategies (i.e., randomized comparative studies) that use cognitive behavioral therapy to address the maladaptive beliefs (e.g, perceived social costs, perceived social self-efficacy, and interpersonal beliefs) of individuals suffering from loneliness appear to hold promise in alleviating loneliness in older adults. The results are consistent with the hypothesis that maladaptive social cognition plays a key role in the development and persistence of loneliness (Cacioppo & Hawkley, 2009). Further, a sophisticated social intervention considering the varying social context and the quality of social interactions as well as the individual risk factors, such as low education, living alone, the severity of loneliness, or social conflict with others, appears to be more effective. It is also noteworthy that cognitive improvement can occur without the abatement of loneliness, as reported in the Finnish study. Therefore, it is necessary to develop diverse intervention programs and examine their effectiveness at multiple levels to provide effective social interventions according to the individual's or the group's characteristics and needs.

12.2.4 Promising Interventions for Older Adults to Improve Their Social Life and Well-Being

Higher socioeconomic status, especially higher education, can help individuals overcome and alter the effects of early experience of adversity on social life and well-being during adulthood, possibly through greater social support and recreational activities (Andersson & Stevens, 1993; Sheikh, 2018; Van Groenou & Van Tilburg, 2003). Can we say, then, that environmental factors, including intervention in adulthood, improve our social life and well-being as well? Although many of the existing studies are correlational, which make it difficult to infer causal direction, there have been a few studies on training or intervention programs that were demonstrated to be effective in the younger population, which could be applied to older adults to improve their social well-being and brain functions.

Socio-cognitive and socio-emotional functions, such as the theory of mind (ToM) and empathy, have been found to improve with training. For instance, conversation training (i.e., talking about others' mind: Bianco et al., 2016; Lecce et al., 2014) and acting (i.e., activities requiring perspective-taking: Goldstein & Winner, 2012) improved the ToM and empathic capacities of children and adolescents. Such training effects were also found in older adults (Lecce et al., 2015; Rosi et al., 2016). For example, older adults aged 58 and above who received a couple of two-hour-long ToM training sessions (e.g., reading stories and having a group conversation to discuss the character's mental states and behavior) displayed improved ToM compared to their counterparts who received the same length of physical conversation training sessions (e.g., reading stories and having a group conversation to discuss physical, not mental, inference) or social contact sessions (e.g., having a group discussion on age-related changes and well-being: Lecce et al., 2015). A recent magnetic resonance imaging study (Valk et al., 2017) found positive structural change in the social brains of young and middle-aged adults with similar training sessions. More specifically, a nine-month socio-affective (e.g., feeling compassion toward oneself and others, empathic listening) and socio-cognitive training (e.g., perspective-taking exercises) led to cortical thickening of the social brain regions, such as the frontoinsular, the inferior frontal, and the lateral temporal regions in adults aged 20–55.

Another well-documented way of improving the social life and well-being of a person is to boost one's sense of belonging. The need to belong is critical to one's psychological, cognitive, and physical well-being (Walton & Brady, 2017). Feelings of social isolation can be perceived as a social threat and are found to be detrimental to health and cognitive functions. Such a harsh social environment is pronounced in underrepresented (e.g., minority) or stereotyped groups (see Walton & Brady, 2020 for review). To meet the needs of belonging and ultimately improve one's social life and well-being, an intervention was designed to increase the sense of social belonging in young adults utilizing a subtle attitude-change strategy (Walton & Cohen, 2007, 2011). Its goal was to improve the sense of belonging by changing the subjective interpretation of negative social situations to less- or non-threatening. For example, participants read stories of others who experienced social adversity conveying that belongingness-related worries and challenges are common, normal, and transient. The study found that only minority students benefited from the intervention. Moreover, the social belonging intervention was found to change one's interpretation of the negative social situations, which resulted in improvement in the academic performance and physical well-being of African American college students. Surprisingly, the same participants reported greater psychological well-being and career satisfaction, and were more successful seven to eleven years after they had received the short intervention (Brady et al., 2020). Such benefits of the intervention have been found in other socially disadvantaged or stigmatized groups as well (i.e., English as a second language students: LaCosse et al., 2020; individuals of higher body weights: Logel et al., 2021; racial/ethnic minority populations: Murphy et al., 2020; Williams et al., 2020; socially or economically disadvantaged populations: Yeager et al., 2016; women in the engineering field, Walton et al., 2015). Boosting the sense of belonging in older adults, however, would require careful assessment of the sociocultural context as well as age- or generation-appropriate narratives to be successful in changing the older adults' interpretation of the unfavorable situation.

12.3 The Interplay between Cognitive Capacity and Social Life in Older Adults

In the ongoing process of aging, cognitive decline can have numerous ramifications. An important one would be its effects on social interaction, as it requires complex cognitive processes, including proficient encoding of social information, capturing subtle cues, inhibiting contextually inappropriate behaviors, and inferring the abstract mental states of others (Henry et al., 2009; Krendl et al., 2021). In other words, higher-order cognitive functions are crucial in maintaining a good social life. An individual's preexisting social life can be disrupted if cognitive decline affects his/her functioning significantly. Conversely, psychosocial functions can be protected if the older adult's cognitive functions are well managed or intensively boosted with interventions.

Numerous intervention strategies are being developed to counteract cognitive and neural decline that could accompany aging. The enhanced neurocognitive function not only serves as an ongoing protective guard against cognitive decline but also enriches social activities that could promote lifelong indirect benefits. The interventions that target cognitive, psychosocial, or physical components may not directly change the neural substrates underlying loneliness or social well-being, but the effects can be explained with the concepts of cognitive reserve, brain maintenance, and compensation; that is, theoretical frameworks that represent cognitive or brain health factors across the lifespan (Cabeza et al., 2018; Stern et al., 2018; Reuter-Lorenz & Park, 2014; see Chapter 5 for details).

The intervention approaches include (a) acquiring skills and strategies of instrumental and social activities of daily life, (b) increasing efficiency in specific cognitive processes, or (c) improving brain health through physical activity (Brehmer et al., 2014). First, the direct and explicit approach targets the basic skills of daily activities that are needed in social well-being and independent functioning. For example, if an older adult suffers from frequent memory failures that disturb daily activities, he/she can benefit from acquiring skills that actively bind memory cues or utilizing compensatory skills (e.g., mnemonic skills, leaving memos). Such interventions are also accompanied by functional changes in the brain (Dresler et al., 2017; Engvig et al., 2014). Education on instrumental skills (e.g., digital devices, riding public transportation) can also be effective and has been shown to improve mood and enhance independent abilities (Orellano et al., 2012). Randomized control trials of cognitively stimulating activities have also shown improvements. Engaging in web-based conversations enhanced cognitive functions of language and processing speed in addition to the broadening opportunity for social interaction through on-line media (Dodge et al., 2015). Moreover, the Synapse Project, which involved older adults randomly assigned to either a socializing condition or a cognitively challenging condition, such as learning photography or quilting, demonstrated that processing speed improved significantly in the cognitively challenging activities, while only marginal improvement was observed in the socializing condition (McDonough et al., 2015; Park et al., 2014).

The processing-specific intervention strategy, frequently implemented in cognitive training, is based on the cognitive models of one's real-world functioning. A specific cognitive processing ability can be targeted for intervention, very much as particular muscular functions are strengthened during physical rehabilitation. For example, repetitively practicing core cognitive processes (e.g., task-switching, inhibition, updating, or sustained attention) can enhance the coping abilities required in a real-world environment. Unlike acquiring skills and strategies, practicing cognitive processes strengthens the general capacity to cope with the cognitively demanding situation. Accordingly, stimulating a specific information-processing module seems to affect the corresponding neural substrates (Dahlin et al., 2008; Jaeggi et al., 2011; Thompson et al., 2016). In accordance with the specific cognitive domain of the intervention target, the improvements are typically observed in the relevant behavioral performance or brain structures, as demonstrated in the spatial navigation training that resulted in protection of the hippocampus in late life (Lövdén et al., 2012). A prolonged mismatch between cognitive supply and external demand during the intervention may induce neural plastic changes that persist through a relatively longer timescale (Lövdén et al., 2013). Although these interventions may not explicitly involve social components, the benefits can propagate to other psychological or social outcomes, such as self-efficacy and social participation in the community, respectively. More specifically, cognitive training of processing speed appears to alleviate depressive symptoms, possibly through efficacious behavioral changes and improved self-concepts (Wolinsky et al., 2009).

Lastly, social enrichment can be promoted alongside a physically active lifestyle. Typically, social activity requires a certain level of physical activity that is known to counteract the effect of cognitive aging by preserving cerebrovascular conditions similar to younger adults, which can be a critical pathway to increase or at least maintain the brain's structural resources. Although it is hard to pinpoint the exact neurobiological basis of the benefit (e.g., cerebrovascular expansion, neurogenesis, glial changes, or reduction of inflammageing), the empirical evidence is consistent and robust in the role of physical exercise in increasing brain structural capacity and cognitive functions (Erickson et al., 2015; Stillman et al., 2020). The effect of physical activity in both short-term intervention and individual differences in lifestyles in a longer timescale was associated with counteracting degeneration of white matter integrity (Burzynska et al., 2017). Therefore, long-term persistence of social engagement that involves physical activities could be one of the most effective methods to delay cognitive aging and prevent dementia, since it is beneficial not only for providing motivations to exercise persistently, but also for improving the social well-being of older adults (Kim et al., 2020).

12.4 Dementia Prevention Strategies and Policies for Social Integration and Brain Health

It was only half a century ago when the proportion of young children was three times more than the older people in the world. In 2018 young children under five were outnumbered by the older population 65 years and above for the first time since the beginning of world history (Ritchie, 2019). As life expectancy grows, multiple generations of family members are now coexisting (WHO, 2011), yet they tend to live separately and frequently alone in urban dwellings, with significant challenges in finding social support and developing a sense of belonging. The "village effect" popularized by Susan Pinker (2015), which protects the health and well-being of its constituents, is diminishing generally and much faster in developing countries (WHO, 2011). International organizations, such as the United Nations (UN) and the Organization for Economic Cooperation and Development (OECD), have been monitoring the social integration of their member countries for decades, but in recent years they have emphasized the issue to national members and urged them to adopt policies to consider the impact of social disintegration and support communities to reinforce social infrastructures that can foster and promote social connections (OECD, 2020; UN DESA, 2021). Consistent with these global efforts, we propose three key strategies a government or community can adopt to improve the social life and well-being of people, which can also reduce the risk of dementia.

Access to Public Education in Youth
Among the modifiable factors to reduce the risk of dementia, lack of formal education is one of the most significant factors, accounting for 8–9% of all dementia cases around the world (Livingston et al., 2020; Norton et al., 2014). Formal education is critical for cognitive development during childhood and youth, acting as a cognitive reserve that protects cognitive functioning in late life or delays the effects of neurodegeneration (Kremen et al., 2019). A robust body of research has

found that low education is a significant risk for dementia (see Chapter 5 for details), despite its variable definition (Maccora et al., 2020). Therefore, establishing and expanding compulsory education as a dementia prevention strategy is particularly relevant for developing countries whose many rural residents do not have access to community-based schools. The alarming increase in dementia cases in these countries since 2010 is projected to make up more than 70% of all dementia cases in the world by 2050 (Alzheimer's Disease International, 2010; Livingston et al., 2020). One of the key factors contributing to this increase is the fact that a significant proportion of these countries' older adults, especially women, have received little education. Since the effects of education or experience on general cognitive ability plateau in late adolescence and early adulthood (Kremen et al., 2019), access to and quality of education during this critical developmental period would contribute significantly to one's cognitive reserve.

An unusual randomized control trial to examine the effects of accessibility of public schooling has been conducted in remote northwestern Afghanistan villages (Burde & Linden, 2013). The study tested the efficacy of a village-based school program because there had been arguments that educational funds from government and international agencies should be invested in bigger city schools (since the demand for schools was greater in cities), which could also house better teachers and facilities. Surprisingly, however, the trial demonstrated that the village-based schools significantly increased enrollment and boosted the test scores of children living in rural areas, closing the gender gap in both these measures within just a year. The results have significant implications for building village-based schools in terms of dementia prevention in countries with strong patriarchal traditions. A slightly different but equally important reason to build village- or community-based schools up to secondary level is that this can be a critical component in reinforcing the social infrastructure that could halt the dissolution of rural communities and social integration, frequently observed during rapid industrialization, which can be another major contributing factor to increases in the incidence of dementia.

The protective effects of education are likely to increase as the number of years in education increases, according to the cognitive reserve hypothesis. Secondary education appears to afford significant cognitive reserve capacity that can mitigate the effect of brain aging and neurodegeneration. The three-decade report of the Framingham Heart Study into the incidence of dementia illustrates the preventive effect of completing secondary education (i.e., twelve years of formal education). More specifically, having a high school diploma was able to reduce the five-year hazard ratio to 0.54, 0.55, and 0.77 from the 1.46, 0.97, and 1.66 observed in older adults without a high school diploma during the follow-up studies of three successive decades (Satizabal et al., 2016). The case of South Korea, with unusually high dementia prevalence compared to its Asian neighbors with similar Confucian traditions and economic development (e.g., Taiwan and Japan, which were able to introduce compulsory middle school education more than three decades earlier) supports the importance of secondary education for a national dementia prevention strategy. Despite cautions that varying operational definitions of low education as a risk for dementia might hinder the translation of the evidence for the robust effects of education into practical policy recommendations (Maccora et al., 2020), a scientific commission has recently recommended childhood education, including primary and secondary schools, as a specific population-based goal to prevent dementia, especially in low- and middle-income countries (Livingston et al., 2020).

Developing Leisure and Volunteering Activities within Communities and Workplaces from Midlife
As modern societies are characterized by larger urban areas, the rise in social isolation and the effects of loneliness have been observed for decades. Although it is difficult, if not impossible, to build villages or social networks based on kinship and neighborhood communities as in the past, it is possible to extend and promote activities and programs that can facilitate social connection in various forms of community. Leisure activities have been found to moderate the effects of brain aging and neurodegeneration (Akbaraly et al., 2009; Verghese et al., 2003), while physical exercise has been proven to prevent cognitive decline and dementia (Colcombe et al., 2006; Erickson et al., 2011). When these activities are practiced in groups for extended periods of time in communities or workplaces, the benefits of social relationships could be added (see Chapter 9 for details). In the Kungsholmen project conducted in Stockholm Sweden, participation in social activities was associated with less cognitive decline six years later (Wang et al., 2002), and many other studies reported similar benefits (Barnes et al., 2004; Bassuk et al., 1999; Ertel et al., 2008; James et al., 2011; Kelly et al., 2017). If these evidence-based activities and programs are to be adopted by local communities and workplaces, community residents and workers could possibly build social connections as well as cognitive reserves, which are both beneficial for preventing dementia in the long run. Moreover, community-based programs can provide

neutral platforms where community newcomers can meet existing residents and start building their social network in the community while benefiting from the programs and activities, especially in urban areas.

The EC program, introduced in Section 12.2.2, can be another promising example that involves community-based volunteering. This intergenerational mentoring program, which took place in community elementary schools, improved the cognitive functions of the older participants in urban areas (Carlson et al., 2008) as well as increasing their brain functioning, which could decline with age (Carlson et al., 2009). In addition, the schoolchildren benefited from the older adults' mentoring and reading, which could give communities further incentives to adopt the program. Consistently, persistence of participation in community volunteering proved effective in slowing the cognitive decline and temporal lobe atrophy in older adults in the rural communities of the Korea Social Life, Health and Aging Project (KSHAP; Jo et al., 2021).

Not all social activities studied so far were effective, nor have all the benefits persisted in the long term (Seeman et al., 2001), but evidence-based interventions involving leisure and volunteering activities in communities have shown the greatest mitigating effects on cognitive decline and brain aging. It is noteworthy that volunteering in communities, possibly tailored to the sociodemographics of older adults, has consistently proven to be effective. Further, social engagement combined with leisure activities, especially those involving physical exercise, appear to protect brain integrity throughout life and possibly mitigate the risk of dementia in late life.

Networks for Social Support and Sense of Belonging in Late Life
Aging is associated with personal losses, physical illness, and disabilities that can make people vulnerable to psychological suffering, loneliness, and depression, especially in very late life. Social support has been found to ameliorate these negative emotions and mood, yet it has been found that older adults have less social support than younger generations (OECD, 2020), particularly in recently industrialized countries such as South Korea and Greece, which have rapidly growing older populations whose traditional care and support from the family are increasingly unstable. Considering that social isolation is a major risk for dementia, policies for dementia prevention in societies with low social support should take this factor seriously, recognizing that younger family members would be increasingly unavailable for social support due to their increased mobility via occupational and educational opportunities. For example, the fact that

South Korea has the widest discrepancy between young and old generations (i.e., 93% of people aged 15–29 reported having relatives or friends they can count on in times of need, compared to only 63% of those aged 50 years old or more [OECD, 2020], the lowest among OECD member countries) calls for government attention. The low social integration of older Koreans may be in part due to the fact that the health and welfare systems of South Korea are mainly focused on physical well-being, such as universal health insurance and the elderly living-assistance service, and not psychological well-being. The quality of social support and the issue of loneliness in older adults, which can be critical for one's psychological well-being (Diener & Tay, 2015), have been relatively neglected, and this may have contributed to the increased dementia prevalence in South Korea (Kim et al., 2019, 2021).

One key issue related to the quality of social support is the need for a sense of belonging, which has been found to be part of human nature or a fundamental human motivation (Baumeister & Leary, 1995), yet it is often lacking in late life. Older adults, especially in developing countries, can feel excluded in societies that are changing at a fast pace and may feel uncomfortable in environments with new technologies and social norms. This can lead to a diminished sense of belonging and loss of purpose in life. Moreover, it has been found that the social networks of older Koreans decreased with age compared to those of their U.S. counterparts, which remained relatively stable with age, possibly due to the fact that older Korean's networks were mostly based on kinship (Youm et al., 2014). Although it may seem like a daunting task to change these critical perceptions about one's self and life in old age, there are innovative programs that can be benchmarked, such as the EC program (Carlson et al., 2008, 2009), which provided a meaningful role for the older adults in the community to help children with academic achievement and emotional support. Also, the experiments with subtle attitude-change strategies that improved the sense of belonging in college communities have the potential to be developed for older adults to help them feel more secure in their social environment (Walton & Cohen, 2007, 2011). Interestingly, a longitudinal all-cause mortality investigation examining the effects of three types of social relationships during the five waves of the KSHAP found that a lack of social relationships observed at the village level (i.e., group-level segregation) predicted the mortality of the older adults significantly even after controlling for the bias of sample attrition during the eight years, whereas the associations with loneliness and social disengagement did not survive after controlling for the attrition (Youm et al., 2021). The results highlight the importance of the need to belong to a larger community or society and have implications for policies concerning the social integration of older adults in a modern society with diverse composition.

Lastly, as one of the few psychosocial interventions proven effective in reducing loneliness in older adults was cognitive therapy that addressed the maladaptive social cognitions associated with loneliness, older adults' better access to evidence-based psychotherapy can be an important policy and strategy recommendation in preventing dementia as well as improving overall mental health in late life. Moreover, depression has been recognized as one of the significant modifiable risk factors for dementia independent of social isolation (Livingston et al., 2020). Although this volume has not included the issue of mental health's role in cognitive decline and dementia, partly due to the extensive nature of its literature that may not be aligned with this book's scope and objective, it should be noted that mental health should be an essential component in any policy or strategy targeting dementia prevention.

12.5 Conclusions

The chapter has extracted three components of social life that have been found to be consistently significant in the scientific literature reviewed throughout the rest of the volume and translated them into policies and strategies that could be effective in reducing the risk of dementia throughout the life course. As social isolation has been recognized as an important modifiable risk for dementia, we reviewed studies examining the effectiveness of various interventions that aimed to increase social engagement, support, and networks in order to slow down cognitive and brain aging. As social relationships and engagements afford the reserve through activation of the social brain as well as brain maintenance by reducing neuroinflammatory responses (see the schematic pathways of these effects in Figure 5.3), promoting the maintenance and building of social connection among older adults can be an effective component in dementia prevention policies and strategies. Studies have found varying effectiveness in these strategies, however, with weaker effects in interventions aimed at reducing loneliness directly or enhancing cognitive and brain functioning with social activities that were not cognitively challenging, while relatively stronger effects in social engagement programs that involve volunteering, which not only demanded a higher level of cognitive and social functioning but also may have provided a sense of belonging or purpose in life. On the other hand, effective intervention strategies to build cognitive reserve can facilitate social life and well-being in late life, and vice versa. Strategies and programs that target skills for daily activities, focus on process-specific cognitive training, and promote social enrichment through physical activities have demonstrated effectiveness.

Lastly, we conclude by mentioning a couple of government policies to address the increasing problem of social isolation and loneliness. Based on the awareness that social isolation or loneliness is a serious health risk (Hawkley & Capitanio, 2015; Holt-Lunstad et al., 2015), the first ministry of loneliness was established in the UK in 2018. High-level leadership is being called in to address the agenda and meet three specific objectives. This process started with efforts to remove the stigma of loneliness and build a national-scale conversation on the problem. In order to take significant government action for change, loneliness will be considered in all government policy-making, while endeavors to connect people in communities will be supported to amplify their impact in civil society. Further, the ministry purports to improve the evidence base for tackling loneliness so that everyone can make informed decisions concerning the matter. Other countries are following suit, and Japan recently appointed a cabinet member to deal with social isolation (Kodama, 2021). It would be no surprise if other governments join the efforts to address increasing social isolation and loneliness at the national level.

REFERENCES

Akbaraly, T. N., Portet, F., Fustinoni, S., Dartigues, J. F., Artero, S., Rouaud, O., Touchon, J., Ritchie, K., & Berr, C. (2009). Leisure activities and the risk of dementia in the elderly: Results from the Three-City Study. *Neurology, 73* (11), 854–861. https://doi.org/10.1212/wnl.0b013e3181b7849b

Alzheimer's Disease International (2010). *World Alzheimer Report 2010: The Global Economic Impact of Dementia.* Alzheimer's Disease International.

Andersson, L., & Stevens, N. (1993). Associations between early experiences with parents and well-being in old age. *Journal of Gerontology, 48*(3), P109–P116. https://doi.org/10.1093/geronj/48.3.P109

Banerjee, D., & Rai, M. (2020). Social isolation in Covid-19: The impact of loneliness. *International Journal of Social Psychiatry, 66*(6), 525–527. https://doi.org/10.1177/0020764020922269

Barnes, L. L., De Leon, C. M., Wilson, R. S., Bienias, J. L., & Evans, D. A. (2004). Social resources and cognitive decline in a population of older African Americans and whites. *Neurology, 63*(12), 2322–2326. https://doi.org/10.1212/01.wnl.0000147473.04043.b3

Bassuk, S. S., Glass, T. A., & Berkman, L. F. (1999). Social disengagement and incident cognitive decline in community-dwelling elderly persons. *Annals of*

Internal Medicine, *131*(3), 165–173. https://doi.org/10.7326/0003-4819-131-3-199908030-00002

Baumeister, R., & Leary, M. (1995). The need to belong: Desire for interpersonal attachments as a fundamental human motivation. *Psychological Bulletin, 117* (3), 497–529. https://doi.org/10.1037/0033-2909.117.3.497

Béland, F., Zunzunegui, M. V., Alvarado, B., Otero, A., & Del Ser, T. (2005). Trajectories of cognitive decline and social relations. *The Journals of Gerontology Series B: Psychological Sciences and Social Sciences, 60*(6), P320–P330. https://doi.org/10.1093/geronb/60.6.p320

Bennett, D. A., Schneider, J. A., Tang, Y., Arnold, S. E., & Wilson, R. S. (2006). The effect of social networks on the relation between Alzheimer's disease pathology and level of cognitive function in old people: A longitudinal cohort study. *The Lancet Neurology, 5*(5), 406–412. https://doi.org/10.1016/s1474-4422(06)70417-3

Berkman, L.F., Ertel, K.Q., & Glymour, M.M. (2011). Aging and social intervention: Life course perspectives. In R. H. Binstock, L. K. George (Eds.), *Handbook of Aging and the Social Sciences*, 7th ed, pp. 337–351. Academic Press. https://doi.org/10.1016/B978-0-12-380880-6.00024-1

Bianco, F., Lecce, S., & Banerjee, R. (2016). Conversations about mental states and theory of mind development during middle childhood: A training study. *Journal of Experimental Child Psychology, 149*, 41–61. https://doi.org/10.1016/j.jecp.2015.11.006

Bielak, A. A. (2010). How can we not "lose it" if we still don't understand how to "use it"? Unanswered questions about the influence of activity participation on cognitive performance in older age – A mini-review. *Gerontology, 56*(5), 507–519. https://doi.org/10.1159/000264918

Brady, S. T., Cohen, G. L., Jarvis, S. N., & Walton, G. M. (2020). A brief social-belonging intervention in college improves adult outcomes for black Americans. *Science Advances, 6*(18), eaay3689. https://doi.org/10.1126/sciadv.aay3689

Brehmer, Y., Kalpouzos, G., Wenger, E., & Lövdén, M. (2014). Plasticity of brain and cognition in older adults. *Psychological Research, 78*(6), 790–802. https://doi.org/10.1007/s00426-014-0587-z

Burde, D., & Linden, L. L. (2013). Bringing education to Afghan girls: A randomized controlled trial of village-based schools. *American Economic Journal: Applied Economics, 5*(3), 27–40. https://doi.org/10.1257/app.5.3.27

Burzynska, A. Z., Jiao, Y., Knecht, A. M., Fanning, J., Awick, E. A., Chen, T., Gothe, N., Voss, M. W., McAuley, E., & Kramer, A. F. (2017). White matter integrity declined over 6-months, but dance intervention improved integrity of the fornix of older adults. *Frontiers in Aging Neuroscience, 9*, 1–15. https://doi.org/10.3389/fnagi.2017.00059

Cabeza, R., Albert, M., Belleville, S., Craik, F. I. M., Duarte, A., Grady, C. L., Lindenberger, U., Nyberg, L., Park, D. C., Reuter-Lorenz, P. A., Rugg, M. D., Steffener, J., & Rajah, M. N. (2018). Maintenance, reserve and compensation: The cognitive neuroscience of healthy ageing. *Nature Reviews Neuroscience, 19*(11), 701–710. https://doi.org/10.1038/s41583-018-0068-2

Cacioppo, J. T., & Hawkley, L. C. (2009). Perceived social isolation and cognition. *Trends in Cognitive Sciences*, *13*(10), 447–454. https://doi.org/10.1016/j.tics.2009.06.005

Cao, Q., Tan, C. C., Xu, W., Hu, H., Cao, X. P., Dong, Q., Tan, L., & Yu, J. T. (2020). The prevalence of dementia: A systematic review and meta-analysis. *Journal of Alzheimer's Disease*, *73*(3), 1157–1166. https://doi.org/10.3233/jad-191092

Carlson, M. C., Erickson, K. I., Kramer, A. F., Voss, M. W., Bolea, N., Mielke, M., McGill, S., Rebok, G. W., Seeman, T., & Fried, L. P. (2009). Evidence for neurocognitive plasticity in at-risk older adults: The Experience Corps program. *Journals of Gerontology Series A: Biomedical Sciences and Medical Sciences*, *64*(12), 1275–1282. https://doi.org/10.1093/gerona/glp117

Carlson, M. C., Saczynski, J. S., Rebok, G. W., Seeman, T., Glass, T. A., McGill, S., Tielsch, J., Frick, K. D., Hill, J., & Fried, L. P. (2008). Exploring the effects of an "everyday" activity program on executive function and memory in older adults: Experience Corps®. *The Gerontologist*, *48*(6), 793–801. https://doi.org/10.1093/geront/48.6.793

Chan, D., Shafto, M., Kievit, R., Matthews, F., Spink, M., Valenzuela, M., & Henson, R. N. (2018). Lifestyle activities in mid-life contribute to cognitive reserve in late-life, independent of education, occupation, and late-life activities. *Neurobiology of Aging*, *70*, 180–183. https://doi.org/10.1016/j.neurobiolaging.2018.06.012

Chang, K. S. (2009). Normalized Crisis of Korean Family. In *Family, Life, and Politico-Economics: Micro-Foundation of Compressed Modernity*, pp. 293–313. Seoul Changbi.

Chey, J., & Lee, H. (2022). Improving effectiveness of mental health system with licensed psychologists in OECD member countries. *Journal of Korean Psychological Association: General*, *41*(3), 221–242. https://doi.org/10.22257/kjp.2022.8.41.3.221

Cohen, S. (2004). Social Relationships and Health. *American Psychologist*, *59*(8), 676–684. https://doi.org/10.1037/0003-066X.59.8.676

Colcombe, S. J., Erickson, K. I., Scalf, P. E., Kim, J. S., Prakash, R., McAuley, E., Elavsky, S., Marquez, D. X., Hu, L., & Kramer, A. F. (2006). Aerobic exercise training increases brain volume in aging humans. *Journals of Gerontology Series A: Biological Sciences and Medical Sciences*, *61*(11), 1166–1170. https://doi.org/10.1093/gerona/61.11.1166

Dahlin, E., Neely, A. S., Larsson, A., Backman, L., & Nyberg, L. (2008). Transfer of learning after updating training mediated by the striatum. *Science*, *320*(5882), 1510–1512. https://doi.org/10.1126/science.1155466

Diehl, M., Hay, E. L., & Chui, H. (2012). Personal risk and resilience factors in the context of daily stress. In B. Hayslip & G. C. Smith (eds.), *Annual Review of Gerontology and Geriatrics: Vol. 32. Emerging Perspectives on Resilience in Adulthood and Later Life*, pp. 251–274. Springer Publishing. https://doi.org/10.1891/0198-8794.32.251

Diener E, & Tay L. (2015). Subjective well-being and human welfare around the world as reflected in the Gallup World Poll. *International Journal of Psychology*, *50*(2), 135–149. https://doi.org/10.1002/ijop.12136

Dodge, H. H., Zhu, J., Mattek, N. C., Bowman, M., Ybarra, O., Wild, K. V., Loewenstein, D. A., & Kaye, J. A. (2015). Web-enabled conversational interactions as a method to improve cognitive functions: Results of a 6-week randomized controlled trial. *Alzheimer's and Dementia: Translational Research and Clinical Interventions*, *1*(1), 1–12. https://doi.org/10.1016/j.trci.2015.01.001

Dresler, M., Shirer, W. R., Konrad, B. N., Müller, N. C. J., Wagner, I. C., Fernández, G., Czisch, M., & Greicius, M. D. (2017). Mnemonic training reshapes brain networks to support superior memory. *Neuron*, *93*(5), 1227–1235. https://doi.org/10.1016/j.neuron.2017.02.003

Engvig, A., Fjell, A. M., Westlye, L. T., Skaane, N. V., Dale, A. M., Holland, D., Due-Tønnessen, P., Sundseth, Ø., & Walhovd, K. B. (2014). Effects of cognitive training on gray matter volumes in memory clinic patients with subjective memory impairment. *Journal of Alzheimer's Disease*, *41*(3), 779–791. https://doi.org/10.3233/JAD-131889

Erickson, K. I., Voss, M. W., Prakash, R. S., Basak, C., Szabo, A., Chaddock, L., Kim, J. S., Heo, S., Alves, H., White, S. M., Wojcicki, T. R., Mailey, E., Vieira, V. J., Martin, S. A., Pence, B. D., Woods, J. A., McAuley, E., & Kramer, A. F. (2011). Exercise training increases size of hippocampus and improves memory. *Proceedings of the National Academy of Sciences*, *108*(7), 3017–3022. https://doi.org/10.1073/pnas.1015950108

Erickson, K. I., Hillman, C. H., & Kramer, A. F. (2015). Physical activity, brain, and cognition. *Current Opinion in Behavioral Sciences*, *4*, 27–32. https://doi.org/10.1016/j.cobeha.2015.01.005

Ertel, K. A., Glymour, M. M., & Berkman, L. F. (2008). Effects of social integration on preserving memory function in a nationally representative US elderly population. *American Journal of Public Health*, *98*(7), 1215–1220. https://doi.org/10.2105/ajph.2007.113654

Findlay, R. A. (2003). Interventions to reduce social isolation amongst older people: Where is the evidence? *Ageing and Society*, *23*(5), 647–658. https://doi.org/10.1017/S0144686X03001296

Fratiglioni, L., Paillard-Borg, S., & Winblad, B. (2004). An active and socially integrated lifestyle in late life might protect against dementia. *The Lancet Neurology*, *3*(6), 343–353. https://doi.org/10.1016/s1474-4422(04)00767-7

Goldstein, T. R., & Winner, E. (2012). Enhancing empathy and theory of mind. *Journal of Cognition and Development*, *13*(1), 19–37. https://doi.org/10.1080/15248372.2011.573514

Hawkley, L. C., & Capitanio, J. P. (2015). Perceived social isolation, evolutionary fitness and health outcomes: A lifespan approach. *Philosophical Transactions of the Royal Society B: Biological Sciences*, *370*(1669), 20140114. https://doi.org/10.1098/rstb.2014.0114.

Henry, J. D., von Hippel, W., & Baynes, K. (2009). Social inappropriateness, executive control, and aging. *Psychology and Aging*, *24*(1), 239–244. https://doi.org/10.1037/a0013423

Holt-Lunstad, J., Smith, T. B., Baker, M., Harris, T., & Stephenson, D. (2015). Loneliness and social isolation as risk factors for mortality. *Perspectives on Psychological Science*, *10*(2), 227–237. https://doi.org/10.1177/1745691614568352

Hughes, T. F., Andel, R., Small, B. J., Borenstein, A. R., & Mortimer, J. A. (2008). The association between social resources and cognitive change in older adults: Evidence from the Charlotte County Healthy Aging Study. *The Journals of Gerontology Series B: Psychological Sciences and Social Sciences*, *63*(4), P241–P244. https://doi.org/10.1093/geronb/63.4.p241

Jaeggi, S. M., Buschkuehl, M., Jonides, J., Shah, P., Morrison, A. B., & Chein, J. M. (2011). Short-and long-term benefits of cognitive training. *Proceedings of the National Academy of Sciences*, *108*(25), 46–60. https://doi.org/10.1073/pnas.1103228108

James, B. D., Wilson, R. S., Barnes, L. L., & Bennett, D. A. (2011). Late-life social activity and cognitive decline in old age. *Journal of the International Neuropsychological Society: JINS*, *17*(6), 998–1005. https://doi.org/10.1017/s1355617711000531

Jarvis, M. A., Padmanabhanunni, A., Chipps, J. (2019). An evaluation of a low-intensity cognitive behavioral therapy mhealth-supported intervention to reduce loneliness in older people. *International Journal of Environmental Research and Public Health*, *16*(7), 1305. https://doi.org/10.3390/ijerph16071305

Jo, J., Kim, H., Youm, Y., & Chey, J. (2021). Late-life social activity moderates the association between temporal lobe atrophy and episodic memory decline. Poster presentation, Alzheimer's Association International Conference (AAIC), July 26–30, 2021.

Kelly, M. E., Duff, H., Kelly, S., McHugh Power, J. E., Brennan, S., Lawlor, B. A., & Loughrey, D. G. (2017). The impact of social activities, social networks, social support and social relationships on the cognitive functioning of healthy older adults: A systematic review. *Systematic Reviews*, *6*(1), 1–18. https://doi.org/10.1186/s13643-017-0632-2

Kim, C., Kim, J., & Thapa, B. (2020). Bidirectional association between leisure time physical activity and well-being: Longitudinal evidence. *Journal of Leisure Research*, *51*(5), 559–580. https://doi.org/10.1080/00222216.2020.1807428

Kim, H., Kwak, S., Kim, J., Youm, Y., & Chey, J. (2019). Social network position moderates the relationship between late-life depressive symptoms and memory differently in men and women. *Scientific Reports*, *9*, 6142. https://doi.org/10.1038/s41598-019-42388-3

Kim, H., Kwak, S., Youm, Y., Chey, J. (2021). Social network characteristics predict loneliness in older adults. *Gerontology*, *68*(3), 309–320. https://doi.org/10.1159/000516226

Kodama, S. (2021). Japan appoints "minister of loneliness" to help people home alone. *Report on NikkeiAsia* on February 13, 2021. https://asia.nikkei.com/

Spotlight/Coronavirus/Japan-appoints-minister-of-loneliness-to-help-peo ple-home-alone

Kremen, W. S., Beck, A., Elman, J. A., Gustavson, D. E., Reynolds, C. A., Tu, X. M., Sanderson-Cimino, M. E., Panizzon, M. S., Vuoksimaa, E., Toomey, R., Fennema-Notestine, C., Haggler, D. J. Jr., Fang, B., Dale, A. M., Lyons, M. L., & Franz, C. E. (2019). Influence of young adult cognitive ability and additional education on later-life cognition. *Proceedings of the National Academy of Sciences, 116*(6), 2021–2026. https://doi.org/10.1073/pnas.1811537116

Krendl, A. C., Kennedy, D. P., Hugenberg, K., & Perry, B. L. (2021). Social cognitive abilities predict unique aspects of older adults' personal social networks. *The Journals of Gerontology: Series B, 77*(1), 18–28. https://doi.org/10.1093/geronb/gbab048

Kuiper, J. S., Zuidersma, M., Oude Voshaar, R. C., Zuidema, S. U., van den Heuvel, E. R., Stolk, R. P., & Smidt, N. (2015). Social relationships and risk of dementia: A systematic review and meta-analysis of longitudinal cohort studies. *Ageing Research Reviews, 22*, 39–57. https://doi.org/10.1016/j.arr.2015.04.006

Kwak, S., Kim, H., Chey, J., & Youm, Y. (2018). Feeling how old I am: Subjective age is associated with estimated brain age. *Frontiers in Aging Neuroscience, 10*. https://doi.org/10.3389/fnagi.2018.00168

LaCosse, J., Canning, E. A., Bowman, N. A., Murphy, M. C., & Logel, C. (2020). A social-belonging intervention improves STEM outcomes for students who speak English as a second language. *Science Advances, 6*(40). https://doi.org/10.1126/sciadv.abb6543

Lecce, S., Bianco, F., Devine, R. T., Hughes, C., & Banerjee, R. (2014). Promoting theory of mind during middle childhood: A training program. *Journal of Experimental Child Psychology, 126*, 52–67. https://doi.org/10.1016/j.jecp.2014.03.002

Lecce, S., Bottiroli, S., Bianco, F., Rosi, A., & Cavallini, E. (2015). Training older adults on Theory of Mind (ToM): Transfer on metamemory. *Archives of Gerontology and Geriatrics, 60*(1), 217–226. https://doi.org/10.1016/j.archger.2014.10.001

Le Penne, S. (2017). Longing to belong: Needing to be needed in a world in need. III Young perspectives. *Society, 54*(6), 535–536. https://doi.org/10.1007/s12115-017-0185-y

Livingston, G., Huntley, J., Sommerlad, A., Ames, D., Ballard, C., Banerjee, S., Brayne, C., Burns, A., Cohen-Mansfield, J., Cooper, C., Costafreda, S. G., Dias, A., Fox, N., Gitlin, L. N., Howard, R., Kales, H. C., Kivimäki, M., Larson, E. B., Ogunniyi, A., ... Mukadam, N. (2020). Dementia prevention, intervention, and care: 2020 report of the Lancet Commission. *The Lancet, 396*(10248), 413–446. https://doi.org/10.1016/s0140-6736(20)30367-6

Logel, C., Le Forestier, J. M., Witherspoon, E. B., & Fotuhi, O. (2021). A social-belonging intervention benefits higher weight students' weight stability and academic achievement. *Social Psychological and Personality Science, 12*(6), 1048–1057. https://doi.org/10.1177/1948550620959236

Lopes, M. A., Hototian, S. R., Reis, G. C., Elkis, H., & Bottino, C. M. D. C. (2007). Systematic review of dementia prevalence-1994 to 2000. *Dementia & Neuropsychologia, 1*(3), 230–240. https://doi.org/10.1590/s1980-57642008dn10300003

Lövdén, M., Schaefer, S., Noack, H., Bodammer, N. C., Kühn, S., Heinze, H. J., Düzel, E., Bäckman, L., & Lindenberger, U. (2012). Spatial navigation training protects the hippocampus against age-related changes during early and late adulthood. *Neurobiology of Aging, 33*(3), 620.e9–620.e22. https://doi.org/10.1016/j.neurobiolaging.2011.02.013

Lövdén, M., Wenger, E., Mårtensson, J., Lindenberger, U., & Bäckman, L. (2013). Structural brain plasticity in adult learning and development. *Neuroscience & Biobehavioral Reviews, 37*(9), 2296–2310. https://doi.org/10.1016/j.neubiorev.2013.02.014

Luo, Y., Hawkley, L. C., Waite, L. J., & Cacioppo, J. T. (2012). Loneliness, health, and mortality in old age: A national longitudinal study. *Social Science & Medicine, 74*(6), 907–914. https://doi.org/10.1016/j.socscimed.2011.11.028

Maccora, J., Peters, R., & Anstey, K. J. (2020). What does (low) education mean in terms of dementia risk? A systematic review and meta-analysis highlighting inconsistency in measuring and operationalising education. *SSM Population Health, 29*(12), 100654. https://doi.org/10.1016/j.ssmph.2020.100654

Masi, C. M., Chen, H. Y., Hawkley, L. C., & Cacioppo, J. T. (2011). A meta-analysis of interventions to reduce loneliness. *Personality and Social Psychology Review, 15*(3), 219–266. https://doi.org/10.1177/1088868310377394

McDonough, I. M., Haber, S., Bischof, G. N., & Park, D. C. (2015). The Synapse Project: Engagement in mentally challenging activities enhances neural efficiency. *Restorative Neurology and Neuroscience, 33*(6), 865–882. https://doi.org/10.3233/rnn-150533

Mortimer, J. A., Ding, D., Borenstein, A. R., DeCarli, C., Guo, Q., Wu, Y., Zhao, Q., & Chu, S. (2012). Changes in brain volume and cognition in a randomized trial of exercise and social interaction in a community-based sample of non-demented Chinese elders. *Journal of Alzheimer's Disease, 30*(4), 757–766. https://doi.org/10.3233/jad-2012-120079

Murphy, M. C., Gopalan, M., Carter, E. R., Emerson, K. T., Bottoms, B. L., & Walton, G. M. (2020). A customized belonging intervention improves retention of socially disadvantaged students at a broad-access university. *Science Advances, 6*(29), eaba4677. https://doi.org/10.1126/sciadv.aba4677

Newsom, J. T., Rook, K. S., Nishishiba, M., Sorkin, D. H., & Mahan, T. L. (2005). Understanding the relative importance of positive and negative social exchanges: Examining specific domains and appraisals. *The Journals of Gerontology Series B: Psychological Sciences and Social Sciences, 60*(6), P304–P312. https://doi.org/10.1093/geronb/60.6.p304

Norton, S., Matthews, F. E., Barnes, D. E., Yaffe, K., & Brayne, C. (2014). Potential for primary prevention of Alzheimer's disease: An analysis of population-based data. *The Lancet Neurology*, 13(8), 788–794. https://doi.org/10.1016/s1474-4422(14)70136-x

Nyberg, L., Lövdén, M., Riklund, K., Lindenberger, U., & Bäckman, L. (2012). Memory aging and brain maintenance. *Trends in Cognitive Sciences*, 16(5), 292–305. https://doi.org/10.1016/j.tics.2012.04.005

OECD (2020), Social Connections. In *How's Life? 2020: Measuring Well-Being*, OECD Publishing. https://doi.org/10.1787/b2090ea8-en

Orellano, E., Colón, W. I., & Arbesman, M. (2012). Effect of occupation- and activity-based interventions on instrumental activities of daily living performance among community-dwelling older adults: A systematic review. *American Journal of Occupational Therapy*, 66(3), 292–300. https://doi.org/10.5014/ajot.2012.003053

Park, D. C., Lodi-Smith, J., Drew, L., Haber, S., Hebrank, A., Bischof, G. N., & Aamodt, W. (2014). The impact of sustained engagement on cognitive function in older adults: The Synapse Project. *Psychological Science*, 25(1), 103–112. https://doi.org/10.1177/0956797613499592

Pinker, S. (2015). *The Village Effect: How Face-To-Face Contact Can Make Us Healthier and Happier*. Vintage Books Canada.

Pitkala, K. H., Routasalo, P., Kautiainen, H., Sintonen, H., & Tilvis, R. S. (2011). Effects of socially stimulating group intervention on lonely, older people's cognition: A randomized, controlled trial. *The American Journal of Geriatric Psychiatry*, 19(7), 654–663. https://doi.org/10.1097/jgp.0b013e3181f7d8b0

Qualls, S. H. (2014). Family Therapy with Ageing Families. In N. A. Pachana & K. Laidlaw (eds.), *The Oxford Handbook of Clinical Gerontology*, pp. 710–732. Oxford Library of Psychology. https://doi.org/10.1093/oxfordhb/9780199663170.013.020

Rafnsson, S. B., Orrell, M., D'Orsi, E., Hogervorst, E., & Steptoe, A. (2020). Loneliness, social integration, and incident dementia over 6 years: Prospective findings from the English Longitudinal Study of Ageing. *The Journals of Gerontology: Series B*, 75(1), 114–124. https://doi.org/10.1093/geronb/gbx087

Reuter-Lorenz, P. A., & Park, D. C. (2014). How does it STAC up? Revisiting the scaffolding theory of aging and cognition. *Neuropsychology Review*, 24(3), 355–370. https://doi.org/10.1007/s11065-014-9270-9

Ritchie, H. (2019) The world population is changing: For the first time there are more people over 64 than children younger than 5. https://ourworldindata.org/population-aged-65-outnumber-children#licence

Rosi, A., Cavallini, E., Bottiroli, S., Bianco, F., & Lecce, S. (2016). Promoting theory of mind in older adults: Does age play a role? *Aging & Mental Health*, 20(1), 22–28. https://doi.org/10.1080/13607863.2015.1049118

Routasalo, P. E., Tilvis, R. S., Kautiainen, H., & Pitkala, K. H. (2009). Effects of psychosocial group rehabilitation on social functioning, loneliness and well-being of lonely, older people: Randomized controlled trial. *Journal of Advanced Nursing, 65*(2), 297–305. https://doi.org/10.1111/j.1365-2648.2008.04837.x

Satizabal, C. L., Claudia, L., Beiser, A. S., Chouraki, V., Chêne, G., Dufouil, C., & Seshadri, S. (2016). Incidence of dementia over three decades in the Framingham Heart Study. *New England Journal of Medicine, 374*(6), 523–532. https://doi.org/10.1056/nejmoa1504327

Scott, A. J. (2008). Resurgent metropolis: Economy, society and urbanization in an interconnected world. *International Journal of Urban and Regional Research, 32*(3), 548–564. https://doi.org/10.1111/j.1468-2427.2008.00795.x

Seeman, T. E., Lusignolo, T. M., Albert, M., & Berkman, L. (2001). Social relationships, social support, and patterns of cognitive aging in healthy, high-functioning older adults: MacArthur studies of successful aging. *Health Psychology, 20*(4), 243–255. https://doi.org/10.1037/0278-6133.20.4.243

Sheikh, M. A. (2018). The potential protective effect of friendship on the association between childhood adversity and psychological distress in adulthood: A retrospective, preliminary, three-wave population-based study. *Journal of Affective Disorders, 226,* 21–27. https://doi.org/10.1016/j.jad.2017.09.015

Stern, Y. (2012). Cognitive reserve in ageing and Alzheimer's disease. *Lancet Neurology, 11*(11), 1006–1012. https://doi.org/10.1016/s1474-4422(12)70191-6

Stern, Y., Arenaza-Urquijo, E. M., Bartrés-Faz, D., Belleville, S., Cantilon, M., Chetelat, G., Ewers, M., Franzmeier, N., Kempermann, G., Kremen, W. S., Okonkwo, O., Scarmeas, N., Soldan, A., Udeh-Momoh, C., Valenzuela, M., Vemuri, P., Vuoksimaa, E., Arenaza Urquijo, E. M., Bartrés-Faz, D., ... Vuoksimaa, E. (2018). Whitepaper: Defining and investigating cognitive reserve, brain reserve, and brain maintenance. *Alzheimer's & Dementia,* 1–7. https://doi.org/10.1016/j.jmarsys.2011.03.015

Stillman, C. M., Esteban-Cornejo, I., Brown, B., Bender, C. M., & Erickson, K. I. (2020). Effects of exercise on brain and cognition across age groups and health states. *Trends in Neurosciences, 43*(7), 533–543. https://doi.org/10.1016/j.tins.2020.04.010

Stine-Morrow, E. A., Parisi, J. M., Morrow, D. G., & Park, D. C. (2008). The effects of an engaged lifestyle on cognitive vitality: A field experiment. *Psychology of Aging, 23*(4), 778–786. https://doi.org/10.1037/a0014341

Thompson, T. W., Waskom, M. L., & Gabrieli, J. D. E. (2016). Intensive working memory training produces functional changes in large-scale fronto-parietal networks. *Journal of Cognitive Neuroscience, 28*(4), 575–588. https://doi.org/10.1162/jocn_a_00916

Tilvis, R. S., Pitkala, K. H., Jolkkonen, J., & Strandberg, T. E. (2000). Social networks and dementia. *Lancet, 356*(9223), 77–78. https://doi.org/10.1016/s0140-6736(05)73414

UN DESA (2021). *World Social Report.* United Nations.

Valk, S. L., Bernhardt, B. C., Trautwein, F. M., Böckler, A., Kanske, P., Guizard, N., Collins. D. L., & Singer, T. (2017). Structural plasticity of the social brain: Differential change after socio-affective and cognitive mental training. *Science Advances*, *3*(10), e1700489. https://doi.org/10.1126/sciadv.1700489

Van Groenou, M. I. B., & Van Tilburg, T. (2003). Network size and support in old age: Differentials by socio-economic status in childhood and adulthood. *Ageing & Society*, *23*(5), 625–645. https://doi.org/10.1017/s0144686x0300134x

Verghese, J., Lipton, R. B., Katz, M. J., Hall, C. B., Derby, C. A., Kuslansky, G., Ambrose, A. F., Sliwinski, M., & Buschke, H. (2003). Leisure activities and the risk of dementia in the elderly. *New England Journal of Medicine*, *348*(25), 2508–2516. https://doi.org/10.1056/nejmoa022252

Walton, G. M., & Brady, S. T. (2017). The many questions of belonging. In A. J. Elliot, C. S. Dweck, & D. S. Yeager (eds.), *Handbook of Competence and Motivation: Theory and Application*, 2nd ed., pp. 272–293. The Guilford Press.

(2020). The social-belonging intervention. In G. M. Walton & A. J. Crum (eds.), *Handbook of Wise Interventions: How Social-Psychological Insights Can Help Solve Problems*, pp. 36–62. Guilford Press.

Walton, G. M., & Cohen, G. L. (2007). A question of belonging: Race, social fit, and achievement. *Journal of Personality and Social Psychology*, *92*(1), 82–96. https://doi.org/10.1037/0022-3514.92.1.82

(2011). A brief social-belonging intervention improves academic and health outcomes of minority students. *Science*, *331*(6023), 1447–1451. https://doi.org/10.1126/science.1198364

Walton, G. M., Logel, C., Peach, J. M., Spencer, S. J., & Zanna, M. P. (2015). Two brief interventions to mitigate a "chilly climate" transform women's experience, relationships, and achievement in engineering. *Journal of Educational Psychology*, *107*(2), 468–485. https://doi.org/10.1037/a0037461

Wang, H.-X., Karp, A., Winblad, B., & Fratiglioni, L. (2002). Late-life engagement in social and leisure activities is associated with a decreased risk of dementia: A longitudinal study from the Kungsholmen project. *American Journal of Epidemiology*, *155*(12), 1081–1087. https://doi.org/10.1093/aje/155.12.1081

Williams, C. L., Hirschi, Q., Sublett, K. V., Hulleman, C. S., & Wilson, T. D. (2020). A brief social belonging intervention improves academic outcomes for minoritized high school students. *Motivation Science*, *6*(4), 423–437. https://doi.org/10.1037/mot0000175

Wilson, R. S., Barnes, L. L., Krueger, K. R., Hoganson, G., Bienias, J. L., & Bennett, D. A. (2005). Early and late life cognitive activity and cognitive systems in old age. *Journal of the International Neuropsychological Society*, *11*(4), 400–407.

Wilson, R. S., Boyle, P. A., James, B. D., Leurgans, S. E., Buchman, A. S., & Bennett, D. A. (2015). Negative social interactions and risk of mild cognitive impairment in old age. *Neuropsychology, 29*(4), 561–570. https://doi.org/10.1037/neu0000154

Wilson, R. S., Krueger, K. R., Arnold, S. E., Schneider, J. A., Kelly, J. F., Barnes, L. L., Tang, Y., & Bennett, D. A. (2007). Loneliness and risk of Alzheimer disease. *Archives of General Psychiatry, 64*(2), 234–240. https://doi.org/10.1001/archpsyc.64.2.234

Wolinsky, F. D., Vander Weg, M. W., Martin, R., Unverzagt, F. W., Ball, K. K., Jones, R. N., & Tennstedt, S. L. (2009). The effect of speed-of-processing training on depressive symptoms in ACTIVE. *Journals of Gerontology Series A: Biological Sciences and Medical Sciences, 64*(4), 468–472. https://doi.org/10.1093/gerona/gln044

World Health Organization (WHO) (2011). *Global Health and Aging*. WHO.

Yeager, D. S., Walton, G. M., Brady, S. T., Akcinar, E. N., Paunesku, D., Keane, L., Kamentz, D., Ritter, G., Duckworth, A. L., Urstein, R., Gomez, E. M., Markus, H. R., Cohen, G. L., & Dweck, C. S. (2016). Teaching a lay theory before college narrows achievement gaps at scale. *Proceedings of the National Academy of Sciences, 113*(24), E3341-E3348. https://doi.org/10.1073/pnas.1524360113

Youm, Y., Baldina, E., & Baek, J. (2021). All-cause mortality and three aspects of social relationships: An eight-year follow-up of older adults from one entire Korean village. *Scientific Reports, 11*(1). https://doi.org/10.1038/s41598-020-80684-5

Youm, Y., Laumann, E. O., Ferraro, K. F., Waite, L. J., Kim, H. C., Park, Y. R., Chu, S. H., Joo, W.-t., & Lee, J. A. (2014). Social network properties and self-rated health in later life: Comparisons from the Korean Social Life, Health, and Aging Project and the National Social Life, Health and Aging Project. *BMC Geriatrics, 14*, 1–15. https://doi.org/10.1186/1471-2318-14-102

Zunzunegui, M. V., Alvarado, B. E., Del Ser, T., & Otero, A. (2003). Social networks, social integration, and social engagement determine cognitive decline in community-dwelling Spanish older adults. *The Journals of Gerontology Series B: Psychological Sciences and Social Sciences, 58*(2), S93–S100. https://doi.org/10.1093/geronb/58.2.s93

Index

Affective systems, 70
Aging, 11, 126, 127, 130, 132, 133, 134
    Aged society, 11
    Aging society, 11
    Global aging, 11, 12, 270
    Population aging, 11, 16, 17, 19–28, 37
Agricultural, 12, 13, 17, 34
Air pollution, 33, 36, 123, 131
Alzheimer's disease (AD), 22, 31, 32, 119, 122, 126, 184
Amygdala network, 144, 145, 148, 152
Antisocial behavior, 231, 247
APOE4, 122
APOE ε4 alleles, 109
Authoritarian, 13, 15

Belongingness hypothesis, 69, 70, 92
    Need to belong, 70–72, 76
    Birth control, 16
    Birth rate, 16, 17
Brain connectivity, 217–222, 224–225
Brain health, 123, 132, 133
Brain injury, 33, 35–37, 120, 123, 127, 131, 133
Brain maintenance (BM), 121, 124, 131, 134, 269, 278, 285
Brain metabolism, 127, 128
Brain network, 120, 124
Brain pathology, 119, 120, 126
Brain size, 32, 72, 73, 119, 120, 124, 126
Brain structure, 217–218, 223–224
    Brain volume, 32, 120, 146, 152, 273
    Entorhinal cortex, 32, 184
    Gray matter density, 223, 227
    Hippocampus, 32, 130, 279
    Medial temporal lobe, 31
    Precuneus, 32, 130
    Prefrontal cortex, 30, 32, 130
    See Social brain for more brain structures

Cardiovascular
    Cardiovascular disease, 16, 36, 122, 133, 142, 206
    Cardiovascular function, 206
    Cardiovascular health, 107, 205, 206, 209, 271
Cerebrovascular health, 142, 149
Chronic low inflammation, 164
Clock Drawing Test (CDT), 29–31
Cognition
    Cognitive ability, 127, 130, 281
    Cognitive function, 273
    Cognitive test, 12, 28, 31, 37, 146
    Higher cognitive function, 30, 32, 120, 200, 206, 207, 278
    Low cognitive performance (LCP), 29, 31–33, 130
Cognitive aging, 12, 37, 124, 131, 133, 196, 197, 199, 200, 202, 206, 207, 208–210
Cognitive behavioral therapy (CBT), 272, 274, 275
Cognitive decline, 6, 32, 33, 34, 105, 109, 112, 122, 125, 126, 148, 151, 164–165, 195, 197, 200, 201, 202, 203, 204, 205, 206, 207, 227, 274, 277, 278, 282, 283, 285
Cognitive development, 2, 12, 27, 28, 123, 127, 280
Cognitive health, 50, 53–55, 61, 62, 64, 132–133, 195–210
Cognitive reserve (CR), 4, 22, 33, 120, 121, 124–132, 133, 199, 201, 205, 209, 269, 270, 271, 278, 280, 281, 282, 285
Cognitive stimulation, 141, 147, 153, 270, 272, 273
Cognitive systems, 70
Cognitive training, 269, 279, 286
Cognitively stimulating activities, 126
Community-based, 273, 281, 282
Compressed modernization, 12, 19, 34, 37
Concept, 30
    Conceptual error, 30
    Conceptualization, 30

Confucian, 18, 19, 34, 35
Confucianist, 13
Conserved transcriptional response to adversity (CTRA), 108, 111
C-reactive protein (CRP), 150, 164, 165, 167
Cultural intelligence hypothesis, 72, 74, 92

Dementia, 119, 120, 121, 125, 126, 127, 131, 132, 133, 184–185
  Alzheimer's disease (AD), 22, 31, 32, 119, 122, 126, 184
  Cost of dementia, 11
  Dementia assessment, 31
  Dementia diagnosis, 31
  Dementia incidence, 28, 37, 121, 122, 269, 281
  Dementia prevalence, 2, 11, 12, 22–28, 37, 121, 124, 126, 282, 284
  Dementia risk, 2, 4, 12, 22, 33, 35, 36, 109, 121, 122, 123, 126, 133, 148, 151, 184, 199, 201–203, 208, 209, 269, 270, 280, 283, 285
Dementia Rating Scale (DRS), 28
Demographic cliff, 17
Depression, 274, 283, 285
Developing country, 272, 280, 281, 284
Diffusion Tensor Imaging (DTI), 142, 150
DNA methylation, 234, 235, 251, 253

Early experience
  Attachment, 232, 234, 245, 246
  Early adversity, 239, 246, 248, 250, 252, 253
  Institutionalization, 239, 248, 250
  Maltreatment, 239, 245, 246, 247, 248, 251
  Parenting, 232, 234, 239, 246, 247, 248, 249, 250, 253
Ecological intelligence hypothesis, 72, 73, 92
Economic development, 13, 16, 17, 18, 22, 27, 37
Economy, 2, 12–17, 18, 34, 37
Education, 30, 32, 120, 121, 122, 123, 124, 126, 127, 130, 271
  Compulsory education, 2, 16, 17, 27–28, 38, 281, 282
  Education effect, 12, 28, 29, 281, 282
  Education fervor, 18
  Formal education, 2, 4, 12, 18, 19, 22, 27, 29, 30, 31, 32, 33, 120, 280
  Higher education, 16, 17, 18, 19, 28
  Low education, 2, 22, 28, 30, 33, 35, 126, 128, 269, 281–282
  Minimal education, 2, 27, 31, 32, 33, 130
  Primary education, 17, 19, 27, 28
  Public education, 16, 19
  Secondary education, 17, 19, 27, 28, 29, 38, 281
Electroencephalogram (EEG), 250

Empathy, 76–80, 82–83, 89, 235, 236, 244, 276
  Mirror neuron system, 78
Estrangement, 270, 271
Eudaimonia, 90
Evidence-based
  Evidence-based intervention, 283
  Evidence-based program, 282
  Evidence-based psychotherapy, 285
Experience corps (EC), 272

Family fatigue, 271
Family therapy, 272
Framingham Heart Study, 281
Functional magnetic resonance imaging (fMRI), 75, 142, 237
  Resting-state fMRI, 224
  Task-based fMRI, 225, 227

Gender, 181–182
  Gender differences in loneliness, 181–182
  Social support, 181–182
Gene, 122, 123
Genetic variants (single nucleotide polymorphism [SNP]), 107, 108, 112
Genome-wide approach study (GWAS), 107, 108, 109, 111
Genotype, 232, 234, 235, 238, 251, 252
Godoksa, 35
Gray matter atrophy, 152
Gross National Product (GDP), 15
Gut microbiome, 166, 168

Harmonized Cognitive Assessment Protocol (HCAP), 31
Health, 50–56, 59–62, 64–65
  Biomarkers, 51, 64
  Brain, 64–65
  Cognitive health, 50, 53–55, 61, 62, 64, 132–133, 195–210
  Mental health, 50, 53–55, 272, 285
  Mortality, 50, 60, 61, 63
  Physical health, 3, 4, 50, 53–55, 56, 61, 62, 65
  Psychological health, 3, 56, 185, 198, 202, 208, 209, 274
  Self-rated health, 52, 55–60
Healthy lifestyle, 168
Hedonia, 90
Human development, 121
Hypothalamic–pituitary–adrenal axis (HPA axis), 182–184
  Stress response, 183

Illiterate, 22, 27, 29, 33
Industrialization, 13, 17, 27, 36, 37, 270
  Industrialized, 12

Industrialized country, 270, 272, 283
Inflammageing, 133, 164, 168
Inflammatory responses, 162–164, 166, 169
Intelligence, 32, 33, 126, 127
Interleukin-6 (IL-6), 150, 163, 164–165, 167

Korea, 11, 12, 13, 17, 22, 28, 30, 31, 35, 37
Korean, 13, 14, 18, 19, 27, 34, 234
   Elderly Korean, 2, 12, 22, 29, 34, 36
   Older Korean, 2, 12, 19, 22–31, 33, 34, 35, 37, 64, 127, 168, 284
   South Korean, 2, 16, 17, 19, 34, 36, 51, 56, 60, 64, 271
   Korean Economic Development Plan (KEDP), 13, 14–17, 19, 36
Kungsholmen Project, 199, 201

Leisure activity, 126, 271, 282, 283
Life course approach, 121, 123, 131, 134
Life expectancy, 2, 16, 27, 181, 280
Lifestyle factors, 126
Literacy, 4, 12, 23, 253
Loneliness, 106–107, 108, 111–112, 181, 198, 202, 205, 269, 270, 272, 273, 274, 275, 278, 282, 283, 284, 285
Low- to middle-income countries (LMIC), 12, 27, 37

Magnetic resonance imaging (MRI), 142
Memory
   Episodic memory, 32, 109, 127, 273
   Memory impairment, 19, 119
Mental health, 50, 53–55, 272, 285
Mentalizing, 78, 80–86, 89, 90, 91, 224–226, 235, 241, 244, 246, 247
Mentalizing network, 76, 79, 87, 92, 144–145, 148, 217–222, 227, 244
Mild cognitive impairment (MCI), 31–32
Moderating effect, 121, 126, 127, 133
Modifiable factors, 123
Modifiable risks, 123, 126, 131
Morphometry, 130

Neural resource, 269
Neurochemicals
   Arginine-vasopressin, 231, 236, 237, 252, 253
   Oxytocin, 231, 232, 234, 236, 238
   Oxytocin receptor gene (OXTR), 234, 235, 251, 253
   Serotonin (5-HTT), 237, 238, 252, 253
Neurodegeneration, 4, 12, 33, 36, 122, 126, 130, 131, 133, 151, 269, 280, 281, 282
Neurofibrillary tangles, 119, 122, 184
Neurogenesis, 120, 128
Neuroinflammatory response, 132, 133

Neuropathology, 119, 120, 121, 122, 125, 126, 132, 133
Neuropsychological, 29, 31
Nun study, 119

Occupation, 120, 126, 271, 283
Organisation for Economic Co-operation and Development (OECD), 34, 176, 280, 283–284

Pesticide, 36
Plaques, 119, 122
   Amyloid beta, 119, 122
   Neocortical, 119
   Neuritic, 122
   Senile, 122
Polygenic scores, 107, 110, 111, 112
Poverty, 12, 16, 34
Premorbid intelligence, 130
Preventive
   Preventive effect, 6, 27, 281
   Preventive factor, 199
   Preventive intervention, 6, 133
Process-specific intervention strategy, 286
Prosocial behavior, 77, 79, 80, 83, 231, 235, 237, 238, 247, 251
Protective factor, 162, 253
Proxy, 126, 127
Psychological well-being, 270, 275, 277, 284
Psychoneuroimmunology, 133
Psychosocial approaches, 270, 274
Purpose in life, 111, 167–168

Quality of life, 6, 17, 70, 89, 91, 185, 195, 197

Relational conflict, 272
Reserve, 4, 119, 120, 121, 124, 127, 130, 134
   Brain reserve (BR), 120, 124, 126, 133
   Cognitive reserve (CR), 4, 22, 33, 120, 121, 124–132, 133, 199, 201, 205, 209, 269, 270, 271, 278, 280, 281, 282, 285
Resilience, 120, 121, 124, 130, 133
Resistance, 120, 121, 124

Scaffolding, 269
Sense of belonging, 270, 272, 277, 280, 284, 285
Social acceptance, 71, 76, 77, 78, 92
Social activity, 1, 133, 148–149, 153, 272, 273, 278, 279, 282, 283, 285
Social bonding, 76–80, 231, 232, 234, 235, 236, 237, 238, 241, 253
Social brain, 69, 72–76, 86–92, 217–228
   Amygdala, 80, 82, 88, 90, 217–222, 227, 235, 236, 237, 238, 242, 243, 247, 248, 249, 250

Social brain (cont.)
  Anterior cingulate cortex (ACC), 90
  Anterior insula, 76, 78, 79, 84, 87, 249
  Anterior middle cingulate cortex (aMCC), 78, 79, 87
  Dorsal anterior cingulate cortex (dACC), 76, 77, 78, 79, 91, 248, 249
  Dorsolateral prefrontal cortex (dlPFC), 243
  Dorsomedial prefrontal cortex (DMPFC), 87, 244
  Fusiform gyrus (FFG), 80, 82, 236
  Inferior anterior prefrontal cortex (PFC), 236, 237
  Inferior frontal cortex, 79, 235, 236, 249
  Inferior parietal lobule (IPL), 79
  Inferior temporal gyrus, 236
  Lateral prefrontal cortex, 80
  Medial prefrontal cortex (mPFC), 79, 80, 83, 84–86, 90, 91, 243, 244
  Nucleus accumbens (NAC), 80, 82, 90
  Orbitofrontal cortex (OFC), 90, 247, 248, 249, 251
  Posterior cingulate cortex (PCC), 86, 90, 244
  Precuneus, 79, 86, 91, 244
  Rostrolateral prefrontal cortex, 91
  Somatosensory cortex, 78, 79
  Subgenual ACC (sgACC), 76, 77, 80, 91
  Superior frontal gyrus (SFG), 247, 248, 249
  Superior temporal sulcus (STS), 80, 82, 86, 236
  Supplementary motor area (SMA), 79
  Temporal pole (TP), 80, 86
  Temporoparietal junction (TPJ), 80, 83–84, 86, 90
  Ventral anterior cingulate cortex (vACC), 77
  Ventral striatum, 76, 77, 80, 90, 249
  Ventrolateral prefrontal cortex (vlPFC), 242, 243
  Ventromedial prefrontal cortex (VMPFC), 76, 77, 79, 80, 82, 90, 91
Social brain hypothesis, 151, 152, 217, 226, 227
Social cognition, 232, 237, 272, 275, 285
  Empathy, 76–80, 82–83, 89, 235, 236, 244, 276
  Mentalizing, 78, 80–86, 89, 90, 91, 224–226, 235, 241, 244, 246, 247
  Perspective-taking, 82, 83, 84, 86
  Theory of mind (ToM), 82, 83, 84, 87, 89, 276
Social connectedness, 178–181
Social connection, 121, 124, 131, 132, 133, 280, 282, 285
  Social relationship, 132, 133
  Social support, 120, 132, 133
Social disconnection, 177, 179, 186
Social disengagement, 270, 274, 284

Social disintegration, 34–35, 37, 270, 280
Social engagement, 269, 270, 272, 273, 274, 280, 283, 285
Social enrichment, 279, 286
Social evaluation, 80
Social genomics, 107
Social group, 69, 71, 72, 73
Social integration, 270, 280, 281, 284, 285
Social intelligence hypothesis, 69, 72–75, 92
Social intervention, 208, 210, 272, 273, 275–276
  Psychosocial intervention, 6, 7, 274, 285
Social investment, 18, 34, 37
Social isolation, 34, 37, 123, 133, 269, 270, 274, 277, 282, 283, 285, 286
Social learning, 72, 73, 74, 80
Social life, 270, 274, 276, 277, 278, 280, 285
Social network, 69, 71, 72, 82, 86, 87, 88, 90, 91, 92, 240, 245, 253
  Complete social networks, 51, 60, 61, 64, 65
  Ego-centric social networks, 51, 56, 60, 64
Social network analysis (SNA), 50, 179
  Distal social characteristics, 179
Social network positions, 50, 51–60, 64–65, 179
  Social network brokerage, 53–55, 59, 64, 222
  Social network closure, 52–55, 59, 65, 222
  Social network size, 52–53, 59, 65, 222–224
Social network structure, 217–228
  Social network diversity, 224–225, 227
  Social network embeddedness, 224–225, 227
  Social network size, 217–224, 225, 227
Social perception, 76, 80, 82
Social rejection
  CyberBall, 76
  Social exclusion, 76, 78, 91
Social relationship, 132, 133, 177, 178, 179, 182, 185, 270, 271, 272, 273, 275, 282, 284, 285
Social relationships, functional aspects of, 202–204
  Loneliness, 198, 202, 205–207
  Social conflict, 198, 203, 207
  Social support, see Social support
Social relationships, structural aspects of, 198–202
  Social activity, 198, 201–202
  Social contact, 198, 199–201
  Social network, 197–202
Social support, 35, 37, 52, 59, 88, 120, 132, 133, 146, 149, 152, 166, 176, 181–182, 198, 203–204, 240–241, 246, 252, 253, 270, 271, 274, 276, 280, 283
Socioaffective, 276
Sociocognitive, 276

Socio-cognitive and socio-emotional function, 231, 232, 234, 235, 236, 238, 240, 241, 246, 247, 253
Socioeconomic, 11, 19, 35
　Socioeconomic burden, 19
　Socioeconomic factor, 122, 131
Socioeconomic status (SES), 22, 110, 239–245
　Education, 239, 240, 241, 242, 253
　Income, 239, 241, 242, 243
　Occupation, 239, 240, 241, 242, 253
　Poverty, 239, 242, 243, 250
Socioemotional regulation, 80
Socioemotional selectivity theory, 86, 88, 176
　Emotional regulation, 176
　Positivity effect, 88, 176
Sociometer theory, 70

Stress, 4, 5, 34, 52, 70, 71, 133, 142, 163, 176, 182, 202, 205–207, 242, 244, 247, 250, 271
Stress response, 5, 142, 150, 151
Stressful experience, 149, 205, 252
Stressful life events, 183, 250, 271
Stressor, 34, 36, 241, 244
Structural magnetic resonance imaging (MRI), 217, 227

Tau, 122, 127
Theory of mind (ToM), *see Social cognition*

Well-being, 3, 70–71, 88–92, 250, 252, 253
White matter microstructure, 150, 152, 153

For EU product safety concerns, contact us at Calle de José Abascal, 56–1°,
28003 Madrid, Spain or eugpsr@cambridge.org.

www.ingramcontent.com/pod-product-compliance
Ingram Content Group UK Ltd.
Pitfield, Milton Keynes, MK11 3LW, UK
UKHW020910191025
464020UK00015B/1434